Beginning with Disability: A Primer brings togeth emergent scholars to offer an exciting and accessib.. ...r.uuucuun to the interdisci-plinary field of disability studies. An excellent resource for those new to this field.

Dan Goodley, Professor of Disability Studies and
Education, University of Sheffield

Davis has deftly curated an indispensable introduction to the field of disability studies. With its accessible and engaging prose, *Beginning with Disability: A Primer* is the disability studies 101 text that will be required reading for every introductory course in the field.

Beth A. Ferri, Professor of Inclusive Education and
Disability Studies, Syracuse University

Beginning with Disability gathers established and emerging disability studies scholars and disability activists to reflect on what it means to center disability in analyses of history, culture, politics, and lived experience. The result is a powerfully diverse array of methods, archives, and voices, and a series of thought-provoking questions that will be an asset to college instructors and students of disability studies at all levels.

Julie Passanante Elman, Assistant Professor of Women's and
Gender Studies, University of Missouri and
Author of *Chronic Youth: Disability, Sexuality,
and U.S. Media Cultures of Rehabilitation*

Beginning with Disability is an indispensable resource for scholars and students of disability studies. For students new to the field, it offers a clear and accessible introduc-tion to the major interventions and ongoing debates in the field; for more seasoned scholars, it compiles classic texts in one location for convenient reference.

Julie Avril Minich, Assistant Professor of English and
Mexican American and Latina/o Studies,
University of Texas at Austin

With zest, *Beginning with Disability* shows us the social relations that make disability a complex set of meanings, experiences, and ways of knowing that should no longer be taken for granted. The various works collected here together with the compelling use of examples from popular culture promise to makes this *Primer* a great one— enabling us to encounter the significance of the mystery that disability is all around us, but as Davis says, "it's often hiding in plain sight."

Tanya Titchkosky, Professor of Disability Studies, Ontario Institute
for Studies in Education, University of Toronto and
Author of *Disability, Self and Society, Reading and
Writing Disability Differently*, and *The Question of
Access: Disability, Space, Meaning*

Beginning with Disability

While there are many introductions to disability and disability studies, most presume an advanced academic knowledge of a range of subjects. *Beginning with Disability* is the first introductory primer for disability studies aimed at first- and second-year students in two- and four-year colleges. This volume of essays across disciplines— including education, sociology, communications, psychology, social sciences, and humanities—features accessible, readable, relatively short chapters that do not require specialized knowledge.

Lennard Davis, along with a team of consulting editors, has compiled a number of blogs, vlogs, and other videos to make the materials more relatable and vivid to students. "Subject to Debate" boxes spotlight short pro and con pieces on controversial subjects that can be debated in class or act as prompts for assignments.

Lennard J. Davis is Distinguished Professor of Liberal Arts and Sciences at the University of Illinois at Chicago in the departments of Disability and Human Development, English, and Medical Education. He is the author of *Enabling Acts: The Hidden Story of How the Americans with Disabilities Act Gave the Largest US Minority Its Rights*; *Obsession: A History*; *Enforcing Normalcy: Disability, Deafness and the Body*; *Bending Over Backwards: Disability, Dismodernism and Other Difficult Positions*; and *The End of Normal: Identity in a Biocultural Era*. He is also the editor of Routledge's *Disability Studies Reader*.

Jay Dolmage is Associate Professor and Associate Chair of English at the University of Waterloo in Canada. He is the founding editor of the Canadian *Journal of Disability Studies* and the author of award-winning books and articles on disability and rhetoric.

Nirmala Erevelles is Professor of Social and Cultural Studies in Education at the University of Alabama. Her research focuses on the unruly, messy, unpredictable, and taboo body in the intersecting areas of disability studies, critical race theory, transnational feminism, sociology of education, and postcolonial studies. Her book *Disability and Difference in Global Contexts: Towards a Transformative Body Politic* was published by Palgrave in November 2012.

Sarah Parker Harris is an Associate Professor and the Director of Graduate and Undergraduate Studies in the Department of Disability and Human Development at the University of Illinois at Chicago. Her interdisciplinary areas of scholarship include Disability Studies, Social Policy, and Sociology. She is co-author of *Disability Through the Lifecourse* (SAGE Reference Series on Disability). Her current research projects focus on comparative and national disability policy and legislation, employment, entrepreneurship and social entrepreneurship, and theories of social justice, human rights, and citizenship.

Alexander Luft is a Ph.D. candidate in the Program for Writers at the University of Illinois at Chicago. His fiction has appeared in *Midwestern Gothic*, *Yemassee*, *The Coachella Review*, and other literary journals. He worked as a research assistant on the fifth edition of Routledge's *Disability Studies Reader*.

Susan Schweik is Professor of English and Disability Studies at University of California, Berkeley and author of *The Ugly Laws: Disability in Public* (NYU Press, 2009). Her new book in progress concerns IQ testing, eugenics, institutionalization, and a group of incarcerated so-called "feeble-minded" women whose collective work in the Depression profoundly challenged all these things.

Linda Ware has published widely in leading journals that evidence her inter-disciplinary interests in disability studies—*Hypatia*, *Equity and Excellence*, *National Women's Studies Journal*, *Disability Studies Quarterly*, *Journal of Teacher Education*, *Learning Disability Quarterly*, *Research in Disability Studies*, *International Journal of Inclusive Education*, *Review of Disability Studies*, and the *Journal of Literary and Cultural Disability Studies*. Her edited book *Ideology and the Politics of (In)Exclusion* (2004, Peter Lang) launched the conversation on disability studies in education within an international context. She is also completing work on *Critical Readings in Interdisciplinary Disability Studies: An International Reader* (Springer).

Beginning with Disability

A Primer

Edited by
Lennard J. Davis

Consulting Editors
Jay Dolmage, Nirmala Erevelles,
Sarah Parker Harris, Alexander Luft,
Susan Schweik, Linda Ware

Routledge
Taylor & Francis Group

NEW YORK AND LONDON

First published 2018
by Routledge
711 Third Avenue, New York, NY 10017

and by Routledge
2 Park Square, Milton Park, Abingdon, Oxon, OX14 4RN

Routledge is an imprint of the Taylor & Francis Group, an informa business

© 2018 Taylor & Francis

Library of Congress Cataloging in Publication Data
A catalog record for this book has been requested

ISBN: 978-1-138-21136-0 (hbk)
ISBN: 978-1-138-21137-7 (pbk)
ISBN: 978-1-315-45321-7 (ebk)

Typeset in Optima
by Florence Production Ltd, Stoodleigh, Devon, UK

Contents

Preface

The purpose of this book is to present material to a beginning student or a general reader who is completely unfamiliar with disability studies and with cultural theory. Many introductions to disability and disability studies on the market presume an advanced academic knowledge of a range of subjects. Such works are valuable, but often present obstacles for a neophyte. That is why we created this collection. As far as can be told, there is no disability-related book like this introduction on the market today.

We envision this book being used in composition courses, introductory disability studies classes, and other introductory courses in a wide variety of disciplines. To that end, we have chosen articles that are very accessible, readable, relatively short, and that do not require a lot of specialized knowledge. These selections are reprinted from a variety of sources, including newspapers, magazines, personal blogs, academic books and journals, and transcripts of live speeches. You'll also find some original material developed for this *Primer*. We have tried to group articles together in areas likely to be of importance to our readers—and we have included a variety of essays in education, sociology, communications, psychology, social sciences, and humanities. We have included a number of blogs and vlogs as well as other videos to make the materials more direct and vivid to students. In addition, we have a section called "Subject to debate" that has short pro and con pieces on controversial subjects that can be debated in class or can act as prompts for assignments.

We have tried to keep the text simple and free from overly academic language, citation, and footnotes. For those who wish to have a deeper look at disability studies, the *Disability Studies Reader* covers that ground. Since we have focused on short and accessible texts, the writings of many well-known scholars of disability studies do not appear in these pages. Their absence is no reflection on the enduring quality of their work. But fortunately, the insights of many other people may get some attention here.

We do not claim that this book is exhaustive nor that disability studies is one coherent field of study. Like any field, disability studies, critical disability studies, crip studies, or any of the allied areas of study, are evolving sets of knowledges that overlap, compete, and even refute each other. What is certain is that disability is a valid subject to consider and that in many cases its importance has been minimized in the past by other areas of study. This book aims to open disability to as many new readers as possible.

PART

1

Defining Disability

Introduction

Lennard J. Davis

As a reader of this text, you may consider yourself normal or you may consider yourself disabled. The decision you make about what to call yourself will determine your feelings about disability. If you're considering yourself normal or able-bodied, you might have feelings of interest and concern (perhaps even pity) for the disabled—for "them." If you're disabled, you might have an insider's knowledge of your disability but be fairly clueless about other disabilities. If you have a family member with a disability or who is Deaf, you may consider yourself between those two perspectives.

You may not consider yourself disabled, but you might have some physical or cognitive limitations that you are used to and don't think a big deal—like being depressed, being somewhat obsessive-compulsive, having a learning disability or attention deficit disorder, having a slight hearing or vision loss, being over or underweight, and the like. But even so you might not identify yourself as disabled and others around you might not either.

If you are disabled you may be reading this book using a screen-reader or some other type of computer program. "Normal"[1] people might assume that something as straightforward as reading would be what all readers of this book have in common. But if you are blind you might be reading this book by non-visual means; if you have a learning disability, you might find an audio version of the book easier to process. If you are Deaf you might find that reading the captions of some of the blogs mentioned in the book is the best way to go.

In any case, you can begin to see disability isn't a simple thing. It isn't necessarily a person using a wheelchair anymore than it is a blind person or someone who is HIV positive. If it isn't a simple thing, what is it? One way to think of disability is as a set of social relations. Simply looking at someone might not reveal much—social context is all. I might think you are disabled if I see you holding a cane with a red tip, but I might not think of you as disabled if you are swinging a fancy cane. I might not think of my grandfather as really deaf just because he recently began wearing hearing aids, but I might see a young person with hearing aids and using sign language and conclude that the person is Deaf.[2] I might not think of you as disabled if you are wearing glasses. I'd assume you are disabled if I see you navigating with a wheelchair but not if you are navigating with an ATV or a car. Society and social convention set up the terms about who is disabled and who isn't.

BOX 1.1

What are the most common myths about disability? See just a few of them here:

www.huffingtonpost.com/sarah-blahovec/basic-myths-about-the-dis_b_9560556.html

Talking About Disability: Terminology and Identity

Before we go any further, we need to get terminology right. In the old days, people with disabilities used to be called "handicapped." That word still survives in the term "handicap parking." The term "handicapped" was largely abandoned in the 1970s and 1980s and replaced with "people first" language. The reason for this was the term handicap was thought of negatively by disability activists as relating to someone with "cap in hand"—in other words a beggar, particularly a disabled one. That explanation of the origin of the expression was incorrect. Linguists call this a false etymology in which a current phrase or word is given an incorrect origin story. The actual term "handicap" comes from a game of chance that then became associated with horseracing. A horse that was very fast was saddled with extra weights so that it could fairly compete with other horses. Handicapping in racing was meant to create a level playing field. Thus handicapped meant that someone was burdened (like the horse with the weights on it) over someone who was not. In any case the term was dropped in favor of "person with a disability," along with other people's first language expressions like "person of color." The idea was that the modifying term shouldn't determine who you were—you were a person *first*, then *secondly* someone who just happened to have a disability or happened to be African-American.

But the person-first language began to be opposed by those who wanted to foreground their identity first. People who were proud of their status wanted to be known for that thing that made them unique. In that case, a person of color became an African-American. A person with a disability became a disabled person or simply disabled. Not everyone has come to agree on this shift, and many people who came to consciousness during the people-first movement still feel comfortable using that terminology. But many other people are actively arguing for identity-first language. Those people often use the term "crip" as well "disabled." That term derives from the pejorative term "cripple," but has been re-appropriated and revitalized, as has been the term "queer," removing it from the mouths of those who would humiliate people and placing it squarely in the camp of liberation and freedom. Crip is roughly used the way queer is now, as a term that aims to empower people and also give them a tool to reconsider conventional ways of thinking about disability. Just as queer upsets the traditional ways of thinking about gender and sexuality, so crip gets us to rethink disability, normality, and the evolving accepted methods of studying disability. In this book, you'll see all these terms being used since there still isn't unanimous agreement on which is the preferred term.

By the way, when you try to figure out what "disability" means, you might also want to try and figure out what "able-bodied" means as well. The two terms live in a dynamic relationship with each other. To be "able" might mean to be "normal" or "free of defects." But the word "able" isn't so simple either. Some people have called "ableism" the insistence on being normal and the accompanying conscious or unconscious discrimination against disabled people. Ableism is like racism, sexism, and other forms of discrimination. Another term, coined by a disability studies scholar, is "normate." Rosemarie Garland-Thomson came up with the idea to make "normal" seem problematic rather than just a routine term. For example, when "normates" act in "ableist" ways they are assuming that being normal is, well, the norm and that it's OK to discriminate against people with disabilities.

And not all people with impairments consider themselves disabled. For example, many Deaf people do not consider themselves disabled. Rather they think of themselves as a linguistic minority. They say that they are not disabled, just surrounded by people who do not speak their language. Deaf people are certainly not disabled within all-Deaf environments like Gallaudet University, the national institution of higher education for the Deaf.

Disability Politics

When people argue about language, they are often really arguing about politics. It actually does matter if you say you're more concerned about your identity and don't want it to play a second-place role in who you are. As with race and gender, disability came to national and international attention through an alliance between political action and scholarly analysis. The disability rights movement was influenced strongly by the civil rights movement in the United States. Activists protested when laws concerning disabled people weren't enforced, and they protested when there were laws on the books that discriminated against people with disabilities. They also protested when they wanted new laws and regulations made. Some of the issues that concerned these activists were and are about accessible public and private transportation, voting rights, access to public and private accommodations like movie theaters, hotels, stores, and restaurants, and the right to live independently. They protested the inaccessibility of public and private schools and colleges. They fought to make books, television, movies, and the Internet accessible to all kinds of people.

Why make all this fuss about disabled people? Aren't they a tiny fraction of the able-bodied population? Aren't there more ethnic and racial groups than there are people with disabilities? Actually, no. People with disabilities make up the largest minority in the United States as well as in most other countries. One in five people in the U.S. are disabled. More than half of the people over 65 are disabled. If you think about it, you can surely find disabled people in your family. Your grandfather with a hearing aid. Your aunt with arthritis. Someone who has vision problems. Someone who walks with the assistance of a cane, a walker, or uses a wheelchair. Someone who needs an inhaler to function. But disabilities aren't only visible. There are invisible ones like chronic diseases, hearing loss, learning disabilities, depression, and the like. Even obesity can be a disability. The more you think about it, the more you'll see disability all around you. In fact, it's often hiding in plain sight.

But what is a disability? Some of the conditions I mentioned don't necessarily seem like a disability. According to the U.S. Americans with Disabilities Act of 1990 a disability is an impairment that limits a person in one or more life activities. Under that definition you could be obese and not be disabled; or you could be obese and be disabled. The key would be if you were limited in a life-activity such as dressing yourself, communicating, ambulating, and so on. That expansive definition eventually got into trouble in the courts because it opened a can of worms. What if you had a condition like high blood pressure or nearsightedness? You could correct those conditions and yet still be discriminated against for having the condition in the first place. That happened to twin sisters who were air pilots and wore glasses when flying a plane. They applied for a job with United Airlines and were told they didn't qualify because of their nearsightedness. When they tried to sue, they were prevented when the courts said that since their vision was correctible they didn't have a disability. Sounds like a catch-22, and it was: they were discriminated against for their impairment but not covered by the law for that same impairment. You can see that disability isn't that easy to define. Eventually the ADA had to be amended to make sure that people with disabilities were protected whether or not the disability was corrected.

Ways of Approaching Disability: Historical Models

Another way of approaching a definition was tried. According to what is called "the social model" there is a distinction to be made between being impaired and being disabled. An impairment is something that limits you physically or mentally. So you might not be able to walk and therefore might have to use a wheelchair. That is your impairment, but in a college or city that has ramps and elevators that impairment isn't really a limitation. In fact, as we all know, wheels are very good things, and we can probably date the beginning of most civilizations to the invention of the wheel among other things. If you want to get somewhere, you take a car, bus, or train and speed along. In fact, most marathons are actually won by wheelchair racers who tend to come in an hour ahead of the best runners. Wheels work!

But they don't work when they come screeching to a halt at a set of stairs. In the social model, the impairment becomes a disability when the environment is not accessible. That disabling could arise as a physical accessibility issue if there are no ramps or elevators, or it might occur if there are no sign language interpreters in a classroom or a lecture. The environment can be thought of broadly to include the political, cultural, and even social environments. If someone gives a lecture on a college campus and there are no sign language interpreters, then a virtual barrier is created that will keep Deaf people out. A YouTube video that has no captioning (or faulty captioning) will also keep a Deaf person out. Facebook postings that include photographs without visual descriptions will keep blind people out. These kinds of cultural and social exclusions are very much a part of life for many people with disabilities.

BOX 1.2

Check out this viral YouTube video about caption technology gone wrong:

www.youtube.com/watch?v=hVNrkXM3TTI

Social discrimination is subtler but just as powerful. Staring at people with visible disabilities creates barriers. Asking probing questions about how a person got their disability creates barriers. And while you might be thinking you are not one of those who are involved in disabling disabled people, stop and consider. Are you friends with people with impairments? Do you date people who are disabled? Have you learned sign language and know how to talk to Deaf people? Are you in fact creating a barrier around you and then allowing access depending on whether people are disabled or not?

We can say that the social model provides one definition of disability—society disables a person with disabilities when it fails to create a barrier-free environment.

What preceded the social model? People speculate that the earliest historical model might be called "the charity model." In that model religious organizations in the past like the church, the mosque, the synagogue, or the temple were the main organizations that dealt with disability (aside from the family). In the charity model, the disabled person was deemed worthy of charity, alms, and the like. Some religious institutions created hospitals and schools that cared for the blind, the deaf, and other people with disabilities. In the charity model, there were various explanations for the existence of disabilities. Some thought that the sins of the parents were visited on the child. Others saw the disability as a test by God to give suffering and insight to the person and those around him or her. In either case, the disability was related to sin and the remedy was alms and prayer.

The charity model was succeeded, in this view, with the medical model. In the medical model a disability is seen as a disease in need of cure. The institutions involved are the clinic, the hospital, and the residential nursing home for those who were severely disabled. Doctors, nurses, and therapists, not priests, imams, rabbis, or ministers, were the ones seen as the appropriate protectors of the disabled and the Deaf. With the medical model sin, alms, and prayer are no longer central because the cause of disability is scientifically determined as defective genes or trauma. And the remedy is cure, prosthetic devices, or other kinds of technological or surgical interventions.

The social model is then the next step historically in this sequence. The social model arose in the latter half of the 20th century and refuted both the charity and the medical models. It proposed the disability/impairment paradigm and saw disability as a socially constructed concept. Impairments only became disabilities in a barrier-filled and unreceptive environment. The goal of the social model concept was to reimagine and agitate for barrier-free environments, increased accommodations for disabilities, and the removal of political, social, and cultural stigmas surrounding disability. In the social model, as opposed to the charity and medical ones, the problem is discrimination by society and the remedy is removal of barriers and addition of accessibility and accommodation. In addition, the social model was initially formulated as a Marxist model that saw impairment, along with class and race, as qualities selected by a capitalist society for disabling discrimination.

As with all ideas, the social model has come in for its share of criticism. The social model seemed like a good way to explain the role of society and government in creating categories of oppression. But it is less robust in explaining the actual living conditions of people with disabilities—many of whom experience periodic or chronic pain, weakness, and other embodied problems. You can critique the negative aspect of disability that is political, but it's harder to say that things like pain are socially constructed. In addition, it isn't so clear that impairment isn't socially constructed as well. In the case of many mental impairments, for example, there are strong societal inputs. For example, some cultures consider certain behaviors part of mental illness while other cultures don't. Mental diseases are defined differently over time. A hundred years ago you might have suffered from hysteria or neurasthenia. Now those terms are gone. If you were homosexual 50 years ago, you would have been considered mentally ill, while now you obviously would not.

Differences Between the U.S. and the U.K.

As you have seen, at first disability seems simple, but the more you look at it the more complex it gets. In the U.K. and the U.S. there were different origins to the disability activism movement and so there are differences in the ways that each country has seen disability. In the Marxist U.K. model, disability is actually a negative term. Disablement is what turns an impairment into a bad or disabling thing. In the U.S., where the Marxist model was far less important than the civil rights model, disability was seen as a positive thing. Using the template of the civil rights movement that led to enforcement of rights for people of color and women, the disability movement in the U.S. chose its songs, demonstration techniques, and inspiration from the fight for civil rights, most notably led by Martin Luther King and other African-Americans in the 1960s. In the same way that black people stressed the cultural uplift carried by "black is beautiful" and "black power," so the U.S. disability activists stressed the positive sides of their own identity. Rather than something negative that had to be overcome, disability was seen as an identity category that had to be uplifted and that claimed the rights it had been denied.

The U.K. model, given its Marxist bent, tended to be associated with the academic fields of the social sciences. In the U.S., disability studies tended to focus on the humanities. The older U.K. model looked with suspicion on critical and literary theory, seeing the U.S. branch as being too intellectual and not political enough. Both of those strands, however, have merged in the past ten years—especially with the rise of critical disability studies in the U.K. and elsewhere—which incorporates the theoretical framework of the humanities into the study of disability. It's probably true that the rift between the U.K. and the U.S. is now no longer a problem.

Disability Activism: Victories and Remaining Obstacles

One of the key things about disability studies is that it has a strong connection with activism. In the U.K. the fight for disability rights dovetailed nicely into the political analysis. In the U.S., disability activism preceded disability studies. The activism around disability began to ramp up in the 1970s and 1980s. Before then, people with disabilities were discriminated against in powerful ways. For example, if you were a wheelchair user, there were no curb cuts and so you couldn't easily move from block to block. There were no forms of public transportation that were accessible. There weren't resources to help people live independently at home. So basically if you could get out of the house, you'd only be able to go around your block. Commuting to work was out of the question. And for many people, living in squalid and understaffed institutions was a reality.

Disabled soldiers returning from the Vietnam War were involved in a lot of disability activism, as were a new coalition of cross-disability groups rallying around disability civil rights. In the 1970s there were a lot of protests and demonstrations around the Nixon and Carter administrations' delaying implementing crucial civil rights legislation concerning disabled people. Those demonstrations culminated in a 1977 takeover by people with disabilities of the Health, Education, and Welfare offices in San Francisco in what was the longest occupation of a federal building in U.S. history. Also many related demonstrations and arrests involved getting city public transportation, railroads, and over-the-road buses like those of Greyhound and Trailways to install lifts and other means by which disabled people could get around on their own. Finally, the Americans with Disabilities Act (ADA) was passed in 1990, accompanied by its own set of demonstrations, the most famous of which included mobility impaired people crawling up the steps to the U.S. Capitol building. Known as "the Capitol Crawl" this action to force Congress to pass the ADA without weakening amendments lives on in disability history as a shining moment of solidarity and political resistance.

The press covered the Capitol Crawl and the publicity helped. Indeed the media and the press can be avenues for lessening discrimination against people with disabilities, but more often they further disability discrimination. Newspapers love the "inspiring" disabled person. The usual and customary story carried by local news publications and television reportage is of some person in the community with a disability who has "overcome" barriers and faced "challenges." Their story of personal triumph serves to inspire "us." While such stories seem to be the opposite of insulting, many disabled people resent having to be the inspiration for nondisabled people. "Inspiration porn" is the term used by Stella Young to describe such reporting. Linked to this is the veneration of the "super-crip," often an athlete who again lives out the template story of overcoming. Early in the disability rights movement, people began to critique "pity" as the dominant way that the normal world related to the disabled. Both pity and inspiration reduce any complex human being with a disability to a mere icon cheerleading normal people's need to hear stories about overcoming difficult obstacles or triumphing over adversity.

BOX 1.3

Watch Stella Young talk about "inspiration porn":

https://youtu.be/SxrS7-I_sMQ

Political activism that revolved around HIV-AIDS was also a disability issue. LGBTQ folks have and have not seen disability as an issue related to sexuality and sexual identity. The idea of intersectionality—that identity groups intersect, overlap, and need to forge alliances rather than think of themselves as separate and apart—has become an important way to regard disability in relation to other groups and categories. When we think of women, transgender people, LGBTQ, people of color, different cultures and peoples throughout the world—we also want to think about how disability intersects and overlaps with those groups. The aim is to avoid having a white, patriarchal, hetero-normative, ableist viewpoint that disguises itself as a universal point of view.

Disability in Popular Culture

Hollywood could also help break down clichés and stereotypes about people with disabilities, but again far too many shows and films reinforce those. The standard stories about people with disabilities follow routine patterns. In the past, many villains were seen to have a disability—whether being one-eyed, one-armed, disfigured, walking with a limp, and the like. Another type of disabled person in film is the pitiable character who is the object of others' support. Sometimes disabled people are given super powers, like the autistic person who can remember dates or has other superhuman abilities. What you don't often see is just a disabled character who isn't living some extraordinary life. Most people with disabilities aren't tied up in plots involving disabilities—they are just folks living their lives.

The plot problem is tied up with a casting problem. Most disabled characters on TV and in film are played by nondisabled actors. Most screenplays about them are written by nondisabled writers, and most films are directed by nondisabled directors. Because of that, most viewers are getting a very skewed and biased view of what disabled people are like.

How did we get to the point that films are made this way and that disabled people don't get into the popular media? To know that we should turn to history. It is hard to say if people with disabilities had it better or worse in the past and that would depend on which country or culture they were part of. Some people speculate that the past was better because families cared for their own and disability was quite common, especially in warrior cultures like the Greeks and Romans, where injuries sustained in battle were signs of courage. Also, before industrialization, people with disabilities might have specialized roles depending on their disability. Deaf people could work in professions where high noise levels would bother hearing people. Blind people were often bards and poets or might work in ways that use their hands. Mobility impaired people could do sedentary jobs at home. Some people with mental differences might even have been seen as seers or prophets. On the other hand, many cultures stigmatized disabled people.

Standardization, Normality, and Eugenics

One thing we can say for certain is that industrialization and particularly factory work made it harder for people with different bodies and minds. The principle of factory work is that every worker is potentially interchangeable with every other worker. Standardization of workers would mean that non-standard workers would be left out of the mix. Further, factory work often caused injuries including loss of limbs, blinding, burning, crushing, and general deterioration of the body and mind. Workers could only be hired if they were not disabled, and would be fired if they became disabled.

Around the time of industrialization in the 19th century, particularly in countries like England and the U.S., there arose an important concept that did not exist before. That concept is tied to the new use of the word "normal." While we use that word all the time, the word was not used until about 1830 in English and a bit later in other languages. The word "normal" has the tremendous power to define and enforce ways of being, looking, working, and doing. Try to imagine a time when the concept did not exist. Think about how much the word is used now and how much it affects your ideas of bodies and minds.

It also turns out that "normal" came at the same time as, and was very much involved with, "eugenics." Eugenics was a "scientific" way of thinking about the human body and mind. I put "scientific" in scare quotes because although the past thought of eugenics as a genuine science, we don't now. Eugenics was the science of breeding better humans. The idea was that since humans had done so well in breeding livestock and pets, why should those accomplishments not be applied to human beings? The goal was to make humans smarter, bigger, stronger, and better behaved. The "science" of eugenics was spurred on by wealthy, white, English and American people who looked around them and saw a growing and restless working class. In the U.S. slavery and the fear of African-Americans encouraged eugenics. The fear of immigration from Southern Europe and Ireland led to seeing the new citizens as a group that contained hereditary traits that would pollute the better stock of native citizens. So along with eugenics, scientific racism was born.

It doesn't take much to see that eugenics combined with the idea of normality created a very bad environment for those who were not "normal." If you weren't normal, then clearly you were abnormal. And if you were abnormal, eugenics said that your hereditary burden needed to be eliminated to improve the human race. People with disabilities, Deaf people, and those from undesirable ethnic and racial groups, as well as poor people, were considered "feeble-minded" and undesirable. In England and the U.S., eugenicists argued for policies that would encourage the marriage of people with superior traits and discourage the mating of people with undesirable traits. In some cases, sterilization was seen as a logical extension of this policy. Germany, a country that came late to eugenics but wanted to show the U.K.

and the U.S. that they were equally devoted to the cause, enforced what was known as negative eugenics—they began a program to sterilize and kill those with "lives not worth living." Beginning with disabled people, in what was known as the T-4 program, Nazis isolated people with disabilities and began the first attempts to systematically kill by gassing them and then disposing of the bodies in crematoriums. Once having established the efficacy of that system, the Nazis used similar techniques against Jews, Romani people (known then as Gypsies), and homosexuals—all of whom were thought of as having "lives not worth living."

While we'd like to think that eugenics ended with the defeat of the Nazi regime, eugenics continues today under a different name. After World War II, the term eugenics became so closely associated with Hitler that the main center in the U.S., the Center for Eugenics at Cold Springs Harbor in Long Island, changed its name to the Center for Genetics. It is in the realm of genetics that some eugenic ideas still hold sway. Most notably, we see this concern in prenatal genetic testing. When couples are deciding to have a child they may be tested for genetic diseases like Down syndrome or Tay-Sachs. A pregnant woman may be tested and if a genetic abnormality is found in the fetus, the opportunity to abort could be offered. While some people with disabilities may support abortion in general, they are concerned that the reason a fetus might be aborted is that they are not "normal," "perfect," or "fit"—words that echo the underlying argument of the eugenics movement.

Why We Study Disability

One thing to be said about disability, disability studies, or crip studies is that these are evolving fields. While the focus of study is on the person with disabilities—mental, physical, invisible, and more—there is no certainty about definitions and approaches. Rather the field has stayed open to new interpretations and insights. Why that is important for you is that your views and insights can contribute to the evolution of the field. While it is unusual for medical students to change the course of medicine, it is very possible for students studying disability to effect change within this field. There are conferences that you can attend, blogs you can start, and papers you can write that may have an influence.

I'll give you one example of this. I had a master's student named Chris Bell who wrote a paper for my class. In it he wrote about how disability studies at that point was based on the work of mainly white people. As his professor, I saw that this paper written for a class had wide applicability. So I published it in an anthology, and his work has become very widely read and influential. There are many other students like Chris whose work has become read and whose voices and words have influenced the direction of the field. I hope you'll feel free to share your experiences and insights as you read this book and learn about disability.

Discussion Questions

1. What does it mean to be considered "normal"? Can someone be both disabled and normal?

2. Identify the major models used to describe and understand disability. What did people find useful about some of these models? What are the problems with them?

3. Give some examples of the kinds of barriers, physical or otherwise, that disabled people often face. What responsibility does society have to address these barriers?

4. How might disability studies change the way you think about other subjects in school: history, psychology, cultural studies, medicine, or any other discipline?

Notes

1 Some words that usually don't carry "scare quotes" are actually in need of rethinking. The word "normal" is one of those. We use the word all the time, but what does it really mean? Read on in this chapter to find out.

2 Another word that needs explaining: When big "D" is used in the word "Deaf" it means that the person is part of the Deaf community, uses sign language, and is identified with Deaf culture. Little "d" in "deaf" means that the person has a hearing loss but doesn't consider themselves to be part of the Deaf community. For "Deaf" think of a person who grew up speaking sign language and went to a Deaf college like Gallaudet University in Washington DC. For "deaf" think of an older person who just started wearing hearing aids.

Becoming Disabled

2

Rosemarie Garland-Thomson

Not long ago, a good friend of mine said something revealing to me: "I don't think of you as disabled," she confessed.

I knew exactly what she meant; I didn't think of myself as disabled until a few decades ago, either, even though my two arms have been pretty significantly asymmetrical and different from most everybody else's my whole life.

My friend's comment was meant as a compliment, but followed a familiar logic—one that African-Americans have noted when their well-meaning white friends have tried to erase the complications of racial identity by saying, "I don't think of you as black," or when a man compliments a woman by saying that he thinks of her as "just one of the guys."

This impulse to rescue people with disabilities from a discredited identity, while usually well meaning, is decidedly at odds with the various pride movements we've come to know in recent decades. Slogans like "Black Is Beautiful" and "We're Here, We're Queer, Get Used to It!" became transformative taunts for generations of people schooled in the self-loathing of racism, sexism and heterosexism. Pride movements were the psycho-emotional equivalents of the antidiscrimination and desegregation laws that asserted the rights of full citizenship to women, gay people, racial minorities and other groups. More recently, the Black Lives Matter and the LGBTQ rights movement have also taken hold.

Yet pride movements for people with disabilities—like Crip Power or Mad Pride —have not gained the same sort of traction in the American consciousness. Why? One answer is that we have a much clearer collective notion of what it means to be a woman or an African-American, gay or transgender person than we do of what it means to be disabled.

A person without a disability may recognize someone using a wheelchair, a guide dog or a prosthetic limb, or someone with Down syndrome, but most don't conceptualize these people as having a shared social identity and a political status.

"They" merely seem to be people to whom something unfortunate has happened, for whom something has gone terribly wrong. The one thing most people do know about being disabled is that they don't want to be that.

Yet disability is everywhere once you start noticing it. A simple awareness of who we are sharing our public spaces with can be revelatory. Wheelchair users or people with walkers, hearing aids, canes, service animals, prosthetic limbs or breathing devices may seem to appear out of nowhere, when they were in fact there all the time.

A mother of a 2-year-old boy with dwarfism who had begun attending Little People of America events summed this up when she said to me with stunned wonder, "There are a lot of them!" Until this beloved child unexpectedly entered her family, she had no idea that achondroplasia is the most common form of short stature or that most people with the condition have average-size parents. More important, she probably did not know how to request the accommodations, access the services, enter the communities or use the laws that he needs to make his way through life. But because he is hers and she loves him, she will learn a lot about disability.

The fact is, most of us will move in and out of disability in our lifetimes, whether we do so through illness, an injury or merely the process of aging.

The World Health Organization defines disability as an umbrella term that encompasses impairments, activity limitations and participation restrictions that reflect the complex interaction between "features of a person's body and features of the society in which he or she lives." The Americans with Disabilities Act tells us that disability is "a physical or mental impairment that substantially limits one or more major life activities."

Obviously, this category is broad and constantly shifting, so exact statistics are hard to come by, but the data from our most reliable sources is surprising. The Centers for Disease Control and Prevention estimates that one in five adults in the United States is living with a disability. The National Organization on Disability says there are 56 million disabled people. Indeed, people with disabilities are the largest minority group in the United States, and as new disability categories such as neurodiversity, psychiatric disabilities, disabilities of aging and learning disabilities emerge and grow, so does that percentage.

Disability growth areas—if you will—include diagnostic categories such as depression, anxiety disorders, anorexia, cancers, traumatic brain injuries, attention deficit disorder, autoimmune disease, spinal cord injuries, autistic spectrum disabilities and dementia. Meanwhile, whole categories of disability and populations of people with certain disabilities have vanished or diminished significantly in the 20th century with improved public health measures, disease prevention and increased public safety.

Because almost all of us will experience disability sometime in our lives, having to navigate one early in life can be a great advantage. Because I was born with six fingers altogether and one quite short arm, I learned to get through the world with the body I had from the beginning. Such a misfit between body and world can be an occasion for resourcefulness. Although I certainly recognized that the world was built for what I call the fully fingered, not for my body, I never experienced a sense of losing capacity, and adapted quite readily, engaging with the world in my preferred way and developing practical workarounds for the life demands my body did not meet. (I used talk-to-text technology to write this essay, for example.)

Still, most Americans don't know how to be disabled. Few of us can imagine living with a disability or using the technologies that disabled people often need. Since most of us are not born into disability but enter into it as we travel through life, we don't get acculturated the way most of us do in our race or gender. Yet disability, like any challenge or limitation, is fundamental to being human—a part of every life. Clearly, the border between "us" and "them" is fragile. We just might be better off preparing for disability than fleeing from it.

Yet even talking about disability can be a fraught experience. The vocabulary of this status is highly charged, and for even the most well-meaning person, a conversation can feel like stepping into a maze of courtesy, correctness and possible offense. When I lecture about disability, someone always wants to know—either defensively, earnestly or cluelessly—the "correct" way to refer to this new politicized identity.

What we call ourselves can also be controversial. Different constituencies have vibrant debates about the politics of self-naming. "People first" language asserts that if we call ourselves "people with disabilities," we put our humanity first and consider our impairment a modification. Others claim disability pride by getting our identity right up front, making us "disabled people." Others, like many sign language users, reject the term "disability."

The old way of talking about disability as a curse, tragedy, misfortune or individual failing is no longer appropriate, but we are unsure about what more progressive, more polite, language to use. "Crippled," "handicapped" and "feeble-minded" are outdated and derogatory. Many pre-Holocaust eugenic categories that were indicators for state-sponsored sterilization or extermination policies—"idiot," "moron," "imbecile" and even "mentally retarded"—have been discarded in favor of terms such as "developmentally delayed" or "intellectually disabled." In 2010, President Obama signed Rosa's Law, which replaced references to "mental retardation" with "intellectual disability" in federal statutes.

The author and scholar Simi Linton writes about learning to be disabled in a hospital after a spinal cord injury—not by way of her rehabilitation but rather by bonding with other young people new to disability. She calls this entering into community "claiming disability." In "Sight Unseen," an elegant explication of blindness and sight as cultural metaphors, Georgina Kleege wryly suggests the difference between medical low vision and blindness as a cultural identity by observing that,

"Writing this book made me blind," a process she calls gaining blindness rather than losing sight.

Like them, I had no idea until the 1980s what it meant to be disabled, that there was a history, culture and politics of disability. Without a disability consciousness, I was in the closet.

Since that time, other people with disabilities have entered the worlds in which I live and work, and I have found community and developed a sturdy disability identity. I have changed the way I see and treat myself and others. I have taken up the job of teaching disability studies and bioethics as part of my work. I have learned to be disabled.

What has been transformed is not my body, but my consciousness.

As we manage our bodies in environments not built for them, the social barriers can sometimes be more awkward than the physical ones. Confused responses to racial or gender categories can provoke the question "What are you?" Whereas disability interrogations are "What's wrong with you?" Before I learned about disability rights and disability pride, which I came to by way of the women's movement, I always squirmed out a shame-filled, "I was born this way." Now I'm likely to begin one of these uncomfortable encounters with, "I have a disability," and to complete it with, "And these are the accommodations I need." This is a claim to inclusion and right to access resources.

This coming out has made possible what a young graduate student with a disability said to me after I gave a lecture at her university. She said that she understood now that she had a right to be in the world.

We owe much of this progress to the Americans with Disabilities Act of 1990 and the laws that led up to it. Starting in the 1960s, a broad disability rights movement encouraged legislation and policy that gradually desegregated the institutions and spaces that had kept disabled people out and barred them from exercising the privileges and obligations of full citizenship. Education, transportation, public spaces and work spaces steadily transformed so that people with disabilities came out of hospitals, asylums, private homes and special schools into an increasingly rebuilt and reorganized world.

That changed landscape is being reflected politically, too, so much so that when Donald Trump mocked the movement of a disabled reporter, most of the country reacted with shock and outrage at his blatant discrimination, and that by the time the Democratic National Convention rolled round, it seemed natural to find the rights and dignity of people with disabilities placed front and center. Hillary Clinton's efforts early in her career to secure the right to an education for all disabled children was celebrated; Tom Harkin, the former Iowa senator and an author of the Americans with Disabilities Act, marked the law's 26th anniversary and called for improvements to it. People with disabilities were featured speakers, including Anastasia Somoza, who received an ovation for her powerful speech. President Obama, in his address, referred to "black, white, Latino, Asian, Native American; young, old; gay, straight; men, women, folks with disabilities, all pledging allegiance, under the same proud flag."

Becoming disabled demands learning how to live effectively as a person with disabilities, not just living as a disabled person trying to become nondisabled. It also demands the awareness and cooperation of others who don't experience these challenges. Becoming disabled means moving from isolation to community, from ignorance to knowledge about who we are, from exclusion to access, and from shame to pride.

Discussion Questions

1. What would it take for America or the U.K. to see a widespread disability pride movement?

2. Why don't most Americans "know how to be disabled"?

3. In what ways are disabled people a separate community, and in what ways are they working to become part of other communities?

3 Reassigning Meaning

Simi Linton

The present examination of disability has no need for the medical language of symptoms and diagnostic categories. Disability studies looks to different kinds of signifiers and the identification of different kinds of syndromes for its material. The elements of interest here are the linguistic conventions that structure the meanings assigned to disability and the patterns of response to disability that emanate from, or are attendant upon, those meanings.

The medical meaning-making was negotiated among interested parties who packaged their version of disability in ways that increased the ideas' potency and marketability. The disability community has attempted to wrest control of the language from the previous owners, and reassign meaning to the terminology used to describe disability and disabled people. This new language conveys different meanings, and, significantly, the shifts serve as metacommunications about the social, political, intellectual, and ideological transformations that have taken place over the past two decades.

Naming Oppression

It has been particularly important to bring to light language that reinforces the dominant culture's views of disability. A useful step in that process has been the construction of the terms ableist and ableism, which can be used to organize ideas about the centering and domination of the nondisabled experience and point of view. Ableism has recently landed in the Readers Digest Oxford Wordfinder,[1] where it is defined as "discrimination in favor of the able-bodied." I would add, extrapolating from the definitions of racism and sexism, that ableism also includes the idea that a person's abilities or characteristics are determined by disability or that people with disabilities as a group are inferior to nondisabled people. Although there is probably greater consensus among the general public on what could be labeled racist or sexist language than there is on what might be considered ableist, that may be because the nature of the oppression of disabled people is not yet as widely understood.

Naming the Group

Across the world and throughout history various terminologies and meanings are ascribed to the types of human variations known in contemporary Westernized countries as disabilities. Over the past century the term disabled and others, such as handicapped and the less inclusive term crippled, have emerged as collective nouns that convey the idea that there is something that links this disparate group of people. The terms have been used to arrange people in ways that are socially and economically convenient to the society.

There are various consequences of the chosen terminology and variation in the degree of control that the named group has over the labeling process. The terms disability and disabled people are the most commonly used by disability rights activists, and recently policymakers and health care professionals have begun to use these terms more consistently. Although there is some agreement on terminology, there are disagreements about what it is that unites disabled people and whether disabled people should have control over the naming of their experience.

The term disability, as it has been used in general parlance, appears to signify something material and concrete, a physical or psychological condition considered to have predominantly medical significance. Yet it is an arbitrary designation, used erratically both by professionals who lay claim to naming such phenomena and by confused citizens. A project of disability studies scholars and the disability rights movement has been to bring into sharp relief the processes by which disability has been imbued with the meaning(s) it has and to reassign a meaning that is consistent with a sociopolitical analysis of disability. Divesting it of its current meaning is no small feat. As typically used, the term disability is a linchpin in a complex web of social ideals, institutional structures, and government policies. As a result, many people have a vested interest in keeping a tenacious hold on the current meaning because it is consistent with the practices and policies that are central to their livelihood or their ideologies. People may not be driven as much by economic imperatives as by a personal investment in their own beliefs and practices, in metaphors they hold dear, or in their own professional roles. Further, underlying this tangled web of needs and beliefs, and central to the arguments presented in this book is an epistemological structure that both generates and reflects current interpretations.[2]

A glance through a few dictionaries will reveal definitions of disability that include incapacity, a disadvantage, deficiency, especially a physical or mental impairment that restricts normal achievement; something that hinders or incapacitates, something that incapacitates or disqualifies. Legal definitions include legal incapacity or disqualification. *Stedman's Medical Dictionary* (1976) identifies disability as a "medicolegal term signifying loss of function and earning power," whereas disablement is a "medicolegal term signifying loss of function without loss of earning power" (400). These definitions are understood by the general public and by many in the academic community to be useful ones. Disability so defined is a medically derived term that assigns predominantly medical significance and meaning to certain types of human variation.

The decision to assign medical meanings to disability has had many and varied consequences for disabled people. One clear benefit has been the medical treatments that have increased the well-being and vitality of many disabled people, indeed have saved people's lives. Ongoing attention by the medical profession to the health and well-being of people with disabilities and to prevention of disease and impairments is critical. Yet, along with these benefits, there are enormous negative consequences that will take a large part of this book to list and explain. Briefly, the medicalization of disability casts human variation as deviance from the norm, as pathological condition, as deficit, and, significantly, as an individual burden and personal tragedy. Society, in agreeing to assign medical meaning to disability, colludes to keep the issue within the purview of the medical establishment, to keep it a personal matter and "treat" the condition and the person with the condition rather than "treating" the social processes and policies that constrict disabled people's lives. The disability studies' and disability rights movement's position is critical of the domination of the medical definition and views it as a major stumbling block to the reinterpretation of disability as a political category and to the social changes that could follow such a shift.

While retaining the term disability, despite its medical origins, a premise of most of the literature in disability studies is that disability is best understood as a marker of identity. As such, it has been used to build a coalition of people with significant impairments, people with behavioral or anatomical characteristics marked as deviant, and people who have or are suspected of having conditions, such as AIDS or emotional illness, that make them targets of discrimination.[3] As rendered in disability studies scholarship, disability has become a more capacious category, incorporating people with a range of physical, emotional, sensory, and cognitive conditions. Although the category is broad, the term is used to designate a specific minority group. When medical definitions of disability are dominant, it is logical to separate people according to biomedical condition through the use of diagnostic categories and to forefront medical perspectives on human variation. When disability is redefined as a social/political category, people with a variety of conditions are identified as people with disabilities or disabled people, a group bound by common social and political experience. These designations, as reclaimed by the community, are used to identify us as a constituency, to serve our needs for unity and identity, and to function as a basis for political activism.

The question of who "qualifies" as disabled is as answerable or as confounding as questions about any identity status. One simple response might be that you are disabled if you say you are. Although that declaration won't satisfy a worker's compensation board, it has a certain credibility with the disabled community. The degree and significance of an individual's impairment is often less of an issue than the degree to which someone identifies as disabled. Another way to answer the question is to say that disability "is mostly a social distinction . . . a marginalized status" and the status is assigned by "the majority culture tribunal."[4] But the problem gets stickier when the distinction between disabled and nondisabled is challenged by people who say, "Actually, we're all disabled in some way, aren't we?"[5] Gill says the answer is no to those whose difference "does not significantly affect daily life and the person does not [with some consistency] present himself/herself to the world at large as a disabled person."[6] I concur with Gill; I am not willing or interested in erasing the line between disabled and nondisabled people, as long as disabled people are devalued and discriminated against, and as long as naming the category serves to call attention to that treatment.

Over the past 20 years, disabled people have gained greater control over these definitional issues. "The disabled" or "the handicapped" was replaced in the mid-1970s by "people with disabilities" to maintain disability as a characteristic of the individual, as opposed to the defining variable. At the time, some people would purposefully say "women and men with disabilities" to provide an extra dimension to the people being described and to deneuter the way the disabled were traditionally described. Beginning in the early 1990s "disabled people" has been increasingly used in disability studies and disability rights circles when referring to the constituency group. Rather than maintaining disability as a secondary characteristic, disabled has become a marker of the identity that the individual and group wish to highlight and call attention to. In this book, the terms disabled and nondisabled are used frequently to designate membership within or outside the community. "Disabled" is centered, and "nondisabled" is placed in the peripheral position in order to look at the world from the inside out, to expose the perspective and expertise that is silenced. Occasionally, "people with disabilities" is used as a variant of "disabled people." The use of "nondisabled" is strategic: to center disability. Its inclusion in this chapter is also to set the stage for postulating about the nondisabled position in society and in scholarship in later chapters. This action is similar to the strategy of marking and articulating "whiteness." The assumed position in scholarship has always been the male, white, nondisabled scholar; it is the default category. As recent scholarship has shown, these positions are not only presumptively hegemonic because they are the assumed universal stance, as well as the presumed neutral or objective stance, but also undertheorized. The nondisabled stance, like the white stance, is veiled. "White cannot be said quite out loud, or it loses its crucial position as a precondition of vision and becomes the object of scrutiny."[7] Therefore, centering the disabled position and labeling its opposite nondisabled focuses attention on both the structure of knowledge and the structure of society.

Nice Words

Terms such as physically challenged, the able disabled, handicapable, and special people/children surface at different times and places. They are rarely used by disabled activists and scholars (except with palpable irony). Although they may be considered well-meaning attempts to inflate the value of people with disabilities, they convey the boosterism and do-gooder mentality endemic to the paternalistic agencies that control many disabled people's lives.

Physically challenged is the only term that seems to have caught on. Nondisabled people use it in conversation around disabled people with no hint of anxiety, suggesting that they believe it is a positive term. This phrase does not make much sense to me. To say that I am physically challenged is to state that the obstacles to my participation are physical, not social, and that the barrier is my own disability. Further, it separates those of us with mobility impairments from other disabled people, not a valid or useful partition for those interested in coalition building and social change. Various derivatives of the term challenged have been adopted as a description used in jokes. For instance, "vertically challenged" is considered a humorous way to say short, and "calorically challenged" to say fat. A review of the Broadway musical *Big* in the *New Yorker* said that the score was "melodically challenged."

I observed a unique use of challenged in the local Barnes and Nobles superstore. The children's department has a section for books on "Children with Special Needs." There are shelves labeled "Epilepsy" and "Down Syndrome." A separate shelf at the bottom is labeled "Misc. Challenges," indicating that it is now used as an organizing category.

The term able disabled and handicapable have had a fairly short shelf life. They are used, it seems, to refute common stereotypes of incompetence. They are, though, defensive and reactive terms rather than terms that advance a new agenda.

An entire profession, in fact a number of professions, are built around the word special. A huge infrastructure rests on the idea that special children and special education are valid and useful structuring ideas. Although dictionaries insist that special be reserved for things that surpass what is common, are distinct among others of their kind, are peculiar to a specific person, have a limited or specific function, are arranged for a particular purpose, or are arranged for a particular occasion, experience teaches us that special when applied to education or to children means something different.

The naming of disabled children and the education that "is designed for students whose learning needs cannot be met by a standard school curriculum"[8] as special can be understood only as a euphemistic formulation, obscuring the reality that neither the children nor the education are considered desirable and that they are not thought to "surpass what is common."

Labeling the education and its recipients special may have been a deliberate attempt to confer legitimacy on the educational practice and to prop up a discarded group. It is also important to consider the unconscious feelings such a strategy may mask. It is my feeling that the nation in general responds to disabled people with great ambivalence. Whatever antipathy and disdain is felt is in competition with feelings of empathy, guilt, and identification. The term special may be evidence not of a deliberate maneuver but of a collective "reaction formation," Freud's term for the unconscious defense mechanism in which an individual adopts attitudes and behaviors that are opposite to his or her own true feelings, in order to protect the ego from the anxiety felt from experiencing the real feelings.

The ironic character of the word special has been captured in the routine on *Saturday Night Live*, where the character called the "Church Lady" declares when she encounters something distasteful or morally repugnant, "Isn't that special!"

Nasty Words

Some of the less subtle or more idiomatic terms for disabled people such as cripple, vegetable, dumb, deformed, retard, and gimp have generally been expunged from public conversation but emerge in various types of discourse. Although they are understood to be offensive or hurtful, they are still used in jokes and in informal conversation.

Cripple as a descriptor of disabled people is considered impolite, but the word has retained its metaphoric vitality, as in "the exposé in the newspaper crippled the politician's campaign." The term is also used occasionally for its evocative power. A recent example appeared in *Lingua Franca* in a report on research on the behaviors of German academics. The article states that a professor had "documented the postwar careers of psychiatrists and geneticists involved in gassing thousands of cripples and schizophrenics."[9] Cripple is used rather loosely here to describe people with a broad range of disabilities. The victims of Nazi slaughter were people with mental illness, epilepsy, chronic illness, and mental retardation, as well as people with physical disabilities. Yet cripple is defined as "one that is partially disabled or unable to use a limb or limbs"[10] and is usually used only to refer to people with mobility impairments. Because cripple inadequately and inaccurately describes the group, the author of the report is likely to have chosen this term for its effect.

Cripple has also been revived by some in the disability community who refer to each other as "crips" or "cripples." A performance group with disabled actors call themselves the "Wry Crips." "In reclaiming 'cripple,' disabled people are taking the thing in their identity that scares the outside world the most and making it a cause to revel in with militant self-pride."[11]

A recent personal ad in the *Village Voice* shows how "out" the term is:

> TWISTED CRIP: Very sexy, full-figured disabled BiWF artist sks fearless, fun, oral BiWF for hot, no-strings nights. Wheelchair, tattoo, dom. Shaved a+ N/S. No men/sleep-overs.

Cripple, gimp, and freak as used by the disability community have transgressive potential. They are personally and politically useful as a means to comment on oppression because they assert our right to name experience.

Discussion Questions

1. Is the term "disability" more useful than other terms that preceded it? How so?
2. Why does Linton caution against the use of "nice words" in discussing disability? How are these words different from those she calls "nasty words?"

Notes

1 Tulloch 1993.
2 Various authors have discussed issues related to definitions of disability. See Wendell (1996), Longmore (1985,1987), and Hahn (1987), and also the June Issacson Kailes (1995) monograph *Language is More Than a Trivial Concern!*
3 The definition of disability under the Americans with Disabilities Act is consistent with the sociopolitical model employed in disability studies. A person is considered to have a disability if he or she: has a physical or mental impairment that substantially limits one or more of his or her major life activities; has a record of such an impairment; or is regarded as having such an impairment. The last two parts of the definition acknowledge that even in the absence of a substantially limiting impairment, people can be discriminated against. For instance, this may occur because someone has a facial disfigurement or has, or is suspected of having, HIV or mental illness. The ADA recognizes that social forces, such as myths and fears regarding disability, function to substantially limit opportunity.
4 Gill 1994, 44.
5 Ibid, 46.
6 Ibid.
7 Haraway 1989, 152.
8 *American Heritage Dictionary* 1992.
9 Allen 1996, 37.

10 *American Heritage Dictionary* 1992.
11 Shapiro 1993, 34.

References

Allen, A. (1996). Open Secrets: a German academic hides his past—in plain sight. *Lingua Franca* 6(3), 28–41.

American Heritage Dictionary (3rd edn). (1992). Boston: Houghton Mifflin.

Gill, C. J. (1994). Questioning continuum. In B. Shaw (Ed.), *The ragged edge: The disability experience from the pages of the first fifteen years of "The Disability Rag,"* (pp. 42–49). Louisville, KY: Advocado Press.

Hahn, H. (1987). Disability and capitalism: Advertising the acceptably employable image. *Policy Studies Journal*, 15(3), 551–570.

Haraway, D. (1989). *Primate visions: Gender, race, and nature in the world of modern science.* New York: Routledge.

Isaacson Kailes, J. (1995). *Language is More Than a Trivial Concern!* Center for Disability and Health Policy.

Longmore, P. (1985, December). The life of Randolph Bourne and the need for a history of disabled people. *Reviews in American History*, 13(4), 581–587.

Longmore, P. (1987, September). Uncovering the hidden history of people with disabilities. *Reviews in American History*, 15(3), 355–364.

Shapiro, J. P. (1993). *No pity: People with disabilities forging a new civil rights movement.* New York: Times Books.

Stedman's Medical Dictionary (23rd edn). (1976). Baltimore, MD: Williams and Wilkins.

Tulloch, S. (Ed.). (1993). *The Reader's Digest Oxford Wordfinder.* Oxford, England: Clarendon Press.

Wendell, S. (1996). *The rejected body: Feminist philosophical reflections on disability.* New York: Routledge.

Disability Rhetoric

Jay Dolmage

Here we are in what is currently Alabama, USA, in 1818, in the forge of a Cherokee metalworker, Sequoyah, a silversmith. His name comes from *siqua*, a Cherokee word meaning hog, a word that also connotes disability or deformity. Historians have suggested that the specific reference was to the pig's foot, suggesting that his own foot was deformed.[1] He was the son of a white soldier and a Cherokee mother. Sequoyah is often mythologized reverently with what disability studies scholars call a "compensation" narrative, common to many disability stories: "because Sequoyah was physically limited, he developed other kinds of skills."[2] Indeed, Sequoyah became much more than a metalsmith—he become a rhetorical inventor. His foremost accomplishment was that he invented the Cherokee syllabary, a system of representing the syllables of Cherokee language so that it could be written and recorded. He is now legendary as "the only member of an illiterate group in human history to have single-handedly devised a successful system of writing."[3] The syllabary has been recognized as having offered linguistic (and thus rhetorical) means to build solidarity in the face of genocide; it has also been since recognized as responsible for allowing Native political speeches and autobiographies to be retained and preserved. In turn, Sequoyah has become a controversial figure, his stories the focus of debate and rhetorical negotiation. He has become a symbol system himself. But through the complicated history of Sequoyah as a rhetorical inventor, there is much to learn about the interconnection between bodies, languages, literacies, and cultures. In the multiple myths and legacies of Sequoyah, we see two key trends or directions that will ground what I define in this chapter as *disability rhetoric*. The first direction is the rhetoric around, about, and over the top of disability. The second direction is the rhetoric that comes *from* disability. Sequoyah as a disabled historical figure has common tropes and metaphors and ideas about disability superimposed upon him, so that we see him as overcoming or compensating for his disability, so that we are urged to pity the disabled part of him. But the other direction that we often neglect to examine is his role as a disabled rhetorical inventor—his rhetorical power coming from, rather than in spite of his disability.

Here we are, then, in a chapter focused on disability rhetoric. Here, we will explore the ways that we define and describe disability, and the meanings that get generated from disability and by disabled people. How do we talk and write about disability? How does this impact the experience of disabled people, or the rules and possibilities for any body? How does disability create new possibilities for making meaning?

To begin, zooming out a little bit: what is rhetoric? You probably recognize the term rhetoric in a negative sense—as the intentional misuse of language to mangle and obscure meaning. But in truth, rhetoricians focus on the uses of language for positive and persuasive ends—the ways that rhetoric shapes what we say and what we write, as well as beliefs, values, institutions, and even bodies. One simple way to define rhetoric is to say that it is the study of all of communication. But more specifically, rhetoricians argue that all texts and expressions are argumentative or persuasive—about actively shaping belief as much as they are about reflecting truths. Language is power. Rhetoric can be seen as the powerful use of communication to shape identity, community, cultural processes, art, and everyday life. Rhetoric not only impacts all of those variables in our lives that are uncertain and thus subject to opinion and persuasion; rhetoric also works to whittle away our sense that any part of our lives could be static, certain, or unchanging.

Sequoyah is an intensely rhetorical figure because when people tell stories about him overcoming his disability, this persuades the public (both disabled and temporarily able-bodied people) that disability must be overcome or compensated for in order for the disabled individual to have value. He is also intensely rhetorical because, like many other disabled people throughout history, he used his unique subject position to develop new means of communication, new ways to record language and to use it politically. And once we begin to examine any body rhetorically, we can't stop: what does it mean that a mainstream, white historical tradition might champion his syllabary while ignoring other forms of indigenous rhetoric, for instance? No matter which angle you examine Sequoyah from, you can find multiple meanings, all of them potentially persuasive and potentially powerful.

So let's define rhetoric as the *study of the movement of power through communication,* how the power of language shapes how we can move, and how we use language to make powerful moves. And disability rhetoric is a way of centering the body in this study—and in particular, in centering non-normative bodies and minds in this study. Why? Because, we need rhetoric to understand the meanings that circulate around and come from bodies. And we use our bodies to be rhetorical. Rhetoric needs disability studies as a reminder to pay critical and careful attention to diverse bodies. Disability studies needs rhetoric to better understand and negotiate the ways that discourse or language represents and impacts the experience of disability. Thus, as students and citizens, we need disability rhetoric.

Meanings *Around* Disability

As Rosemarie Garland-Thomson writes, "seeing disability as a representational system engages several premises of current critical theory: that representation structures reality, that the margins constitute the center, that human identity is multiple and unstable, and that all analysis and evaluation has political implications."[4] With this in mind, the first thing I want to show is that, rhetorically, the ways we tell particular stories about disability condition our understanding of disability (and thus of all identity and all bodies). These "particular stories" are the meanings that get written and spoken around, over, and into disability. To understand disability rhetoric, we need to begin to understand how these messages and arguments work, as well as what patterns we can identify in such messages and arguments.

To begin with, we know that certain words related to disability have power— words like retard, spaz, idiot, and moron carry with them the history of the oppression and mistreatment of disabled people. As rhetorical students, we have a responsibility to understand this history. But beyond individual words, there are also myths of disability that can be found, repeatedly, across cultures and eras. The vast majority of these myths work to mark and construct disability as undesirable, strange, outside of common experience, and *other*. In this way, these myths reach into all bodies; and yet they also very particularly structure roles for people with disabilities. Regardless, like the words mentioned above, these myths shape both stories and lives. As Joseph Shapiro has shown,

> disabled people find constant descriptions of a disabled person's proper role as either an object of pity or a source of inspiration. These images are internalized by disabled and nondisabled people alike and build social stereotypes, create artificial limitations, and contribute to discrimination.
>
> (Shapiro, 1993: 30)

Some of the more straightforward of these myths or stories include the myth of overcoming or compensation, which we already explored through the figure of Sequoyah. In this myth, the person with a disability overcomes their impairment through hard work, or has some special talent that offsets their deficiencies. Shapiro calls this figure the "super crip." In this myth, the audience doesn't have to focus on the disability, or challenge the stigma that this disability entails, but instead re-focuses attention toward the "gift." This works as a management of the fears of the temporarily able-bodied (if/when I become disabled, I'll compensate or overcome) and it acts as a demand placed upon disabled bodies (you better be very good at something). And this myth shapes reality. Think, for instance, of the celebration of Paralympic athletes, despite the lack of real access to modest recreation facilities for most disabled people.

Another common rhetorical story is the myth of disability as object of pity and/or charity. Much of the language of disability relies on symbols and stories of pity: myths of powerlessness which demand to be answered with charity. People with disabilities are represented as sad and helpless, isolated, a problem that can be solved via the good hearts, and the wallets, of well-meaning nondisabled people.

Other times, we see physical deformity as a sign of an internal flaw. Leonard Kriegel argues that Captain Ahab from *Moby Dick* "is not merely crippled—his leg torn from his body by the white whale—he is crippled in the deepest metaphysical sense. His injury became his selfhood."[5] This interacts with the myth of disability as inherently evil. Often, in fiction, a character with a disability is evil because he or she is "mad at the world." We can recognize this stereotype in almost the entirety of children's literature, which is overrun with disfigured pirates and witches, outfitted with the requisite crutches and eye-patches. Children are then encouraged to fear people with disabilities, or to associate disability with anger and revenge. Think of some of the books that you read as a child—how was disability represented and how might this have conditioned your idea of disability?

Of course, just as disability can be read as evil, disability can also be represented as pure good, through the creation of equally one-dimensional characters. The result of this myth is that people with disabilities are disallowed from being bad or fallible, and thus they can't really be fully human—or if they somehow fail to live up to this standard, their failure is particularly pronounced. There is a clear rhetorical relationship between disability-as-good and disability-as-evil as well: as soon as a disability is no longer profitable, curable, rehabilitible, infantile, and/or unassuming, it can be quickly made evil. As Colin Cameron writes, "resisting categorisation in terms of one stereotype (passive, uncomplaining victim) simply leads to being identified in terms of another (bitter and twisted)."[6]

Unfortunately, these are just a few of the dozens of damaging tropes we could explore. Instead of cataloguing them, I'm going to look at one extended example. Both Tom Couser and Ato Quayson recognize that disability often "acts as some form of ethical background to the actions of other characters, or as a means of testing or enhancing their moral standing."[7] How a protagonist treats these disabled figures then establishes the hero's character, and tells us whether we should like or trust that person. This is the trope or myth of disability as an ethical test. Take for example the character of Walter White, Jr. from the TV series *Breaking Bad*. Walt Jr. is the son of the series "hero." The show's website identifies him as being "born with cerebral palsy" but also, in the same sentence, as a "typical high school kid." Walt Jr.'s character is indeed quite well-rounded, and instead of being written through many stereotypical disability myths, he twists them. He creates a website to raise donations for his father, who has cancer, making his dad extremely uncomfortable, as the last thing Walt Sr. wants is to be viewed as an object of pity and charity—but then he doesn't want any attention at all, really, considering that he is moonlighting as a large-scale drug manufacturer. The son is also clearly an "ethical test" for his father, and thus propels the plot. When Walt Sr. believes he is going to die from cancer, he justifies starting a lucrative career making meth through the belief that he needs to provide for his son's care after he himself is gone. This reasoning makes the entire plot not just believable, but much more appealing than if Walt Sr. were just greedy. This said, as the series developed, the question of Walt's ethics became much more nuanced, and we were invited to question what his true priorities and motivations were—the simple story of a man-gone-bad to provide for his disabled son transforms into a range of other more difficult possibilities. Thus the entire plot, in a way, centers around the ethical test of Walt Jr.'s disability.

But we have come to expect that the character (or the person) with the disability will not be central to the story. Instead, they will be secondary, a narrow reflective thread sewn into the narrative that allows us to see the able-bodied heroes or protagonists more clearly. This extends out from fictional depictions on TV, at the movies, or on the pages of novels. We want to judge politicians, for example, by how they react to disability. When American presidential candidate Donald Trump mocked a disabled reporter, it was framed nearly unanimously as exposing a severe flaw in Trump's character. When Canadian Prime Ministerial candidate Justin Trudeau lifted a man in a wheelchair down a set of stairs, the story got a lot of traction. He is now the Prime Minister, and the story and images still get circulated. No one seems to ask what the story of that man being lifted might be. And why, in the first place, was the Subway station in which both Trudeau and this man found themselves so inaccessible? These become key rhetorical questions around disability because they reveal dominant opinions and arguments and values about disability, but also because they obscure so many other possible meanings and arguments and values. Remember: the power of language shapes how we can move, and how we use language to make powerful moves. The power of language and discourse centers some things and hides others. This hiding might lead us to avoid taking action to make public space accessible, or might lead us to seek leaders who are attuned to disability rights issues, rather than ridiculing them.

Rhetoric *From* Disability

So, where do we land after we have examined myths like these? Surely, we can recognize that, for instance, myths of pity and evil and compensation offer really limited, and often very damaging, representations of disability, and thus also shape lives negatively. But hopefully, recounting some of these myths gives you tools to interrogate any text or artifact that you examine, and to look for similar rhetoric. What are some of the other ways that disability gets over-represented or under-scored? In the readings provided in this book, you'll encounter the analyses and critiques of other authors who utilize disability studies to examine similar myths and tropes, and you should be able to both recognize and argue for a different range of representations in the culture and the society around you.

It is worth noting that R.J. Mitte, who plays Walt Jr. on *Breaking Bad*, has cerebral palsy himself, which is notable mainly because there are almost no actors with disabilities on TV or in the movies. Since the conclusion of *Breaking Bad*, Mitte has visibly pushed for more acting roles for disabled people, as he has argued for equitable employment for all disabled people. In this way, expanding outwards from his role representing disability on a popular TV series, he has become a rhetorician arguing for societal change. He has become a disability activist.

Such activism is, of course, at the heart of disability studies and at the heart of disability rhetoric. Disability studies as a political movement has been about claiming disability (see Simi Linton's chapter, "Reassigning Meaning," in this book), owning disabled identity and the right to define this lived experience. In the face of the medical model of disability, in which the individual was often reduced to the sum of their dysfunctional parts, disability rights has been an identity movement—a reclamation of the symbolic power of self-definition. While medical discourse framed disability in the negative and reductive terms of affliction and symptomology, applied labels, and placed individuals in passive and disempowered roles, the disability rights movement made powerful linguistic and rhetorical moves to critique ableist culture. Essential to this movement was the message that disability is beautiful and valuable, that people who experience disability do not want to be cured, do not want to overcome their disabilities, and that they can and will lead very valuable lives in the face of oppression.

A key to the movement has been the concept that we live in an ableist society, one in which barriers are *created* that impede the ability of disabled people to participate, live fully, join the public conversation, and determine their own lives. For instance, in an ableist society, people with disabilities like R.J. Mitte are seen as incapable even of playing characters with disabilities on the screen, despite the advantage of actually living *with* the disability. The derogatory myths *about* and *around* disability drastically interfere with the right of disabled people to determine their own lives and advocate from their own lived experience. And at what cost?

Well, let's return to Sequoyah for a moment. Without his invention of the syllabary, something made possible by his inclusion and employment, his skill as a metalsmith, we'd likely know a lot less about Cherokee life, about their political struggles. And what we would know would be narrated by colonizers. The syllabary may seem like one isolated example, but the truth is that our current world is full of innovations created by and for disabled people, and often centered around rhetoric and communication. Back in 1999, Steve Jacobs wrote about the "Electronic Curb-Cut Effect," showing that "unusual things happen when products are designed to be accessible to people with disabilities. It wasn't long after sidewalks were redesigned to accommodate wheelchair users that the benefits of curb cuts began to be realized by everyone." And Jacobs created a long list, with links, of the technologies that were originally developed for (and by) people with disabilities but now benefit all: from the first typewriter, created in 1808 for a blind woman, to 1972 when Vinton Cerf developed email within ARPANET, in part because he was hard-of-hearing and used a kind of early email to communicate with his deaf wife. We could add recent examples like Optical Character Recognition (OCR), revolutionized by Ray Kurzweil to create a reading machine for blind people. This then quickly led to scanners, online research databases like *Google Books*, and now a million smartphone apps allowing people to translate foreign-language signs, solve equations by taking pictures of them, and on and on. Put together speech recognition and OCR, both developed by and for disabled people, and smartphones can be seen as terrific assistive devices for people with disabilities—but we also start to see these "assistive" features as the keys to almost everything a smartphone does. Peter Goggin and Christopher Newell have looked at the history of cell phones suggesting that "disability has played a crucial yet overlooked role" in the development of the technology.[8] As Graham Pullin writes, "this challenges the so-called trickle-down effect whereby advances in mainstream design are expected to find their way into specialist products for people with disabilities, smaller markets that could not have supported their development."[9] Instead, things created for these smaller markets become useful—terrifically, unforeseeably useful—for all. As Sara Hendren argues, "all technology is assistive technology." The power of disability shapes how we all communicate, how we all move through the world.

We began this chapter in Sequoyah's forge. But here we are today, perhaps even reading this text online or having it read aloud to us by a computer or smartphone. Technologies that were first developed for people with disabilities are now an integral part of our communicative world, reshaping language use. Body values continue to shift, to the degree that we may even fantasize that technologies can erase disability. Technology is supposed to make the body obsolete, right? Or at least technology will allow us to choose our bodies, heal them, perfect them? Yet so many of the technologies that suggest to us that we are perfectible have been invented specifically because we are not perfect or normal. Bodies continue to change, as do attitudes about them; and the rhetorical impact of these bodily transformations continue to be negotiated. What we know is that we cannot overlook—or overwrite—the value of disability.

So we will need disability rhetoric, not just to recognize the negative language, metaphors, tropes, and myths of disability in the public sphere, in art and politics and culture. We will need disability rhetoric to invent, create, and harness new technologies, languages, arguments, and artifacts, each of which are likely to transform us all.

Discussion Questions

1. What makes "disability rhetoric" distinct from other kinds of rhetorical study?

2. Discuss how Dolmage uses the example of Sequoyah. What's the connection between disability and his linguistic inventions?

3. Dolmage suggests that a story of "overcoming" is one of the most popular disability myths. Why do people keep repeating this kind of story and other stereotypes about disabled people?

4. Disability activism requires us to see disability as "beautiful and valuable." How might this be different from other ways society approaches disability?

Notes

1 Basel (2007), p. 19.
2 Ibid.
3 Wadley, n.p.
4 "The New Disability Studies," 19.
5 Kriegel, 18.
6 Cameron, 385.
7 Quayson, p. 36.
8 Goggin and Newell, p. 155.
9 Pullin, p. xiii.

References

Basel, Roberta. (2007). *Sequoyah: Inventor of Written Cherokee*. Capstone.

Cameron, Colin. (2009). Tragic but Brave or Just Crips with Chips? Songs and Their Lyrics in the Disability Arts Movement in Britain. *Popular Music* 28(3), 381–396.

Garland-Thomson, Rosemarie. The New Disability Studies. *ADFL Bulletin*, 31(1) (Fall), 49–53.

Goggin, Gerald and Christopher Newell. (2003). *Digital Disability: The Social Construction of Disability in New Media*. Rowman & Littlefield.

Hendren, Sara. (2013). All Technology is Assistive Technology. *Abler* (Sept. 17).

Jacobs, Steven. (1999). Fueling the Creation of New Electronic Curbcuts. www.accessibilitysociety.org.

Kriegel, Leonard. (1998). Disability as a Metaphor in Literature. *Kaleidoscope*, 17.

Pullin, Graham. (2009). *Design Meets Disability*. MIT Press.

Quayson, Ato. (2012). *Aesthetic Nervousness: Disability and the Crisis of Representation*. Columbia University Press.

Shapiro, Joseph P. (1993). *No Pity: people with disabilities forging a new civil rights movement*. Times Books.

Wadley, Ted. *Sequoyah (ca. 1770-ca. 1840)*. New Georgie Encyclopedia. Web.

A Comparison of Disability With Race, Sex, and Sexual Orientation Statuses

Beth Omansky and Karen Rosenblum

This chapter offers a preliminary examination of the *shared* characteristics of American constructions of race, sex and gender, sexual orientation, and disability.[1] In the discussion that follows, we will consider how each of these is constructed through social processes in which categories of people are (1) named, (2) aggregated and disaggregated, (3) dichotomized and stigmatized, and (4) denied the attributes valued in the culture. What does disability look like when its context is the social construction of race, sex and gender, and sexual orientation categories?

Naming Categories of People

Naming—whether of self or others—is a key process in the creation of categories of people. For example, the relevance of naming to the construction of social identities is illustrated in the historical transformation of Americans of African ancestry from "colored," to "Negro," to "black" or "Afro-American," and most recently "African-American." This evolution of terminology reflected both the imposition of a category name through law and public policy and the self-conscious assertion of a new name and new identity by members of the category and the social change leadership lobbying on their behalf. Thus, "Negro" was first affirmed by black leadership in the late nineteenth century as a positive collective identity in opposition to "colored." But when "Negro" had become ensconced in discriminatory public policy and social prejudice, "black" and "Afro-American" were offered by social movement leaders as a signal of a reborn collective power.[2] When feminists affirmed they were "women" rather than "girls," or when gay rights activists rejected "homosexual" for "gay" the same assertion of collective power and re-formed identity was at play.

Affirmation of a new name as signal of a new identity has also been the case for the disability rights movement, most specifically in the movement's rejection of the term "handicapped" based on the assertion by some that the term originated in disabled people having to beg—"cap in hand"—for their subsistence.[3] Currently, the movement offers "disability," "disabled people," and "people with disabilities," as conceptual alternatives. As is true for all social movements, there is intense debate about use of such terms especially among activists, since the category name is a significant part of the collective carving-out of social identity and movement goals. David Pfeiffer (1993), editor of the American journal, *Disability Studies Quarterly,* illustrates:

> Some persons use the term [disabled] to identify with the disability movement while others use it to indicate a functional limitation. The term *handicapped* is also used in different ways by different persons. Some disability activists may be comfortable saying "I am disabled because I have paralyzed limbs, but I am not handicapped because I have a job and a family." For the same circumstances, others might say, "I am handicapped because I have paralyzed limbs, but I am not disabled because I can move around quite well in a wheelchair."[4]

While those outside the group may see such distinctions as arcane, for many of those "inside" naming is part of the collective carving-out of social identity, movement goals, and ideological orientations. For example, in the United Kingdom those who subscribe to a materialist, neo-Marxist social model and those creating a postmodern constructionist model of disability often prefer "disabled person," asserting that this phrasing best describes the disablement of the person by society *in reaction to* his or her impairment. Making a different point, some American activists, along with scholars who support a "minority model" of disability, use "person with a disability" because it puts the human being first and the impairment second. Thus, choice of terminology reflects ideological stance.

Linton (1998) describes the metamorphosis of naming within the disability movement:

> *The disabled* or *the handicapped* was replaced in the mid-70s by *people with disabilities* to maintain disability as a characteristic of the individual as opposed to the defining variable . . . Beginning in the early 90s *disabled people* has been increasingly used in disability studies and disability rights circles when referring to the constituency group. Rather than maintaining disability as a secondary characteristic, *disabled* has become a marker of the identity that the individual and group wish to highlight and call attention to.[5]

Corker and French (1999) explains the implications of the two names:

[I]f we look at how language is actually used by a range of users, "people with" language and terms like "the disabled" are what might be called hybrid discourses which by their nature are ambiguous from the semantic point of view. So, "people with disabilities" can NOW mean putting the person first AND it can mean distancing oneself from the social model AND it can mean internalised oppression. The key is then in how language use is contextualised, who is using the term, why, etc. . . . and also whether changing language means changed attitudes, which lead to social change.[6]

In either case, "the term *disability* (like African-American, gay, woman, etc.) is a linchpin in a complex web of social ideals, institutional structures, and government policies. As a result, many people have a vested interest in keeping a tenacious hold on the current meaning because it is consistent with the practice and policies that are central to their livelihood or their ideologies."[7]

As names of these categories are contested, we can observe who has the power to establish and police the categories, the criteria by which individuals are included in a category, and what rights and privileges are denied or allowed category members. For example, in *Plessy v. Ferguson*—the landmark 1896 U.S. Supreme Court decision that defined those with *any* African ancestry as fully black and thereby subject to legalized segregation—the Supreme Court effectively created two mutually exclusive categories of "white" and "black" Americans.[8] A similar "opportunity" for the discussion of the criteria for category membership was provided in 1930 when the United States Census categories for "Race and Color" offered "White, Negro, Mexican, Indian, Chinese, Japanese, Filipino, Hindu, and Korean." When Mexican-Americans and the Mexican government objected to the use of "Mexican" as a *racial* category, the term was removed from the list and over the next several censuses Mexican-Americans were defined as "persons of Spanish mother tongue," and later "white persons of Spanish surname."[9] Thus, at least on the census, the category "Mexican" was transformed from a distinct racial category to a white subgroup.

With disability statuses, conflicts over category names provide the opportunity to explicate the criteria by which individuals are to be included in a category, to identify who has the power to establish and police such criteria, and to define the rights and privileges allowed or disallowed those in the category. In this case, laws, regulations, and policies at all levels of government encompass criteria for the identification of disability and the consequent eligibility for services and support. Some regulations are quite specific in their gradation of physical and/or mental functioning. For example, the United States National Center for Health Statistics lists specific categories of physical impairment: visual impairment, hearing impairment, speech impairment, absence of extremities, paralysis of extremities, and deformity or orthopedic impairment. Each of these categories encompasses one or more subcategories of physical impairment including which part of the body is "malformed," and each category is located within an overall ranking of type and severity of disability which determines the amount of monetary compensation and "appropriate" service modality.

The naming and defining of these master-status categories cultivates the misconception—common among lay as well as scientific communities—that individuals can be easily located within the discontinuous categories that such names construct. For example, despite the significant presence of mixed-race people in the United States, American social practices continue to assume that individuals can be fairly easily slotted into the categories black, white, or Asian—a premise which has generally been reproduced in public policy, law, and social science (as when, for example, social science investigates "race" differences in crime). In the area of sexual orientation, popular opinion and science have treated "gay," "straight," and even "bisexual" as discrete, non-overlapping categories—and this despite the continuum in sexual behavior that has been documented since Kinsey's work over 50 years ago.

The notion that people can be easily classified into "able-bodied" and "disabled" is similarly pervasive, despite the fact that many impairment-related conditions have transient symptoms or play out differently under varying personal and environmental considerations. For example, people living with multiple sclerosis may awaken one morning unable to move their legs, then later the same day find themselves able to walk for miles. Should they be classified as disabled and thus entitled to disability benefits and services because of the few hours of paralysis? Or, are they "not disabled" because they were "able" to walk most of that day, even though there is no promise that they will be able to walk at all the day after that? Suppose some eye diseases cause people to have enough visual acuity to pass a driver's license eye test in sunny weather conditions, but not on cloudy days. Does this mean that they should be considered eligible to drive? Or, should they be refused the privilege even though they may live in a climate where the sun shines 275 days a year and so are "able" to drive most of the time? Does this imply that they ought to be granted the privilege of a driver's license with a "sunny-days-only-no-nights" restriction? How many days would the sun have to shine in order for them to be eligible? Even disability law, which has the potential to protect rights, also functions to create categories that may subvert equity:

> Law works by categorizing, isolating, ostracizing, dehumanizing, rather than by just punishing identifiable acts of wrong doing . . . The study of the

way the law constructs and deconstructs people with impairments and the way in which the ideology of disability is a feature in the construction and process of law provides a perfect opportunity for putting "crime and punishment" into perspective.[10]

While disability categories are constructed as discontinuous, the Americans with Disabilities Act (ADA) of 1990 offers a broadly inclusive definition of disability. The ADA defines a person with a disability as someone who has a "physical or mental impairment that substantially limits one or more major life activities . . . a record of such impairment . . . [or is] regarded as having such an impairment."[11] The ADA definition is both broader and less tied to medical or materialist assessments than that used for Supplemental Security Income (SSI) or Social Security Disability Insurance (SSDI), both of which define "disability" as "an inability to engage in work."[12] It is this work-related definition that is used in the decennial Census of Population and Housing.[13]

Still, the restrictive definitions of entitlement programs or the expanded definition of the ADA occupy only a small (albeit materially consequential) part of the social landscape. More often, social life and social science share the culture's commonsense practices that people are either "in the basket or out of it," for example that one is either blind or not blind. The distinction between "legally blind" and "totally blind"—and the fact that the former is the much larger category—is a gradation not accessed in most social interaction. The assumption of discrete categories emerges in social science as well, as when surveys pose yes/no questions about being disabled.[14] Equally,

> The way we report statistics vis-à-vis disability and disease is generally misleading. If we speak of ratio figures for a particular disease . . . [we] convey that 1 person in 10 *does get* a particular disease, [and that] 9 out of 10 *do not.* This means, however, only that those 9 people do not get *that* particular disease. It does not mean they are disease-free, nor are they likely to be so. . . . The issue of disability for individuals . . . is not *whether* but *when,* not so much *which one* but *how many* and *in what combination.* . . . The paradigm of disability as fixed and dichotomous is so pervasively embedded that it is evident in the work of any of us.[15]

In all, like race, sex, or sexual orientation categories, disability categories are named, those names are subject to debate and change, they are acted upon by law and public policy, and they imply that the categorizations are more discrete than they are.

Aggregating and Disaggregating the Categories

Once named, defined, and rendered discrete by law, public policy, or social convention, categorizations are available for aggregation and disaggregation by category members as well as others. For example, the category "gay" is often used to imply that shared sexual orientation will override differences of race, sex, disability, and social class.[16] Similarly, the 1964 Civil Rights Act aggregated Puerto Ricans, Mexican-Americans, and Spanish-Americans into a federal category called "Hispanic" or "Latino," and the Asian-American movement of the 1960s offered the identity "Asian American" as somehow overriding differences of national origin, language, and religion.[17] While such aggregate terms may be used by members of the category for lobbying and social movement building, they are not necessarily based on a sense of collective identity among category members.[18] Thus, a variety of functions may be served by aggregation: "the presupposition in favour of conceptualising the object of moral respect as collective rather than individualised, is that to equalise a group is to equalise its members, to transport them collectively from a devalued to an esteemed status."[19]

BOX 5.1

Many historians compare the civil rights movement for disabled people with those movements of other groups. What are the similarities between disability rights and feminism? Read more here:

www.huffingtonpost.com/sarah-blahovec/four-reasons-that-feminis_b_6160774.html

In the case of disability, in the United States "people with disabilities" has been offered as an aggregate term for those who are heterogeneous not only in race, sex/gender, and sexuality, but also in terms of the nature and extent of their disability. As with other social movements, the putative members of the category may or may not respond to the appeal. Many people with impairments do not perceive themselves as disabled and may recoil from alignment with a social movement. And, like others struggling with the significance of categorical memberships, people with impairments must regularly assess the relative significance of their statuses: Which is more important, their sex, race, social class, sexual orientation, or disability? At points and for some, the answer is clear:

> Disability is the primary problem in our lives. Once we identify ourselves as powerful disabled individuals, we can go back into our secondary communities, whether it is to be the black community, or the Chicano community, the women's community, or some combination of these.[20]

More often, just as in social movements founded on race, ethnicity, sex, and sexuality, the aggregate "disabled people" or "people with disabilities" offers only a temporary and strategic alliance susceptible to disaggregation at virtually any point. As a matter of course, disintegration besets the disability movement because of people's variant needs. Curb cuts provide a graphic example. Wheelchair users need curb cuts because they create level surfaces between sidewalks and roadways, allowing them to maneuver their wheelchairs across streets and driveways. Blind people who use white canes, however, have traditionally used curbs as warnings that they are at the edges of sidewalks and about to step into roadways— cutting the curb eliminates that guidepost. Disability advocacy groups vie for architectural redesign and funding from the same limited budgets of local, state, and federal governments, just as all those in the aggregate category "minority" are in competition for resources allocated to the category as a whole. One group's gain may be another's loss.

Ideological splits occur within each sub-category of disability, too. Some Deaf organizations reject the idea that "Deaf" is a disability, arguing instead that it is a culture. In a stance that mirrors the separatist wing of any social movement, the case is made that Deaf people should rely exclusively on sign language and that those who learn to vocalize are "sell-outs." (The first deaf Miss America found herself embroiled in this controversy.) Other deaf organizations assert that deaf people should be taught to use their voices and that this effort will allow them to function within the nondisabled majority society. The two factions distinguish themselves through the use of the letter *d*, with the capitalized Deaf signaling the disability-as-culture model, which rejects "Deaf" as either impairment or disability, and the lower-case *d* the "sensory impairment" construction. Within the blindness community, the ideological split rests on issues of environmental accommodation. One school asserts that truly independent living eschews environmental accommodations—such as audible or large-print signage, or tactile warning strips on railway platforms—and that only blind people are qualified to train other blind people in blindness skills. In all, aggregate categorizations regularly decompose into sub-populations—which may also then re-consolidate around the shared experience of discrimination and oppression.

Dichotomizing and Stigmatizing

The categories of people produced by naming and aggregating may be put to a variety of social uses, but our interest here is how they may be constructed into dichotomies that both functionally erase ambiguities of membership and stigmatize one half of the set. In such a binary process, "race" becomes black or white, "sex" becomes male or female, "sexual orientation" becomes gay or straight, and people are either disabled or "normal." In each case, one "side" of the dichotomy is stigmatized. For example, in the constructed binary of blindness/sightedness, the assumption is that blindness is "adversity" while sightedness is "trouble-free."[21] Indeed, the social assumption that blindness is an aberration requiring professional intervention remains largely unchallenged. Thus, impairment is socially constructed as "deficit" rather than an alternate ontology.

> Whatever the physically [cognitively or sensory] impaired person may think of [themselves], [they are] given a negative identity by society, and much of social life is a struggle against this imposed image. It is for this reason that we can say that stigmatization is less a by-product of disability than its substance. The greatest impediment to a [disabled] person's taking full part in society is . . . the tissue of myths, fears, and misunderstanding that society attaches to them . . . There is a clear pattern in the United States, and in many other countries, of prejudice toward disabled people and debasement of their social status. This is manifested in its most extreme forms by avoidance, fear, and outright hostility.[22]

Disabled persons have also endured the same segregation as those in stigmatized race, sex/gender, and sexuality categories. "Special" education in separate classrooms, schools, and day-care centers, segregated housing, sheltered workshops, and separate transportation vehicles all contribute to physical segregation, as do mundane architectural and information systems barriers.[23]

> The present forms of architectural structures and social institutions exist because statutes, ordinances, and codes either required or permitted them to be constructed in that manner. These public policies imply values, expectations and assumptions about the physical and behavioral attributes that people ought to possess in order to survive or to participate in community life. Many everyday activities, such as the distance people walk, the steps they climb, the materials they read, and the messages they receive, impose stringent requirements on persons with different levels of functional skills.
>
> (Hahn, 1988, p. 40)

Stairs, curbs, or small-print signs hung over doorways make admission nearly impossible. They may lack discriminatory intent, but they have the effect of exclusion nonetheless. This separation from mainstream society keeps disabled people hidden, thus out of public consciousness, and so supports the continuance of such policies.

BOX 5.2

Misconceptions about disability can create barriers for disabled people even in groups that work for social justice. Do mainstream feminists leave disabled women out of the discussion?:

www.thedailybeast.com/articles/2014/11/24/yesallwomen-but-not-really-how-feminism-leaves-the-disabled-behind.html

Physical segregation also contributes to problematic interaction between disabled and nondisabled people, just as it does between race or sexual orientation groups. Thus, relations may run the gamut from awkward to aggravating to frightening. For disabled people, the reality of being observed (discreetly or explicitly), of possessing "defects" that cannot be "fixed," the need to anticipate "normals'" production of intrusive or offensive behavior, the relief of self-isolation, and the lack of interactional practice that such isolation yields were detailed by Goffman over 50 years ago (1963). His work also reflects the experience of those in stigmatized race, sex, and sexual orientation categories.

Finally, in dichotomies like these, the non-stigmatized member of the set can be described as curiously "absent" while the stigmatized member is quite "vividly" present. For example, in American culture, "whites are the non-defined definers of others"; they name but are not themselves named; their dominance is reflected in the ability to impose names on others but remain invisible themselves.[24] A similar invisibility attends being able-bodied—indeed there are few names that even refer to that status except those in currency within the disability community.

Denied the Attributes Valued in the Culture

Perhaps the equivalence of disability to the other stigmatized race, sex, and sexuality statuses becomes most vivid when we consider the characteristics attributed to people with impairments. For example, attitudes among the general population about blind people include that they are pitiful, miserable, helpless, useless, and mysterious.[25] Those who are physically impaired are viewed as childlike and dependent.[26] With disability, such characterizations also draw on biblical liturgy, since disability was historically used to frighten people into "moral" behavior and adherence to religious doctrine. Constructed as the punishment wrought by God on sinners, impairment became a metaphor for evil, immorality, and treachery.

These "defects" have been attributed to people in virtually every category of disability, but also to those who are in stigmatized race, sex, and sexuality categories.

With disability—as with the others—such characterizations presume that "biological deficiency [or difference] confers social deficiency"[27]—although it may also sometimes confer exceptional demonstrations of insight, forgiveness, sexuality, intelligence, or physical prowess.

Americans' current equation of physical beauty with fitness and health certainly underscores the degree to which disabled people are presumed to lack what the culture values:

> The pursuit of the slim, well-muscled body is not only an aesthetic matter, but also a moral imperative. . . . It hardly needs saying that the disabled, individually and as a group, contravene all the values of youth, virility, activity, and physical beauty that Americans cherish, however little most individuals may embody them.[28]

Thus, the person with a visible physical disability inhabits a body rejected by society—and the consequences of that are much the same as they are for those in race and sexual minority groups.

Not only are those with physical disabilities perceived to be aesthetically deficient, they are often mistakenly believed to be weak or ill. Indeed, disability is typically constructed in social science and commonsense practices as "illness," despite the fact that most people with disabilities are healthy. While some diseases do cause disabling conditions, there is no necessary equation of disability and ill health, just as there is no necessary equation of aging and disability. Many disabilities are congenital and have nothing to do with age, just as age does not necessarily impose disability. Even in work roles, disability need not be a negative:

> Through high school and college, when in my immediate post-polio phase I used crutches, wore leg braces, and, most important . . . [a] back-stomach support, I worked on a quasi-assembly line. My on-line productivity exceeded that of any other worker. This was not due to heroics or motivation—economic or psychological—on my part. It was due essentially to one thing I had that others did not—a full back support which allowed me to sit ramrod straight, comfortable, and untired so that I could work with-out interruption. For virtually every other worker, the strain on their back and stomach muscles (muscles which in my case were clinically far weaker than theirs) was enormous, requiring frequent stretches, breaks, or slow downs.[29]

Finally, people with impairments—just like those in stigmatized race, sex, and sexuality categories—are presumed to lack or be unable to realize the values and attributes the culture esteems. They are not expected to be dominant, active, independent, competitive, adventurous, sexual, self-controlled, healthy, intelligent, attractive, or competent. Like those in other stigmatized categories, they risk being seen as *nothing but a problem*—because they are assumed to suffer from problems and are expected to be a problem for "the rest of us."[30]

Similarities and One Significant Difference

In all these ways, the lives of people with impairments parallel the experience of those in stigmatized American race, sex, and sexuality categories. Disability is created through many of the same social processes that construct race, sex, and sexual orientation. The attitudes, patterns of behavior, and artifacts that characterize blind people, for example, are not inherent in their condition but socially created. When totally blind people wear dark glasses, it is not for their benefit, rather it is to shield sighted persons from the appearance of blind persons' eyes. A similar stigma encourages people to hide their prosthetic devices or partially amputated limbs, so as not to offend a squeamish nondisabled majority. Thus,

> there is nothing in the condition of blindness [or other impairments] that requires that a person be dependent, melancholy, or helpless; nor is there anything about it that should lead [them] to become independent or assertive. Blind [people] are made, and by the same processes of socialization that have made us all.[31]

Similarly, disability is itself socially constructed. Oliver (1996) reports:

> since the politicization of disability by the international disabled people's movement a growing number of academics, many of whom are disabled people themselves, have reconceptualized disability as a complex and sophisticated form of social oppression or institutional discrimination on a par with sexism, heterosexism and racism.[32]

Each sub-category of impairment within the broader category "disability" is subject to social construction with all that implies.

Still, there are significant differences between disability and the other stigmatized statuses we have considered here, perhaps the most important being that in the other cases the non-stigmatized have little fear of suddenly joining the ranks of the stigmatized. Disability, however, is always a potential status and in that it is perhaps closest to sexual orientation, whether the latter is considered a choice or biologically determined.

Discussion Questions

1. Why are categories (and names for those categories) so pervasive? How does power work within or through these categories?

2. Is disability as important to people as other kinds of identity categories? How is it understood as similar or different for people who assume these identities?

3. How does disability relate to various cultural values described by the authors? Discuss how these values are further disabling themselves.

4. What do the authors say is the "one significant difference" between disability and other identity categories?

Notes

1 Rosenblum & Travis, 2016
2 Smith, 1992.
3 Biklen & Bogden, 1977. Editor's note: This explanation of the term "handicap" has since been disputed and revised. See Davis's introduction (Ch. 1) for further discussion.
4 Pfeiffer, 1993, p. 79, emphasis in original.
5 Linton, 1998, p. 13, emphasis in original.
6 Personal correspondence.
7 Linton, 1998, p. 10, emphasis in original.
8 Davis, 1991.
9 Espíritu, 1992, p. 114.
10 Jones & Basser Marks, 1999, p. 4.
11 U.S. Congress, 1990.
12 Bowe, 1993, p. 86.
13 Ibid.
14 Zola, 1993, p. 18
15 Ibid., pp. 18 and 22. Emphasis in original.
16 Spelman, 1988.
17 Espíritu, 1992; Wei, 1993.
18 e.g., de la Garza et al., 1992.
19 Silvers, 1999, p. 79.
20 Saxon & Howe, 1988, pp. 211–212.
21 Michalko, 1998.
22 Murphy, 1995, p. 140.
23 Higgins, 1995, p. 31.
24 Frankenberg, 1993.
25 Monbeck, 1973, p. 25.
26 Luborsky, 1994.

27 Liachowitz, 1998, p.1.
28 Murphy, 1995, p. 143.
29 Zola, 1993, p. 29.
30 Rosenblum and Travis, 1996.
31 Scott, 1969, p. 143.
32 Oliver, 1996.

References

BARNES, C. (1996) Theories of Disability and the Origins of the Oppression of Disabled People in Western Society, in: L. BARTON (Ed.), *Disability and Society: Emerging Issues and Insights* (London: Longman).

BIKLEN, D. & BOGDAN, R. (1977) Media Portrayals of Disabled People: A Study in Stereotypes. *Interracial Books for Children Bulletin*, (v)8.

BOWE, F.G. (1993) Statistics, Politics, and Employment of People with Disabilities, *Journal of Disability Policy Studies* 4, 83–91.

CORKER, M. & FRENCH, S. (1999) *Disability Discourse* (Buckingham: Open University Press).

DAVIS, F.J. (1991) *Who is Black? One Nation's Rule* (University Park, PA: Pennsylvania State Press).

DE LA GARZA, R.O., DESIPIO, L., GARCIA, F.C., GARCIA, J. & FALCON, A. (1992) *Latino Voices: Mexican, Puerto Rican, and Cuban Perspectives on American Politics* (Boulder, CO: Westview Press).

ESPIRITU, Y.L. (1992) *Asian American Panethnicity: Bridging Institutions and Identities* (Philadelphia, PA: Temple University Press).

FRANKENBERG, R. (1993) *White Women, Race Matters: The Social Construction of Whiteness* (Minneapolis, MN: University of Minnesota Press).

GOFFMAN, E. (1963) *Stigma: Notes on the Management of Spoiled Identity* (Englewood Cliffs, NJ: Prentice-Hall).

HAHN, H. (1988) The Politics of Physical Difference: Disability and Discrimination, *Journal of Social Issues* 44, 39–47.

HIGGINS, R.C. (1995) *Making Disability: Exploring the Social Transformation of Human Variation* (Springfield, IL: Charles C. Thomas).

JONES, M. & BASSER MARKS, L.A. (1999) *Disability, Divers-ability and Legal Change* (The Hague: Kluwer Law International).

LIACHOWITZ, C.H. (1988) *Disability as a Social Construct* (Philadelphia, PA: University of Pennsylvania Press).

LINTON, S. (1998) Disability Studies: Not Disability Studies, *Disability & Society* 13, 525–541.

LUBORSKY, M.R. (1994) The Cultural Diversity of Physical Disability: Erosion of Full Adult Personhood, *Journal of Aging Studies* 8, 239–253.

MICHALKO, R. (1998) *The Mystery of the Eye and the Shadow of Blindness* (Toronto, Ont: University of Toronto Press).

MONBECK, M.E. (1973) *The Meaning of Blindness: Attitudes Toward Blindness and Blind People* (Bloomington, IN: Indiana University Press).

MURPHY, R.F. (1995) "Encounters: The Body Silent in America", in B. INGSTAD & S. WHYTE (Eds), *Disability and Culture* (Berkeley: University of California Press). OLIVER, M. (1996) *Understanding Disability: From Theory to Practice* (London: Macmillan).

PFEIFFER, D. (1993) The Problem of Disability Definition, *Journal of Disability Policy Studies* 4, 77–82.

ROSENBLUM, K.E. & TRAVIS, T.C. (2016) *The Meaning of Difference: American Constructions of Race and Ethnicity, Sex and Gender, Social Class, Sexuality, and Disability*, 7th edn (New York: McGraw Hill).

SAXON, M. & HOWE, F. (Eds) (1988) *With Wings: An Anthology of Literature By and About Women with Disabilities* (New York: Feminist Press at City University of New York).

SCOTT, R.A. (1969) *The Making of Blind Men: A Study of Adult Socialization* (New York: Russell Sage Foundation).

SILVERS, A. (1999) Double Consciousness, Triple Difference: Disability, Race, Gender and the Politics of Recognition, in: M. JONES & L.A. BASSER MARKS (Eds), *Disability, Divers-ability and Legal Change* (The Hague: Martinus Nijoff).

SMITH, T.W. (1992) Changing Racial Labels: From Colored, to Negro, to Black, to African American, *Public Opinion Quarterly* 56, 496–514.

SPELMAN, E. (1988) *Inessential Woman* (Boston, MA: Beacon Press).

UNITED STATES CONGRESS (1990) 'The Americans With Disabilities Act,' Public Law 101.

WEI, W. (1993) *The Asian American Movement* (Philadelphia, PA: Temple University Press).

ZOLA, K. (1993) Disability Statistics, What We Count and What It Tells Us, *Journal of Disability Policy Studies* 4, 9–39.

Neurodiversity Rewires Conventional Thinking About Brains

Steve Silberman

In the late 1990s, a sociologist named Judy Singer—who is on the autism spectrum herself—invented a new word to describe conditions like autism, dyslexia, and ADHD: neurodiversity. In a radical stroke, she hoped to shift the focus of discourse about atypical ways of thinking and learning away from the usual litany of deficits, disorders, and impairments. Echoing positive terms like biodiversity and cultural diversity, her neologism called attention to the fact that many atypical forms of brain wiring also convey unusual skills and aptitudes.

Autistic people, for instance, have prodigious memories for facts, are often highly intelligent in ways that don't register on verbal IQ tests, and are capable of focusing for long periods on tasks that take advantage of their natural gift for detecting flaws in visual patterns. By autistic standards, the "normal" human brain is easily distractible, is obsessively social, and suffers from a deficit of attention to detail. "I was interested in the liberatory, activist aspects of it," Singer explained to journalist Andrew Solomon in 2008, "to do for neurologically different people what feminism and gay rights had done for their constituencies."

The new word first appeared in print in a 1998 Atlantic article about *Wired* magazine's website, HotWired, by journalist Harvey Blume. "Neurodiversity may be every bit as crucial for the human race as biodiversity is for life in general," he declared. "Who can say what form of wiring will prove best at any given moment? Cybernetics and computer culture, for example, may favor a somewhat autistic cast of mind."

Thinking this way is no mere exercise in postmodern relativism. One reason that the vast majority of autistic adults are chronically unemployed or underemployed, consigned to make-work jobs like assembling keychains in sheltered workshops, is because HR departments are hesitant to hire workers who look, act, or communicate in non-neurotypical ways—say, by using a keyboard and text-to-speech software to express themselves, rather than by chattering around the water cooler.

One way to understand neurodiversity is to remember that just because a PC is not running Windows doesn't mean that it's broken. Not all the features of atypical human operating systems are bugs. We owe many of the wonders of modern life to innovators who were brilliant in non-neurotypical ways. Herman Hollerith, who helped launch the age of computing by inventing a machine to tabulate and sort punch cards, once leaped out of a school window to escape his spelling lessons because he was dyslexic. So were Carver Mead, the father of very large-scale integrated circuits, and William Dreyer, who designed one of the first protein sequencers.

Singer's subversive meme has also become the rallying cry of the first new civil rights movement to take off in the 21st century. Empowered by the Internet, autistic self-advocates, proud dyslexics, unapologetic Touretters, and others who think differently are raising the rainbow banner of neurodiversity to encourage society to appreciate and celebrate cognitive differences, while demanding reasonable accommodations in schools, housing, and the workplace.

A nonprofit group called the Autistic Self Advocacy Network is working with the U.S. Department of Labor to develop better employment opportunities for all people on the spectrum, including those who rely on screen-based devices to communicate (and who doesn't these days?). "Trying to make someone 'normal' isn't always the best way to improve their life," says ASAN cofounder Ari Ne'eman, the first openly autistic White House appointee.

Neurodiversity is also gaining traction in special education, where experts are learning that helping students make the most of their native strengths and special interests, rather than focusing on trying to correct their deficits or normalize their behavior, is a more effective method of educating young people with atypical minds so they can make meaningful contributions to society. "We don't pathologize a calla lily by saying it has a 'petal deficit disorder,'" writes Thomas Armstrong, author of a new book called *Neurodiversity in the Classroom*. "Similarly, we ought not to pathologize children who have different kinds of brains and different ways of thinking and learning."

In forests and tide pools, the value of biological diversity is resilience: the ability to withstand shifting conditions and resist attacks from predators. In a world changing faster than ever, honoring and nurturing neurodiversity is civilization's best chance to thrive in an uncertain future.

Discussion Questions

1. What are the possible benefits of valuing neurodiversity?
2. What steps might we take in education and employment to embrace neuro-diversity?

Deafness and Deaf Culture

Talking Culture
Deaf People and Disability Studies
Carol A. Padden

The history of disability studies overlaps nicely with the history of deaf studies. Both came into being roughly at the same time, in the last two decades. Just as there are new programs of disability studies in universities across the United States and around the world, there are new programs of deaf studies at places like the University of Iowa, Gallaudet University, Northeastern University, and California State University, Northridge. The idea of a "deaf studies" is still so new that the phrase feels novel and unexpected, but the idea gained a certain inevitability as a field of inquiry began to develop around the history of deaf people, their lives, their communities and cultures.

Truth be told, deaf people see themselves an odd fit in disability studies. We've been segregated for such a long time that we see our history as set apart from others, and it feels strange to have the company of other disabled people. For most of America's history, deaf children have lived in institutions designed exclusively for them in nearly every state of the country. Some states had more than one institution: New York, for example, had as many as eight schools for deaf children through most of the 20th century. By the late 1970s, these institutions began to decline as deaf children were moved into public schools with hearing children as part of a wider trend toward deinstitutionalization. Considering that the first school for deaf children in the United States was founded in 1817, we have little experience outside deaf schools and the segregated lives that developed around them. Without question, mainstreaming has had a huge effect on deaf people, but it is part of a much broader social change.

I intend with my brief overview of the recent history of deaf people to show how disability studies as a field will need to acknowledge that different disabilities have their own histories, each defined by unique trajectories. This might seem like a confusing cacophony of voices, but the broadcasts at the same time pictured people without disabilities as their opposites: physically healthy and whole, giving rather than receiving charity, socially valid.

And by having nondisabled presenters do almost all the talking, the charities reinforced the power of nondisabled people in general to define the social meaning of "disability" and the social identities of people with disabilities. Telethons empowered nondisabled emcees to explain to nondisabled viewers the daily experience of disability. "We hope to give you a little more understanding of what life is like for someone with a disability," announced a local Easter Seals host in 1990. But, admitted another in 1988, one of the frustrating things about hosting this show is that one is often asked "to describe what someone in a wheelchair is going through, and frankly we can only imagine what it is like." Yet, undaunted by their ignorance and authorized by the charities, the hosts talked on and on.

During the latter half of the 20th century, growing numbers of Americans with disabilities resisted their relegation to social invalidity. They organized themselves into a movement—more accurately, an assemblage of movements—that challenged dominant views of disability. Instead of attributing disabled people's social and economic marginalization to pathology, their campaign adopted a minority-group perspective. More urgent than remedial measures to fix individuals was the instatement of equal access, reasonable accommodations, and antidiscrimination protections. Rejecting the charity approach that beseeched attention to disabled people's needs, the movement demanded civil rights enforcement to ensure their right of access to society.

This activism led in the 1980s and 1990s to criticism of and then protests against the telethons. Whereas those broadcasts assumed that "affliction" and "misfortune" were inevitably and self-evidently the state of being of anyone with a disability, disabled activists scorned those suppositions as not objective statements of biological facts but social prejudices that justified discriminatory practices. The charities could not ignore the demonstrations or the emergent minority-group mentality that fueled them. In fact, some of the agitation came from activist constituents in the organizations themselves. And so, in various ways, the telethons sought to co-opt or criticize, address, assimilate, or adopt the activist perspective.

On and off the broadcasts, the controversy generated public debate that touched on, without deeply exploring, let alone resolving, a clutch of questions: Is disability inherent defectiveness, socially constructed devaluation, or human variation and difference? What are the real needs and interests of people with disabilities, and who is qualified to determine them? Could Americans with disabilities legitimately demand equal dignity and equal rights while insisting that society provide for their distinctive disability-related needs and alternative modes of functioning as a matter of right? Could disabled citizens assert their fundamental equality if they admitted that some conditions involve intrinsic limitation and suffering? Is it possible for charity publicists to promote amelioration of genuine human suffering without demeaning the people they ostensibly seek to help? Are American values about need, justice, equality, and difference compatible with one another or irreconcilably at odds?

Neither the critics of the telethons outside the disability rights movement nor the broadcasts' apologists examined the complexity or significance of these issues, ideologies, and messages. They didn't wonder why the infantilizing and sentimentalizing of disabled people had such appeal with the American public. They didn't seek to explain why and how these forms of mendicancy worked. They didn't ask if the telethons' solicitation techniques were, in fact, "the only way" to fund medical research and medical treatments and social services, as Bob Greene and others had learned to take for granted. They did not ponder how the telethon mode of fund-histories offer a pathway to understanding both deaf studies and disability studies. I believe these new fields of inquiry can address what many deaf people see as some of the most pressing questions of our lives: What is the future of our bodies, and how will science and technology use us to address questions about the future?

The Problem of Voice

Among the first signs of change in deaf communities in the United States is the emergence of a changed language about ourselves, our language, and our culture. Over the last 40 years, we have devised new vocabulary and new ways of talking about ourselves. My frequent collaborator and coauthor, Tom Humphries, describes this change as a transition from "culture talking" to "talking culture," borrowing from Jim Clifford's characterization of modern cultures.[1] Deaf people have acquired not only a new vocabulary but also a new consciousness, indeed a self-consciousness about themselves and their behaviors.

In a 1913 film of the president of the National Association of the Deaf, George William Veditz, giving a signed oratory, we see examples of the voice of deaf people in the early part of the century. Titled "The Preservation of the Sign Language," Veditz's delivery is a fiery and impassioned defense of sign language in the face of attempts to banish it from schools across the country. As we read a letter Veditz wrote containing the English text of his signed speech, we see how he used the vocabulary of his time to refer to himself and his community as "deaf-mutes" using "the beautiful sign language." He warns of "a new race of pharaohs that knew not Joseph" who advocate the banishment of sign language from deaf schools, and he strikes out at the "oral Moloch that destroys the mind and soul of the deaf." Veditz's speech is a beautifully constructed example of the problem of voice that plagued deaf people at the time. Douglas Baynton explains in his history of the deaf community in the 19th century that deaf people persisted in using religious and divine accounts of their language and their existence while their opposition was shifting to the language of rationality and science that shaped much of oratory at the close of the century. As impassioned as the protests on film were, deaf people were essentially silent and silenced—deemed to be without sound and comprehensible only to those few who knew sign language.

BOX 7.1

What is Deaf culture? Watch a sign language explanation from Flavia Fleischer:

www.youtube.com/watch?v=U1xQaRbWHus

As they moved into the 20th century, deaf people agreed to modernize their language, first ceasing to refer to one another as "deaf-mutes" and "deaf and dumb" in an effort to end the perception of themselves as silenced.[2] Whereas once their language was simply, as Veditz called it, "the sign language," which conveyed "their thoughts and souls, their feelings, desires and needs,"[3] deaf people now use "American Sign Language," capitalized and labeled for its country of origin, and they refer to their lives in terms of a deaf culture. The divine language has yielded to a changed perception of sign languages as one type in the array of natural human languages around the world. Sign languages have grammars, and these grammars vary. These new ways of talking about sign languages are part of a broader shift, moving deaf people toward the family of languages and cultures. This is what we mean by "talking culture."

To illustrate the recent history of deaf people, I focus on three aspects: the legacy of deaf schools; deaf people's transition from private, segregated lives to more public ones; and how deaf people exploit technology in a struggle for voice.

The Legacy of Deaf Schools

Beginning in 1817, America embarked on a prolonged effort of building asylums and institutions specifically for deaf children, an impulse that continued until 1953, when the last school of this type was built in Riverside, California.[4] Hartford was the site of the first asylum in 1817, followed by a school near New York City and another in Philadelphia by 1820. Ohio opened its state school in 1829, and South Carolina's appeared in 1849. New schools continued to open at a steady rate until the end of the century, when nearly every state had at least one. Many, though not all, of these schools had blind departments on the same campus. (The joint histories of blind and deaf children on these campuses are rarely described, but worthy of attention.)[5]

Such faith was invested in these asylums and institutions that they came to dominate education of deaf children for nearly 150 years. Today, if you ask deaf men and women older than 30 where they are from, they will name the deaf school they attended—"Berkeley" refers to the original site of the California School for the Deaf (it has since relocated to Fremont). My father was born in Chicago, but he will say he is from Faribault, where he attended the Minnesota School for the Deaf his entire childhood. Built in the centralized and separate asylum architecture characteristic of the 19th century, deaf schools created a strong sense of delineation, separating deaf children from other children living outside the school. My colleague Ted Supalla remembers how a child from the neighborhood once pierced the iron walls surrounding Ted's school and rode a bicycle across campus, drawing incredulous stares from deaf students and teachers. Asylums were places of respite, apart and separate, and outsiders rarely came on campus.

The schools rearranged the geography of deaf communities in the United States. Whereas deaf communities of the American colonial period existed on a small scale throughout the country,[6] by the 19th century these clusters were reorganized into larger communities with schools at their center. This geography continues to this day; there are robust deaf communities in Philadelphia, Washington, New York City, and Rochester, all of which had large deaf schools at their core.

Within the schools, deaf children were carefully grouped. They were always taught separately from blind children. Some deaf schools segregated children by gender as well. By the mid-19th century, racial segregation was instituted in deaf schools throughout the South. In Tennessee, Virginia, South Carolina, and Arkansas, black deaf children attended school in separate buildings. In Louisiana, West Virginia, Maryland, and Florida, they attended separate campuses, sometimes in different parts of the state.[7]

This is a complicated legacy, both alienating and comforting. Deafness is an uncommon condition. Often deaf children are alone in early childhood, without siblings or parents who are deaf. What asylums and institutions provided for deaf children through the 19th century was a chance to be with other deaf people. As the schools sought out deaf children and brought them under the protective care of the institution, deaf children met others like themselves. In his account of asylums, Michel Foucault describes the coming together of inmates as creating in one another "recognition by mirror," a realization that one's insanity is not so unusual.[8] The effect of this realization deflates the inmate's sense of uniqueness, leading eventually to demoralization and then oppression by the caretaker. For deaf people, the flip side of recognition by mirror is the possibility of elation—not deflation—at being surrounded for the first time in their lives by real life versions of the self, in deaf teachers and fellow deaf students.

On the one hand, deaf schools are places of overbearing management of children's bodies, which, sadly, leads often to physical and sexual abuse. At the same time, these are places where deaf children meet others like themselves. Children who do not learn sign language at home can acquire it at school. Today, facing a changed sentiment about institutions, many of these schools closed doors and no longer operate. Others have redesigned their buildings to seem more like smaller-scale private schools and not as massively institutional as they were in the 19th and 20th centuries. Maryland School for the Deaf tore down its large Old Main Hall and replaced it with a more modest brick building. When Pennsylvania School for the Deaf faced a decline in enrollment, it sold its rambling grassy campus in the Germantown section of the city and moved to smaller location, a former boys' military academy. Modern deaf schools are more likely to be regional schools than state schools, downscaling their ambition and drawing their population of deaf children from urban areas like the San Francisco Bay Area, the Washington metropolitan area, New York City, and Riverside, California. Far fewer children board at such schools today, now known in deaf education by the more suitable term "special schools."

Deaf Theater and How It Went From Private to Public

Though deaf theater has been a mainstay of the community since its earliest history, the first professional national deaf theater was founded in 1967. Funded with a federal grant and headed by a hearing artistic director who had worked in Broadway theater, the National Theatre of the Deaf brought together deaf actors who were popular performers in deaf clubs. These were small social clubs found in cities and towns throughout the United States. New York City had 12 such clubs in its boroughs, catering to those who played sports or poker. At least as many existed in Ohio, where deaf men and women were employed in the defense industries during the First and Second World Wars. Deaf clubs were nearly always made up of deaf patrons (except for hearing spouses and children), and their activities were separate and private. Signed performances on deaf club stages were often not voice-interpreted. Much like Yiddish theater of the 1930s and 1940s, deaf club theater was presented for deaf people by deaf actors and deaf directors. They staged vaudevillian skits, beauty pageants, and sign translations of popular plays, pleasing their loyal club patrons.

When the first professional theater company was established, the actors began with translated performances of poetry by Elizabeth Barrett Browning and plays by Dylan Thomas. A few years later, they mounted an original production called *My Third Eye*, in which they told vignettes about being deaf, including a segment on sign language. This was arguably their first performance in public featuring an original piece intended for an audience who knew neither sign language or deafness. I have written elsewhere that this was a pivotal moment in the history of the community, when deaf poets and actors began to imagine how to present themselves, their language, and their practices to others (Padden and Humphries, 2005). At about the same time, not coincidentally, the name for their language changed first to "the

American sign language" and a few years later to the fully capitalized "American Sign Language" as they acquired a new vocabulary for describing the elements of the language.

Technologies of Voice

As they began to tour the country performing their brand of sign language theater, the deaf actors were accompanied onstage by hearing actors, who spoke the lines simultaneously in English. Whereas in deaf clubs the deaf actors performed alone and silently in their language, on a public stage they shared the spotlight. The intent was to give voice to performance that was formerly intelligible only privately, but interaction transformed the performance. As the deaf actors performed alongside the spoken word, they found that their signing could be too slow or too fast for the spoken translation. The signing had to be coordinated with speaking, and in the process, the actors lost full control of the stage. Their signing changed its tempo, increasing in rhythm from the comfortable pacing of the deaf club theater to the more choreographed and fast-paced style of the public theater. Deaf and hearing actors moved around on the stage delicately, trying to accommodate each other's presence, but once the performance was spoken, it lost its exclusive signed quality. Like Yiddish theater, deaf club theater faded in the light of professional mainstream performance. Voice technology made public signed performance possible while it diminished what was formerly private. As deaf people became more public and brought their sign language out for others to see, they lost much of what they had privately.

As did the actors in the national theater, deaf people in their everyday lives initially used the spoken voice strategically: to interpret, to explain, to convey what was previously silent and unreachable. But like all forms of communication technology, the spoken voice reorganizes and repositions as it reveals. Voice technology in the community has advanced to where we have professional sign language interpreters who lend voice to those of us who sign. We have captioning where voice is translated to the visual in alphabetic form. Deaf people can connect on the Web to a relay service, where they have access through a webcam to a sign language interpreter who can make voice calls for them. The interpreter dials up another caller on behalf of the deaf person and voice-interprets through the medium of the Internet. As sign is mediated, it is broadcast in voice. In the days of the deaf club, voice was provided by an intimate, a good friend or a relative who knew the sign language and could speak English. Today it can be purchased on demand from a professional. On the Internet, interpreters identify themselves only by number, not by location or name— and they are just as anonymous as voice operators. The intimacy of private lives is replaced by the anonymity of public participation.

The Problem of Voice in the 21st Century

The community has changed what it says. Deaf people have changed how they explain themselves. Using technology, deaf people manage the resource of voice for their needs. But what remains is the problem of voice: how do deaf people speak in the time of the microchip and the genome? We find it hard to be heard in the public discussion about prostheses and genetic engineering. This is a problem we share with our disabled colleagues. Here I return to where I began: disability studies and deaf studies have a common project. What is the future of our bodies, and how will science and technology use us to address questions about the future?

The cochlear implant may be a prosthesis, as many of its developers say, but it has also led to an alarming social trend of segregating deaf children—again. There are school districts with separate classrooms for those who have implants. In 1850 deaf schools separated black and white children because of a belief that they could not be educated together, and again in 2004 there were classrooms where deaf children are kept apart from other deaf children in the belief that mixing them would injure their education. Children with implants receive the prosthesis so that they can learn to hear and speak, and in some hospitals sign language is judged not compatible with postoperative treatment: what would be the point of a prosthesis if the patient were to use sign language? Deaf people don't see the two as incompatible, but is their voice being heard? How can they explain that speaking and signing are layered skills and should not be viewed as competing?

In April 2003, the National Institutes of Health announced that scientists had completed the sequencing of the human genome. The Human Genome Project has invited disabled people to say what we think about the scientists' goals for the future. The symbolic conclusion of the genome project represents the beginning of a new age: how will disability and diversity fare as genetic research moves forward? It has been stated that the goal of understanding the human genome is to relieve human beings of debilitating and fatal genetic conditions. One condition deserving of a cure is deafness. As deafness is cured, the individual is returned to speech. Though the scientists do not say so, a related goal of the project must be to eliminate the need for sign language as well. In the genetic project, sign languages are seen not as among the thousands of human languages of the world but as an adjustment by or even a by-product of those who do not, but should, have speech.

Disability studies and deaf studies have divergent interests, even as they have convergent issues. I believe that deaf people do not view their legacy of segregation in the United States in the same way that other disabled groups do theirs. We who are deaf view our schools' history as constitutive of who we are, even as we acknowledge their troubled past. Our segregated past shaped our social history, from our clubs to our theaters. We build and consume technologies of voice as apparatuses to convey to others what we say. We see the world in visual terms, acknowledging that throughout our history we are, as George Veditz called us, "first, last and for all time, the people of the eye."[9] This is why we must have a deaf studies project apart from disability studies.

Yet together these fields of inquiry can be brought to bear on some of the most important issues of our time. Who better to discuss issues of body and society than we who have long suffered social projects inscribed on ourselves? Where better to discuss these issues than in academic programs on university campuses, where the resources of scholars from across disciplines are available? What disability studies and deaf studies can offer are the shared and separate perspectives that are needed to make some of the most important human issues intelligible to everyone.

Discussion Questions

1. Why might one understand Deafness as different from other disabilities? Are there similarities nonetheless?

2. How have institutions like schools and theaters changed in the course of Deaf history?

3. What are the different meanings of "voice" in Padden's analysis? Why is voice such a relevant issue for this Deaf culture?

4. As you learn more about disability studies, how can Deaf people be best included in analyses and topics you might encounter?

Notes

1 Clifford; Padden and Humphries.
2 Fay.
3 Veditz, George. Letter to Roy Stewart. 1915.
4 Gannon.
5 Crockett and Dease; Bickley.
6 Lane, Pillard and French; Lane.
7 Hairston and Smith; Padden and Humphries; Joyner; Bickley.
8 Foucault, p. 152.
9 Veditz, "Resolutions," p. 30.

References

Baynton, Douglas. *Forbidden Signs: American Culture and the Campaign against Sign Language.* Chicago: University of Chicago Press, 1996.

Bickley, Ancella. *In Spite of Obstacles: A History of the West Virginia Schools for the Colored Deaf and Blind, 1926–1955*. Charleston: West Virginia Dept. of Education and the Arts, Division of Rehabilitation Service, 2001.

Clifford, James. *The Predicament of Culture: Twentieth-Century Ethnography, Literature, and Art.* Cambridge, MA: Harvard University Press, 1988.

Crockett, Manuel, and Barbara Dease. *Through the Years 1867–1977: Light out of Darkness.* Raleigh, NC: Barefoot, 1990.

Fay, Edward A. "Miscellaneous: 'How *Dumb* Was Dropped.'" *American Annals of the Deaf and Dumb* 34 (1889): 82–83.

Foucault, Michel. "The Birth of The Asylum." *The Foucault Reader.* Ed. Paul Rabinow, New York: Pantheon, 1984, 141–167.

Gannon, Jack. *Deaf Heritage: A Narrative History of Deaf America.* Silver Spring, MD: National Association of the Deaf, 1981.

Hairston, Ernest, and Linwood Smith. *Black and Deaf in America. Are We That Different?* Silver Spring, MD: TJ Publishing, 1983.

Joyner, Hannah. *From Pity to Pride: Growing Up Deaf in the Old South.* Washington: Gallaudet University Press, 2004.

Lane, Harlan. *A Deaf Artist in Early America: The Worlds of John Brewster, Jr.* Boston: Beacon. 2004.

Lane, Harlan, Richard Pillard, and Mary French. "Origins of the American Deaf-World: Assimilating and Differentiating Societies and Their Relation to Genetic Patterning." *The Signs of Language Revisited: An Anthology to Honor Ursula Bellugi and Edward Klima.* Ed. Karen Emmorey and Harlan L. Lane. Mahwah, NJ: Erlbaum, 2000, pp. 77–100.

Padden, Carol, and Tom Humphries. *Inside Deaf Culture.* Cambridge, MA: Harvard University Press, 2005.

Veditz, George. Letter to Roy Stewart, 1915, Roy Stewart Papers. Gallandet University Lib.

———. *The Presentation of the Sign Language.* Film. Natl. Assn. of the Deaf, 1913.

———. "Resolutions on Methods of Education." *Proceedings of the Ninth Convention of the National Association of the Deaf and the Third World's Congress of the Deaf, 1910.* Philadelphia: Philocophus, 1912, 27–31.

Stop Sharing Those Feel-Good Cochlear Implant Videos

8

Morgan Leahy

The video opens with a cute baby lying in his mother's arms. They are sitting in a doctor's office, about to activate a cochlear implant, a device that will help the child hear. The doctor turns on the implant, the baby's mother says his name . . . and he smiles so wide his pacifier falls out of his mouth. "A tear jerker if I ever saw one," say the comments. "I cry every time I watch this." "Science be praised!" "God be praised!" It's been viewed over 4.5 million times.

There are dozens of videos like this one online, and they often get millions of views and hundreds of comments about how miraculous it is for a person to suddenly be able to hear. But these videos, and the responses they generate, demonstrate an ignorance about cochlear implants and perpetuate dangerous misconceptions about deafness.

A cochlear implant is a medical device surgically placed in the inner ear, which transmits sound signals to the brain and can allow some deaf people to hear again, or hear for the first time. For hearing people, a video of a deaf person experiencing sound may look like a scientific and personal triumph. But for a deaf person, even a cochlear implant user like me, these "feel-good" videos are often a bit tasteless at best, ableist at worst.

In my experience, a majority of the Deaf community typically embraces those who take interest in deafness, including sign language, Deaf history, deafness-related technology, etc.—as long as they have good intentions, for instance if they're trying to educate themselves on what it is like to be culturally and medically deaf. But these videos can create misconceptions about cochlear implants, deaf technology, and what it means to be deaf.

For starters, cochlear implant technology is not as perfect as these videos make it seem. Hearing is not a switch you can just turn on. It takes months or years of hard work, therapy, and effort before the cochlear implant can be fully functioning—and that doesn't even include the speech therapy and other audiology appointments.

A majority of deaf people who get their implant turned on for the first time cannot even understand the sound that their brain is receiving. The brain needs to rewire itself before it can even comprehend the new sensory input.

I had my hearing for 20 years before going fully deaf, meaning that my brain did not need to rewire as much when I chose to get a cochlear implant. But even though I was the most prepared patient at my hospital, I could not understand a single thing that was said to me for two months after my activation. Yes, I could hear sound, but it was extremely difficult to comprehend. The artificial sound a cochlear implant provides is not the same as the sound hearing people experience. It takes practice and hard work in order to obtain something close to audibility. Using a cochlear implant can be quite demanding, even for the most promising candidates. So when a person without this knowledge watches the activation video they are led to think that the deaf person can fully hear everything, which is not the case.

Responses from hearing people on activation videos make it clear that they are unaware of the cochlear implant's limitations. One YouTube commenter, for instance, responded to a video with "take her to an orchestra, now!" To a majority of implant users, music is the last thing they want to hear on the first day of hearing sound. Sound is strenuous at first and it is a struggle to even keep the implant on for the first few weeks.

Once you know how overwhelming the new sounds from the cochlear implant can be, it's clear that people in some of these videos may not be crying tears of joy, but tears of confusion and discomfort due to sensory overload—although, of course, it's the "happy" results that tend to go viral. One commenter on a cochlear implant video writes: "It's interesting to me that deaf children always seem to smile when they hear for the first time." But the children who cry from the sudden flood of new sensory information aren't seen online.

These videos also tend to get comments from hearing people like "this is a miracle cure!" For several reasons, it's troubling to hail cochlear implants as a miracle. Cochlear implants aren't accessible to everyone; they cost a minimum of $30,000, require a lot of therapy and effort, and aren't appropriate for every person or every type of deafness. More important for the Deaf community, though, is the implication that deafness is something that needs to be cured, rather than accommodated by our hearing-dominated society. Though the community is generally supportive of cochlear implants as a technology, as long as they're handled ethically, the perception of them as a "miracle cure" is offensive.

The implant itself isn't a problem. The issue is that when people view these activation videos as tear-jerking material of disabled people being "cured," it perpetuates many foundations of ableism. For some members of the Deaf community, glamorizing and celebrating cochlear implants this way amounts to saying "your existence is impaired and diminished and needs to be fixed for you to have a full life."

BOX 8.1

Nyle DiMarco is famous for shows like *America's Next Top Model* and *Dancing with the Stars*. He also stars in a short film about how technology might improve the future for deaf people. Watch "Beyond Inclusion" here:

http://attitude.co.uk/nyle-dimarco-stars-in-politically-charged-short-film-about-the-future-of-disability/

Romanticizing cochlear implant technology puts further pressure onto deaf people to conform. Deaf people feel that they must reject their identity as a culturally Deaf or medically deaf individual. This pressure is a form of ableism, since it makes Deaf people feel as though something is wrong with them, and even feel that their culture is under threat.

Cochlear implant activation is the start of a long and hard journey, but these activation videos give the impression that it is instead the end of one. When a hearing person shares these videos with the belief that they show deaf people being "cured," they're perpetuating misinformation about cochlear implants, deafness, and the role of the Deaf community in society. The cochlear implant is merely an assistive medical tool and it does not redefine a deaf person's medical condition. We can't cure deafness, and more to the point, we don't need to.

Discussion Questions

1. Why do people like the "feel-good" cochlear implant videos to begin with? How would you explain to someone who posts one of these videos that they aren't making everyone "feel good?"

2. What is the danger in promoting a "cure" for Deafness (or any other disability)?

"Everyone Here Spoke Sign Language"
Nora Groce

The fifth of April, 1715, had not been a good day for Judge Samuel Sewell of Boston. On his way to the island of Martha's Vineyard there had been trouble finding a boat to cross Nantucket Sound. The vessel then lay for hours without wind, and once it was across, the horses had to be pushed overboard to swim for shore on their own. Sewell and his company reached shore at dusk—cold, hungry, and in bad humor. Finding a group of local fishermen nearby, the judge engaged one of them to guide him to Edgartown and later noted in his diary: "We were ready to be offended that an Englishman . . . in the company spake not a word to us. But," he continued by way of explanation, "it seems he is deaf and dumb."

This Englishman was indeed deaf, as were two of his seven children. His is the first recorded case of what we now know to be a form of inherited deafness that was to appear consistently within this island population for more than 250 years and affect dozens of individuals. Probably one or several of the small number of settlers who originally populated the area brought with them a trait for hereditary deafness. As long as the "gene pool" remained limited in the small island population, this trait appeared with high frequency in subsequent generations. Put another way, the founders of this isolated society had a greater likelihood of perpetuating the trait for congenital deafness than if they had been part of a larger, changing population.

Martha's Vineyard offers what I feel to be a good example of the way in which a community adapts to a hereditary disorder. Lying some 5 miles off the southeastern coast of Massachusetts, the island was first settled by Europeans in the early 1640s. The population, of predominantly English stock with some admixture of indigenous Wampanoag Indian, expanded rapidly, owing to a tremendously high birthrate. Families that had 15 to 20 children were not uncommon and 25 to 30 not unheard of. Although several hundred households are listed in the census records of the mid-18th century, only about 30 surnames are to be found, and during the next century and a half only a handful more were added to the original group of names.

After the first generation, marriage "off-island" was rare. While Vineyard men sailed around the world on whaleships, merchantmen, and fishing vessels, they almost invariably returned home to marry local girls and settle down. Women married off-island even less frequently than did the men. Contact with the mainland was said to be more sporadic than with foreign countries. In the 19th century, islanders claimed that more of their men had been to China than to Boston, only 80 miles away. Even today, many islanders have never been to the island of Nantucket, barely 8 miles to the east.

Throughout the 17th, 18th, and 19th centuries, marriage patterns on the island followed the customs of any small New England community. Most of the islanders, however, could trace their descent to the same small nucleus of original settlers, indicating that although they were unaware of it, considerable "inbreeding" took place. The result was that during these two and a half centuries, within a population averaging little more than 3,100 individuals, hereditary deafness occurred at a rate many times that of the national population. For example, in the latter part of the 19th century, an estimated one out of every 2,730 Americans was born deaf. On Martha's Vineyard the rate was closer to one out of every 155. But even this figure does not accurately represent the distribution of deafness on the Vineyard.

Marriages were usually contracted between members of the same village, creating smaller groups *within* the island's population characterized by a higher frequency of deafness. The greatest concentration occurred in one village on the western part of the island where, by my analysis, within a population of 500, one in every twenty-five individuals was deaf. And even there the distribution was not uniform, for in one area of the village during this time period, one out of every four persons was born deaf.

The high rate of deafness on the island brought only occasional comment from island visitors over the years. Because most of the island deaf lived in the more remote areas of the island, few off-islanders were aware of their presence. Vineyarders themselves, used to a sizeable deaf population, saw nothing unusual in this, and many assumed that all communities had a similar number of deaf members. Almost nothing exists in the written records to indicate who was or was not deaf, and indeed, only a passing reference made by an older islander directed my attention to the fact that there had been any deaf there at all.

While most of my information on island deafness has been obtained from the living oral history of islanders now in their seventies, eighties, and nineties, part of my genealogical data was acquired from the only other study of this deaf population. I came to know of it when an 86-year-old woman I was interviewing recalled that her mother had mentioned a "teacher of the deaf from Boston" at one time taking an interest in the island deaf. This "teacher of the deaf" turned out to be Alexander Graham Bell, who, having recently invented the telephone, turned his attention back to his lifelong interest in deafness research. Concerned with the question of heredity as it related to deafness, Bell began a major research project in the early 1880s, which was never completed.

Nineteenth-century scholars, without the benefit of Mendel's concept of unit factor inheritance (which only received widespread circulation at the turn of the century, although it had been published in the 1860s), were at a loss to explain why some but not all children of a deaf parent were themselves deaf. Selecting New England because of the older and unusually complete records available, Bell believed that by tracing back the genealogy of every family with two or more deaf children, he could establish some pattern for the inheritance of deafness. He soon found that practically every family in New England with a history of deafness was in some way connected with the early settlers of Martha's Vineyard, but he was unable to account for the fact that a deaf parent did not always have deaf children and so he abandoned the study. Although Bell never published his material, he left dozens of genealogical charts that have proved invaluable for my research—particularly because they corroborate the information I have been able to collect from the oral history of the older islanders.

Since Bell's time, scientists have found, through the construction and analysis of family pedigrees and the use of mathematical models, that congenital deafness may result from several causes: spontaneous mutations involving one or more genes; an already established dominant or recessive inheritance, as Mendel demonstrated; or factors otherwise altering normal development of the ear and its pathways to the brain. Human populations, of course, cannot be studied with the same exactness as a laboratory experiment. However, the appearance of apparently congenitally deaf individuals is far too frequent on Martha's Vineyard to be mere coincidence, and the evidence collected thus far points to a recessive mode of inheritance.

While the genetic nature of a hereditary disorder in small populations is something that both anthropologists and geneticists have studied, there is another question, rarely addressed, that is of equal importance: How does the population of a community in which a hereditary disorder exists adjust to that disorder—particularly one as prominent as deafness? In modern society the emphasis has been on having "handicapped" individuals adapt to the greater society. But the perception of a handicap, with its associated physical and social limitations, is tempered by the community in which it is found. The manner in which the deaf of Martha's Vineyard were treated provides an interesting example of how one community responded to this type of situation. "How," I asked my informants, "were the island deaf able to communicate with you when they could not speak?" "Oh," I was told, "there was no problem at all. You see, everyone here spoke sign language."

From the late 17th century to the early years of the twentieth, islanders, particularly those from the western section where the largest number of deaf individuals lived, maintained a bilingual speech community based on spoken English and sign language. What is of particular interest is that the use of sign language played an important role in day-to-day life.

Islanders acquired a knowledge of sign language in childhood. They were usually taught by parents, with further reinforcement coming from the surrounding community, both hearing and deaf. For example, recalling how she learned a particular sign, one elderly woman explained:

> When I was a little girl, I knew many of the signs, and the manual alphabet of course, but I didn't know how to say "Merry Christmas," and I wanted to tell Mr. M. "Merry Christmas." So I asked Mrs. M., his wife. She could hear and she showed me how. And so I wished Mr. M. "Merry Christmas"—and he was just so delighted.

This woman then described how she taught her son, now in his late seventies, how to speak the language.

> When my son was perhaps three years old, I taught him to say in sign language "the little cat and dog and baby." This man, who was deaf, he used to like to go down to our little general store and see people come and go. One day when I went down there, I took my son there and I said to him, "Go over and say 'how-do-you-do' to Mr. T.," the deaf man. So he went right over, and then I told him to tell Mr. T. so-and-so—a cat, a dog, and whatever. And wasn't Mr. T. tickled! Oh, he was so pleased to know a little bit of a boy like that was telling him all those things, and so he just taught my son a few more words. That's how he learned. That's how we all learned.

Particularly in the western section of the island, if an immediate member of the family was not deaf, a neighbor, friend, or close relative of a friend was likely to be. Practically all my "up-island" informants above the age of 70 remembered signs, a good indication of the extent to which the language was known and used. In this section, and to a lesser extent in the other villages on the island, sign language formed an integral part of all communications. For example, all informants remembered the deaf participating freely in discussions. One remarked:

> If there were several people present and there was a deaf man or woman in the crowd, he'd take upon himself the discussion of anything, jokes or news or anything like that. They always had a part in it, they were never excluded.

As in all New England communities, gathering around the potbellied stove or on the front porch of what served as a combination general store and post office provided a focal point for stories, news, and gossip. Many of the people I have talked to distinctly remember the deaf members of the community in this situation. As one man recalled:

> We would sit around and wait for the mail to come in and just talk. And the deaf would be there, everyone would be there. And they were part of the crowd, and they were accepted. They were fishermen and farmers and everything else. And they wanted to find out the news just as much as the rest of us. And oftentimes people would tell stories and make signs at the same time so everyone could follow him together. Of course, sometimes, if there were more deaf than hearing there, everyone would speak sign language—just to be polite, you know.

The use of sign was not confined to small group discussions. It also found its way into assembled crowds. For example, one gentleman told me:

> They would come to prayer meetings; most all of them were regular church people, you know. They would come when people offered testimonials, and they would get up in front of the audience and stand there and give a whole lecture in sign. No one translated it to the audience because everyone knew what they were saying. And if there was anyone who missed something somewhere, somebody sitting near them would be able to tell them about it.

The deaf were so integral a part of the community that at town meetings up-island, a hearing person would stand at the side of the hall and cue the deaf in sign to let them know what vote was coming up next, thus allowing them to keep right on top of things. The participation of the deaf in all day-to-day work and play situations contrasted with the manner in which those handicapped by deafness were generally treated in the United States during the same time period.

Sign language on the island was not restricted to those occasions when deaf and hearing were together, but was used on a regular basis between the hearing as well. For example, sign language was used on boats to give commands and among fishermen out in open water to discuss their catch. I was told:

> Fishermen, hauling pots outside in the Sound or off Gay Head, when they would be heaven knows how far apart, would discuss how the luck was running—all that sort of thing. These men could talk and hear all right, but it'd be too far to yell.

Indeed, signs were used any place the distance prohibited talking in a normal voice. For example, one man remembered:

Jim had a shop down on the shore of Tisbury Pond, and his house was a ways away, up on the high land. When Trudy, his wife, wanted to tell Jim something, she'd come to the door, blow a fish horn, and Jim would step outside. He'd say, "Excuse me, Trudy wants me for something"; then she'd make signs to tell him what she needed done.

On those occasions when speaking was out of place, such as in church, school, or at some public gatherings, the hearing communicated through signs. Such stories as the following are common: "Ben and his brother could both talk and hear, but I've seen them sitting across from each other in town meetings or in church and telling each other funny stories in sign language."

Island people frequently maintained social distance and a sense of distinct identity in the presence of tourists by exchanging comments about them in sign language. The occurrence of what linguists call code switching from speech to sign also seems to have been used in certain instances. For example, I was told:

People would start off a sentence in speaking and then finish it off in sign language, especially if they were saying something dirty. The punch line would often be in sign language. If there was a bunch of guys standing around the general store telling a [dirty] story and a woman walked in, they'd turn away from her and finish the story in sign language.

Perhaps the following anecdote best illustrates the unique way island sign language was integral to all aspects of life:

My mother was in the New Bedford hospital—had an operation—and father went over in his boat and lived aboard his boat and went to the hospital to see her every night. Now the surgeon, when he left him in her room, said they mustn't speak, father couldn't say a word to her. So he didn't. But they made signs for about half an hour and mother got so worked up, they had to send father out, wouldn't let him stay any longer.

Sign language or rather sign languages—for even within this country there exist a number of distinct languages and dialects—are languages in their own right, systems of communication different from the spoken languages used by hearing members of the same community. It has often been noted that American Sign Language, the sign system commonly used among the deaf in the United States today, is influenced by French Sign Language, introduced to America in 1817. The data from Martha's Vineyard, however, clearly support the hypothesis, made by the linguist James Woodward, that local sign language systems were in use in

America long before this. By 1817 (the year the American School for the Deaf was founded in Hartford, Connecticut), deaf individuals on Martha's Vineyard had been actively participating in island society for well over a century. Because they were on an equal footing, both socially and economically, with the hearing members of the community, and because they held town offices, married, raised families, and left legal and personal documents, there must have existed some sort of sign language system that allowed full communication with family, friends, and neighbors.

It may prove difficult to reconstruct the original sign language system used on the island during the 17th and 18th centuries, but study of this question is currently underway. Whatever the exact nature of the original language, we know that it later grew to acquire many aspects of the more widely used American Sign Language, as increasing numbers of deaf island children were sent to the school in Hartford during the 19th century. This combination of the indigenous sign system with the more standardized American Sign Language seems to have produced a sign language that was, in many respects, unique to the island of Martha's Vineyard. The most common remark made by islanders who still remember the language is that they find it very difficult or are completely unable to understand the sign language spoken by off-islanders or the translations for the deaf that are beginning to be seen on television.

The use of sign language as an active system of communication lessened as the number of individuals in the community with hereditary deafness gradually disappeared, the last few dying in the 1940s and early 1950s. This decrease in the number of deaf can be attributed to a shift in marriage patterns that began in the latter part of the nineteenth century, when both hearing and deaf islanders began to marry off-islanders. The introduction of new genes into the once small gene pool has reduced the chance of a reappearance of "island deafness."

As the number of islanders born deaf dwindled, younger generations no longer took an interest in learning sign language, and the older generations rarely had the need to make use of it. Today, very few people are left who can speak the language fluently, although bits and pieces of it can be recalled by several dozen of the oldest islanders. A few signs are still kept alive among those who knew the language and on a few of their fishing boats. As one gentleman, well along in his seventies, told me recently:

> You know, strangely enough, there's still vestiges of that left in the older families around here. Instinctively you make some such movement, and it means something to you, but it doesn't mean anything to the one you're talking to.

Discussion Questions

1. How does the idea of deafness change in a population where hearing impairments are common?

2. What are the benefits to using sign language for a community made up of both Deaf and hearing people?

The History of Disability

Disability History

Susan Burch and
Kim E. Nielsen

10

Historians grapple with and learn from disability via two distinct but overlapping methods of analyzing change over time. First, they examine the daily and structural lives of those considered disabled and others who interact with them; second, they analyze changing historical conceptualizations of disability, able-bodiedness, and able-mindedness. Many disability historians also explore disability and ableism's relation to other frameworks of power—such as race, class, sexuality, age, gender, and family. Central to disability history is the analytical and archival task of unpacking the largely Western and contemporary cross-impairment category we now call disability.

Historical scholarship differs from other disciplines because of its reliance on evidentiary materials from the past and interest in change and continuities over time. Primary sources vary, but traditionally historians have drawn primarily on "official" text-based resources, such as proclamations and laws, newspapers, memoirs, court proceedings, and church records. Because of a historian's power to select which sources to examine, and because of a society's power to retain and/or rid itself of some evidentiary sources, history also forces questions about knowledge: what counts as knowledge, who is authorized to provide knowledge, who is the intended recipient of knowledge, and how it is preserved and disseminated. These issues are significant for all historical research, but because those in power (particularly medical and institutional experts) have frequently dismissed people with disabilities as unworthy and deficient—unable to accurately document their own lives—these questions are particularly salient to historicizing disability.

The increased engagement of people with disabilities in the production of historical knowledge, the concomitant rise of disability scholarship, and the increased use of disability as an analytical tool have encouraged archivists, librarians, museum curators, and others to expand and redefine their own historical work. There is literally more *history* available because of this. More reflective and inclusive indices, exhibits, libraries and collections, and courses in disability history have changed how the broader discipline "gets done." Part of this change includes reflecting upon and learning from historical terminology used to describe disability, such as "cripple," "abnormal," "retard," "incompetent," "lunatic," "delinquent," "deviant," "feeble-minded," and "special"; as well as nondisability status: "normal," "competent," "fit," and "citizen." Providing new data and interpretations contributes to the broader increase of understanding; this movement transcends disciplines as well as cultural and geographic boundaries.

The cultural meanings and lived experience of disability are marked both by continuities and by changes over time. Understandings of epilepsy and epileptics, for example, illustrate both tendencies. Since ancient times and across the globe, epileptics have appeared in historic sources. Considerable interest in the causes of what today is considered epilepsy figured prominently in these stories. According to many cultures, the evil eye, jinn possession, or God's punishment produced "the falling sickness."[1] In other communities, "the sacred disease" has denoted positive divine intervention, and those so touched have held exalted status. Other interpretations, also sustained to varying degrees across millennia, have cast epileptics as mentally ill, "unfit," or mentally disabled. Epileptics themselves have offered widely ranging expressions of their experiences, but especially in the past several decades, and in specific geographic contexts, an additional framework has emerged that emphasizes epileptic community as an authentic cultural identity.

Historical study draws attention to dynamic relations and outcomes. Hostility, fear, and wonderment were among the varied responses to epileptics across different times and places. While the experience of epileptics— mirroring the broader history of numerous disability groups—changed sharply in the modern era in the global north, certain themes remain constant across a broader history. In the 19th- and 20th-century United States, as just one era and location, epileptics often were forcibly institutionalized, subjected to forced sterilizations, and prohibited from marrying or having sexual relations with others. Foreign epileptics were prohibited from entering the country. By the late 20th century, many of these restrictions had been lifted. At the same time, erroneous and long-standing beliefs that epilepsy was contagious and that epileptics were unfit to parent or to work continue to shape daily experiences of epileptics, their families, and the broader society. Historians of disability assess these diverse interventions across time and place—including exorcisms, trepanning (drilling holes in the skull), homeopathic and pharmaceutical remedies, invitations to serve as shamans, institutionalization, immigration and employment bans, forced sterilizations, and marriage restrictions—to demonstrate wide-ranging and culture-specific understandings of epilepsy. Such historical developments also point to the ways that epileptics have been situated in the overlap of religious and spiritual traditions, magic and science, and legal and economic systems.

Historians' rigorous consideration of context and developments across time is particularly important for the social (relational) model of disability. According to this model, bodily and mental impairments encompass different meanings and experiences depending on the environments in which they exist. For example, the Arab-Islamic world in the early modern period, which emphasized oral dissemination of knowledge, presented unique opportunities for some people who were blind or had low vision. Ottoman sources detail numerous, prominent roles that blind men filled in Muslim society: muezzin (the man who calls other Muslims to prayer), mullahs, Qur'an teachers and reciters, and Hadith scholars.[2] Indeed, what blind has meant, and how blind—as a category and a lived experience—has been expressed have varied as widely as its definitions.

A historical approach also makes transparent the ways that people with disabilities have both been shaped by and responded to broader forces in history. Disabled slaves in the United States, like all enslaved peoples, sought to resist slavery and shape their own lives. In 1840, for example, a New Orleans slave named Bob who had an amputated leg stole away from his master with the assistance of a crutch. Similarly, a slave named Peggy was "very much parrot toed and walks badly," but she ran away from her Virginia master in 1798. Although slave owners tended to dismiss disabled slaves as *refuse* or *unsound,* disabled slaves often engaged in significant skilled and unskilled work that included working in the fields, caring for children, and household labor. Sojourner Truth, the noted abolitionist and women's rights activist, had, in her words, "a badly diseased hand, which greatly diminished her usefulness" to her master. But such self-acknowledged impairment did not limit her future political activism or leadership.[3]

Similarly, many institutionalized people left abundant evidence of their efforts to shape their own surroundings. Young women institutionalized in early 20th-century Chicago as "feebleminded" and "defective," for example, quickly realized that by responding as expected when they were questioned, they could better and shape their circumstances—in essence, manipulating the institutional experts who determined much of their lives.[4] Between 1851 and 1860, residents of the New York State Lunatic Asylum in Utica, New York, created a monthly journal of poetry, editorials, essays, plays, and art. While rigorously supervised, *The Opal* also became a means by which asylum residents criticized medical practices, such as physical restraints and isolation, offered their own political and social commentary on national events, established community, and expressed anger and resistance.

Wars and conflict provide additional and vivid examples of the relationship between historical forces and historical actors shaping the experiences and meanings of disability. The Bolshevik revolution profoundly shaped the course of 20th-century history, bearing human marks across generations. The ensuing civil war exacerbated the loss of human life, contributing to especially dire economic circumstances of the Soviet regime. Amid this complex, sometimes inspiring, and often harrowing wave of change, deaf citizens experienced unprecedented opportunities. During the previous century, deaf schools, funded exclusively and sporadically by secular and religious philanthropists, privileged only a select few. By the 1920s, however, deaf youth generally had access to primary, secondary, and—to some degree—higher education. As in other nations, sustained residential schools for Soviet deaf students became the touchstones for vibrant cultural communities. Emerging from this increasingly unified world, deaf leaders like Pavel Savel'ev cultivated profitable ties to the Soviet regime based on common interests, particularly employment. Recognizing that deaf people had long struggled to gain full access to the workplace, Savel'ev's proposal to establish deaf-only factory-educational facilities (*rabfacs*) achieved multiple goals. The state benefitted from the influx of engaged, capable laborers who expressed gratitude for the opportunity to work; deaf people, in turn, enjoyed greater social status and concomitant resources: food rations, homes, funding for deaf art exhibits, sports clubs, newspapers, and other community projects. For most of the 20th century, the state supported deaf cultural oases: towns where members communicated in Russian Sign Language, lived and worked together, and shared richly in deaf cultural traditions.[5]

Disability history is inextricably entangled with all other topics of history. For instance, disability rights movements in all of their manifestations share central themes in history: struggle, citizenship, labor, power, violence, health, representation, and community. The rise of disability rights activism in Germany, particularly since the 1960s, points to the powerful role of transnational activism. Early activists in Germany, drawing on examples of African-Americans and their antiracist allies in the United States, challenged mainstream discriminatory attitudes and policies. Invoking the civil rights rhetoric of integration and inclusion, these activists demanded a reckoning with their nation's history of violence against people with disabilities. Collective action focused on self-empowerment, dismantling of environmental and attitudinal barriers, and greater access to the workplace. Specifically rejecting patronizing representations in the United Nations Year of the Disabled platform, German disability activists in 1981 challenged philanthropists who relied on the charity model of disability and demanded full and equal citizenship rights. One leader, Franz Christoph, applied unsuccessfully for political asylum, claiming that Germany persecuted disabled people. A "cripple tribunal" (*Krüppeltribunal*) drew public attention to a litany of abuses: under- and unemployment, inaccessible transportation and health care, limited housing options, and other forms of daily marginalization and oppression.[6] The efforts, while uneven in their impact, galvanized the emerging disability cultural community in Germany. As these stories illustrate, disability history can teach much about larger historical questions and themes.

This is partly why historical scholarship is foundational to disability studies. At its core, disability studies is built on the premise that neither disability nor able-bodiedness and able-mindedness are simply and wholly biologically determined. As the examples of disabled American slaves, institutionalized white men and women, and Russian deaf activists illustrate, people with disabilities have in all circumstances sought to shape their daily and structural lives. Simultaneously, larger historical forces and incidents have influenced the options and methods before them. The study of history provides means by which to substantiate this argument and reflect on its implications. When examined historically and across cultures, it is clear that definitions of disability and related terms are variable, culturally shaped, influenced by other power structures, and built in interaction with major historical forces such as (but not limited to) religion, politics, and economic systems. Historical scholarship also provides evidence of the rich lives and activism of people with disabilities, providing lessons and resources for contemporary activists. Knowledge of others' activism and efforts nourishes contemporary communities. The stories and debates of the past invite questions into the present and lend insight into how current positions, relations, and understandings have been shaped by the past. Disability history facilitates a richer imagining of alternatives and structural opportunities for change.

Discussion Questions

1. What are the challenges of historicizing disability? The unique opportunities? Give at least one example of history here that most people aren't familiar with yet.

2. How might the histories of other civil rights movements help us understand the history of disability rights?

Notes

1   Dwyer, 1992; Carod-Artal and Vázquez-Cabrera, 2007; Wolf, 2010; Fadiman, 1998.
2   Scalenghe, 2014, 47; Weygand, 2009; Barasch, 2001.
3   Gilbert and Truth, 1850, 39; Boster, 2009.
4   Rembis, 2011.
5   Burch, 2000.
6   Poore, 2007, 281; Köbsell, 2006; Bosl, 2014.

References

Barasch, Moshe. *Blindness: The History of a Mental Image in Western Thought.* New York: Routledge, 2001.

Bosl, Elsbeth. "The Contergan Scandal: Media, Medicine, and Thalidomide in 1960s West Germany" in *Disability Histories,* edited by Susan Burch and Michael Rembis, 136–162. Urbana: University of Illinois Press, 2014.

Boster, Dea. "An 'Epeleptick' Bondswoman: Fits, Slavery, and Power in the Antebellum South." *Bulletin of the History of Medicine* 83 (2009): 271–301.

Burch, Susan. "Transcending Revolutions: The Tsars, the Soviets and Deaf History." *Journal of Social History* 34 (2000): 393–402.

Carod-Artal, F. J. and Vázquez-Cabrera, C. "An Anthropological Study About Headache and Migraine in Native Cultures From Central and South America." *Headache: The Journal of Head and Face Pain,* 47 (2007): 834–841.

Dwyer, Ellen. "Epilepsy Stories, 1880–1930" in *Framing Disease: Studies in Cultural History,* edited by Charles E. Rosenberg and Jane Goldern, 248–272. New Brunswick, N.J.: Rutgers University Press, 1992.

Fadiman, Anne. *The Spirit Catches You and You Fall Down.* New York: Farrar, Straus and Giroux, 1998.

Gilbert, Olive and Truth, Sojourner. *Narrative of Sojourner Truth: A Northern Slave, Emancipated from Bodily Servitude by the State of New York in 1828.* Boston: privately printed, 1850.

Köbsell, Swantje. "Towards Self-Determination and Equalization: A Short History of the German Disability Rights Movement." *Disability Studies Quarterly* 26, no.2 (2006). Accessed September 17, 2014. http://dsq-sds.org/article/view/692/869

Poore, Carol. *Disability in Twentieth-Century German Culture.* Ann Arbor: University of Michigan Press, 2007.

Rembis, Michael A. *Defining Deviance: Sex, Science, and Delinquent Girls,* 1890–1960. Chicago: University of Chicago Press, 2011.

Scalenghe, Sara. *The Body Different: Disability in the Arab-Islamic World, 1500–1800.* Cambridge: Cambridge University Press, 2014.

Weygand, Zina. *The Blind in French Society: From the Middle Ages to the Century of Louis Braille.* Translated by Emily-Jane Cohen. Stanford: Stanford University Press, 2009.

Wolf, Peter. "Sociocultural History of Epilepsy" in *Atlas of Epilepsies, Part 2,* edited by C.P. Panaylotopoulos, 35–43. London: Springer-Verlag, 2010.

Defectives in the Land

Disability and American Immigration
Policy, 1882–1924

Douglas C. Baynton

Sophie Fuko of Hungary embarked from Hamburg aboard the SS Kaiserin Auguste Victoria in late November 1912, with her 6-year-old son, Kaiman. Fuko's husband had died four years earlier and now, at the age of 46, with no remaining relatives in her native land, she had decided to emigrate to the United States to join her two adult sons, Laszlo and Bela. She and Kaiman arrived at Ellis Island December 4. They immediately encountered difficulties. The medical inspectors certified Sophie Fuko as "practically blind in right eye," her son as "afflicted with deaf mutism," and therefore both of them as "likely to become public charges."

When their hearing before the Board of Special Inquiry was held four days later, Fuko's adult sons were there to testify on her behalf. Fuko testified that she had $20 with her and had been self-supporting in Hungary as a housekeeper. Her sons Laszlo and Bela testified that they were employed and earning decent wages. They had spent $170 for a second-class cabin for their mother and brother and $100 to furnish a home for them, as well as paying for the passage from Hungary for Bela's wife and child who were due to arrive soon. Ordinarily, the family's finances would have been more than sufficient, but for the medical certificates. The Board ruled that Fuko and her son were "suffering from physical defects, the nature of which will affect their ability to earn a living" and were therefore "likely to become public charges." It ordered them to be deported, informing her of her right to appeal to the Secretary of the Department of Commerce and Labor.

Fuko did appeal. In her letter to the Secretary, she said that her sons were prepared to furnish bonds guaranteeing that she and her son would not become public charges. She added that while she had little cash, she owned a house in her native town that she would soon sell, "promisery [sic] notes" on which she would soon collect, and a substantial life insurance policy covering herself and her young son. In addition, she claimed that her son was neither deaf nor mute, but could hear when spoken to loudly and that "of late he begain [sic] to talk very nicely." He could also read and write. Finally, she appealed to the Secretary's sympathy by stressing that she had no one left in Hungary to return to, that her only family was here in the United States.

William Williams, the Commissioner of Immigration at Ellis Island, had built a reputation as a strict enforcer of the immigration laws, particularly those related to physical and mental defects. He urged the Secretary to dismiss Fuko's appeal, because "her child will always be physically defective, and it would be improper to admit merely because of the relatives here." The Commissioner General of the Bureau of Immigration agreed, saying that "the Bureau does not think the mere presence here of two sons affords any good ground for admitting these physically defective aliens." The Secretary, deferring as he usually did to the Commissioner of the station and the Commissioner General when they were in agreement, dismissed the appeal. Sophie Fuko and her son were put aboard the USS Pennsylvania on December 21 and returned to an unknown fate in Hungary.[1]

One of the driving forces behind early federal immigration law, beginning with the first major Immigration Act in 1882, was the exclusion of people with mental and physical defects (as well as those considered criminal or immoral, problems seen at the time as closely related to mental defect). Congressional legislation throughout this period repeatedly, and with ever increasing urgency, identified defective immigrants as a threat to the nation. The desire to keep out immigrants deemed defective was not an isolated development, but rather was one aspect of a trend toward the increasing segregation of disabled people into institutions and the sterilization of the "unfit" and "degenerate" under state eugenic laws.

While anti-immigrant sentiment in the United States has long been a significant area of scholarly research, disability has held a marginal place in that scholarship. John Higham's *Strangers in the Land* identified three main currents of anti-immigrant sentiment: anti-Catholicism, fear of foreign radicals, and racial nativism. Roger Daniels stated in *Coming to America* that "by 1917 the immigration policy of the United States had been restricted in seven major ways," with admission being denied to "Asians . . .; criminals; persons who failed to meet certain moral standards; persons with various diseases; paupers; assorted radicals; and illiterates." Alan Kraut's *Silent Travelers* and Amy Fairchild's recent book, *Science at the Borders*, brought a welcome focus to medical inspection, but did not examine communicable disease and disability as distinct issues, nor explore the cultural stigmatization of disability that formed the background to these laws.[2]

Sophie Fuko does not fit into any of the categories that historians of immigration policy have described as fundamental to anti-immigrant sentiment or the enactment of exclusionary immigration policies in the United States. Though she had little money at hand, she was by no definition a pauper. Neither she nor her son was a carrier of disease. The only charge against Fuko, and many other similar immigrants, was that they were defective. Countless other immigrants passed through Ellis Island with fewer financial resources, no family in the United States to turn to in case of difficulty, and certainly less poignant personal circumstances. Disability was a crucial factor in deciding whether an immigrant would be allowed to enter the United States.

The first major immigration law, the Act of 1882, prohibited entry to any "lunatic, idiot, or any person *unable* to take care of himself or herself without becoming a public charge." Those placed in the categories "lunatic" or "idiot" were automatically excluded. The "public charge" provision was intended to encompass individuals with disabilities more generally, and was left to the examining officer's discretion.[3] The criteria for excluding disabled persons were steadily tightened as the eugenics movement and popular fears about the decline of the national stock gathered strength. The Act of 1891 replaced the phrase "unable to take care of himself or herself without becoming a public charge," with "*likely* to become a public charge." The 1907 law then required a medical certificate for anyone judged "mentally or physically defective, such mental or physical defect being of a nature which *may affect* the ability of such alien to earn a living." While nondisabled immigrants continued to be admitted unless found to be "likely to become a public charge," disabled people were subject to this more rigorous standard.[4]

Exclusions for mental defect were steadily expanded. In 1903 people with epilepsy were added, as well as "persons who have been insane within five years previous [or] who have had two or more attacks of insanity at any time previously." In 1907 "imbeciles" and "feeble-minded persons" had been barred, in addition to "idiots." In 1917 the classification of "constitutional psychopathic inferiority" was added, which inspection regulations described as including "various unstable individuals on the border line between sanity and insanity, such as . . . persons with abnormal sex instincts." Officials were instructed to exclude persons with "any mental abnormality whatever . . . which justifies the statement that the alien is mentally defective." This provision, the regulations explain, was intended "as a means of excluding aliens of a mentally inferior type, not comprehended in the other provisions of the law, without being under the necessity, as formerly, of showing that they have a defect which may affect their ability to earn a living."[5]

The rules governing exclusion for physical disabilities were equally vague and expansive. Regulations instructed inspectors that "each individual should be seen first at rest and then in motion," in order to detect "irregularities in movement" and "abnormalities of any description." It listed defects that could be cause for exclusion, a few examples of which were arthritis, asthma, bunions, deafness, deformities, flat feet, heart disease, hernia, hysteria, poor eyesight, poor physical development, spinal curvature, vascular disease of the heart, and varicose veins.[6] An Ellis Island medical inspector later wrote that his task was "to detect poorly built, defective or broken down human beings."[7] In short, the exclusion of disabled people was central to the laws governing immigration. As the Commissioner General of Immigration reported in 1907, "The exclusion from this country of the morally, mentally, and physically deficient is the principal object to be accomplished by the immigration laws."[8]

These laws were usually presented as simply a matter of economics. The issue, however, was rarely so straightforward. Many rejected immigrants had been self-supporting in their home countries. Others received job offers while awaiting their hearing, but still were deported as likely to become public charges. More importantly, to the extent that some people with disabilities might indeed encounter difficulties in finding employment, the public charge law also assumes that the unemploy-ment or underemployment of disabled people is a problem centered in bodies rather than in the relationship between particular bodies and the constructed physical and social environments in which they live. This may have been the only practical assumption for immigration officials, but historians should put immigration restriction into context as one element in a larger system of discrimination that made it difficult for disabled people to live and move about independently. Leaving aside, however, complex questions of what factors made (and still make) it difficult for disabled people to find work, the economic explanation for exclusion remains an incomplete one. Two examples of the mixed motives and reasoning that went into these exclusions were the diagnoses "poor physique" and "lack of sexual development."

In his *Annual Report* of 1904, the Commissioner of Ellis Island, William Williams, suggested that the country was "receiving too many immigrants whose physical condition is poor." The only disabled persons specifically excluded under law at that time were idiots, insane persons, and epileptics (the category of "physical and mental defects" came in 1907). As Williams explained, to exclude immigrants certi-fied with physical impairments required finding that they were likely to become public charges, "yet it is obviously impossible to exclude on this ground all persons whose physical condition is poor." He urged that the exclusion of immigrants certified as having "poor physique" be made mandatory in all cases.[9] Soon thereafter, Robert DeCourcey Ward of the Immigration Restriction League wrote to the Commissioner General of Immigration, Frank Sargent, urging him to take up Williams's cause before Congress.[10]

The specific diagnostic category was never embodied in law, but within a year "poor physique" was being widely used as a diagnosis by immigration officials to exclude immigrants on grounds of being "likely to become a public charge." The immigration service defined poor physique as covering individuals "who have frail frame, flat chest, and are generally deficient in muscular development," or who are "undersized–markedly of short stature–dwarf."[11] As one medical officer explained, the "immigrant of poor physique is not able to perform rough labor, and *even if he were able*, employers of labor would not hire him."[12] That is, the belief that an immigrant was unfit to work justified exclusion, but so did the belief that an immigrant *was likely to encounter discrimination* because of a disability.

Eugenic considerations also played an important role in both the creation and the application of immigration law. In a letter to the Commissioner General, the Ellis Island Commissioner wrote that the Bureau had no more important work to perform than that of picking out all mentally defective immigrants, for these are not only likely to join the criminal classes and become public charges, but by leaving feebleminded descendents they start vicious strains which lead to misery and loss in future generations and influence unfavorably the character and lives of hundreds of persons.[13]

This inter-generational "contagion" of defect worried the Commissioner General about immigrants with "poor physiques." In a 1905 memorandum, he explained that "a certificate of this nature implies that the alien concerned is afflicted with a body but illy adapted . . . to the work necessary to earn his bread," and further that the immigrant is "undersized, poorly developed [and] physically degenerate, and as such, not only unlikely to become a desirable citizen, but also very likely to transmit his undesirable qualities to his offspring, should he unfortunately for the country in which he is domiciled, have any."[14]

On January 30, 1906, Israel Bosak was certified at Ellis Island for "poor physique." He was not destitute, having $65 in his possession, a respectable sum for an immigrant at the time. Bosak testified that he had owned a tailor shop in Russia before it was destroyed by a mob during an anti-Jewish pogrom. He intended to send for his wife and children as soon as he had gotten himself established, explaining that he had "plenty of countrymen here who are just as good as relatives, to help me." After a brief hearing, the Board of Special Inquiry voted unanimously to exclude. Bosak had a second hearing when two distant relatives appeared to assure the Board that they would assist him in finding work and provide for him until he did so. Such testimony rarely changed a Board's decision, but this time the Board had a new member, Philip Cowen, who was not a regular member of the service but rather a political appointee of Theodore Roosevelt. Cowen proved to be a maverick in many cases. He questioned Bosak about his business in Russia and the pogrom in which it was destroyed, then made a short speech:

> The alien before the Board has come here because of the unsettled condition of affairs in his home; the rioters having despoiled him of the property which he held in his business, and prevented him from earning a livelihood; he is thus practically driven from his home by the mob; he comes to this country to establish a home for himself and family; a man who has once been possessed of a home and property seems to me to be valuable material for immigration and needs nothing more than a helping hand of friends to become self sustaining; these friends appear in the persons of the witnesses before the board; and it seems to me that there is no danger whatever of the man becoming a public charge. . . . I therefore move his admission.

Inspector Smiley, who had been on the previous Board and voted to exclude, was moved to change his vote: "From the excellent showing of the witnesses made in the alien's behalf, I second the motion to admit." Inspector Paul, however, voted to exclude which meant that the Secretary of Labor would have to decide the matter. In his letter to Washington, Inspector Paul noted that he wished to "particularly call attention to Department letter 48,462," the circular that had emphasized the danger to the eugenic health of the nation in admitting people "whose offspring will reproduce, often in an exaggerated degree, the physical degeneracy of their parents." The Commissioner at Ellis Island "strongly" recommended deportation, and he too called attention to the same Bureau circular on the eugenic dangers of admitting immigrants of poor physique. The Commissioner General concurred, and the Secretary ordered Israel Bosak returned to Russia.[15]

Since the screening of immigrants was mostly a matter of detecting visual abnormality, the appearance of immigrants played an important role. Inspectors prided themselves on their ability to make a "snapshot diagnosis" as immigrants streamed past them single file. For most immigrants, a normal appearance usually meant an uneventful passage through the immigration station. An abnormal appearance, however, meant a chalked letter on the back. Once chalked, a closer inspection was required—"L for lameness, K for suspected hernia, G for goiter, X for suspected mental illness," and so on.[16] The inspection then would be general, not confined to the abnormality that set them apart, which meant that visibly different people—as well as those whose ethnic appearance was abnormal to the inspectors—were more likely to be set apart for close examination, and therefore more likely to have other problems discovered and to be excluded.

Donabet Mousekian had an abnormal appearance. On April 23, 1905, this Armenian Turk stood before the Board of Special Inquiry with an inspection certificate that read "feminism." In other instances the term used was "lack of sexual development." In this case, it meant an absence of male sexual organs, in others, insufficient development (now known to be caused by a hormonal deficiency). Mousekian's hearing was extraordinarily brief. No one mentioned the diagnosis or questioned him about it. After asking only the most basic questions concerning his identity and background, and noting that he brought $48 with him, the transcript reads as follows: "Mr. Rotz: In view of the Doctor's certificate I move to exclude him as likely to become a public charge. Mr. Ryan: Second motion. Mr. Smiley: Excluded." This was all the hearing that Mousekian received.

In his appeal, Mousekian explained that he had fled the violent oppression of Armenians in Turkey and had officially renounced his citizenship. Since he would never be permitted to return to Turkey and remain free, rather than send him back, "it would be much better that you kill me," he wrote. His relatives were all in America, including his two brothers who were citizens and well employed. He was a photographer by trade, as well as a skilled weaver and dyer of rugs and a cook, and could work at any of these trades. He wrote,

> I am not ill, have no contagious disease; my eyes, feet, hands and ears are sound; only I am deprived of male organs; this is not a fault because it has come from God and my mother: what can I do? It won't do any harm to my working; or what harm can I do to the U.S. by my being deprived of male organs?

His brothers wrote letters in much the same vein, asking plaintively,

> How is it his fault? Our father and mother are dead; he is our only brother . . .; we guarantee that he will not be a public charge; we are able to give the required guarantee; he cannot return to Turkey; we are US citizens, hence we beg US government not to separate our brother from us.

The Commissioner at Ellis supported the Board's decision, largely on the basis of an unfavorable appearance: "Appellant is devoid of every external evidence of desirability. He is weak . . ., repulsive in appearance, the doctor's certificate . . . furnishing sufficient indication of his physical defects." Mousekian was returned to Turkey where, if he remained and lived that long, he would be caught up in the Armenian genocide ten years later.[17]

In cases of lack of sexual development, the files rarely explained the reasons for exclusion. The Surgeon General, however, did explain in a memo the reasoning behind this exclusion:

> These persons present bad economic risks . . . [T]heir chief failure to adjust is due to the fact that their abnormality soon becomes known to their associates who make them the butt of coarse jokes to their own despair, and to the impairment of the work in hand. Since this is recognized . . . among employers, it is difficult for these unfortunates to get or retain jobs, their facial and bodily appearance, at least in adult life, furnishing a patent advertisement of their condition.[18]

The disability that justified exclusion in these cases was a matter of an abnormal appearance that might invite discrimination and therefore poverty. Thus it was an economic argument, but at two steps removed.

The justification given was not always economic, however, whether directly or indirectly. Nicolaos Xilomenos was refused entry in 1912 for "lack of sexual development." The Commissioner noted that while "the individual may appear strong and robust" and brought with him sufficient cash, his condition indicates the probability of "perversions or mental instability." In a similar case in 1908, Helena Bartnikowska was refused entry. The physician explained that "this supposed woman" was a hermaphrodite, who were "usually of perverted sexual instincts, and with lack of moral responsibility," adding significantly that her voice was masculine and that she had facial hair. Although her family was willing and able to guarantee her support, she was also deported.[19]

In March 1905, Domenico Rocco Vozzo, a 35-year-old Italian immigrant, was puzzled to find himself barred from entering the country at the port of Boston. Vozzo was a "bird of passage," a migrant worker who intended to earn some money and then return to Italy. This was his second trip to the United States, and he had encountered no difficulty his first time three years earlier. The medical inspector certified him for "debility," and he was excluded as likely to become a public charge. Vozzo retained an attorney who explained in his appeal that Vozzo was strong, robust, and healthy. In fact, he "looks perfectly healthy below the head," but has a "curiously shaped head, and his skin looks rather white, almost bleached, and his ears are quite thin." He had never been ill, had always worked, and during his recent two-year sojourn in the United States had fully supported himself while saving money. He brought with him $20 in cash and had friends who filed affidavits on his behalf. The Commissioner at the Boston station, however, recommended against admission and sent to the Secretary this evidence: "I enclose his picture which I think will convince you that he is not a desirable acquisition." Vozzo was deported.[20]

The principle that persons of abnormal appearance were not "desirable acquisitions" was not universally held nor consistently applied. For example, when Abraham Hoffman, a 25-year-old tailor with a prosperous brother working in the same trade in New York, was ruled likely to become a public charge by the immigration board because of his curved spine, his attorney labeled this assumption "ridiculous and absurd." "The axiom," he continued, "that one who is unfortunate enough to suffer from a certain infirmity, is likely for that reason alone, to become a public charge, is entirely new to us." Warming to the subject, the attorney asked,

> Are we living in this enlightened Twentieth Century where everyone is supposed to be given a fair opportunity, or are we going back to the times of the Salem witch-craft, when, because a woman was old and afflicted with a high back (spinal curvature), she was considered and treated as a witch? . . . The immigrants [sic] affliction can in no wise affect his earning capacity as a tailor.

The Commissioner at Ellis was torn. The evidence on the basis of appearance was conflicting. On the one hand, visually "the spinal curvature for which he is certified is quite obvious." On the other, "I may state in appellant's behalf, that he is a man of considerable intelligence, is very well dressed, and came as a second cabin passenger." With appearance working both against and in favor of the immigrant, the Commissioner made the unusual decision to forward the case files to Washington without recommendation. In his summary for the Secretary, the

Commissioner General re-emphasized the immigrant's appearance: "The Commissioner states that the alien is intelligent looking and is well dressed; he came in second cabin." In this case, the positive aspects of his appearance and his class status trumped the negative appearance of his disability. Hoffman was admitted on appeal.[21]

The precise number of those turned back for physical and mental defects each year is difficult to pin down. Until 1908, exclusions based on physical defects were mixed with nondefectives in the category of "likely to become a public charge." After 1908, rejected immigrants were counted in the category of "mental or physical defective" if they were deemed defective but not likely to become public charges, and counted in the "public charge" category if they were determined to be both defective and potential paupers.[22] In any case, taken together, exclusions in both categories grew considerably, if erratically, over the years. In 1895, 1,720 were excluded, or .6 percent of all immigrants. By 1905, the number excluded had increased to just over 8,000, or .7 percent of all immigrants. And in 1910, 16,000 or 1.6 percent were excluded. Due to wartime disruptions, the numbers during and just after World War One fluctuated widely, making useful comparisons difficult.[23]

BOX 11.1

From "ugly laws" to the Americans with Disabilities Act, disabled people in America have long fought to replace discriminatory public policies with more just practices. Listen here for audio history stories from "The American History Guys":

http://backstoryradio.org/shows/body-politics/

These numbers are all likely to be just the tip of the iceberg, however. Those who arrived at American shores to be inspected had already been through several screens. First, many would be deterred by the general inaccessibility of transportation. Second, since American immigration laws were widely advertised and easily available to people interested in immigrating, a significant number must have decided not to risk the journey and the expense knowing they might be turned back. Third, American law required ship captains to examine all passengers and certify that none appeared to be mentally defective. The manifest was to describe "the immigrant's condition of health mentally and physically, and whether deformed or crippled, and if so, from what cause."[24] Fourth, ships were required to return rejected immigrants at no charge and pay a fine for each, and if the immigrant was admitted but later discovered to have an excludable disability that initially passed unnoticed, they could be deported up to three years later at the expense of the company. Shipping companies therefore had strong incentives to refuse passage to anyone they thought unlikely to get by the inspectors, and ship captains became, in effect, an unofficial arm of the immigration service.[25] Finally, ticket agents, who were stationed throughout inland Europe, also became inspectors, because they were fined by the shipping companies if they sold tickets to anyone who was rejected when they tried to board the ship. The superintendent of immigration in 1894 noted approvingly that steamship lines instructed their agents to refuse tickets to "the blind, deaf and dumb, and crippled persons." There is good reason, then, to suppose that those turned away at the borders were a small minority of those who would have emigrated to America but were deterred because of disability. A federal commission in 1911 estimated that about ten times as many were refused transportation for medical reasons as were barred at U.S. ports.[26]

In 1924, a new quota system was instituted, based on national origin, that severely limited immigration from southern and eastern Europe. In the debate leading up to this legislation, disability figured prominently. Quota advocates warned that particular nationalities were disproportionately prone to be mentally defective. Rhetoric about "the slow-witted Slav," the poor physique of Jews," the "neurotic condition of our Jewish immigrants," and the "degenerate and psychopathic types, which are so conspicuous and numerous among the immigrants," was pervasive.[27] Restrictionists emphasized the inferior appearance of recent immigrants. One avowed that "the physiognomy of certain groups unmistakably proclaims inferiority of type." When he observed immigrants, he saw that "in every face there was something wrong . . . There were so many sugar-loaf heads, moon-faces, slit mouths, lantern-jaws, and goose-bill noses that one might imagine a malicious jinn had amused himself by casting human beings in a set of skew-molds discarded by the Creator." Most were physically inadequate in some way:

> South Europeans run to low stature. A gang of Italian navvies filing along the street present, by their dwarfishness, a curious contrast to other people. The Portuguese, the Greeks, and the Syrians are, from our point of view, undersized. The Hebrew immigrants are very poor in physique . . . the polar opposite of our pioneer breed.[28]

The issues of ethnicity and disability were inextricably intertwined.

While disability has been largely overlooked as a category of analysis in the literature on immigration, this is by no means unique to immigration studies. Disability is conspicuously absent from all fields of histories. In areas of study where disability is clearly central, such as the consequences of war, industrialization, and the rise of the automobile, even in the history of the eugenics movement, the literature has focused elsewhere, emphasizing better established categories of analysis such as race, gender, and class, and leaving disability unexamined at the periphery. When historians do take note of disability, they usually treat it merely as personal tragedy rather than a cultural construct to be questioned and explored.[29] In immigration historiography, as in so many other areas of historical inquiry, disability has long been present but rendered either invisible or insignificant. A disability analysis is essential, however, to making sense of the depth of anti-immigrant sentiment and the workings of immigration policy at the turn of the twentieth century. While it is certain that immigration restriction rested in good part on a fear of "strangers in the land," in John Higham's phrase, it was fueled at least as much by a fear of *defectives* in the land.

Discussion Questions

1. How did immigration policy both follow and shape public opinion about disability?

2. Baynton points out that discrimination against disability was often justified as a matter of economics. What are the problems with this line or argument?

3. In what ways did sexuality or sexual identity come under the scrutiny of immigration inspectors? Discuss how disability affected these judgments.

4. How does immigration discrimination against disability overlap with other immigration policies, especially considering race or national origin?

Notes

1 National Archives, Record Group 85, Records of the Immigration and Naturalization Service, Accession 60A600, File no. 53550/580.

2 John Higham, *Strangers in the Land: Patterns of American Nativism, 1860–1925* (1955; New York, 1963), p. 5; Roger Daniels, *Coming to America: A History of Immigration and Ethnicity in American Life* (New York, 1990), p. 279; Alan M. Kraut, *Silent Travelers* (New York, 1994), p. 55; Amy L. Fairchild, *Science at the Borders: Immigration Medical Inspection and the Shaping of the Modern Industrial Labor Force* (Baltimore, 2003).

3 An earlier immigration act, passed in 1875, excluded criminals and prostitutes (this also was a disability issue, as immorality was thought to be closely associated with mental defect). *United States Statutes at Large*, Vol. 22 (Washington, DC, 1883), 214.

4 Emphases added. United States Statutes, Vol. 26 (1891), 1084; United States Statutes, Vol. 34 (1907), 899.

5 United States Statutes, Vol. 32 (1903), 1213. United States Statutes, Vol. 34 (1907), 898. United States Public Health Service, Regulations Governing the Medical Inspection of Aliens (Washington, DC, 1917), 25–26, 28–29, 30–31.

6 Regulations, 16–19.

7 Victor Safford, *Immigration Problems: Personal Experiences of An Official* (New York, 1925), pp. 244–245, 246.

8 U.S. Bureau of Immigration, *Annual Report of the Commissioner of Immigration* (Washington, DC, 1907), p. 62.

9 William Williams, "Ellis Island Station," in *Annual Report of the Commissioner General of Immigration, 1904* (Washington, DC, 1904), 105.

10 Robert DeCourcey Ward to Frank P. Sargent, Commissioner General of Immigration, Washington, DC, dated January 11, 1905, National Archives, Record Group 85, Records of the Immigration and Naturalization Service, Entry 9, File no. 51490/19.

11 Letter from George Stoner, Chief Medical Officer, Public Health and Marine Hospital Service, to Surgeon General of the Public Health and Marine Hospital, Nov. 29, 1912, National Archives, Record Group 90, Records of the Public Health Service, Entry 10, File no. 219.

12 Allan McLaughlin, "The Problem of Immigration," *Popular Science Monthly* 66 (April 1905): 532 (emphasis added).

13 Letter dated March 31, 1913, National Archives, Record Group 85, Records of the Immigration and Naturalization Service, Entry 9, File no. 51490/19.

14 Letter from F. P. Sargent, Commissioner General of the Bureau of Immigration, to the Commissioner of Immigration on Ellis Island, April 17, 1905, National Archives, Record Group 90, Records of the Public Health Service, Entry 10, File no. 219.

15 National Archives, Record Group 85, Records of the Immigration and Naturalization Service, Entry 7, File no. 49968/4.

16 Alan M. Kraut, *Silent Travelers* (New York, 1994), p. 55.

17 National Archives, Record Group 85, Records of the Immigration and Naturalization Service, Entry 7, File no. 48599/4.

18 Letter from W.W. Husband, Commissioner General, Bureau of Immigration, to H.S. Cumming, Surgeon General, United States Public Health Service, September 27, 1922; and reply from Cumming to Husband, September 29, 1922; National Archives, Record Group 90, Records of the Public Health Service, Entry 10, File no. 219.

19 National Archives, Record Group 85, Records of the Immigration and Naturalization Service, Accession No. 60A600, File No. 53542–952. National Archives, Record Group 85, Records of the Immigration and Naturalization Service, Accession No. 60A600, File no. 51806–16.

20 National Archives, Record Group 85, Records of the Immigration and Naturalization Service, Entry 7, File no. 48462. Aside from several days' beard growth and a scowl, it is hard to see to what the Commissioner was referring.

21 National Archives, Record Group 85, Records of the Immigration and Naturalization Service, Entry 7, File no. 49951–1 (the immigrant's name is rendered Abram Hofmann and Abram Hofman by immigration officials, Abraham Hoffman by his attorney). Spinal curvature was a common reason for rejection. A 50-year study at the University of Iowa recently concluded that persons with late-onset scoliosis (occurring during puberty) "are productive and functional at a high level at 50-year follow-up" and experienced "little physical impairment," with "cosmetic concerns" being the only significant problem. This finding contradicts the common perception among

physicians and the general public that this is a serious and debilitating condition. Stuart Weinstein, et al., "Health and Function of Patients With Untreated Idiopathic Scoliosis: A 50-Year Natural History Study," *Journal of the American Medical Association* 289 (February 5, 2003): 559–568.

22 The LPC or pauper category was always the largest category of exclusion, but the criteria used are not entirely clear. Lack of money in itself was not a primary factor, though it was taken into consideration. Disability appears to have been a major factor. The definition of "pauper" for the immigration service was "one who is actually dependent upon public funds for support and who, in addition, is unable to work by reason of mental or physical infirmity, or who is unwilling to work." The Dillingham Commission reported in 1911 that, "At the present time . . . pauperism among newly admitted immigrants is relatively at a minimum, owing to the fact that the present immigration law provides for the admission only of the able-bodied, or dependents whose support by relatives is assured." United States Government, *Abstracts of Reports of the Immigration Commission*, Vol. I (Washington, DC, 1911), 35. The Report of the Commissioner General of Immigration in 1912 states that while 3,055 were rejected as mentally or physically defective, 12,004 were rejected as "likely to become a public charge," and of those "a considerable portion . . . were excluded on the additional ground of being mentally or physically defective. . . . Where the exclusion occurs on both grounds, it is not an easy matter properly to classify the cases in the statistical reports; and the figures representing those 'LPC' and those 'mentally and physically defective' should be considered together." *Annual Report of the Commissioner General of Immigration, 1912* (Washington, DC, 1912), 125.

23 United States, *Abstracts of Reports of the Immigration Commission*, Vol. I (Washington, DC, 1911), also known as the Dillingham Report. In 1915, nearly 5 percent were excluded, probably because the reduced number of immigrants during the war allowed more careful inspection.

24 United States Statutes, Vol. 27 (1893), 569; United States Statutes, Vol. 34 (1907), 901–902.

25 The Act of 1882 required vessel owners to provide return passage and reimburse inspection costs. The 1891 Act added that immigrants could be deported up to one year after entry, at the cost of the shipping company, if discovered to have had a disability that initially passed unnoticed. In 1903, companies were made responsible for returning a deported immigrant for two years after landing, and in 1907, for three. Significant fines were added in 1907 for ships that carried immigrants deemed mentally defective.

26 E. Abbott, *Immigration: Select Documents and Case Records* (Chicago, 1924), 71; U.S. Bureau of Immigration, *Annual Report of the Commissioner of Immigration* (Washington, DC, 1907), 10; U.S. Immigration Service, *Annual Report of the Superintendent of Immigration* (Washington, DC, 1894), 12–13; Abstract of Reports of the Immigration Commission [Dillingham Commission], Vol. 1 (Washington, DC, 1911), 26; Amy Fairchild's *Science at the Borders* (56–63) gives an excellent account of the multiple inspections immigrants faced along the way.

27   James W. Trent Jr., *Inventing the Feeble Mind: A History of Mental Retardation in the United States* (Berkeley, 1994), pp. 166–169; Thomas Wray Grayson, "The Effect of the Modern Immigrant on our Industrial Centers," in *Medical Problems of Immigration* (Easton, PA, 1913), pp. 103, 107–109. I examine how disability has been used to deny citizenship rights to women and minority groups in "Disability and the Justification of Inequality in American History," in Paul Longmore and Lauri Umansky, eds., *The New Disability History: American Perspectives* (New York, 2001), pp. 33–57.

28   Edward Alsworth Ross, *The Old World and the New: The Significance of Past and Present Immigration to the American People* (New York, 1914), pp. 285–290. Disability scholars have emphasized the importance of appearance to the construction of disability. For example, Martin Pernick has described the importance of aesthetics in eugenics literature, how fitness was equated with beauty and disability with ugliness, and Lennard Davis has maintained that disability presents itself "through two main modalities—function and appearance." Martin Pernick, *The Black Stork: Eugenics and the Death of 'Defective' Babies in American Medicine and Motion Pictures Since 1915* (New York, 1996) pp. 60–71; Lennard Davis, *Enforcing Normalcy: Disability, Deafness, and the Body* (London, 1995), pp. 11–12. See also Harlan Hahn, "Antidiscrimination Laws and Social Research on Disability: The Minority Group Perspective," *Behavioral Sciences and the Law* 14 (1996): 54.

29   One of the first to point out the distorting effects of this omission on our understanding of history was Paul Longmore, in two review essays in the 1980s: "The Life of Randolph Bourne and the Need for a History of Disabled People," *Reviews in American History* 13 (December 1985): 581–587; and "Uncovering the Hidden History of Disabled People," *Reviews in American History* 15 (September 1987): 355–364. Longmore and David Goldberger also demonstrated the importance of disability in the history of the Great Depression and the New Deal in "The League of the Physically Handicapped and the Great Depression: A Case Study in the New Disability History," *Journal of American History* 87 (December 2000): 888–922. A recent corrective to the lack of attention given to disability among war veterans is David A. Gerber, ed., *Disabled Veterans in History* (Ann Arbor, MI, 2000). For a review of recent work on disability in history, see Catherine J. Kudlick, "Disability History: Why We Need Another 'Other'," *The American Historical Review* 108 (June 2003): 763–793.

On the Margins of Citizenship

Disability Activism and the Intellectually Disabled

Allison C. Carey[1]

In 1990, self-advocates met in Estes Park, Colorado, for the First North American People First Conference. At that meeting, a steering committee was formed to plan for the establishment of a national organization to unify the state and local chapters and exert political influence at the national level. The steering committee drafted a statement of belief that read,

> We believe people with disabilities should be treated as equals. That means that people should be given the same decisions, choices, rights, responsibilities, chance to speak up to empower themselves, and to make new friendships and old friendships. Just like everyone else. They should also be able to learn from their mistakes. Like everyone else.[2]

A year later, more than 800 self-advocates attended the second North American People First Conference and voted to establish an organization based on the recommendations of the steering committee. Later that year they selected a name: Self-Advocates Becoming Empowered.

Members of SABE positioned it as an organization within the disability rights movement, not as a charity to help people with disabilities or as an offshoot of a professional or parent organization. They took care to ensure that people with disabilities, not professionals, would provide its leadership. Any person with a disability could join as a voting member of the organization, whereas people without disabilities could join only as non-voting members. They also restricted the role of "advisers," who provided support but could not engage in substantive decision making. In solidarity with the disability rights movement, they framed their movement in terms of self-determination and drew on disability rights slogans such as "Free Our People" and "Nothing about Us without Us." Through their alliance with disability organizations such as ADAPT, SABE members learned an array of techniques for activism, including demonstrations, the education of policymakers, collaboration with state agencies, and the development of programs to assist individual residents to leave institutional settings if they so desired. They also collected stories from the people who had resided in institutions and began to build a history and a set of heroes from their own perspective. In SABE's early history, it established a particularly strong relationship with Justin Dart, an iconic figure of the disability rights movement who is best known for his role in the passage of the ADA. Dart helped establish ties between SABE and other national organizations such as ADAPT, the President's Committee on Employment of People with Disabilities, and the National Council on Disability.

Whereas parents and professionals in the 1970s had taken a cautious stand on the autonomy of people with mental retardation,[3] SABE stridently supported self-determination. According to SABE, all people with disabilities could exercise control over their lives, including people with developmental disabilities. No person, they argued, should have to sacrifice his or her rights for the receipt of services. All individuals should choose where to live, how to live, with whom to build relationships, and so on. Some might need support to make these choices; however, they did not need professionals who claimed to be experts determining the details of their lives. *They* were the experts in disability, and they should shape their own lives, influence the policies that affected them, and determine which services they needed. The self-advocate Liz Obermayer explained,

> I live in America, the land that gives me the right to make choices and speak my mind. But I have a disability. . . . Nobody allows me to make choices. People tell me all the time what to wear, what to eat, what job to have and who are my friends. Is that fair? I say no! But I have a disability. . . . [P]eople don't listen to me anyway. . . . [W]hy should I give my opinions? I fight so hard for someone to listen . . . just want someone to listen . . . and give a damn about what I want. If people with disabilities can live with everyone else, than why can't I make choices like anyone else . . . if that's my right as a citizen of the U.S.A.[4]

SABE's emphasis on choice and self-determination stood in stark contrast with the institutional and agency-run group-home models of service delivery. Institutions and even most group homes were run by administrators who continued to make rules based on bureaucratic efficiency and legal liability rather than on the wishes of their residents. For example, many group homes still compelled residents to attend programs, work, or school during the day so they could reduce staffing. Similarly, many did not allow residents to have privacy with members of the opposite sex. Thus, to receive services, people with disabilities had to accept a host of restrictions on their lives.

Support of deinstitutionalization became one of SABE's first and most pressing political tasks. It defined an institution as "any facility or program where people don't have control of their lives," a much broader definition than typically used.[5] In contrast with many other organizations in the field of developmental disabilities, SABE demanded the closure of traditional group homes, sheltered workshops, day facilities, and any other segregated group services, in addition to large-scale residential facilities, in favor of individualized support controlled by the person with a disability. In alliance with ADAPT and other disability organizations, SABE demanded that the government and professional agencies "Free Our People," comparing institutions to prisons and their residents to prisoners.[6] A former resident of an institution in Oklahoma argued, "Everybody has rights, just because we are different or look different does not make us have to be in institutions. We are people just like you and anyone else, so start treating us like other people, not animals."[7] Activists and self-advocates emphasized the abuse people had experienced in institutions and compared this with the better quality of life they experienced in the community. For example, a self-advocate named Leon remembered that in the institution in which he had lived, "They used to pound me and beat me up." As a member of the community, he explained, "I have a good life now. Make my own coffee . . . I live by myself now, and I have my own apartment." He continued, "When I was in the institution, I was shy. I like where I am now. I like myself. I am better off now."[8]

Tackling the service system ultimately meant tackling the structure of government benefits. Disability activists had argued for decades that the Medicaid funding structure contained an "institutional bias" toward reimbursing services provided in institutional settings (including nursing homes and Intermediate Care Facilities for the Mentally Retarded (ICR-MFs)) rather than services provided in the home and the community. Twice as many people received their services in community-based setting as institutional settings, yet only about one-quarter of Medicaid's budget for long-term care was spent on community-based services. Therefore, many individuals with disabilities were forced to reside in an institutional setting to receive services, to live in the community without services, or to pay out of pocket for their services. Moreover, by directing funding to agencies rather than individuals, the funding structure encouraged agency control over the lives of people with disabilities and limited consumer choice and empowerment.

Self-advocates and other disability rights activists imagined a system in which services were disaggregated and could be purchased without an expectation regarding one's residence or other aspects of one's life. The Disability Rights Movement espoused the use of "personal assistants," people hired by people with disabilities to support them in their daily tasks. Self-advocates believed that this model of service provision could also work for them. Because individuals with disabilities hired and directed their personal assistants, they held power in this relationship to direct and individualize the services provided. Moving from agency control to consumer control, though, required that government funds "follow the person" to give individuals the power to use their disability benefits to purchase services as they felt appropriate.

SABE also worked on other major initiatives, including reforms of the criminal-justice system. People with developmental disabilities were disproportionately likely to be victims of crime, yet they were unlikely to report their experiences to the authorities for several reasons. Most commonly, those who decided not to report feared the possible consequences (especially if the perpetrator was a caregiver), had difficulties articulating their experiences, or were unaware that they had been a victim of a criminal act. Those who did report often found that legal officials discounted them as incompetent and unreliable and that the agencies' staff members treated their experiences as administrative problems rather than as crimes requiring legal intervention.[9]

People with developmental disabilities suspected of crimes experienced similar problems. On arrest, some people with developmental disabilities did not understand their Miranda rights and waived them, seemingly "voluntarily"; sought to please authority figures and avoid stressful questioning, leading them to offer false confessions; and hid their disability rather than requesting accommodation. In addition, they often had difficulty assisting their counsel, if they became confused, forgot timelines, or struggled to communicate their thoughts. Defendants with developmental disabilities also had difficulty impressing jurors, as they at times failed to follow the expected rules of "impression management." Defendants, for example, might appear bored or sleepy during their trials, leading jurors to conclude that they were indifferent or hostile. Due to these issues, people with developmental disabilities faced higher rates of arrest and conviction as well as longer sentences than people without disabilities who committed similar crimes. National organizations, including SABE, took on this issue, demanding accommodation in the criminal-justice system for people with disabilities.

In addition to deinstitutionalization and reform in the criminal-justice system, SABE worked on a broad array of policy areas, such as health insurance and the education of health professionals, accessible transportation, SSI and Medicaid regulations, the ADA, and the ADA Restoration Act. It demanded a place at the political table when policies that would affect people with disabilities were at issue. By the end of the twentieth century, SABE had grown into a respected organization within the disability rights movement and in the field of developmental disabilities. Indeed, as the only national organization predominantly of people with developmental disabilities, SABE found it held a position of symbolic power, and its participation and approval was increasingly sought, especially among those claiming to fight for the rights and inclusion of people with developmental disabilities. For example, in 2003 11 major organizations, including the Center on Human Policy, TASH, The Arc, and SABE, joined forces to create the Alliance for Full Participation (AFP), an organization designed to promote the full participation of people with developmental disabilities in communities of their choice. Members of SABE withdrew their support from the AFP, however, because they felt that professionals were excluding them by using jargon, moving discussions along too quickly, and creating goals and objectives without them. In a statement to the AFP, SABE made clear its agenda for full participation and its dissatisfaction with the way in which the alliance was run:

The Founding groups are looking for priorities for the future

Our answer is:

JUST DO IT!!!

Many have listened, some have taken action and we thank you.
But we have talked enough and waited too long!!!

We have told you what is important to us
Get rid of the infamous and hurtful "r" word, do not label us

We will not put up with
the "r" word continuing as part of an organization's name
even as initials
If you are working with me and for me then do not disrespect me

We have been prepared enough
ASK the people who are living in institutions
Would you trade places

Close institutions

Get us real jobs
Close sheltered workshops

Give us the money to live **OUR** lives
Money follows the person means it is **OURS** not programs

We have the right to make our own decisions
with or without the support from others
WE CAN RUN OUR LIVES

Support our movement,
IT IS OURS
YOU RECEIVE MILLIONS OF DOLLARS IN OUR NAME
We want to control this money
As we are the **EXPERTS**

You must change, we have changed, we are taking the power
Walk the Walk, Respect Us or We will go on without you!

The AFP wrote an apology, and SABE rejoined its efforts. For the other organizations to proceed in the fight for full inclusion without this national self-advocacy group would have been embarrassing and ineffective.

SABE also did not hesitate to take on parents' groups, especially Voice of the Retarded (VOR), which continued to support the provision of state funding for institutions as part of the "continuum of choice." SABE found VOR's name and mission to be offensive:

> This organization doesn't speak for us. They do not agree with what we want—the freedom to live in the community, authority to make decisions for ourselves and to spend money the way that we want, the support we need to be successful, and the responsibility to give back to our communities, help others learn to speak-up for themselves so they will become self-determined individuals.[10]

While less adversarial, perhaps, SABE's condemnation of the provision of group services such as group homes and sheltered workshops also placed it in conflict with The Arc and with many service providers that administered these services.

Thus, as SABE joined the national political fray, it quickly grew into a respected organization that consistently and stridently demanded social change. At the heart of its mission was a belief in the rights of all people to make choices, exercise control over their lives, receive support in exercising their rights, and, ultimately, be treated as respected members of the community. As such, it positioned people with developmental disabilities within the liberal requirements for the exercise of rights, arguing that all people with support could make self-determined choices and pursue their own happiness.

Individuals with developmental disabilities who were not formally affiliated with the self-advocacy movement also burst into the public limelight. Chris Burke, an actor with Down syndrome, made history when executives at the ABC television network decided to cast him in the lead role in a show about a teenager with Down syndrome and his family. From 1989 to 1993, *Life Goes On* portrayed the challenges and joys experienced by the Thatcher family as Burke's character, "Corky," received an education in an integrated school, pursued a job, dated, and eventually married. As an actor, author of a best-selling autobiography, musician, and spokesperson for the National Down Syndrome Society, Burke stressed,

> We need to be out there in the community. We need to have our voices heard. When I have a job, I do my job and I like to work. Everyone should have that chance. I say to people "Give them a chance! Make their dreams come true!"[11]

In 1994, Jason Kingsley and Mitchell Levitz published *Count Us In,* a book of their conversations about living with Down syndrome, school, work, relationships, religion, and many other topics. Like Burke, Kingsley and Levitz emphasized their pride in themselves and their accomplishments and their desire to participate fully in mainstream society. They joked that, rather than Down syndrome, the term should be "Up Syndrome" to emphasize the abilities and sense of self-worth of individuals with Down syndrome. Describing life as a "learning adventure" that required participating, taking risks, and making choices, they explained that they wanted to participate in the adventure along with everyone else.

Controversies Over Terminology

The new image of the self-determined citizen with intellectual disabilities was very positive, stressing group pride and demanding self-determination. In this context, the label "mental retardation"—once seen as an improvement over terms such as "feeble-minded," "idiot," and "moron"—now seemed pejorative. The definition of "mental retardation" relied on a "deficit model" that defined the condition as a permanent, individual-based limitation. The social model of disability promoted by the disability rights movement, however, called the deficit model into question. According to the social model, disability resulted from the interaction between an individual and his or her environment and thus was fluid and contextual. This model emphasized the importance of removing environmental and social barriers to improve the opportunities and quality of life for people with disabilities rather than "fixing" individuals with disabilities. "Retardation" was seen as representing the old deficit model, and as such it seemed inappropriate and even offensive. Self-advocates resented this label, referring to it as the "r" word, and demanded that organizations serving them stop using it. Many professionals and parents also voiced concerns that the term was "tarnished" and that its use hindered their activities, offended the people they served, and made their organizations appear outdated.

While many people agreed that the term "retardation" had outlasted its usefulness, there was little agreement about how to proceed. Self-advocates resisted any professional label that placed a "diagnosis" on them. SABE tended to use the phrase "person with a disability," an identification that could be self-defined, was associated with disability pride, and placed them alongside other activists in the disability rights movement. However, the legislative successes achieved in the 1970s and 1980s, such as IDEA and expanded access to income support, were largely predicated on specific professional diagnoses, and some parents and professionals feared that a significant change in terminology or definition might have a negative impact on people who received services or funding.

The term "developmental disabilities" had become popular since its legislative inception in 1970, but its meaning was broad and ambiguous. Initially created to join together particular childhood disabilities affecting development, such as mental retardation and cerebral palsy, the federal government redefined it in the 1978 reauthorization of the DD Act to include any severe, lifelong disability that originated from birth through age 21, including, for example, blindness, paralysis, and schizophrenia. This new definition was much broader than its predecessor and created confusion as some people continued to use the term to refer to a narrow set of disabilities, whereas others began to use it more broadly as intended by the 1978 DD Act.

Because the definition of developmental disability had come to include such diverse disabilities, other terms emerged that identified a narrower set of disabilities related to cognitive functioning, including "cognitive disabilities," "intellectual disabilities," and "learning disabilities." Cognitive disabilities were typically seen as those that involved limitations in mental and intellectual function, such as retardation, autism, traumatic brain injury, and Alzheimer's disease (not including mental illness), but the term carried no specific requirement regarding age of onset. "Intellectual disability" was typically used to refer to a population similar to those diagnosed as "mentally retarded" and referred to limitations rooted in sub-average intellectual and adaptive functioning occurring early in life. "Learning disabilities" included disabilities that affected the brain's ability to receive, process, analyze, or store information. In Europe this term included what Americans referred to as "retardation," but in America it was typically reserved for disabilities such as dyslexia, which affect specific learning activities without necessarily limiting one's overall level of intelligence.

Leading organizations in the field developed different strategies to replace the term "mental retardation." As noted earlier, in 1992 the Association for Retarded Citizens (ARC) decided to drop the acronym and become simply The Arc, redefining itself as an organization of and for people with developmental and intellectual disabilities. Similarly, in 1995 the Association for Persons with Severe Handicaps voted to use its acronym, TASH, without referring to its full name, because that name "didn't reflect current values and directions." It described its mission as the inclusion of all people in all aspects of society, regardless of disability. In organizing SABE, self-advocates purposefully avoided reference to any specific types of disability and instead framed their mission as including all people with disabilities. Whereas The Arc, TASH, and SABE attempted to pursue their missions to some degree without reference to a specific disability, other organizations replaced the term "mental retardation" with the term "intellectual disability." In 2003, President George W. Bush signed an executive order renaming the President's Committee on Mental Retardation the President's Committee for People with Intellectual Disabilities. And in 2007, the American Association on Mental Retardation (AAMR) changed its name to the American Association on Intellectual and Developmental Disability (AAIDD).

Redesigning "Services" Into "Individualized Support"

In the shift toward self-determination and a social-ecological model, some organizations, including TASH and the Center on Human Policy, joined self-advocates in criticizing prepackaged group services controlled by professionals and supporting the individualization of support and self-determination for those receiving support services.[12] John O'Brien, a leading advocate for community inclusion, argued that individualized services should do the following:

- Assist people with developmental disabilities to develop their individual abilities and personal interests.

- Discover and respond to individual choices.

- Support important personal relationships and encourage positive participation in community life.

- Deal effectively with people's vulnerabilities.

- Promote personal and organizational learning which leads to continual improvement of service provider ability to make these our essential contributions.

Person-centered planning (PCP) was designed to serve as a starting point for the provision of individualized support by assisting people with disabilities in defining, planning for, and pursuing their desired futures, including housing arrangements, employment, relationships, and leisure activities. At the outset of the process, the person with a disability typically selects a team of people to provide support. While professionals may serve as important members of these teams, PCP prioritizes the identification and development of informal, community-based relationships that will provide support to people with disabilities as they move toward greater participation in the community. Hence, the process of PCP should enhance an individual's capacity to articulate his or her interests, set goals, and make choices; an individual's social capital—or, in other words, his or her access to relationships that provide various forms of support toward the pursuit of his or her goals; and an individual's access to the resources and services provided in the community for people with disabilities and for all members of the community.[13] In this framework, "support" that is chosen and directed by individuals with disabilities takes the place of "services" that are designed and controlled by professionals.

Transforming the Community

The effective provision of individualized support would require a massive overhaul of the service-delivery system, funding streams, and, ultimately, the community. People with disabilities would need access to a pool of personal assistants and services disentangled from large-scale, prepackaged options; accessible community options, including affordable housing, accommodated employment, and accessible public transportation; members of the community to serve as natural supports; professionals willing to provide support rather than supervision; and state funding structures that offered people with disabilities, instead of agencies, control of their Medicaid dollars. Ironically, perhaps, self-determination cannot be achieved through individual decision making or actions; rather, it requires the redistribution of power across relationships and the transformation of community so that people have feasible options and the power to pursue them.

Activists began to articulate a new ideal of community. In the era of eugenics, policy and law assumed that "the community" included "normal," "productive" citizens and that people who deviated from the norm could and should be segregated for the common good. In the 1950s, parents and professionals sought to retain people with disabilities in "the community" but placed few expectations on communities to value or support people with disabilities. At the end of the twentieth century, activists began to imagine a community that included, valued, and supported all of its members, including its members with disabilities.

According to John McKnight (1995), whereas professional systems were necessarily artificial, segregated, and restrictive, the community could offer natural and creative social support to its members. His proposed "community vision" argued that embedded within each community are the associations, relationships, and other resources necessary to creatively incorporate diverse people. Rather than develop artificial segregated options, we should strive to develop strong natural relationships embedded within communities to encourage inclusion while also strengthening the capacity of communities to include all of their members. In advocating for the inclusion of *all* people with disabilities in the community, a consortium of major organizations described the community in the following way:

> It is not an idealized place, like Lake Wobegon, where all are perfect. Communities have strengths and weaknesses, highs and lows. But community is the place where you make friends, have the choice of things to do or not do, where you share your joys and sorrows, where your parents brought you when you were born, where your grandparents live out their lives, it is where people care about each other or stay distant, again their choice.... Community is where all people belong, disability or not, in need of a lot of

> supports, or some or none. Community is possibility and opportunity and hope for the future. It is not a program, or services or an alternative. It is the only choice.[14]

As this quote suggests, community is not simply a place; it is a network of relationships embedded with roles, rules, and institutional patterns that shape how power is distributed. Building community therefore entails building meaningful relationships, enabling people to participate in social roles of value to them, providing them with valued resources, and appreciating the contributions they make. Building community is not principally about building individual capacity, although this might be part of an overall strategy. It relies on "social capital," a concept that refers to the use of relationships and social networks as resources to achieve one's goals. According to Al Condeluci, executive director of United Cerebral Palsy of the Pittsburgh district,

> It is through our social capital that people get closer to the most basic quality of life indicators: healthfulness, happiness, and longevity. . . . Quite simply, the more relationships in your life, the happier you are, the healthier you are, and the longer you live.[15]

Proponents of the "community vision" imagine a world of freely given, natural support. While they often rely on a language of rights, the community vision goes beyond establishing formal claims that demand access. It attempts to envision and create a world that values its members so that formal claims to rights are largely unnecessary. Some people believe this vision to be unrealistic, due to the inconsistency of natural support and the potential for abuse and exploitation in unmonitored environments. In response, advocates for the community vision argue that segregation and administrative regulations impose unnecessary restrictions, often fail to protect, and impose their own harm. In contrast, increasing the visibility and the value of people with disabilities in the community, incorporating them into mainstream organizations and associations, and building networks of natural relationships will offer people with disabilities maximal support and protection. According to Julie Pratt, "No matter where you live, the more people who know and care about you, the safer you are. We found that caring relationships are central to safety and to people's satisfaction with their lives."[16]

Discussion Questions

1. Why has it been difficult for people with intellectual disabilities to be recognized for self-determination in matters of policy, institutionalization and public perception?

2. What does the shifting terminology of mental disability have to do with issues of justice and fair treatment?

3. What should be the role of nondisabled people in determining the best policies and practices for disabled people?

4. How can we understand the relationship between the "community" at large and the need for personalized support for disabled people?

Notes

1 Editor's note: This chapter is from Allison C. Carey's *On the Margins of Citizenship: Disability and Civil Rights in 20th Century America.*

2 Shoultz and Ward 1996, 222.

3 Allison Carey uses the word "retardation" here to reflect how the word was used at that point in history. Later in this chapter, she explains why people would reject this terminology.

4 Obermayer 2004; ellipses in the original.

5 Self-Advocates Becoming Empowered 1999.

6 Nelis and Ward 1995–1996.

7 Ibid, p. 12.

8 Hayden 1997.

9 Lumley and Miltenberger 1997; McCabe et al. 1994; Sobsey 1994; Stromsness 1993.

10 SABE 2000.

11 Burke and McDaniel 1991, 255.

12 O'Brien 1993; O'Brien and O'Brien 2006; Taylor et al. 1987.

13 Mount 1992; O'Brien and O'Brien 2006.

14 McKnight, "What Is the Community?" *Community for Air Tool Kit.* Asset-Based Community Development Institute. Accessed 2004. Web.

15 Quoted in Lavigne 2004.

16 Pratt, 1998, 8.

References

Burke, Chris, and Jo Beth McDaniel. 1991. *A Special Kind of Hero.* New York: Doubleday.

Hayden, Mary F. 1997. *Living in the Freedom World: Personal Stories of Living in the Community by People Who Once Lived in Oklahoma's Institutions.* Minneapolis: Research and Training Center on Community Living, institute on Community integration, University of Minnesota.

Lavigne, Muffi. 2004. "In profile: Dr. Al Condelucci." UCP press room, November 4. Available online at www.ucp.org/ucp_generaldoc.cfm/1/9/10438/10438-10438/5875 (accessed May 2007).

Lumley, Vicki A., and Raymond G. Miltenberger. 1997. "Sexual Abuse Prevention For Persons With Mental Retardation." *American Journal on Mental Retardation* 101: 459–472.

McCabe, Marita P., Robert A. Cummins, and Shelly B. Reid. 1994. "An Empirical Study of Sexual Abuse of People With Intellectual Disabilities." *Sexuality and Disability* 12.

McKnight, John. 1995. "Regenerating Community." *Social Policy* 25 (4): 54–58.

Mount, Beth. 1992. *Personal Futures Planning: Promises and Precautions.* New York: Graphic Futures.

Nelis, Tia and Nancy Ward. 1995–1996. "Operation Close the Doors: Working for Freedom." *Impact* 9 (1): 12.

Obermayer, Liz. 2004. "Choices." In *"Community for All" Tool Kit: Resources for Supporting Community Living.* Syracuse, N.Y.: Human Policy Press.

O'Brien, John. 1993. "Supported Living: What's the Difference?" report prepared for the Center on Human Policy, Syracuse University, Syracuse, N.Y.

O'Brien, John, and Connie Lyle O'Brien. 2006. *Implementing Person Centered Planning: Voices of Experience.* Toronto: Inclusion Press.

Pratt, Julie. 1998. "Introduction," pp. 1–9 in *On the Outside: A Look at Two Decades of Deinstitutionalization through the Eyes of People with Developmental Disabilities,* ed. Julie Pratt. Charleston: West Virginia Developmental Disabilities Planning Council.

Shoultz, Bonnie, and Nancy Ward. 1996. "Self-Advocates Becoming Empowered: The Birth of a National Organization in the U.S.," pp. 216–236 in *New Voices: Self-Advocacy by People with Disabilities,* ed. Gunnar Dybwad and Hank Bersani Jr. Cambridge, Mass.: Brookline Books.

Sobsey, Dick. 1994. *Violence and Abuse in the Lives of People with Disabilities: The End of Silent Acceptance?* Baltimore, Md.: Paul H. Brookes.

Stromsness, M. M. 1993. "Sexually Abused Women with Mental Retardation: Hidden Victims, Absent Resources." *Women and Therapy* 14: 139–152.

Taylor, Steven J., Douglas Biklen, and James Knoll, eds. 1987. *Community Integration for People with Severe Disabilities.* New York City: Teachers College Press.

4

Disability, Identity, and Social Justice

13 Disability and Race

Nirmala Erevelles

Disability and race are uncomfortable bedfellows. They are bedfellows because both disability and race embody a modality of difference from some hypothetical norm that organizes bodies along an oppressive social hierarchy. Both disability and race as biological categories have been widely accepted as common sense. We read race (rather simplistically) as merely a difference in skin color. A seemingly more complicated reading would identify racial differences as phenotypical (physiological/biological). Similarly, disability as abnormal/deviant biological difference has been the commonly accepted definition of disability. And yet, even while acknowledging that both race and disability do embody some physiological differences, we also know that these observable differences do not equate to the naturalized social hierarchies that justify social inequalities on a global scale.

I stress the term, "naturalized," because we go through our daily lives accepting these social hierarchies as inevitable and more often than not, as acceptable. For example, one such social hierarchy that is justified by appealing to racial difference and disability is via the social practice of compulsory segregation. I contend that compulsory segregation on the basis of race and disability is so commonplace in so many social institutions that often times we fail to even notice it. For example, let us reflect on one social institution we are most familiar with: the public school. We conceive of educational institutions like public schools as hallmarks of our tenuous democracy whose function is to ensure equal (educational) opportunity for all citizens. And yet, students in schools, both public and private, are relentlessly segregated along the axes of race and disability. Think back to your own school days and try and remember when teachers sorted you and your classmates and tracked each of you along very different future trajectories. Think back on what those classrooms looked like in the context of racial diversity. Think back on the racial configuration of college prep courses and those of special education and remedial classes. Think back on how disability was used to justify such forms of segregation as natural and logical and fair. Think back on how such practices were viewed as promising for those who benefitted positively from such segregation. Think back on what the implications are for the continued maintenance of these social hierarchies for those who got the shorter end of the stick.

The above example of school segregation illustrates how race and disability become uncomfortable bedfellows in the social context of education. The discomfort lies in how the politics of race and disability are pitted against each other. In public schools all over the U.S., African-American and Latino/a students are over-represented in special education, remedial education, and alternative educational classrooms, while White and Asian students dominate college prep and advanced courses. This disproportionality is defended on the grounds that African-American and Latino/a students are "naturally" intellectually and behaviorally deficient when compared to their White and Asian classmates. Thus, in attempts to argue against this dubious assumption and its very real negative consequences for African-American and Latino/a students, critical race scholars in education have often attempted to distance themselves from any association with disability. In fact, in a troubling maneuver, critical race scholars feel compelled to repudiate disability by claiming that racialized citizens have very little in common with the presumed deviant pathology that is attributed to disability. In doing so anti-racist scholarship erroneously assumes that while race is a social construction, disability is a biological fact. And it is by invoking this confounding logic that race and disability become uncomfortable bedfellows.

Racism and Ableism as Simultaneous Oppressive Practices

This discomfiture between race and disability extends beyond the segregated context of education to other social spaces in both historical and contemporary contexts. One way that scholars have attempted to resolve this discomfort is to claim that race and disability are synonymous conditions such that being disabled is just like being black (for example) and being black is just like being disabled. However, this kind of circular reasoning does little to capture the complex processes by which race and disability were/are simultaneously constituted via settler colonialism, imperialism, and transnational capitalism. In other words, I call attention to the social conditions and hegemonic practices that authorize the *simultaneous* processes by which disabled bodies become racialized and racialized bodies become disabled.

In an attempt to explain these processes that foreground the simultaneous practices of racism and ableism, let us use a critical intersectional lens and reflect on the historical and contemporary social practices at play. An intersectional lens asks us to consider that a person might occupy several different identities at the same time. For example, how does one engage the historical legacy of settler-colonialism, slavery, indentured labor, Jim Crow, and the involuntary commitment of indigenous people to boarding schools, reservations, and asylums—all racist practices that have produced physical and mental trauma (disability) that has persisted over multiple generations? These racist practices still persist today via the environmental degradation and toxicity in our racially segregated inner cities, small towns, and indigenous-owned lands. Toxic industrial and nuclear waste is dumped in rivers and/or buried underground in landfills in low-income rural areas where local residents acquire illnesses and disabilities that persist across generations. For example, in Flint, Michigan, the city that is mostly black and poor, the drinking water in the town is contaminated by lead that has contributed to the proliferation of both physical and intellectual disabilities among its inhabitants. The poisoned waters of Flint illustrate painfully how race and disability are constitutive of each other. Additionally, lack of access to affordable healthy food in inner-city neighborhoods, high unemployment, run-down housing, high crime rates, and inadequate access to medical care has also led to the proliferation of preventable illnesses that result in disabilities.

Colonial occupation and its more contemporary manifestation of neocolonialism (using economic or political pressures to control vulnerable nations) have also resulted in the proliferation of disability for people of color transnationally. The material conditions of colonial rule supported a violent police state to subdue its colonial subjects who rebelled against the oppressive conditions within which they lived. Even after colonial rule was overthrown, interventions by the former colonists in the internal affairs of the new postcolonial states continued to produce disability using the excuse of stemming the tide of communism to orchestrate assassinations, coups, and civil unrest. As if this kind of human exploitation is not enough, on a regular basis, the United States military deploys drones in Afghanistan and Pakistan that kill and injure civilian populations, the continuation of the U.S. dubbed "War on Terror" initiated via Operation Iraqi Freedom in March 2003 that has generated its own class of casualties of war.

We know that within the internal colonies in the U.S.—also known as the inner cities—the state has enacted immense violence against its own poor citizens of color, many of them with disabilities. On an almost daily basis we have been witnessing police shootings that have both maimed and/or murdered its poor, black, and disabled citizens. The largest civilian population living in incarcerated settings exists in the U.S., most of whom are overwhelmingly people of color and many of them with disabilities. The U.S. public education system, where low income students of color are indiscriminately labeled behaviorally disabled, language disabled, borderline intellectually disabled, and emotionally disturbed are also quite literally ushered via the school-to-prison pipeline to a lifetime of involuntary institutionalization in the prison industrial complex.

Shifting to the economic context, transnational capitalism (typically made up of corporations operating across national borders) is also implicated in the simultaneous deployment of racism and ableism. The now well-established transnational capitalist exploitative machine has enabled capital to flow freely across international borders while at the same time ensuring that labor be confined within the nation states themselves. This has maintained a cheap and docile labor force living in precarious conditions in obeisance to the dictates of the World Bank and the International Monetary Fund. Many of their mandated economic policies have required the dismantling of the already skeletal economic safety nets in these nation states resulting in large shortages of food, inadequate access to health care, and deplorable living conditions that have continued the proliferation of disability. Undocumented workers cross the U.S./Mexico border endure dehydration and other heat-related diseases, risking rape and sexual molestation to end up as laborers in fruit and vegetable farms, cattle ranches, chicken factories, and formal/informal service work and are compensated with the lowest wages, unsafe working conditions, and little to no medical care. Global investment in the so-called "Third World" has resulted in the relocation of multi-national factories from the neo-imperialist north where "third world" laborers in the global south work under sweatshop conditions to produce cheap and affordable goods for consumption by world markets. Recently, a garment factory burned down in Bangladesh and while the newspaper reporters rushed to count the dead, very little was said about the underpaid women laborers who have undergone amputations, suffered burns, and who are working through post-traumatic stress.

Every one of the examples above points to an intimate relationship between race and disability on a global scale and yet scholars in both disability studies and race studies have failed to foreground this critical intersection on a consistent basis. In 2004, the late Chris Bell wrote an essay calling out disability studies scholarship for producing what he called *White Disability Studies.* Acknowledging that this exclusion was not intentional, Bell pointed out that its inadvertent outcome has been a "tendency to whitewash disability history, ontology, and phenomenology." Since Bell's "tongue-in-cheek modest proposal", the field of disability studies has taken heed and there has been a notable increase in scholarship that engages both race and disability. However, more than a decade after Bell's "modest proposal," there is still a paucity of scholarship that moves beyond an additive framework committed to some variation of the rather simplistic analogy: "Being disabled is just like being black." If race and disability are intimately interrelated as mutually constitutive of each other, then disability studies scholarship should reflect this intersectional complexity.

DisCrit: Race and Disability at the Intersections

This recognition of the intimate relationship between race and disability is indebted to the scholarship of critical race feminist Kimberle Crenshaw. Crenshaw critiques identity politics because as she writes it "frequently conflates and ignores intragroup difference." Crenshaw uses, as an example, the implications of legal and policy reform directed to end violence (battering and rape) against women of color who have to deal with both sexism and racism in a bid for their physical and emotional survival. Here, Crenshaw notes that the experiences of violence by women of color are mediated by the intersecting realities of sexism within communities of color and racism within the feminist movement and, as a result, these women are marginalized within both communities. A theory of intersectionality is especially critical in accounting for multiple grounds of identity so as to challenge homogenous groups "that are after all in one sense 'home' to us so that we can name the parts of us that are made at home."

There are perils of being located at the intersections of race and disability. We know that ableism locates disability at the margins of society by denying disabled people access to almost every aspect of social life. When racism intersects with ableism, the lives of disabled people of color are placed in double jeopardy. Take for example, Susan Burch's historical account of the involuntary institutionalization of Elizabeth Fe Alexis Fairbault , a Dakota woman who lived in South Dakota's Canton Asylum from 1915 till her unexplained death in 1928. This historical account foregrounds the political necessity of engaging in an intersectional analysis. Fairbault was forcibly dislocated from her family and community and institutionalized at the Canton Asylum because she was, as her husband asserted, mildly drunk. Hospital records report that she was diagnosed with "Intoxication psychosis"— a medical diagnosis. Fairbault was forcibly held at the institution for more than a decade. She tried to run away twice but was forcibly brought back, and she died there under questionable circumstances a couple of years after she had a child in the asylum. The father of the child was in question, with the institution insisting that the child's biological father was another inmate, a Diné (Navajo) man named Willie Dayea. However, other sources hinted that the Superintendent of the asylum, H. H. Hamner, could have raped Fairbault, and could also have murdered her.

The Canton Asylum, first called the "Hiawatha Asylum," opened in 1902 and it was the only federal psychiatric institution in the United States specifically dedicated to American Indians. The Asylum closed amid scandal in 1934 after nearly 400 men, women, and children from 17 states and 50 tribal nations inhabited its wards. Burch cites researchers Bradley and Jennifer Soule who wrote that the primary reason for the Canton Asylum inhabitants' "discharge" was death: "roughly 120 in twenty years, or 45 percent; the high mortality rate due to tuberculosis (one-third) and the comparatively young age at death—forty two years—were remarkable" (2003, 17). By the 1920s, Canton also held a sizeable and growing Native population diagnosed with intellectual disabilities, which contrasted with all other psychiatric institutions at the time.

Fairbault's story brings to bear a poignant narrative that endures at the intersections of indigenous life, gendered violence, and disability such that we find it almost impossible to disentangle disability from race and gender in trying to understand how Fairbault came to be involuntarily committed to the Canton Asylum. An intersectional analysis would ask the reader to consider the history of forced dislocations of indigenous peoples from land and community in relation to the history of involuntary confinements of disabled people in state asylums and institutions. An intersectional analysis would also ask us to consider the differential treatments meted out to disabled white people and disabled indigenous communities trapped in these state institutions.

In yet another example, Natalia Molina in an article, *Medicalizing the Mexican,* utilizes the intersectional space of race and disability to challenge "the power of biology as a naturalizing discourse." Consider how the very logic of immigration policy supports exclusionary policies based on intersecting practices of racism and ableism. For example, the Immigration Act of 1882 specifically supported the exclusion of any immigrant deemed to be a "convict, lunatic, idiot, or any person unable to take care of himself or herself without becoming a public charge" (24). This exclusion on the basis of disability was then transposed onto certain racialized bodies whose usefulness to the state shifted with the economic and social demands of the times. Chinese immigrants, for example, processed on Angel Island, were believed to be carriers of diseases like leprosy and hookworm and were therefore processed differently from other immigrants at Ellis Island. Similarly, Molina traces the changing fortunes of Mexican immigrants in early 20th-century America. She describes how the corporeal characteristics ascribed to Mexicans during immigration debates became central to the construction of the racial category of "Mexican."

Conclusion: Building Transformative Coalitions

I started this chapter by positing disability and race as uncomfortable bedfellows. I want to end this chapter by calling on you to reflect on what it would mean to imagine race and disability through the prism of a transformative coalition politics (a movement involving groups with differing identities). But coalition politics are difficult when people are caught at the intersections of multiple identities that compete with each other in some kind of oppression Olympics. We have seen this play out in the context of the recent social movement—Black Lives Matter—that came into being in angry response to the violent police brutality against black bodies. The conservative backlash to this movement has been to decry identity politics claiming that ALL Lives Matter. And even some in progressive circles have pointed out that identity politics continue to disrupt calls for solidarity.

I argue, however, that rather than decry identity politics, it is important to recognize the importance of the intersectional politics of race and disability. For example, disabled activists like Leroy Moore and Kerima Cevic have pointed out that many of those murdered by police have been both black and disabled. It is in this context then that it is difficult to ignore the reality of a relentless anti-blackness and its implications for the diverse bodies assembled under the banner of this much disdained identity category (gender, disability, queer, trans, poor, dis-respectable).

One response to this complexity of identity is a personal essay by Sami Schalk, "Coming to claim crip: Disidentification with/in disability studies," which marks her journey as a self-identified "fat black queer woman" as she maps her "personal and political connections to the term 'crip' and a disidentified relationship with disability studies." Schalk borrows the term "disidentification" from queer scholar José Esteban Muñoz to describe "the strategic survival strategies of identification for/of/by those with multiple intersecting marginal identities." Located at the intersections of identity categories, it becomes a difficult task for anyone to either fully conform to or to fully resist any of one's multiple identity categories. Instead, the process of disidentification enables those located at the intersection of differ-ence "to take up and (re)use representations and theories in ways that were not originally intended." Schalk discusses the process by which she has come to call herself "crip-identified" which implies that she identifies "*with* not *as* crip." Thus, Schalk urges us to reflect on the following: "How can we identify *with* social categories we don't identify *as* and how can this benefit us all? What are the similar, but not same, aspects of the lived experiences of people of color and people with disabilities?"

Schalk's questions open up a space that enables us to begin to conceptualize a coalition politics that has transformative promise. However, this vision is not new. Rather, this transformative vision is already being enacted outside the academy by activists who live at the intersections of race and disability. This vision thrives in the intersectional praxis of grassroots communities such as ADAPT, Black Lives Matter, Krips Occupy Wall Street; Sins Invalid; Society for Disability Studies People of Color Collective; Krip-Hop, Neurodiversity Network, etc., to name only a few. In fact, much of the scholarship that is cited in this chapter is informed by the intellectual labor and material struggles of activists of color like the late Chris Bell, Lydia Brown, the late Carlos Drazen, Angel Miles, Stacy Milburn, Mia Mingus, Leroy Moore, Eddie Ndobu, Akemi Nishida, Kerima Cevik among others. You can learn so much from their work in their powerful and passionate writing on desire, struggle, pride, resistance, revolution, and pain. Their work requires that we acknowledge the generosity of their labor and invite us to join them in solidarity with their real life struggles for disability and racial justice.

Discussion Questions

1. Why does Erevelles call race and disability "uncomfortable bedfellows"? Discuss some examples about the intersections of race and disability in oppressing various groups.

2. How does Erevelles envision the possibility of a "coalition politics"? How can we benefit from seeing intersectionality in disability activism?

References

Bell, Chris. "A Modest Proposal." *The Disability Studies Reader* (2006): 275.

Burch, Susan. "'Dislocated Histories': The Canton Asylum for Insane Indians." *Women, Gender, and Families of Color* 2.2 (2014): 141–162.

Crenshaw, Kimberle. "Mapping the margins: Intersectionality, identity politics, and violence against women of color." *Stanford Law Review* (1991): 1241–1299.

Molina, Natalia. "Medicalizing the Mexican: Immigration, race, and disability in the early-twentieth-century United States." *Radical History Review* 2006.94 (2006): 22–37.

Schalk, Sami. "Coming to claim crip: Disidentification with/in disability studies." *Disability Studies Quarterly* 33.2 (2013). http://dsq-sds.org/article/view/3705/3240

Soule, Bradley and Jennifer Soule. "Death at the Hiawatha Asylum for Insane Indians." *South Dakota Journal of Medicine* 56.1 (2003): 15–18.

Coming to Claim Crip

Disidentification With/In Disability Studies

Sami Schalk

As a young gender, race, and disability studies scholar, my entry into and relationship with/in this last field of study is not the story many expect when I tell them that I do disability studies. Unlike many people in the field, I am not (yet) a person with a disability and I am not (yet) the parent, guardian, sibling, or partner of a person with a disability. Ten to 15 years ago, being a nondisabled[1] disability studies researcher[2] with no immediate, personal experience with disability would have been relatively unusual. However, due to the growth of disability studies as an academic field since the 1990s, more people are encountering disability theory in the course of their academic careers whether or not they identify as or have a personal relationship with a person with a disability. Although I do not identify as a person with a disability, I nonetheless have come to identify with the term "crip" as elucidated by feminist and queer crip/disability theorists such as Carrie Sandahl, Robert McRuer, and Alison Kafer. As a fat, black, queer woman, my experiences have led me to have particular personal and political connections to the term "crip" and a disidentified relationship with disability studies. In what follows, I argue that disidentification can be used by minoritarian subjects to disidentify with other minoritarian subjects, communities, and/or representations and that this kind of disidentifying process among/across/between minoritarian subjects can allow for coalitional theory and political solidarity.

By coalitional theory, I mean theories which are inclusive of multiple minority groups without being limited to only those people who occupy multiply minoritized positions. Regarding political solidarity, I follow Chandra Talpade Mohanty who defines solidarity as follows:

> In terms of mutuality, accountability, and the recognition of common interests as the basis for relationships among diverse communities . . . who have chosen to work and fight together. Diversity and difference are central values here—to be acknowledged and respected, not erased in the building of alliances.[3]

My goal here is to show through both my own experiences and existing theory how disidentification with/in disability studies and identification with crip offers transformative possibilities for disability studies to make stronger academic and political connections to other identity-based fields, particularly race/ethnic and sexuality/queer studies—connections that the field has not yet been able to make thus far in substantive and lasting ways.[4]

As an undergraduate first coming into my feminist voice, I began to embrace my many marginal identities and understand how my body/mind/desire/behavior[5] shape(d) my past, present, and future experiences. I became a loud, at times angry, young activist who consistently called out others on their white, straight, upper-class, and/or male privilege. When it came to the oppression Olympics, I was a gold-medal contender, the ultimate minority, and I made it my business to teach those privileged subjects around me how to be allies to feminist, antiracist, and LBGTQIA[6] movements. I thought I knew it all.

Then, during my sophomore year, I took an elective course for my Women's Studies major entitled "Women and Disability" with Drs. Kathy McMahon-Klosterman and Jean Lynch.[7] In that course, I encountered my own unrecognized privilege for the first time. While I was aware of my class and nationality privileges, they didn't bother me because I easily recognized them and tried to act as an ally as a result. The experience of learning about (dis)ability[8] as a social system of oppression and privilege, however, one I had never even remotely considered, shifted my entire worldview. I had previously scoffed at the notion of white guilt,[9] but my initial reaction to the revelation of my ability privilege[10] was also one of guilt. Though it took some time to come out of that emotionally reactive state, I did eventually begin to pay critical attention to the ability privileges I receive each day and before the end of the semester I had declared myself a vocal ally of disability rights communities. I did this not only because I immediately made connections between (dis)ability and other systems of privilege and oppression, but also because I realized that if I ever again wanted to call someone out on their other forms of privilege or encourage them to be an ally to me, I absolutely had to evaluate my own ability privilege and become an ally myself.

The "Women and Disability" class led to other classes on disability and eventually to a disability studies minor, a senior thesis on student activism, and membership in the Society for Disability Studies (SDS). The summer after I graduated I attended the SDS annual conference with Dr. Kathy McMahon-Klosterman to help lead a roundtable discussion about student activism. It was this conference experience that solidified my relationship to disability studies.

Initially, I was simply thrilled to be in the presence of such academic and activist greatness. I met Rosemarie Garland-Thomson at lunch. I attended a workshop with Eli Clare. I sat behind Jim Ferris at a panel. I had never experienced such an interesting, exciting, and friendly intellectual environment. Something felt right about this space. On the last night of the conference I prepared myself for the (in)famous SDS dance. I had read about the spirit of SDS and the unrivaled nature of its culminating dance in Simi Linton's (2006) memoir, *My Body Politic*, so I was more excitedly nervous for this event than I was for my prom. Would the dance live up to everything Linton made it out to be?

As I entered the basement hallway of the CUNY building where the dance would occur, I could hear the music thumping with the strong trembling bass used so people who are Deaf, hard of hearing, or hearing impaired can feel the rhythm pulse. I entered the dark space to see a cornucopia of bodies scattered around the room: people spinning, rolling, jumping, shaking, wriggling, fist-pumping, sashaying, and bouncing in an explosion of movements, large and small. I saw people in chairs (wheeled and not) sitting on the sidelines clapping their hands or tapping their feet as they talked, drank, and laughed, their bodies close, sometimes interlaced. There was ethos of community and love in that room and though I was terrified of knowing no one and not fitting in, I also desperately wanted to dance.

Though still unsure of myself, when I located the unmistakable hair of Simi's husband, David, across the dance floor, I headed over to join their group of dancers. That night, my body moved more freely and less self-consciously than it ever had before because, at this dance, people were not watching me the way they sometimes stare or leer at dance clubs or bars; folks were looking, but here with friendly excitement or admiration. One of my dance partners that night, the beautiful and talented Alice Sheppard of AXIS Dance Company, followed the lead of my movements, adapting and responding to them with her own agile body and wheelchair. Then she helped me learn to watch her as well, to follow her movements, spinning, sliding, touching hands, and shaking our hair. I didn't leave until the wine was gone, the music stopped, and people started to disperse. I replayed the dance in my head as I headed back to my hotel and though I did not yet have the language for it, my first Society for Disability Studies dance was the moment I began to both disidentify with/in disability studies and identify with crip.

I am primarily using disidentification as elucidated by José Esteban Muñoz (1999) in *Disidentifications: Queers of Color and the Performance of Politics*. He defines disidentification as a strategic survival strategy of identification for/of/by those with multiple intersecting marginal identities whom Muñoz refers to as minoritarian subjects.[11]

Muñoz opens the book with a description of Marga Gomez's performance piece, *Marga Gomez Is Pretty, Witty, and Gay*, in which Gomez sees lesbians on television for the first time and is captivated by their mysterious allure because the women are all depicted wearing raincoats, wigs, and sunglasses to hide their identities. Muñoz uses this as an example of a minoritarian subject negotiating and reinterpreting a mainstream image intended as negative. He insists that the act of disidentification is neither assimilationist nor anti-assimilationist, but rather, it's an alternative political resistance strategy that works with and against dominant ideology at the same time for the performative and political purposes of minoritarian subjects.

Disidentification is therefore a way to locate one's self within, take up, and (re)use representations and theories in ways that were not originally intended. Disidentification is not, however, the only useful minoritarian political strategy and may not be appropriate or effective for all subjects or situations.[12]

Taking up this adapted understanding of disidentification, I find myself, a minoritarian subject, disidentifying with disability studies, a minoritarian field of research, because although the field's resistance to the pathologization of non-normative bodies appeals to me as a nondisabled, fat, black, queer woman, the shortage of substantive race analysis within the field and the relatively minor attention given to issues of class and sexuality trouble me deeply and disallow me any direct Good Subject[13] identification. The whiteness of disability studies has already been noted by Chris Bell (2006) in his essay "Introducing White Disability Studies: A Modest Proposal." However, the ubiquitous citation of this essay as the reference for disability studies scholars attempting to acknowledge race in relation to disability simply underscores the need for more critical scholarship on race in the field at this time.[14] While this lack of a substantial amount of research on race and disability does not necessarily mean there are also no people of color within the field (because people of color do not necessarily do research on race), the racial diversity of the disability studies researcher population that I've witnessed is minimal. The continued conspicuous presence of my racialized body at disability studies conferences and events disconcerts me and makes me wary of being tokenized. These emotions further facilitate my disidentification with/in disability studies. Following Ferguson and Muñoz, because this collection of theories and practices do not seem originally intended for me, as a researcher I must take up and revise disability theories and scholarship while refusing to extend its legacy of whiteness and racism.

Despite the disjuncture I experience in the field as it currently exists, I still have a deeply personal, emotional affinity with disability studies scholar and activist communities. This affinity is what facilitates my coming to claim and identify with crip. Note here, that there are a few key differences between disidentification and identifying with as I am using them. Disidentification is primarily in respect to representations, ideologies, and theories which have important, useful aspects that the disidentifying subject takes up, uses, or revamps while leaving behind or being critical of other problematic or damaging elements. To identify with, as I will explain more below, is to personally and politically align oneself with a group one may or may not belong to, but with which one feels a positive connection. I discuss these concepts separately in order to distinguish my relationship to the field of disability studies from my relationship to the concept of crip, not to claim one form of identification is more positive or useful than the other. In fact, disidentification and identifying with have important areas of overlap and intersection.

Crip is a term many people within disability studies and activist communities use not only in reference to people with disabilities, but also to the intellectual and art culture arising from such communities. Crip is shorthand for the word "cripple" which has been (and is) used as an insult toward people with disabilities, but which has been re-appropriated as an intra-group term of empowerment and solidarity. Thus, crip "is a term which has much currency in disability activism and culture but still might seem harsh to those outside those communities."[15] An early proponent of crip's social and political potential, Carrie Sandahl describes crip as a "fluid and ever-changing" term which "expanded to include not only those with physical impairments but those with sensory or mental impairments as well."[16] In a footnote to her use of the term, Sandahl recognizes the still-developing state of disability studies and writes: "If I had my druthers, I would replace the term disability studies with crip theory or crip studies to represent its radical edge."[17]

Robert McRuer, however, proposes that crip theory is not a one-to-one replacement for disability studies, but rather, crip theory has "a similar contestatory relationship to disability studies and identity that queer theory has to LGBT studies and identity, [although] crip theory does not—perhaps paradoxically—seek to de-materialize disability identity."[18] This move away from the postmodern demateriali-zation of identity positions is a key connection between crip theory and queer of color critique by scholars such as Cathy Cohen (2005), Lawrence La Fountain-Stokes (2009), and others who have actively resisted such moves, insisting that to move entirely away from identity and identity politics is not a viable option for those who are multiply marginalized and who need such identity positions for survival and collective action. As Roderick Ferguson (2004) writes, queer of color critique rethinks categories, but does not discard them. Related to Ferguson's rethinking of categories, Alison Kafer argues that crip theory expands and enriches disability studies by departing from the social model's assumption that "disabled" and "nondisabled" are discrete, self-evident categories, choosing instead to explore the creation of such categories and the moments in which they "fail to hold."[19]

I align myself with McRuer's "coming out crip" and Kafer's "crip affiliation" by claiming crip and declaring myself a crip-identified, fat, black, queer woman.[20] Kafer writes:

Claiming crip can be a way of acknowledging that we all have bodies and minds with shifting abilities, and that such shifts have political and social meanings and histories. It can be a way of imagining multiple futures, claiming crip as a desired and desirable location, regardless of one's own embodiment or mental/psychological processes . . . thinking through what nondisabled claims to crip might entail will require exploring whether such claims might be more available, more imaginable, to some people than others (and on what basis).[21]

I argue that my particular relationship to racial, gender, and sexuality systems of oppression and privilege is what makes claiming crip available to me. The ways in which my fat, black, queer, woman's body/mind/desire/behavior is constantly read and reacted to as non-normative, sometimes excessively so, makes me feel particularly akin to those who identify as disabled and/or crip, people whose bodies/minds/desires/behaviors are also outside the social norm. In this way, I argue that I am similarly situated in regard to many vectors of power as people with disabilities and that interrogation into the processes which have so situated us is needed in order to develop coalitional theory and political solidarity.

It is important to emphasize that I am calling myself crip-identified, meaning that I identify with not as crip, a distinction McRuer (2006) suggests in his work, but does not make sufficiently clear. I use "identify with" to mean having acknowledged and prioritized political and personal connections to a group with which one does not identify as a member. To identify with means to feel implicated by the culture and politics of another group and seek to better understand this link. While to identify with could be understood as analogous to being an ally, I contend that there is something more personal, sustained, and affective about it. Identifying with is a careful, conscious joining—a standing/sitting among rather than by or behind a group—which seeks to reduce separation while acknowledging differences in privileges and oppression. I connect identifying with to Cathy Cohen's (2005) call for a radical politics of shared resistance built on identities as they are impacted by and invested with different degrees of normative power. Identifying with is particularly important in the case of disability which, as many have noted, is the only identity category which one can join at any moment without intent. I use crip-identified as something different than disability ally because it is an almost-not-quite-yet identification. I am crip-identified not only because my body/mind/desire/behavior is non-normative in terms of race, gender, sexuality, and size, but also because of its precarious relationship to disability as this term is currently culturally understood.

I want to be clear that I am aware of my ability privileges and I know, as McRuer insists, that I cannot make such privileges "magically disappear" by simply refusing them because "the benefits that accrue to nondisabled people in that [ability/disability] system are bigger than any individual's seemingly voluntary refusal of them."[22] With this recognition of privilege in mind, I contend that fatness represents an important form of embodiment which needs further engagement within the field of disability studies. Fatness is one of the primary avenues through which I identify with crip and therefore I want to discuss a few of the connections between fatness and disability here to further illustrate how I have come to claim crip.

The parallels and overlaps between disability and fatness are striking. Both fatness and disability are highly pathologized, viewed as medical and/or health issues located primarily in the failed body/mind/desire/behavior of the individual. Within disability studies this framework is referred to as the medical model. An aspect of the medical model which also applies to fatness is the representation of disability and fatness as medical/health problems which ought to be "fixed" or "cured" even if such "fixing" goes against the wishes of the person and/or does not improve overall health. As April Herndon notes, "there is very little compelling evidence that losing weight equals a step toward health or that losing weight is even really possible for the vast majority of folks."[23] Additionally, even if weight loss is attainable, in order to achieve or maintain weight loss many people resort to dieting and disordered eating practices that can have negative long-term health effects.[24] In terms of disability, the medical[25] push for cochlear implants for Deaf/deaf people or limb-lengthening for little people as well as the general societal pressure for people with disabilities to perform as much able-ness as possible, even when the strain and fatigue of such effort causes health problems, all represent aspects of the medical/social obligation to be as close to the norm as possible at any cost.

There are also a number of other social conditions that connect fatness and disability. Both terms are highly contextual and socially constructed. Recognition as fat or disabled varies depending on where, when, and with whom one is located. This understanding of fatness and disability falls under the social model of disability that locates problems not within bodies/minds/desires/behaviors, but in the social attitudes and the environment. Both disability and fatness are terms without consistent definitions, either in terms of social or medical understandings. This is illustrated by the open-ended wording of the Americans with Disabilities Act and the continually expansive way it has been legally applied to include categories such as drug and alcohol addiction.[26] Similarly, notions of fatness include a wide range of bodies and body parts. Socially "'fat' can mark any woman, referencing body size in general, a jiggle of a thigh, or the slight swell of a tummy," while medical and professional definitions of and perspectives on fatness are also quite varied.[27] For example, at my current weight I am "obese" according to the most common measurement, the body mass index (BMI); however, I am also "acceptable" according to my body fat percentage and "low risk" according to my waist to hip ratio.[28] According to these standards, I am somehow extremely, moderately, and mildly fat all at the same time.

These various medical, legal, and cultural perspectives all contribute to the social construction of disability and fatness. America is a particularly fatphobic place in which many people "believe that fat is unhealthy, immoral, and often downright disgusting"[29] and thus fat people are often subject to hateful verbal, emotional, and physical abuse.[30] People with disabilities also face attitudes of hatred and contempt, especially in the form of microaggressions: indirect, non-physical interactions which communicate hostility, negativity, and insult toward a marginalized individual.[31] People with disabilities additionally encounter attitudes of pity and infantilization. As Herndon notes, however, discourses of both "weight and disability seem per-petually freighted with issues of choice and frivolity,"[32] notions which stem from what Joyce L. Huff calls our cultural "fiction of absolute corporeal control."[33] In terms of environment, stairs, heavy doors, poor signage, inaccessible bathrooms, and other barriers prevent people with physical disabilities specifically from fully accessing certain spaces. In a related way, the design of airline seats, classroom desks, seatbelts, and more prevent fat people from fully accessing some spaces, at least not without discomfort or shame.[34]

Finally, I find an important connection in the construction of fat and disabled sexualities. Both groups are constructed as nonsexual and undeserving or incapable of having satisfying sexual relationships.[35] Both groups also experience what Abby Wilkerson calls "erotic segregation"[36] which Sarah Smith Rainey explains occurs both socially and environmentally for people with disabilities because of institutions, nursing and group homes, inaccessible dating spaces like clubs, restaurants, or bars, and the social taboo on disabled/nondisabled dating.

It is particularly through these many, varied connections between fatness and disability[37]—medicalization, social construction, cultural attitudes, environmental barriers, and sexuality—that I have come to be crip-identified; however, I also identify with crip because of my own shifting levels of ability in terms of my sight due to early retinal degeneration and because of the impurity of the term disability generally. As the social constructionist argument of disability contends, this category is historically and culturally specific. As a fat, black, queer woman, I cannot help but recall that homosexuality was a psychological disorder in the Diagnostic and Statistical Manual of Mental Disorders until 1973, that runaway slaves were said to experience the mental disorder "drapetomania" which made them run, that free blacks were said to have higher rates of mental and cognitive disability than those still enslaved, and that women have and continue to consciously and unconsciously disable their bodies in order to adhere to beauty norms through practices such as corseting, cosmetic surgery, tanning, and extreme exercise and dieting.[38] Herndon writes that both fatness and disability:

> remind us that bodies are subjected to changing sociocultural contexts as well as physiological changes . . . Many women have times in their lives when they gain weight and/or become disabled. Regardless of whether either is permanent or temporary, the existence of these possibilities removes bodies from solid ground and acknowledges once again that bodies are unstable.[39]

I know that my body/mind/desire/behavior (and the culture which interprets it) is not fixed. I am crip-identified because I am not afraid of this instability. I am not afraid of this instability because I am crip-identified. My identification with crip is neither simply personal nor purely academic. It is both of these things as well as highly political and it is this politics of claiming crip as a nondisabled, fat, black, queer woman that I believe has the most value for the future of disability studies.

My identification with crip is not a cure-all for the problems of race, class, and sexuality within the field of disability studies. It also certainly does not fix the problem of disability being left out of intersectional analyses in race and ethnic studies, queer and sexuality studies, and women's and gender studies. However, I believe being crip-identified is an enactment of solidarity which can be beneficial politically, socially, and academically for multiple minoritarian groups. I want disability studies scholars not only to consider how to bring disability to, for example, black studies or to bring blackness to disability studies, but also consider how we as disability studies scholars and activists might disidentify with people of color, women, queers, or gender non-conforming people. How can we identify with social categories we don't identify as and how can this benefit us all? What are the similar, but not same, aspects of the lived experiences of people of color and people with disabilities? We would do well to ask those who identify as both, but the burden of proof should not lie with them alone. Disability studies has a long history of borrowing from work in other fields and civil rights movements, but this borrowing tends to emphasize the difference or exceptionality of disability[40] rather than its similarities or overlap—the places where disidentification across/between/among minoritarian subjects could occur. This coalitional politics through minoritarian subjects disidentifying with other minoritarian subjects, representations, theories or practices need not, however, be for political or intellectual purposes alone. It can also be, like my coming to claim crip, deeply personal and affective.

Discussion Questions

1. How does Schalk identify with disability without being a disabled person? What does she hope she can gain from this identification, and in what ways does she distance herself from disability studies?

2. What are the connections between the terms "queer" and "crip" in this essay? Discuss how perceptions around these terms might change through their new uses.

3. How does Schalk compare fatness and disability? In what ways are these identities similar and in what ways might they be different?

Notes

1 I use "nondisabled" rather than "able-bodied" not only because, as Sarah Ann Rainey (following the lead of Nancy Mairs and Simi Linton) notes, "nondisabled" moves disability from margin to center, but also because "able-bodied" erases or ignores the experiences of those with non-physical disabilities (Rainey, 2011, p. 11).

2   To be clear here, I mean disability studies as a field arising from the disability rights movement headed by people with disabilities to resist the medical model of disability and introduce the study of disability into the humanities and social sciences in ways not previously performed. Within this field, the majority of researchers are people with disabilities or people who have family or partner relationships with people with disabilities. I recognize that in areas like rehabilitation, medicine, special education, and speech and hearing therapy the majority of researchers and practitioners have been and often continue to be nondisabled.

3   Mohanty, 2003, p. 7.

4   This is not to imply that only disability studies scholars should be doing this work of solidarity and coalition, but it is mainly to this group that I direct this particular article.

5   I use body/mind/desire/behavior in order to imply these things are not distinct entities that can be understood or experienced separately. This is a critical intersectionality approach which refuses to consider my race, gender, sexuality, and (dis)ability identities as "separable analytics" (Puar, 2007, p. 212).

6   Lesbian, Bisexual, Gay, Trans-, Queer and Questioning, Intersex, Asexual, and Ally.

7   I am forever grateful for the many things I gained by being a student of Dr. KMK and Dr. Lynch at Miami University. From them, I learned not only about disability studies, but also about being a teacher and an activist committed to social justice. This essay is dedicated to them.

8   I use "(dis)ability" here to reference the overarching normative body system which includes ability and disability, since unlike terms such as gender, which references man, woman, genderqueer, transgender, and other gender identities, disability without the parenthetical adjustment merely references disability and impairment. Other scholars use "dis/ability," "disAbility," or "ability/disability" to reference this system.

9   White guilt is a liberal idea that white people feel guilty about either their own privilege (past or present) or people of color's oppression (past or present) and often as a result feel as if there is nothing they can personally do about it. Several scholars critique the notion of white guilt. See for example, Price, 2011.

10 I use "ability" rather than "able-bodied" in order to not emphasize physical impairment over mental, c ognitive, emotional, and behavioral impairments. For more, see note 1.

11 Editor's note: A more complete explanation of Munoz's work and other theories of disidentification is available in a longer version of Schalk's article, which is accessible at http://dsq-sds.org/article/view/3705/3240.

12 Munoz, 1999.

13 Good Subject here refers back to Althusser's concept of interpellation. A Good Subject is one who properly responds to being hailed, who is easily interpellated.

14 It's critical for me to acknowledge the work that has been done on race and disability. In addition to Chris Bell, other key scholars include Nirmala Erevelles, Michelle Jarman, Cynthia Wu, Mel Chen, Susan Burch, Ellen Samuels, Anna Morrow, Moya Bailey, and Terry Rowden. At this time the majority of this work is in the form of articles and anthology chapters. There are only five monographs which focus extensively on

disability and race—and most are quite recent. These are: Burch and Joyner, 2007; Rowden, 2009; Erevelles, 2011; Wu, 2012; Chen, 2012.

15 Kafer, 2013, p. 15.

16 Sandahl, 2003, p. 27.

17 Ibid, p. 53.

18 McRuer, 2006, p. 27.

19 Kafer, 2013, p. 10.

20 Further explanation of "crip" identity and theory is available in the long form of Schalk's essay.

21 Kafer, 2013, p. 13.

22 McRuer, 2006, p. 36.

23 Herndon, 2011, p. 36.

24 Lyons, 2009.

25 Note that in terms of cochlear implants in particular, the push is not only medical, but also socio-cultural, stemming from hearing parents of deaf children and even some segments of the Deaf community.

26 Herndon, 2011, pp. 248–249; Vade & Solovay, 2009, pp. 169–70.

27 Herndon, 2011, pp. 258, 50. For more critical investigation of scientific and medical approaches to fatness, see Gard and Wright, 2005 or Wright and Harwood, 2009.

28 The body mass index (BMI) is a body fat indicator which uses height and weight to calculate whether a person is under weight, normal, overweight, or obese. The BMI is known to be a poor indicator for adolescents, the elderly, and athletes. Body fat percentage is a more complex calculation developed by the Navy, which typically uses weight and the circumference of the waist, hips, wrists, and forearms to calculate what percentage of fat the body contains, but other methods such as underwater weighing are also used. Body fat percentage categories are essential fat, athletic, fit, acceptable, and obese. Hip to waist ratio is a simple calculation of the difference between the circumference of the hips and waist to determine fat distribution—where fat is carried on the body—to determine a low, moderate, or high risk fat distribution. BMI, body fat percentage, and hip to waist ratio calculators can all be found online. I determined mine using the Fitter: Fitness Calculator app for iPhone on December 8, 2011.

29 Herndon, 2011, p. 250.

30 Herndon, 2011; Prohaska & Gailey, 2009; Royce, 2009.

31 This term comes from critical race theory, but has been used in relation to a variety of marginalized identities. For more see Sue, 2010a and Sue, 2010b.

32 Herndon, 2001, pp. 249–250.

33 Huff, 2009, p. 176.

34 Hetrick & Attig, 2009; Huff, 2009.

35 Asbill, 2009; Kaufman, Silverberg, & Odette 2003; Pyle & Loewy, 2009.

36 As cited in Rainey, 2011, p. 3.

37 See original essay for more extensive discussion of these connections.

38 Herek, 2012; Jarman, 2012.

39 Herndon, 2011, p. 258.

40 See, for example, Snyder and Mitchell, 2006.

References

Asbill, D. Lacy. (2009). "'I'm Allowed to Be a Sexual Being': The Distinctive Social Conditions of the Fat Burlesque Stage." In Esther D. Rothblum and Sondra Solovay (Eds), *The Fat Studies Reader* (pp. 299–304). New York: New York University Press.

Bell, C. (2006). "Introducing White Disability Studies: A modest proposal." In L. J. Davis (Ed.), *The Disability Studies Reader.* Second ed. (pp. 275–282). New York, NY: Routledge.

Burch, S., and Joyner, H. (2007). *Unspeakable: The Story of Junius Wilson.* Chapel Hill, NC: University of North Carolina Press.

Chen, M.Y. (2012). *Animacies: Biopolitics, Racial Mattering, and Queer Affect.* Durham, NC: Duke University Press.

Cohen, Cathy J. (2005). "Punks, Bulldaggers and Welfare Queens: The Radical Potential of Queer Politics?" In E. Patrick Johnson and Mae Henderson (Eds), *Black Queer Studies: A Critical Anthology* (pp. 21–51). Durham, NC: Duke University Press.

Erevelles, N. (2011). *Disability and Difference in Global Contexts: Enabling a Transformative Body Politic.* New York: Palgrave Macmillan.

Ferguson, R.A. (2004). *Aberrations in Black: Toward a Queer of Color Critique.* Minneapolis, MN: University of Minnesota Press.

Gard, M., and Wright, J. (2005). *The Obesity Epidemic: Science, Morality, and Ideology.* London/New York: Routledge.

Herek, Gregory M. (2012) "Facts About Homosexuality and Mental Health." University of California-Davis [cited 27 Nov 2012]. Available at psychology.ucdavis. edu.

Herndon, A. (2011). "Disparate, but Disabled: Fat Embodiment and Disability Studies." In K. Q. Hall (Ed.), *Feminist Disability Studies* (pp. 245–262). Bloomington, IN: Indiana University Press.

Hetrick, Ashley, and Derek Attig. (2009). "Sitting Pretty: Fat Bodies, Classroom Desks, and Academic Excess." In Esther D. Rothblum and Sondra Solovay (Eds), *The Fat Studies Reader* (pp. 197–204). New York: New York University Press.

Huff, Joyce L. (2009). "Access to the Sky: Airplane Seats and Fat Bodies as Contested Spaces." In Esther D. Rothblum and Sondra Solovay (Eds), *The Fat Studies Reader* (pp. 176–186). New York: New York University Press.

Jarman, Michelle. (2012). "Coming Up from Underground: Uneasy Dialogues at the Intersections of Race, Mental Illness, and Disability Studies." In Chris Bell (Ed.), *Blackness and Disability* (pp. 9–30). East Lansing: Michigan State University Press.

Kafer, A. (2013). *Feminist, Crip, Queer.* Bloomington, IN: Indiana University Press.

Kaufman, M., Silverberg, C., and Odette, F. (2003). *The Ultimate Guide to Sex and Disability: For All of Us Who Live With Disabilities, Chronic Pain, and Illness.* First ed. San Francisco: Cleis Press.

La Fountain-Stokes, Lawrence M. (2009). *Queer Ricans: Cultures and Sexualities in the Diaspora*, Cultural studies of the Americas. Minneapolis: University of Minnesota Press.

Linton, Simi. (2006). *My Body Politic: A Memoir*. Ann Arbor: University of Michigan Press.

Lyons, Pat. (2009). "Prescription for Harm: Diet Industry Influence, Public Health Policy, and the 'Obesity Epidemic'." In Esther D. Rothblum and Sondra Solovay (Eds), *The Fat Studies Reader* (pp. 75–87). New York: New York University Press.

McRuer, Robert. (2006). *Crip Theory: Cultural Signs of Queerness and Disability*, Cultural Front. New York: New York University Press.

Mohanty, C.T. (2003). *Feminism Without Borders: Decolonizing Theory, Practicing Solidarity*. Durham, NC: Duke University Press.

Muñoz, José Esteban. (1999). *Disidentifications: Queers of Color and the Performance of Politics*, Cultural studies of the Americas. Minneapolis: University of Minnesota Press.

Price, M. (2011). Cripping Revolution: A Crazed Essay. Paper presented at the Society for Disability Studies, San Jose, CA. http://margaretprice.files.wordpress.com/2011/06/sds-activism-plenary-6-29-11.pdf

Prohaska, Adriane, and Jeannine Gailey. (2009). "Fat Women as 'Easy Targets': Achieving Masculinity Through Hogging." In Esther D. Rothblum and Sondra Solovay (Eds), *The Fat Studies Reader* (pp. 158–166). New York: New York University Press.

Puar, Jasbir K. (2007). *Terrorist Assemblages: Homonationalism in Queer Times*, Next Wave. Durham, NC: Duke University Press.

Pyle, N.C., and Loewy, M.I. (2009). "Double Stigma: Fat Men and Their Male Admirers." In E. D. Rothblum and S. Solovay (Eds.), *The Fat Studies Reader* (pp. 143–150). New York: New York University Press.

Rainey, Sarah Smith. (2011). *Love, Sex, and Disability: The Pleasures of Care*, Disability in Society. Boulder, CO: Lynne Rienner Publishers.

Rowden, T. (2009). *The Songs of Blind Folk: African American Musicians and the Cultures of Blindness*. Ann Arbor, MI: University of Michigan Press.

Royce, Tracy. (2009). "The Shape of Abuse: Fat Oppression as a Form of Violence Again Women." In Esther D. Rothblum and Sondra Solovay (Eds), *The Fat Studies Reader* (pp. 151–157). New York: New York University Press.

Sandahl, Carrie. (2003). "Queering the Crip or Cripping the Queer?: Intersections of Queer and Crip Identities in Solo Autobiographical Performance." *GLQ: A Journal of Lesbian and Gay Studies*, no. 9 (1–2): 25–56.

Snyder, S.L., and Mitchell, D.T. (2006). *Cultural Locations of Disability*. Chicago: University of Chicago Press.

Sue, D.W. (2010a). *Microaggressions and Marginality: Manifestation, Dynamics, and Impact*. Hoboken, NJ: Wiley.

Sue, D.W. (2010b). *Microaggressions in Everyday Life: Race, Gender, and Sexual Orientation*. Hoboken, NJ: Wiley.

Vade, D., and Solovay, S. (2009). "No Apology: Shared Struggles in Fat and Transgender Law." In E. D. Rothblum, & S. Solovay (Eds.), *The Fat Studies Reader* (pp. 167–175). New York: New York University Press.

Wright, J., and Harwood, V. (2009). *Biopolitics and the "Obesity Epidemic": Governing Bodies.* New York: Routledge.

Wu, C. (2012). *Chang and Eng Reconnected: The Original Siamese Twins in American Culture.* Philadelphia: Temple University Press.

Moving Toward the Ugly

A Politic Beyond Desirability

Mia Mingus[1]

I always think it is important to say that I'm a queer, disabled, Korean woman, transracial/transnational adoptee, raised in a U.S. territory in the Caribbean. None of which are more or less important. For me, these are not just descriptive terms; they are political identities, based out of my own and other people's lived experiences, and I understand them—all of them—to be powerful ways of moving through and understanding the world . . .

What I have learned from living in the south has helped me to survive as a queer person; and what I have learned from being adopted has helped me to survive as a disabled person.

To me, femme must include ending ableism, white supremacy, heterosexism, the gender binary, economic exploitation, sexual violence, population control, male supremacy, war and militarization, and ownership of children and land.

Ableism must be included in our analysis of oppression and in our conversations about violence, responses to violence and ending violence. Ableism cuts across all of our movements because ableism dictates how bodies should function against a mythical norm—an able-bodied standard of white supremacy, heterosexism, sexism, economic exploitation, moral/religious beliefs, age and ability. Ableism set the stage for queer and trans people to be institutionalized as mentally disabled; for communities of color to be understood as less capable, smart and intelligent, therefore "naturally" fit for slave labor; for women's bodies to be used to produce children, when, where and how men needed them; for people with disabilities to be seen as "disposable" in a capitalist and exploitative culture because we are not seen as "productive"; for immigrants to be thought of as a "disease" that we must "cure" because it is "weakening" our country; for violence, cycles of poverty, lack of resources and war to be used as systematic tools to construct disability in communities and entire countries.

I want to say upfront that I don't identify as femme. I have struggled with identifying as Femme. I don't politically identify as "Femme," even though I get the lived experience of being a femme of color in so many ways. And frankly, much of this is because I have had horrible interactions with self-identified femmes of color, much of which has been because of their ableism and ignorance around how ableism, white supremacy and gender oppression get leveraged everyday in service of each other. Much of it has been because of the *palpable* culture of ableism within queer people of color community. And some of it has been because *I have spent most of my life as a physically disabled child, youth and adult adoptee of color trying to find my way into "human," let alone "woman."*

As a disabled child shuffled through the medical industrial complex and as a baby of color shipped across the world to "new parents," I have felt more like a different species, a freak, an object to be fixed/saved, a commodity. Like someone who has been owned and whose body has never felt like it was mine. Like someone who they were trying to make human (read: able-bodied, white), if only the surgeries had worked and the braces had stuck. Like something that never could even get close to "desirable" or "feminine" or "woman" or "queer." Like ugly. Not human.

Many people assume that I identify as femme and even call me femme, but the truth is that "femme" has not felt like a term where I belonged nor was it a place I wanted to be. I rarely see femme being done in a way that actually challenges and transforms gender, rather than colluding in an alternative enforcing of gender. Many of the people in this room are more invested in being beautiful and sexy than being magnificent. Even something as small as the time I nervously asked a comrade femme of color friend of mine to wear sneakers in solidarity with me, instead of her high heels, because I didn't want to be the only one and didn't want to get chided from other femmes of color about my shoes (as so often has happened). She said "no," but she (of course) "totally didn't think there was anything wrong with wearing sneakers."

It seems so basic in our communities, but I think we need to stop making assumptions about each other's identities and make distinctions between **how someone identifies versus what someone's lived experience is.** We need to make the distinction between descriptively femme and politically femme.

In my disability justice work this comes up a lot. Especially for disabled women of color. Over and over I meet disabled women of color who do not identify as disabled, even though they have the lived reality of being disabled. And this is for many complicated reasons around race, ability, gender, access, etc. It can be very dangerous to identify as disabled when your survival depends on you denying it.

When I say "descriptively disabled," I mean someone who has the lived experience of being disabled. They may not talk about ableism, discrimination or even call themselves "disabled," but they know what it feels like to use a wheelchair, experience chronic pain, have people stare at you, be institutionalized, walk with a brace, be isolated, etc. There are many people who are descriptively disabled who never become or identify as "politically disabled." When I say "politically disabled," I mean someone who is descriptively disabled but also has a political understanding about that lived experience. I mean someone who has an analysis about ableism, power, privilege, who feels connected to and is in solidarity with other disabled people (regardless of whatever language you use). I mean someone who thinks of disability as a political identity/experience, grounded in their descriptive lived experience. (The same is true for descriptively queer, descriptively woman of color, descriptively adoptee and so on.)

And just to be clear, I believe that in order to politically identify as queer, disabled, femme, woman of color, one needs to have a descriptive lived experience to ground it in. My political identities come directly out of my lived experience. I never used to identify as disabled, even though my life was extremely disabled. It was not until 1998 that I even started to describe myself as disabled—and even then, it was only descriptively. It wasn't until 2002 that I started identifying politically as disabled.

Doing disability justice work, we struggle with creating spaces that are based on how one identifies, because often times, the disabled people who identify as "(politically) disabled" are white disabled people. As people with multiple oppressed identities doing work with (our) folks on the margins of the margins of the margins, we need to think carefully about how we are inviting people into spaces and how we meet people where they're at.

I am descriptively femme of color. I know this. This has always been my lived experience. I was femme before I was queer. I was grappling with how to navigate gender as a tiny Korean transracial and transnational adoptee disabled girl queered by my physically disabled body. I grew up in a feminist community, around other powerful femmes of color, but none of whom identified that way. There was no word for it, it was . . . just their life. It was how they had to learn to be, to survive. It was what they had crafted out of the fires of their desires and loving. It was part of how they had learned to be magnificent.

Their gender was about being a grounded force to end violence. Their gender was about forging dignity out of invisibility that could slice through femininity that would rather be pretty than useful. Their gender was about answering the question, "what is the work you are doing to end violence and poverty?", not "what shoes are you wearing?" Their gender was about feeding family and raising children collectively; organizing for themselves when no one else would. Their gender was a challenge to the world they lived in that was trying to erase them.

As femmes of color—however we identify—we have to push ourselves to go deeper than consumerism, ableism, transphobia and building a politic of desirability. Especially as femmes of color. We cannot leave our folks behind, just to join the femmes of color contingent in the giant white femme parade.

As the (generational) effects of global capitalism, genocide, violence, oppression and trauma settle into our bodies, we must build new understandings of bodies and gender that can reflect our histories and our resiliency, not that of our oppressor or that of our self-shame and loathing. We must shift from a politic of desirability and beauty to a politic of ugly and magnificence. That moves us closer to bodies and movements that disrupt, dismantle, disturb. Bodies and movements ready to throw down and create a different way *for all of us, not just some of us.*

The magnificence of a body that shakes, spills out, takes up space, needs help, moseys, slinks, limps, drools, rocks, curls over on itself. The magnificence of a body that doesn't get to choose when to go to the bathroom, let alone which bathroom to use. A body that doesn't get to choose what to wear in the morning, what hairstyle to sport, how they're going to move or stand, or what time they're going to bed. The magnificence of bodies that have been coded, not just undesirable and ugly, but un-human. The magnificence of bodies that are understanding gender in far more complex ways than I could explain in an hour. Moving beyond a politic of desirability to loving the ugly. Respecting Ugly for how it has shaped us and been exiled. Seeing its power and magic, seeing the reasons it has been feared. Seeing it for what it is: some of our greatest strength.

Because we all do it. We all run from the ugly. And the farther we run from it, the more we stigmatize it and the more power we give beauty. Our communities are obsessed with being beautiful and gorgeous and hot. What would it mean if we were ugly? What would it mean if we didn't run from our own ugliness or each other's? How do we take the sting out of "ugly?" What would it mean to acknowledge our ugliness for all it has given us, how it has shaped our brilliance and taught us about how we never want to make anyone else feel? What would it take for us to be able to risk being ugly, in whatever that means for us. What would happen if we stopped apologizing for our ugly, stopped being ashamed of it? *What if we let go of being beautiful, stopped chasing "pretty," stopped sucking in and shrinking and spending enormous amounts of money and time on things that don't make us magnificent?*

Where is the Ugly in you? What is it trying to teach you?

And I am not saying it is easy to be ugly without apology. It is hard as fuck. It threatens our survival. I recognize the brilliance in our instinct to move toward beauty and desirability. And it takes time and for some of us it may be impossible. I know it is complicated. . . . And I also know that though it may be a way to survive, it will not be a way to thrive, to grow the kind of genders and world we need. And it is not attainable to everyone, even those who want it to be.

What do we do with bodies that can't change no matter how much we dress them up or down; no matter how much we want them to?

What about those of us who are freaks, in the most powerful sense of the word? Freakery is that piece of disability and ableism where bodies that are deformed, disfigured, scarred and non-normatively physically disabled live. Its roots come out of monsters and goblins and beasts; from the freak shows of the 1800s where physically disabled folks, trans and gender non-conforming folks, indigenous folks and people of color were displayed side-by-side. It is where "beauty" and "freak" got constructed day in and day out, where "whiteness" and "other" got burned into our brains. It is part of the legacy of Ugly and it is part of my legacy as a queer disabled woman of color. *It is a part of all of our history as queer people of color. It is how I know we must never let ourselves be on the side of the gawking crowd ever again in any way.* It is the part of me that doesn't show my leg. It is the part of me that knows that building my gender—my anything—around desirability or beauty is not just an ableist notion of what's important, but will always keep me chasing what doesn't want me. Will always keep me hurling swords at the very core of me.

There is only the illusion of solace in beauty. If age and disability teach us anything, it is that investing in beauty will never set us free. Beauty has always been hurled as a weapon. It has always taken the form of an exclusive club; and supposed protection against violence, isolation and pain, but this is a myth. It is not true, even for those accepted in to the club. I don't think we can reclaim beauty.

Magnificence has always been with us. Always been there in the freak shows— staring back at the gawking crowd, in the back rooms of the brothels, in the fields fresh with cotton, on the street corners in the middle of the night, as the bombs drop, in our breaths after surviving the doctor's office, crossing the border, in the first quiet moments of a bloody face after the attack is done. Magnificence was there.

Magnificence was with me in the car rides home after long days being dehumanized, abused and steeled in the medical industrial complex. It was there with me when I took my first breaths in my mother's arms in Korea, and a week later those first days alone without her realizing I wasn't going home.

Magnificence has always been with us.

Note

1 Editor's note: This chapter is excerpted from a keynote speech that activist-scholar Mia Mingus delivered at a Femmes of Color Symposium in 2011. The full speech, as well as other writings, are available at http://LeavingEvidence.wordpress.com.

Discussion Questions

1. What is the difference between identifying as "femme" politically and having the lived experience of being femme? How does this difference also help explain the political identity of disability?

2. Why does Mingus argue that we stop valuing beauty and instead value ugliness?

What Wounds Enable

The Politics of Disability and Violence in Chicago

Laurence Ralph

We're in Kemo's garage. I sit near a pile of DVD players, cell phones, car stereos, laptops, and Internet routers.[1]

"When wintertime hits, and it's hard to get people to stand on the corner, he goes all bootleg and starts selling everything," Justin mutters.

Justin's back faces me. He's gripping the armrests of his wheelchair, raising his body up and down—slow, fluid movements—his triceps bulge and his breath labors as he finishes his third set of inverted push-ups. He catches me in his peripheral vision, studying the latest contraband from a rusted foldout chair. This "hot" merchandise means it's cold outside, as confirmed by the draft that stings us from the side door someone has left ajar. Kemo closes it when he arrives.

"What's Urkel doin' here?" Kemo says as he enters.

He acknowledges my presence with a snide comparison to the stereotypical TV nerd, but simultaneously distances himself. He refuses to reciprocate the customary head nod, yet stares me down.

"I told you, he's helping out with the forum. He's here to take notes," Justin says.

Kemo keeps his eyes trained on me, suspiciously. Then he casually snaps open a chair and straddles it. Approximately 17 minutes late and in a rush, Kemo is now apparently willing to spell out, in meticulous detail, what can and cannot be discussed at the upcoming forum.

"I don't want you guys mentioning any gang leaders or any sets by name," he says, looking back and forth between the two of us. "No blocks, no streets, nothing like that. I don't know who's gonna be around, you know."[2]

"Nah, I don't do that," Justin replies. "That's not the point of what I do."

"Well, that's good . . . that's good, then." Kemo seems pleased.

"But, I am going to talk about the consequences," Justin continues. "You know, the consequences of gang banging. I am going to talk about what happened to me, and how it's affected my life."

"I ain't got no problem with that," Kemo says with a smirk. "But, good luck getting them to listen. I'll do my part. I'll get them there. Then they're all yours."

Why would a paralyzed, ex-gang-member-turned-activist team up with a gang leader to organize a community forum on violence? What can this event teach us about the concept of disability? And what can this event show us about the seemingly contradictory ways that people disempower themselves in order to empower others?

In 2009 the rate of violent crime in Chicago was almost double that of New York City and Los Angeles. Among the nation's ten largest cities, only Philadelphia had higher rates of murder and violent crime than Chicago.[3] What is more, during the 2008–2009 academic year, a record number of public school students (38) were murdered. The enormity of these numbers naturally focuses our attention on murder and death. Such a focus, however, limits our understanding of urban violence. Unacknowledged in these disheartening statistics is a more complex reality: most victims of gun violence do not die. While the most common cause of violence in urban areas is gun violence, a victim of a gunshot wound is four times more likely to end up disabled than killed. Though guns are no doubt deadly, equally important is that gunshot injuries constitute the second most common cause of disability in urban areas overall (only paralysis as a result of car crashes is more common). And for our purposes, we must note that gun violence is the primary cause of disability among Hispanics and blacks; these two populations, in turn, make up the majority of gang members in Chicago.

This chapter is about what injury allows us to see about the diversity among disabled populations. My argument is that, while admirable, the focus on assuaging social difference within the disability rights movement has served to obscure key distinctions within disabled communities along the axes of race and socioeconomic status. While the larger community of disabled activists in Chicago tends to use the social model of disability, in which there are multiple ways to view ability and physical capacities are not devalued, disabled ex-gang members rely on a medical model of disability that highlights physical differences rather than seeking to diminish them. This chapter contends that the reliance on the medical model is one of many demonstrations of the severity of circumstances for these disabled, African-American ex-gang members. The fact that they are willing to insist on the defectiveness of their own body points to the sheer depth of the problems they have to contend with, and the sheer burden that violence creates in communities like Eastwood.

I demonstrate this point, in what follows, by discussing how notions of debt and obligation surface as critical components of gang sociality. When it comes to the familiar sequence (wherein a gang member shoots an affiliate of a rival gang, and in response, members of the rival gang retaliate) death and injury can be thought of as forms of debt exchange. I show that it is precisely because social relations between gang members are so often solidified through violence that expressive communication by a disabled gang member (which transmits knowledge about the streets and about injury) can be strategically deployed to disrupt a cycle of vengeance. Since the audience now owes it to the disabled affiliate who sacrificed his life, to change theirs, wounds become the precondition that enable social transformation.

Race and the Discourse of Disability

Social scientists interested in race and urban America have long pointed out the underbelly of American exceptionalism. The "land of promise" celebrated in the Constitution of the United States, they argue, has a flipside, which is the construction of the "defective" black subject.[4] Whether in the 1890s, when anthropologists measured the skulls of African descendants to show that behaviors and abilities corresponded to different racial groups, or more recently when scholars and government agencies suggested that the socioeconomic plight of urban blacks was associated with degenerate cultural values, notions of the defective body, born in the 19th century, continue to shape the 21st.[5] Given this fraught legacy, it is all the more striking that, as Philippe Bourgois has recently suggested, there remains a sizeable void on urban scholarship that examines the relationship between forms of bodily injury and forms of social injury.[6] Whether considering the community ramifications of mass incarceration, or the daily effects of the "war on drugs," both of which have exploded in the last three decades, it is clear that we must deepen our understanding of the myriad forms that injury can take, and the myriad manifestations that those injuries can have.

The nascent literature on disability can thus serve as a point of intervention—a way to examine the relationship between biology and culture without invoking ideas of innate dysfunction—since scholars in this field have been attentive to bodily injury, yet have also advanced a "social model" of illness.[7] As these scholars have viewed disability as an institutionalized source of oppression, comparable to inequalities based on race, gender, and sexual orientation, they have argued that it is not an individual's actual "impairments" which construct disability as a subordinate social status and devalued life experience but socially imposed barriers (anything from inaccessible buildings, to limited modes of transportation and communication, to prejudicial attitudes).[8] This "social model," not surprisingly, is a radical step away from the medical model of illness, which has dominated Western thinking since the early 1900s, and which views disabilities and diseases as physical conditions that reduce a person's quality of life, and thus pose clear disadvantages to that person. In this way, the medical model echoes the 19th century notion of the black defective body. It is important to point out that advocates of disability rights have long rejected the medical model of disability, and instead emphasize a rights-based model that "emphasizes people's personal adjustment to impairment and their adaptation to a medical-rehabilitative regimen of treatment."[9]

The medical model is often presumed to silence a disabled person's voice. In *The Wounded Storyteller*, for example, Arthur Frank discusses how medical culture is often experienced as foreign to those who are ill or injured. This is because in our hospitals doctors reinterpret personal feelings of suffering into symptoms. Medical treatment facilities use technical language that is "unfamiliar and overwhelming," language that seems to come from somewhere else. Frank describes how the disabled patient tends to "surrender" his narrative to medical authority. To make his case, he quotes Dan Gottlieb, a quadriplegic turned self-help author who was paralyzed in an automobile accident: "When we're admitted to a hospital or even visiting a doctor the forms ask for 'Patient name.' We stop being people and start being patients . . . our identity as people and the world we once knew both are relinquished; we become their patients and we live in their hospital."

This quote points to the fact that a core expectation of being disabled is surrendering oneself to the care of a physician. The act of telling one's own story is therefore an act of empowerment. In *Crip Theory*, Robert McRuer brilliantly demonstrates how, by turning a story of suffering into testimony, disabled activists who "come out crip," endow the pejorative slur "crippled" with a positive valence. In a similar vein, for Frank, the wounded storyteller's disavowal of medical experience is the basis by which he voices her own experience of suffering. The notion that a person should embrace his own wounded body as an act of empowerment has been greatly influenced by the Americans with Disabilities Act of 1990. The Act makes discrimination based on disability illegal, but just as importantly, it has made acceptable the idea that people with disabilities face systemic societal barriers that impact their worldview and the ways in which they navigate their social environment.

Though the ADA has made great strides in providing resources for disabled people, one unintended consequence has been that in the process of leveling the playing field, both scholars of bodily impairment and the public have glossed over the ways race operates within disabled communities.[10] That is, in striving to attenuate biases for people with different physical and mental capacities, disability scholars have been less concerned with how and why particular populations, in particular areas, acquire particular kinds of impairments.[11] My time in Eastwood reveals the perils of such an omission. Justin's wheelchair-bound life, and the way he uses his disability, as we'll see, would be nearly unrecognizable—not to mention incomprehensible— to, for example, a well-off, white, middle-aged, suburban polio survivor.

In this chapter, I aim to pinpoint how disabled populations have always had to highlight their differences in order to advocate for themselves, typically in ways that are politically strategic and reflective of their marginalized status. I ask: how, within a model of disability rights, do we account for the fact that, depending on the way a disability was acquired, what caused it, and the factors that might stop others from becoming similarly hurt, disabled people may choose to define themselves in terms of their defectiveness? To answer this question I want to turn to a piece of legislation that preceded the Americans with Disabilities Act.

In 1973 Congress passed the Federal Vocational Rehabilitation Act, a statute that "prohibited discrimination of otherwise handicapped persons who are able to perform the duties required by their employment." While this legislation can be said to reify a devalued notion of disability (through its invocation of the "handicapped person"), it has also been significant for groups seeking redress for discrimination. In the Supreme Court's 1987 decision concerning Nassau County v Arline, for example, AIDS was protected as a "handicap" under law: This disease should be protected, the Justices of the Supreme Court argued, "not only because of the physical limitations it imposes, but because the prejudice surrounding AIDS exacts a social death, which precedes the actual physical one." While equating disability to death has rightly been criticized by forbears of the disability rights movement, such as the League of the Physically Handicapped and the National Federation of the Blind, I want to complicate contemporary notions of "impairment" by describing some of the contexts in which it becomes politically strategic to inhabit the role of a defective person (that is, to adopt the language of "social death") in order to illuminate the sheer burden of the injustices with which some people have to contend. Similarly to how refugees have deployed the language of trauma to gain political asylum, examining the ends to which narratives about disability are used in a gang-saturated neighborhood points out the ways that a discourse about disability rights is not always about empowerment, and the disabled person's aim not always to disavow or expand what it means to be "normal."[12]

The success of the disability rights movement has created the impression that the medical model is harmful, an outmoded relic of a discriminatory past, but the efforts of these disabled ex-gang members suggest that perhaps the disability rights movement has eschewed the medical model all too soon. Although these ex-gang members in Chicago face criticism from the wider disability rights community for highlighting variations in social difference (between "the normals" and the stigmatized, the paralyzed and the able-bodied) they feel that they must do so— since, as they put it, their wounds enable them to save lives. Though I focus this chapter on the anti-gang forums hosted by disabled ex-gang members, rather than their positionality within the larger disability rights movement, both these forums, and the tenuous subject position of the people who run them, highlight the ways in which disabled communities are stratified along the lines of race, masculinity, and socioeconomic status.[13] It is the interplay of these culturally constructed identities that maps the contours of oppression that African-Americans face, allowing us to see the extent to which violence becomes both a gang and community-defining feature.[14]

BOX 16.1

Attitudes toward disability can produce violence in many communities. Read more here:

www.autistichoya.com/2016/07/ableism-is-not-bad-words-its-violence.html

Gang Geographies of Commerce

Days after Justin and I met with Kemo, I see him again. Only this time, instead of a garage, he is holding court in an abandoned lot. A group of eight teenage boys sit on the rubbled, glass-strewn ground at his feet. The leader of the local gang set waves his arms, punctures his words with stares. As he scolds the small group for failing to police their neighborhood, Kemo looks like an urban griot.

"You know what? Y'all lack discipline," he says. "That's why you got the Bandits comin' in here shooting up the place." Kemo is referring to a rival gang set, whose members recently infiltrated his territory, injuring two people. Pete, an affiliate who was shot in the leg during that incident, sits next to Kemo. The cane he will use for the rest of his life lies between them. After Kemo praises Pete for his bravery, and announces to the group that he is one of the few among them who has "what it takes" to be a gang leader, he reaches for Pete's curved-handle cane and drags the rubber tip through the dirt, sketching the boundaries of their block. Xs mark the places he predicts rival gangs will attempt to invade. Then he draws a series of arrows that surround the Xs. These are the routes gang members should travel to safeguard their domain.

"Y'all gotta protect your turf," Kemo barks: "That's the most important thing."

Kemo's depiction of his commercial strategy literally relies on a marker of disability—the cane. In other words, the cane is the tool Kemo uses to explain to his foot soldiers how they are going to maintain economic control; the cane is simultaneously a reminder of the consequences of that task.

In her article, "The Prosthetic Imagination," Sarah Jain demonstrates how the mutual constitution between wounding and enabling is a productive way to understand the concept of injury.[15] Though she is specifically preoccupied with understanding the ideas that inform how futuristic fantasies associated with prostheses simultaneously wound and enable, her analysis is useful in thinking about where and how disability is located in a gang. Contemplating what it means to be wounded —and conversely enabled—by a gang allows us to examine both the relationships that are formed through the trade in injury and the discourse on disability that gang members produce.

Since the 1920s, the term "gang" has been used to describe all kinds of collectives, from groups of well-dressed mobsters to petty criminals and juvenile delinquents —everything from substitute family units to religious groups and entrepreneurial drug-dealing cartels.[16] Perhaps the only thing that has remained consistent about gangs in nearly a century of research is their characterization as an internal Other from the vantage point of the law—a group that lives amongst us but does not abide by our "normal" rules.[17] But rather than focus on the processes which regiment a group's juridical status, I want to look at how the gang itself is cultivated out of the uneasy dialectic between wounding and enabling.[18]

As we saw through Kemo's inscription in the dirt, the interplay between wounding and enabling surfaces in the ways in which gang cultures have been said to emerge out of the rationalities and strategies of protecting "turf"—i.e. territory, property, access—as a means to accrue good standing in a society in which people are frequently excluded from participation in the American polity.[19] On the face of it, the violent event associated with injury allows the disabled gang member to rise in social stature and moral standing, similar to the war veteran in contemporary American society. And like the war veteran in contemporary society, the rhetorical effect of this patriotism stands in sharp relief to reality. Unlike the gang member who has been labeled as a police informant (or "snitch"), disabled gang members in Eastwood are not given a "dishonorable discharge"—rather, they are released from service. An "honorable discharge" would be the appropriate analogy here. Of course, some disabled gang members will prefer to resume their activities, and in such cases, they are not so much willfully ignored as forgotten about, marginalized, or neglected. Hence, in contrast to members who die in gang wars and become martyrs—those bygone affiliates often emblematized on graffiti'd R.I.P. t-shirts—the disabled gang member, who cannot contribute to the organization in the way that is most valued (that is, as a street-corner drug dealer), becomes like the presumably honored war veteran who begs for change by day, and is tucked beneath a highway underpass by night.

As disability can signal honor and ignominy at the same time, in this chapter, wounding as it pertains to disabled bodies should be read as a commentary on enabling—whether this is the enabling of gang entrepreneurship and the forms of violence associated with it or, as we will see, the enabling of initiatives to stop violence. Likewise, enabling should be read as a commentary on wounding—whether this is the injury that stems from the drug trade, or the criminalization of black urbanites, which make them prone to debilitation. Hence, if this analysis of wounding is to be read with a negative moral valence, it is not because the notion of disability itself should be devalued. Rather, in this chapter, the disabled subject signals the ways in which the intersection of race and socioeconomics funnels risk of morbidity, unemployment, incarceration, and mortality rates toward young urban residents in Chicago, who are far more likely than most of those who will read this chapter to fall victim to a stray bullet in the midst of drug-related gang warfare.

In My Shoes

In the aftermath of 2009's record number of shootings of public school students, community forums on violence became commonplace in Eastwood, the west side neighborhood where I lived while conducting my research. These forums were typically sponsored by nonprofit organizations, schools, or churches and coordinated by adults who—though well intentioned by all accounts—had only a tangential relationship to the troubled youths they were targeting. Even though the rate of incarceration for women in Chicago was on the rise, in most cases, that prototypical problem child was a young black male.

Justin had attended many such forums over the past year, but had not seen many young men at any of them, so he worried about their efficacy: "I don't know man," he says to me one day, as we put away basketballs in the after-school program where he works and I volunteer, "It's like they're preaching to the choir. The guys who really need to be there, them boys who really need to hear those stories, they're out on the street."

Justin, however, has a solution: sessions offered by a very different group of men, forums which differed from the approaches of what he refers to as the "out-of-touch" gang-prevention programs. And, even though Justin himself does not organize these forums, he identifies with the people who do. The men whom Justin is speaking of are in their early to mid-twenties—young enough to relate. Many of them still communicate with members of the Divine Knights, so they do not underestimate the gang's influence in the lives of young people. Plus, their very presence makes the consequences of gang life salient for everyone who attends their events—these men are all in wheelchairs. This group of paralyzed ex-gang members first met at Eastwood Hospital. Across the last five years, they participated in a rehabilitation program that teaches people suffering from spinal cord injuries how to adapt to their new lives. After finishing the program, a few of these men petitioned the hospital to sponsor the next step in their work: with the "In My Shoes" program, these former gang affiliates—themselves the victims of gun violence—travel to schools to discuss what it feels like to have your life permanently altered by a disability.

One day I accompany Justin to Jackson High, where the school administrators decide to dedicate the bulk of the day to violence prevention programming. To hone in on what they perceive to be the different needs of their male and female students, they separate the sessions by gender: while later in the day the girls will hear from a group of women on leave from an Illinois Correctional facility, the high school boys hear from Justin's group of disabled, ex-gang members.

I watch with the boisterous crowd as four ex-affiliates form a semi-circle on the stage of the school's auditorium. Before them sit 250 students, who shuffle and fidget in creaky wooden seats. The backs of the seats are scarred all over with hastily carved gang signs.

"Welcome to the 'In My Shoes' program," the leader of the group, Darius, starts.

"What we are is a violence prevention program. We're a little different from other programs. Like, we're not here to scare you or anything like that. We're basically here to educate you about the consequences of drug activities and gang life. As you can see, all of us here have wheelchairs," he continues. "And the reason we have wheelchairs is because we were out in the streets gang banging, selling drugs. We got shot, and ultimately we got paralyzed. So what we're gonna do today is tell you what happens to your body when you have a spinal cord injury."

The "In My Shoes" speakers have two primary goals in a situation like this. First, they try to counteract the foundational belief that perpetuating violence unifies the gang. Next, they argue that when the gang is no longer around, gunshot victims have to care for themselves.

"There's two types of spinal cord injuries," Darius begins, "there's a paraplegic and a quadriplegic. Par- meaning two: it means two of your limbs are affected. I'm a paraplegic. I'm paralyzed from the waist down. A quadriplegic is paralyzed from the neck down."

"See, the thing about the spine," he adds, "is that it's one of the few parts of your body that doesn't heal for itself. You know how if you break your arm or you get a cut, your body naturally heals itself, right? Well, when you have a spinal cord injury or a brain injury, that's permanent because there ain't no medicine or no doctor in the world that can fix that."

With a few sentences, Darius establishes his authority through medical expertise. The teenagers in the audience still fidget, hesitant to look directly at the injured bodies on stage. Then he tells the crowd how much his life has changed since he has become paralyzed.

"Aside from your movement, one of the first things that gets affected is your bladder. Y'all know when you gotta use the washroom, you get that feeling, right? Well when you're in a situation like ours, you no longer get that sensation. So what happens is that you gotta be on the clock. You know every four-to-six hours, you have to manually extract the urine. And that's done with one of these. This right here is a catheter."

He holds up a cloudy plastic bag, which is met with a collective groan from the crowd. Then he places his thumb and index finger a couple of inches apart: "For males it'll probably go about tha-a-a-t deep inside the pee hole before it starts draining."

The group of adolescents erupt in a deafening chorus of gags and grimaces—this, at the mere thought of using a device in service of something which seems so natural.

"And this gotta be done every four-to-six hours for the rest of your life. Cause what can happen is, either you're gonna pee all over yourself . . . and you can imagine you're on the corner chillin' and all of a sudden: You're wet."

More groans. Now laughter. Nervous, embarrassed laughter. I worry that the kids in the audience are actually making fun of Darius. Some boys point at the catheter. But Darius waits out the snickers; he smiles with the kids, willing to indulge their nervousness, willing to play the role of the hapless, disabled person.

"Or it can stay in your system," Darius continues as the tittering from the crowd dies down. "And, basically, urine is just waste. So if it stays in your system, you can get sick, catch infections from it, and ultimately be hospitalized. What I'ma do is pass this around so you can check it out. It ain't never been used or nothing like that."

The crowd laughs in relief.

After Darius describes how the most prominent biological feature of manhood is transformed from the penetrator to that which is penetrated, another activist, Aaron, begins to speak.

"One of the most important things that you have to look out for is the health of your skin, cause it can also get infected. Y'all know when you've been sitting down for a long time, how your butt starts to hurt and you get a little uncomfortable. You know, you gotta fidget a little bit. Well in a situation like ours, we can't feel our butts. So what we have to do is, we have to be constantly lifting off our chairs, doing 'pressure reliefs.' So you'll see me every once and a while do this—" he grabs the armrests of his chair and lifts his body above it, holding himself in an inverted push-up.

"'Cause what could happen is, I can develop a 'pressure sore'—also known as a 'bedsore,' or a 'ubiquitous ulcer.' That's when the bone starts digging through the skin. It starts off as a little pimple; but this is one pimple you don't wanna pop, 'cause you could make it worse.

"The thing about these pressure sores is that I can get one in a matter of hours. If I was to sit down in one of those chairs for two or three hours," Darius says, gesturing toward the wooden seats in the crowd, "I could develop a pressure sore."

"The problem is gettin' rid of one," Aaron intervenes. "To get rid of one could take anywhere from two months to a year. And the only way to heal it is to stay off it. Bed rest. So you can imagine if it's the summer. Summer just kicked off, and I got a pressure sore—now I gotta stay in bed to heal it."

"And what a lot of people don't know," Oscar says, taking the reins, "is that Christopher Reeves, you know the actor that played Superman; he actually passed away from one of these. He caught a pressure sore, it got infected, and it got into his blood. And you know how blood is constantly traveling through your body? Well, it hit his heart, and he had a heart attack. What I try to tell people is that this is Christopher Reeves: this is Superman. He had Superman money. And he couldn't prevent one of these? What's gonna happen to one of us from the 'hood? We don't got that kind of money. We don't have that kind of around-the-clock care."

Here, Oscar's reference to Superman does not merely underscore the gulf in access to medical resources between a world-renowned actor and a poor person of color. He highlights another register of wounding: the fact that no one is actually fast enough to dodge a speeding bullet. Even Superman can die from a pimple.

The "In My Shoes" presentation at Jackson High resonates with Arthur and Joan Kleinman's insights about the stakes of telling stories through wounded bodies.[20] They argue that illness stories transcend the bodies of the ill. It is not merely that culture "infolds" into the body through differing ways to define disease, or varying access to, and attitudes toward, health care. Our bodily processes also "outfold" into social space, giving shape and meaning to the society in which we live. Borrowing from the Kleinmans, I want to suggest that the stories of these disabled, ex-gang members are not just about the interpersonal affects of disability. These stories outfold as well, inviting "at risk" teenage, black males to recognize themselves in them.[21] By speaking about what it is like to be disabled former gang members signal the mutual constitution between wounding and enabling as a means to respond to the gang's far-reaching influence in Eastwood.

In contrast to Frank's notion of "narrative surrender" to medical authority, the men at Jackson High show no anger or resentment toward the medical establishment. To the contrary, disabled ex-gang members build their narratives out of the medical model of disability, in order to emphasize the biological reality of their now "broken" body. They do so to amplify the magnitude of urban violence. For members of racial groups who are prone to debilitation through gun violence, highlighting one's body as broken is a political act. Again, the comparison with refugees is appropriate here— though the political ends are different, the means are similar.[22] The members of "In My Shoes," like Justin and every other disabled ex-gang member I have met, speak about the best ways to craft their stories; they borrow narrative techniques from each other; they rehearse, constantly. They learn by hearing themselves tell their own stories, absorbing each others' reactions, and experiencing their stories being shared.[23] On this day, for example, one of the disabled ex-gang members, Sam, did not speak at all. He listened and watched, still honing his own illness narrative in preparation for the next school assembly when, perhaps, he will feel ready to testify. In this way, the "In My Shoes" speakers draw on presuppositions of illness that enable collectively salient descriptions of disability. Crafting their paralysis as undesirable and preventable is crucial since it helps excavate an altered vision of a world, already radically transformed by violence. Disabled ex-gang members hope that by seeing the world through their eyes—the eyes of the injured—these inner city students will come to see the effects of violence more clearly.

Injurious Debts and Enabling Obligations

A couple of days after the assembly I run into Marcus, a neighbor whom I haven't seen on the block in a while. He is a senior at Jackson High; I ask him what he thought about "In My Shoes."

Marcus invites me into his house; his mother is cooking dinner and asks if I want to stay. Marcus and I sit at the dining room table while she prepares food in the adjoining kitchen. He tells me about how the assembly has altered his perspective on gang life.

"Yeah," Marcus begins, "it was real deep to hear them speak, 'cause my mom kept telling me that my associations will lead me to one day, God forbid, be in the same predicament. And my heart was beating like 100 miles an hour, 'cause I could just see myself in the position they're in.

"Most of the people I hang out with are gang bangers," he explains. "And I was the type that always wanted to do right, but did wrong. I didn't want my brothers and them fighting, but I was right there in front—fighting everybody. But it's kinda like . . . over here . . . in this area . . . in the school I go to . . . thinking about tomorrow is the last thing you wanna do. Cause you wanna live through today."

Marcus's statement is meant to set the backdrop for life in Eastwood, where gangs are commonly imagined as stand-in family units, where even a teenager who opts not to join the Divine Knights will be cognizant of who belongs to which set, and the jurisdictions of each, where young people are well aware that although most of the gang sets in their neighborhood fall under the Divine Knights umbrella, two factions can inspire violence at any given moment, becoming de facto rivals.[24] It is for this reason, at least in part, that a gang's legacy is heightened even as the immediacy of "tomorrow" is diminished.

"You know how it is," Marcus says. "We got all the rival gangs. I actually got pulled outta my last high school 'cause me and my friends got into it with some Bandits. My momma feared for my life. And I noticed when she took me out of school that most of the fights I was getting into wasn't because of me, or something I did. It was because of my friends. That's why when the paralyzed speakers came to my new school, it was kinda like a privilege because before I didn't think it was real.

"But two of my friends just died over the past three weeks now," he continues. "And one of my cousin's friends, he died also. I know you heard about the fifteen-year-old boy that was found in the dumpster. That was him."

Marcus takes a sip from a glass of water and looks out of the window. I think about what he has just told me. The notion that he does not start most of the fights in which he is engaged could be read as a convenient excuse (especially with his mother within earshot). But even so, the stakes of the peer pressure that he describes are painfully high in a context in which teenagers are regularly murdered and debilitated. Trade in injury is so common that even a hospital bed doesn't necessarily occasion a person to orient his life away from the gang. It may simply lead him to seek revenge.

"I got jumped on a while back. I got put in the hospital—in the trauma center. She'll tell you," Marcus says, gesturing toward his mother. "When my momma came in there I was talking to the doctor like: 'So, umm . . . What's up? What's your son's name? Can I play video games?' I was having fun—not knowing that something could've seriously been wrong with me. When my friends came I was jumping on the bed like, 'Yeah, man, they ain't do nothing to me! They ain't do nothing to me!'

"I wanted revenge. I didn't think nothing really bad could happen. I even put the hospital band—the one that was on my arm—I put it around my neck and I wore it as a chain, like a trophy. My momma said that scared her. She told me that I could be dead, 'cause I blacked out for a second while I was fighting. In the meantime, I ain't really know what was happening.

"After I got out of the hospital, the next day, my friends came to my house. They were like, 'Man, what up? What you gonna do?'

"Inside my head I'm like, 'Do I really want to go with them, or do I wanna listen to my momma?'"

For the next several minutes, Marcus describes arguing with his friends about his decision not to retaliate, and their response that he would look "weak" if he didn't. It wasn't just his reputation that was on the line, they argued, but that of the whole set. Still, Marcus insists that he remained adamant about resisting the temptation to strike back.

"The point is," Marcus says, "instead of listening to my friends, I listened to what my momma said. And they were looking at me like, 'Dang man, what's wrong with you? Why you actin' like this?'"

He pauses, takes another sip of water. His mother has stopped preparing dinner; I can't tell if she is paying attention.

"So I know how hard it is to get up on stage and do what they did. I saw one of the speakers, Darius, the other day and I told him. I said, 'I take my hat off to y'all. For y'all to come to my school and have the courage to say that in front of everybody, that means a lot. So I thank y'all, man, for real.'"

Marcus's insights allude to the fact that in Eastwood the obligation to seek vengeance is frequently anticipated, and its fulfillment relentlessly planned. Here, vengeance is an enduring ritual of exchange. Still, it is critical to note that in a context in which the Divine Knights cultivate feuds over territory and economic control, violence does not merely wound. More importantly, as we will see, it can enable. The fact that my conversation with Marcus takes place in his mother's house highlights the similarities between their familial bond and a kind of gang sociality in which members habitually express social obligations in an idiom of kinship. Here, the dichotomy between the Divine Knights' imagined community and physical debility does not merely surface through wounds, or the bodily pain that Marcus endures on behalf of his gang. It is also evidenced through the invocation of his mother who, he says, steers him away from gang affiliation.[25] But despite Marcus's discussion of his choice to stay in the house rather than enact revenge in the streets (to listen to "what my momma said"), one should not read my conversation with this teenage gang member as a story of redemption, primarily.

I mention this discussion, first and foremost, because it recalls the ways in which debts carry with them wounds that can either enable—or disable—the solidification of social bonds. This point is evidenced by the shock Marcus's friends experience upon hearing that he will forgo his opportunity for vengeance. In the days after Marcus's beating, as he chooses to listen to his mother, a curious thing happens. He leaves school and comes home. He doesn't dawdle on the corner. He stays inside. His friends stop talking to him. He gets dirty looks. At one point the leader of his local set even visits him at home, and says he has turned his back on his friends and his community. In other words, he is viewed by other affiliates as abandoning the gang. The crucial point here is that in refusing to retaliate, by being willing to look "weak," by extracting himself from social activities outside of his home, Marcus forgoes the opportunity to cultivate bonds with his brethren; and it is primarily because he withdraws from a system in which injury is often proposed as a means for debt settlement, that he is viewed as a deserter.

Cashing In

Intimately felt obligations have an immeasurable impact on the ways in which a teenager like Marcus navigates his social world. But this sense of indebtedness does not always have to wound. It is because Justin knows intuitively that the most significant aspect of gang rivalry is its ability to maintain relationships between affiliates, that he brings a gang leader to the negotiating table to talk about the crippling violence that the gang set he commands has become known for. By re-channeling gang notions of reciprocity—and in the process allowing his wounds to enable peace, rather than violence—Justin frames his community forum as a harmonious way to settle debts between gang members.

In the winter of 2008, Justin decides that he wants the "In My Shoes" program to sponsor a community forum on violence. Even though he is not one of the speakers, he appreciates their approach. But, when he brings his proposal to the administrators at Eastwood Hospital, they decline. The institution is "low on funds," they tell him. In fact, the "In My Shoes" program now has to institute a $250 fee for public appearances. Dismayed by the constraints, Justin decides to organize an independent forum. He gets tips from Darius and Aaron about how to craft his message, while looking for other sources of sponsorship. As he seeks financial support, one of the first people to contact him is Kemo, on behalf of the Divine Knights. He pledges to donate funds for the purchase of food and promises to make the event a mandatory meeting for his constituency.

Even though I know Justin and Kemo's relationship dates back 17 years, when the two of them were budding gang bangers, I am initially taken aback when I hear that Kemo, a gang leader, is contributing to the forum that will talk about the hazards of gang life.

One day I ask about the gang leader's motivation: "So, Kemo is actually telling his crew to go to the forum?" I question. "How did you convince him to do that?"

"I mean, Kemo don't want the killings either," Justin replies. "You gotta remember: some of those boys are his cousins, and the little brothers of people we grew up with. Besides Kemo owes me and now I'm cashin' in."

On the brisk Saturday morning of May 10, 2009—three days after the 36th killing of a Chicago public school student—Kemo delivers. He personally drops off an SUV full of young gang members at the House of Worship for Justin's violence forum. Kemo and some of the leaders from the other neighborhood gang sets linger outside of the church while the members of their respective constituencies file in. They are prepared to quell any tensions that may arise, Justin tells me. But the disabled, ex-gang member does not merely solicit help from gang leaders; a number of probation officers and high school counselors pitch in as well. As a result of this collective effort, affiliates from a number of gang sets that compose part of the Divine Knight diaspora are in attendance. Kemo's boys, like the other affiliates, travel in a pack. The gang leader has demanded that his whole set all see Justin, so some 15 teenage boys shuffle from the parking lot to the church library where he is due to give his speech. The large oval table that is usually at the center of the room has been pushed aside for this event. The teenagers are seated in cushioned armchairs that have been brought in to accommodate upwards of 40 gang members. With many of the young gang members from Eastwood in attendance, the setting reminds me of the spirited summer nights when respected elders gather to recount gang lore. Only, instead of a notorious Divine Knight standing on the corner, Justin is seated in his wheelchair. He quickly grabs the crowd's attention by describing how he got "plugged" into the gang.

"I was raised right here in Eastwood," Justin begins after introducing himself. "And just like today, there was a lot of violence when I was growing up. It was real bad over here.

"You know, Eastwood is not that big of a community," he continues, "but when I was coming up, there was a lot of different gang sets; and they were all at war. To make matters worse, there was only one high school in the entire area. So everybody within those gang boundaries had to attend that high school. Being that the school was within a particular gang's territory, it was pretty rough. I remember in the ninth grade—before I was even in the gang—I would get frustrated because I had to cross rival territories to get to school. I was getting chased, beat up, and robbed constantly. Sometimes the people from my block would stick up for me . . . What would happen was, members of the rival gangs would see me with the boys from my block and would assume I was in the same gang. So now they started treating me like opposition. It got to the point where I was already marked as a gang member, so I just decided to join the gang."

After speaking about how gang ties are solidified through rivalry—whether accurate or not—Justin describes the ways that the devotion generated within his newfound fraternity became naturalized:

"I joined up, and I never really thought twice about it. It seemed like I was where I should be because a lot of my friends, my cousins, and my uncles—even my grandfather—they were all involved in the gang. So it wasn't nothing new to me. But after a while I started going to school less and less, and I was surrounded by violence more and more. I saw close family members and good friends die. I thought, 'If my friends and my family, they all died for the gang, then why not me? What makes me better than them?' I started telling myself, 'Man, I'm willing to die for this.'

"At the time, I needed that mentality because I started dealing drugs. My two closest friends were becoming gang leaders and big-time drug dealers. They were the ones giving the product to everyone in my neighborhood. One day, there was a meeting with the high-ranking gang officials and the guy who was supplying both of them said that they would have to consolidate their gang sets. He said they could play Rock, Paper, Scissors, for all he cared, but someone had to step up, and someone had to fall back. It had to be done, he said. So my two boys decided to set up a meeting.

"It was January 3, 2000," Justin continues after taking a deep breath, "That day, the friend who I worked for picked me up and told me what they decided. They were gonna do it like the old-timers: meet and fight, one-on-one. Whoever won the fight would get the neighborhood drug market. The other person would be the right-hand man, and make his crew fall in line. They would even shake hands afterwards.

"They decided to fight in an abandoned lot. No one was there when we arrived, so me and my boy got out and waited for my other friend to show.

"After a couple minutes, a car came down the street. I made eye contact with the driver, but didn't recognize him. The car kept going. When it reached the dead end, it circled back around. It was creeping up slowly, so my boy said 'Let's get outta here.' But by the time we got back inside, the car was right beside us. I looked up and the person in the passenger seat had pulled out a pistol.

"Tink . . . Tink . . . t-t-tink. Tink. Tink. That's all I heard. I saw flashes. My boy said, 'Pull off. Pull off,' so I started driving. But I was already hit, so I lost control of the vehicle. Eventually, I crashed. That's when I noticed that I was bleeding from my shoulder and my thigh. I started screaming: 'I got shot. I got shot.' Next thing you know, I hear the car door slam shut. Just then I realized: one of my friends had left me, and my other friend wanted me dead."

Justin's voice is shaky. His elbow is on the armrest of his wheelchair and he covers his mouth with his hand, concealing an expression that I can only presume portrays disappointment. Now even the kids who were pretending as if they could care less about what he had to say, seem riveted. They wait patiently every time Justin pauses to compose himself.

During this brief lull, I recall how weeks ago he told me that Kemo "owes" him because they were together when he was shot. It hadn't registered before now: Kemo had been in the car with Justin. His words now resonate with what I already knew about his shooting. Another affiliate, Eric, once told me that Kemo wanted badly to retaliate against the person who shot Justin, but he forbade it. As Justin had made a commitment to God to turn his life around on what he thought was his deathbed, the most he allowed Kemo to do was to confront the perpetrator, tell him to leave the neighborhood, and warn him to never come back. Because Kemo hoped that one day Justin would change his mind and permit revenge, the gang never informed the police about the shooter. The assailant escaped without sanction. As I reflect on these circumstances, Kemo's commitment to the forum makes all the more sense— as does Justin's willingness, to accept his help.

"I just got out of the car and started running," Justin continues. "I cut through an alleyway and stopped at the first house I saw. I knocked on the door. Then I knocked harder.

"All of a sudden the porch lit up. I got excited at first, but then I realized that the light wasn't coming from inside of the house. Headlights were beaming on the door from behind me. The car from before was approaching fast.

"Someone got out and started running towards me with a gun so I hopped over the porch railing. I almost reached the back of the house when I heard a shot go off—BANG.

"I just remember falling to the ground. I wasn't in pain or anything like that. I was in shock. All I knew is that my legs wouldn't work. I was trying and trying, but I couldn't move my legs. I couldn't get up. I just couldn't. I laid my head on the grass, and that's when I heard footsteps running away and a car screeching off.

"I started yelling: 'Help. Help.' I was screaming my boys' names. 'Help.' One-by-one, I screamed my cousins' names and all the people that I was willing to die for: 'Help.'

"Then all of sudden I saw this lady look out her window. I sat up and called out to her, the best I could. I said, 'I've been shot. I've been shot. Please, ma'am, help me. I've been shot.'

"While I was waiting to see if she would come out I tried to get up. I grabbed the storm drain and lifted my upper body. I remember looking at my legs and they were dangling. They were dead. When I saw that, I fell back down.

"The lady came out with a cell phone and called the ambulance. If it wasn't for her, who knows if I'd be here today. She waited with me and tried to comfort me: 'Everything's gonna be alright,' she said. 'Don't worry, everything's gonna be alright.'

"As she's telling me this, I see her eyes watering. Tears are coming down her face. And I just remember thinking, like, 'man, I don't wanna die.' I remember thinking that in my head. All my life I told myself that, I'm willing to die for this. I was willing to get shot. I didn't care. But, when I was lying there. I was scared to die. I didn't want to die. I don't know why, but I didn't want to die."

Justin ends his story with a somber description of the day the doctor informs him that he will "never walk again." As he begins to recount his early days in a wheelchair, what strikes me most is how Justin felt abandoned. The pain of Kemo running from their car, and his recitation of the names of his gang brethren while lying in the woman's yard, seem to eclipse even the pain of the bullets lodged in his body. What's more, the injury of abandonment is correlated with the event that debilitated him, the details of which are practiced, memorized, and packaged into a script that is deployed as a message for gang-affiliated youth. In this way, the trope of wounding is meant to complicate the ideas common among gang affiliates about what membership enables. As opposed to the prestige associated with fleeing from cops or escaping a gun blast, Justin's speech opens up a space to talk about the pressures of gang membership. After Justin speaks, I think about how the sense of abandonment elicited through his testimony relates to the plight of other gang members—people like Marcus who attempt to extract themselves from the cycle of gang vengeance and are ridiculed as a result. Marcus is in the crowd today. Observing him and the others, as Justin rolls his chair through the aisles, talking to the boys, I see that many of the young gang members are unable to look Justin in the face anymore. Perhaps it is out of fear that they might become emotional, like some of the teenagers in the room have already; instead of looking him in the eyes, Kemo's boys stare, stoically, at the spokes of Justin's wheelchair.

Today, Justin's inability to feel—the physical and psychological wounds of paralysis—enables him to elicit rare shades of empathy and sorrow from otherwise unshakeable young gang members. Days prior to the event, I overheard Kemo telling young affiliates of how Justin sacrificed his body so that he could flee in a gun battle. It is for this reason that Justin should be respected, the gang leader said. Watching them now, I hope they understand: not only did Justin sacrifice himself. But after doing so, he forgave the debt that was owed to him and transformed it into a communal project to stop the killings. This sacrifice, Justin hopes, will help youngsters like Marcus break free from the obligations that gang life is built upon.

Wounds That Enable

While traveling to local high schools and talking to "at risk" youth, disabled ex-gang members are willing to insist on the defectiveness of their bodies in order to highlight the burden that violence creates in communities like Eastwood. Their methods contrast sharply with the aims of the disability rights movement, in which constructing physical difference as an inferior identity is routinely and unequivocally criticized. This incongruity suggests that paralyzed ex-gang members and the larger world of disabled activists are not fully visible to each other. The disconnection also points to the fact that the disability rights movement and the field of disability studies have generally been silent about the ways in which race and socioeconomic status intersect. The success of the disability rights movement has created the impression that the medical model of disability breeds pity. My examination, however, reveals another more complex possibility. The sympathy, disgust, fear, and perhaps even the relief at being able-bodied, are all indicative of disabled, ex-gang members' approach to anti-violence. They essentially disempower themselves in order to empower others. Their efforts show that a medical model of disability does not always muffle the voices of the injured, but can demonstrate the scale of the social problems that African-Americans growing up in violent neighborhoods face.

Justin and Kemo, the organizers of the forum, attempt to address gang violence by establishing meaningful bonds between members, a bond that mirrors the sense of debt and obligation intrinsic to their own lifelong friendship. In this regard, it is critical to acknowledge that—even within the violence forum itself—the trans-formation that a young affiliate would ideally achieve takes place over and through a disabled gang member's body. Young gang members from rival gang sets are supposed to use Justin's life story as a conduit through which to become more peaceful. Debilitated gang members' stories of catheters and enemas, pressure sores and bed rest, stories of their mothers warning them about their associations, illuminate an invisible aspect of gang sociality: disability is a distinct, though often frequently invisible, reality.

By discussing the wheelchair, in other words, this chapter makes clear that on the west side of Chicago, the figure of the disabled gang member emerges as a prominent form of life—one that emblematizes the kinds of practices, aesthetics, and dynamics of belonging associated with living in a poor community and coming of age under a persistent cloud of violence. It follows that, by focusing on injury—and the often-ignored notions of race and class it signals—forums like the ones in Eastwood reveal aspects of violence that are scarcely mentioned in ethnographic studies of street gangs. Contemporary gang scholarship fails to acknowledge that victims of gun violence in Chicago, and all across the United States, are more frequently disabled than killed.

Unlike many researchers, gang members themselves acknowledge the fact of disability, and even place paralyzed members on a pedestal in gang lore. Disabled ex-gang members like Justin, however, counter the prominent belief that by sacrificing yourself for the gang you'll become a martyr or time-honored veteran. It is critical that their method of exposing this myth is by fixing themselves as inhabitants of imprisoned bodies—as a disabled gang member, Tony, reminded us in yet another Eastwood forum:

"They say when you gang bang . . . when you drug deal, the outcomes are either death or jail. You never hear about the wheelchair. I ain't know this was an option. And if you think about it, it's a little bit of both worlds cause half of my body's dead. Literally. From the waist down, I can't feel it. I can't move it. I can't do nothing with it. The rest of it's confined to this wheelchair. This is my prison for the choices I've made."

This "imprisoned" body, I would add to Tony's statement, should not be dismissed as an outmoded and narrow-minded conception of disability. Rather, Tony is calling attention to his immobility to make the argument that the violence to which his body bears witness can and should be prevented.

Discussion Questions

1. Most disability activists and scholars resist the idea of the disabled body as defective, but Ralph gives us an example in which focusing on a defective body might produce a social benefit. What are the consequences of ex-gang members in Chicago using a "medical model" of disability as a path to justice?

2. Members of "In My Shoes" reason that if younger people see their disabilities, it will turn them away from gang life. How effective can these efforts be in dissuading potential gang members?

3. How do wounds "enable" people with disabilities? Discuss how a sense of obligation can help those with "broken" bodies speak to other members of a community.

4. What did you find surprising or affecting about how these ex-gang members described living with disability?

Notes

1 In accordance with the Internal Review Board protocol for the University of Chicago (my institutional affiliation when this research was conducted) I have changed the names of people (i.e. "Justin and Kemo"), gangs (i.e. "The Divine Knights"), institutions (i.e. "Eastwood Hospital"), and specific neighborhoods (i.e. "Eastwood") throughout this study.

2 The Divine Knight gang is split into segments, referred to by gang members as "sets." There are currently eight gang sets of the Divine Knight gang dispersed throughout Chicago. These subgroups are overwhelmingly male and African-American. Of this membership, crews of four to six members serve as "foot soldiers," responsible for street level dealing in open-air markets. Approximately eight to ten members fulfill other drug-related duties (i.e., runners, muscle, treasurers) (cf. Levitt and Venkatesh 2000). The rest of the affiliates may or may not have an explicit connection to the gang's drug distribution network. For them, the gang is primarily a social group. Levitt, Steven D., and Sudhir Alladi Venkatesh, 2000: "An Economic Analysis of a Drug-Selling Gang's Finances." *Quarterly Journal of Economics* 115 (3): 755–789.

3 These statistics are from the Annual Crime Statistics released by the Federal Bureau of Investigation in May 2010.

4 See Muhammad, Khalil Gibran, 2010: *The Condemnation of Blackness: Race, Crime, and the Making of Modern Urban America.* Cambridge, Mass: Harvard University Press. See also Parenti, Christian, 1999: *Lockdown America: Police and Prisons in the Age of Crisis.* London: Verso.

5 For an early critique of biologically based theories of innate dysfunction, see: Boas, Franz, 1910: *Changes in Bodily Form of Descendants of Immigrants.* Washington, D.C.: United States Immigration Commission. For a prominent example of a "culture of poverty" thesis, see: Moynihan, Daniel Patrick, 1965: *The Negro Family: The Case for National Action.* Washington, D.C.: Office of Policy Planning and Research, U.S. Department of Labor.

6 Bourgois, Philippe, and Jeffrey Schonberg, 2009: *Righteous Dopefiend.* Berkeley: University of California Press.

7 Linton, Simi, 1998: *Claiming Disability: Knowledge and Identity.* New York: New York University Press.

8 Berger, Ronald and Melvin Juette, 2008: *Wheelchair Warrior: Gangs, Disability, and Basketball.* Philadelphia: Temple University Press. See also Siebers, Tobin Anthony, 2008: *Disability Theory.* Ann Arbor: University of Michigan Press.

9 Berger and Juette, 2008: 10.

10 For a similar critique see Garland-Thomson, Rosemarie, 2009: *Staring: How We Look.* New York: Oxford University Press.

11 See McRuer, Robert, 2006: *Crip Theory: Cultural Signs of Queerness and Disability.* New York: New York University Press.

12 Fassin, Didier, 2009: *The Empire of Trauma: An Inquiry into the Condition of Victimhood.* Princeton, N.J.: Princeton University Press.

13 See Jain, Sarah S., 1999: "The Prosthetic Imagination: Enabling and Disabling the Prosthesis Trope." *Science, Technology & Human Values* 24, no. 1 (Winter 1999): 31–54. Here, I borrow from Jain (1999) who similarly views disabled bodies or bodies "dubbed as not fully whole" through these "richly intertwined (and ultimately inseparable) axes of identity." Only instead of socioeconomic status, Jain's focus on prostheses draws her to "another category that considers identity as a correlate to technology" (32).

14 See Crenshaw, Kimberlé, ed., 1995: *Critical Race Theory.* New York: New Press. See also Lorde, Audre, 1984: *Sister Outsider: Essays and Speeches.* Crossing Press Feminist Series. Trumansburg, N.Y.: Crossing Press.

15 Jain 1999.

16 For the gang as mobsters see: Adler, Jeffrey S., 2006: *First in Violence, Deepest in Dirt: Homicide in Chicago, 1875–1920.* Cambridge, Mass: Harvard University Press; Asbury, Herbert, [1940] 2002: *The Gangs of Chicago: An Informal History of the Chicago Underworld.* New York: Thunder Mouth Press. For the gang as petty criminals and juvenile delinquents see: Thrasher, Frederic Milton, 1926 [1963]: *The Gang: A Study of 1,313 Gangs in Chicago.* Abridged ed. Chicago: University of Chicago Press. For the gang as substitute family units see: Decker, Scott H. and Barrik van Winkle, 1996: *Life in the Gang: Family, Friends, and Violence.* 1st ed. New York: Cambridge University Press. For the gang as religious groups see: Brotherton, David, 2004: *The Almighty Latin King and Queen Nation: Street Politics and the Transformation of a New York City Gang.* New York: Columbia University Press. For the gang as entrepreneurial drug-dealing cartels see: Venkatesh, Sudhir Alladi, 2006: *Off the Books: The Underground Economy of the Urban Poor.* Cambridge, Mass: Harvard University Press.

17 Thrasher 1926, Venkatesh 2006.

18 Jain 1999. See also Jain, Sarah S. Lochlann, 2006: *Injury: The Politics of Product Design and Safety Law in the United States.* Princeton: Princeton University Press.

19 Venkatesh 2006.

20 Kleinman, Arthur and Joan Kleinman, "How Bodies Remember: Social Memory and Bodily Experience of Criticism, Resistance, and Delegitimation Following China's Cultural Revolution." *New Literary History* 25 (1994): 710–711.

21 Frank, Arthur W., 1995: *The Wounded Storyteller: Body, Illness, and Ethics.* 1st ed. Chicago: University of Chicago Press, 50.

22 Fassin 2009.

23 Frank 1995: 1.

24 Decker and Winkle 1996. For the geography of gang territories, see: Jankowski, Martin Sanchez, 1991: *Islands in the Street: Gangs and American Urban Society.* Berkeley: University of California Press. For violence as related to gang rivalries, see: Levitt and Venkatesh, 2000.

25 Though not a central concern of this chapter, I use Marcus's description of his neighborhood, and the recollections of his mother's warnings, to gesture toward the fact that it is one's family members—oftentimes, those who condemn gang life the most—

who become the primary caretakers for black urban youth who are disabled (Devlieger et al. 2007). Devlieger, Patrick J., Gary L. Albrecht, and Miram Hertz, 2007: "The Production of Disability Culture Among Young African-American men." *Social Science & Medicine* 64, no. 9 (May): 1948–1959.

How Misunderstanding Disability Leads to Police Violence

David M. Perry and
Lawrence Carter-Long

On April 29, 2014, the Senate Judiciary Committee met to discuss law-enforcement responses to disabled Americans. The committee, chaired by democratic Senator Dick Durbin from Illinois, met against the backdrop of the death of James Boyd, a homeless man who had been in and out of psychiatric hospitals, shot to death by police in Albuquerque, and Ethan Saylor, a man with Down syndrome who suffocated to death while handcuffed by off-duty deputies working as security guards in a Maryland movie theater. They are just two of many people with psychiatric or intellectual disabilities killed by law enforcement.

In the face of these deaths and many others, the senators and witnesses all argued that something must be done. Suggested solutions included increased funding and support for Crisis Intervention Teams (CIT) training and the Justice and Mental Health Collaboration Act, which would improve access to mental-health services for people who come into contact with the criminal-justice system and provide law enforcement officers tools to identify and respond to mental-health issues.

While the hearing focused on troubling, high profile, and tragic cases such as those of Boyd and Saylor, the scope of the problem extends to virtually every kind of disability. Encounters with police have also taken an unnecessarily violent turn for people with disabilities that are not psychiatric or intellectual, including conditions that are physical or sensory:

- In 2008, Ernest Griglen was removed from his car by police who thought he was intoxicated. He was subsequently beaten. Griglen was, in fact, quite sober, but he is diabetic and was in insulin shock. Judging by media reports alone, people who are diabetic are often mistaken as threatening or drunk.

- In 2009, Antonio Love felt sick and went into a Dollar General store to use the bathroom. Time passed and he didn't come out, so the store manager called the police. The officers knocked on the bathroom door, ordered him to come out, but got no response. They sprayed pepper spray under the door, opened it with a tire iron, then tasered Love repeatedly. Love is deaf. He couldn't hear the police. Again, if news reports are any indication, deaf people are too frequently treated as non-compliant and tasered or beaten by police.

- In 2010, Garry Palmer was driving home from visiting his wife's grave when a dog darted in front of his truck and was hit. Palmer reported the accident as he should have, but because he was slurring his words and shaking, he was arrested for drunk driving. Palmer has cerebral palsy.

- In January 2014, Robert Marzullo filed a lawsuit citing battery, excessive force, false imprisonment, unlawful seizure, and supervisory liability against the town of Hamden, Connecticut and its police department. News reports reveal that Marzullo was tasered by two police officers while having an epileptic seizure in his car.

While specific details vary by case, the common threads that link these stories together are often disconcerting. Law enforcement officials expect and demand compliance, but when they don't recognize a person's disability in the course of an interaction, the consequences can be tragic. Misconceptions or assumptions can lead to over-reactions that culminate in unnecessary arrest, use of pepper spray, or individuals being tasered.

BOX 17.1

The media is missing the story when it comes to disability and police violence. Read more about a groundbreaking study of the issue here:

www.rudermanfoundation.org/blog/in-the-media/media-missing-the-story-half-of-all-recent-high-profile-police-related-killings-are-people-with-disabilities

Sadly, while incidences of this sort aren't necessarily new, for many of us, learning about them is. The Internet, social media, and ubiquitous cell phones have helped catapult stories that were once easily restricted to local police blotters to unprecedented national prominence.

As National Council on Disability (NCD) Executive Director Rebecca Cokley wrote in her testimony to the Senate Judiciary subcommittee, "misunderstandings, fears, and stereotypes about disability have led to tragic outcomes throughout U.S. history. During the American Eugenics movement, pseudo-scientific 'evidence' gave way to popular myths linking disability and criminality, and the inheritability of both." As a result, people with disabilities were devalued, isolated from the rest of society, prevented from attending school, getting married, or becoming active and engaged in their communities.

Fortunately people with disabilities now enjoy far greater civil rights that have come hard fought in the least 50 years. However, harmful attitudes and assumptions, once established, can be difficult to replace even in the face of evidence to the contrary.

In the latest data released by the U.S. Department of Justice's Bureau of Justice Statistics, Americans with disabilities are victims of violent crimes at nearly three times the rate of their peers without disabilities. In 2012 alone, 1.3 million nonfatal violent crimes were perpetrated against people aged 12 or older with disabilities. Statistics bear out that people with disabilities are far more likely to be the victims of crimes than the perpetrators of them, and therefore are arguably in greater need of supportive relationships with and understanding from law enforcement.

Disability is varied and complex. Sometimes disability is visibly apparent, making it easier for law enforcement, to see—if not misinterpret. For others, disability is invisible. Whether it is written in the genetic code and is a companion since birth, or becomes a part of one's experience later because of age, accident, or public service during the course of our natural lifespan many of us will move in and out of states of disability, whether it is due to breaking a limb, becoming diabetic, or conditions related to aging.

The disabled community relies on law enforcement as the first line of defense and protection in countless situations of varying complexity. Strengthening this important relationship could be a step toward preventing the sort of misunderstandings that can result in tragedy.

BOX 17.2

The solution to problems of police violence goes well beyond training programs. Check out one activist's take on how the wider community might address these incidents:

www.poormagazine.org/node/5510

As Patti Saylor, Ethan's mother, testified at Tuesday's hearing:

When you know someone with a disability and have a relationship with that person, it changes your whole being and perspective. At the local level, we have a real opportunity to build relationships with our local law enforcement and public sector officials, the ones that are on the frontlines serving our communities . . . Local disability advocacy organizations and providers should build lasting relationships with their local law enforcement and public sector officials. It doesn't take an act of Congress, federal or state mandate, or even money to make you realize that relationships are everything.

The recent hearing by the Senate Judiciary Committee is an important first sentence in an ongoing dialogue about how law enforcement officials relate to people with psychiatric, developmental, and physical disabilities. Non-compliance isn't automatically criminal, and if more police understood that, it could minimize the violence.

At the end of the hearing, Senator Al Franken remarked, "I think we need CIT training for every law enforcement official." CIT training is one component, along with increased community support, public engagement, and funding. These are all steps we can take to try to decrease the likelihood of more mistreatment of those like Saylor and Boyd.

But as long as disability is misunderstood and criminalized, even unintentionally, nearly everyone will be at increased risk.

Discussion Questions

1. What factors contribute to the prevalence of violence in encounters between disabled people and police?

2. How might changing attitudes about disability improve relations between law enforcement and the disabled community?

Let's Talk About Guns, But Stop Stereotyping the Mentally Ill

Jonathan Metzl

18

Restricting gun rights for people with mental illness is the one gun-control initiative that Republicans feel free to support. In the aftermath of the epic failure of substantive gun-control legislation, they "overwhelmingly" voted for mental-health efforts that "could help prevent killers like Adam Lanza, the gunman in the Newtown, Conn., massacre, from slipping through the cracks." Similar linkages appear in National Rifle Association head Wayne LaPierre's calls for a "national registry" of persons with mental illness, and in conservative commentator Ann Coulter's provocative claims that "guns don't kill people–the mentally ill do."

Of course, links between guns and mental illness arise in the aftermath of many American mass shootings, in no small part because of the mental-health histories of the assailants. Now, however, a number of states have begun to mandate that mental-health professionals report persons they believe to be potentially violent to the police. For instance, New York passed a bill that requires mental-health professionals to report "dangerous patients" to local officials, who would then be authorized to confiscate any firearms that these patients might own. And a senate bill in Tennessee obligates mental-health professionals—but not other types of caregivers—to report to local law enforcement any patients who make "credible threats."

I was a guest on an April 2013 edition of Melissa Harris-Perry's show, where the discussion explored whether psychiatrists should breach doctor–patient confidentiality and report potentially violent patients to the police—like the one treating Aurora shooting suspect James Holmes did—and whether serious mental illness should preclude a person from owning guns.

As a psychiatrist, I feel deep unease about these questions. Persons with violent tendencies should not have access to weapons that could be used to harm themselves or others. At the same time, the notion that "mental illness" becomes the only publicly permissible way for politicians to support gun control is highly problematic.

Psychiatric diagnosis is not a predictive tool. And indeed, the types of information garnered in background checks is far-and-away more relevant for predicting gun crime than is a person's psychiatric history—making the recent legislative setbacks all the more troubling.

In our research, my colleague Ken MacLeash and I find that three misperceptions underlie legislative assumptions about guns and mental illness.

The first is that mental illness causes gun violence. In fact, surprisingly little evidence suggests that persons with mental illness are more likely than anyone else to commit gun crimes. Databases that track U.S. gun homicides find that 3 to 5 percent of American crimes involve "mentally ill shooters."

Research also shows that stereotypes of violent madmen represent an inversion of reality. Many mental illnesses actually reduce a person's risk of violence, since these illnesses often produce social withdrawal. And individuals with severe mental illness are far more likely to be assaulted by others than to commit violent crimes themselves. One study in Los Angeles found that, far from posing threats to others, people diagnosed with schizophrenia had victimization rates 65 to 130 percent higher than those of the general public. Another recent study found that people with mental illness are significantly more likely than the general population to be shot by the police.

As such, associations between gun violence and mental illness represent an oversimplification or a distortion. And reflexively blaming people who have mental disorders for violent crimes overlooks the threats posed to U.S. society by a much larger population—the sane.

Second, psychiatric diagnosis can't predict gun crime before it happens. Actually, it's far from predictive in matters of violence. Psychiatrists using clinical judgment are not much better than chance at predicting which individual patients will commit gun crimes. This lack of prognostic specificity is a matter of simple math: mental-health professionals see many patients who threaten violence, yet most violent impulses are ultimately ignored or resisted by the persons who experience them.

The association between violence and psychiatric diagnosis also shifts dramatically over time. Psychiatrists considered schizophrenia an illness of docility during the first half of the 20th century. Only in the 1960s did American psychiatry link schizophrenia with violence. We now recognize that this transformation did not result from the increasingly violent actions of people with mental illness. Instead, it arose from changes in the way that psychiatry defined mental illness. Before the 1960s, psychiatry defined schizophrenia as a psychological "reaction" that produced "regressive behavior." But in 1968, psychiatry redefined paranoid schizophrenia as a condition of "hostility" and "aggression." This change imbued the mentally ill with an imagined—and highly racialized—potential for violence, and encouraged psychiatrists to conceptualize violent acts as symptomatic of mental illness.

Lastly, American gun culture falsely paints mentally ill persons as dangerous loners. After the Newtown shootings, news reports depicted Adam Lanza as a "Loner Who Felt No Pain." Lanza undoubtedly led a troubled, solitary life—yet sociological research shows that up to 85 percent of shootings occur within social networks, meaning that you are far more likely to be shot by a friend, neighbor, disgruntled employee, or spouse than by a lone stranger.

Questioning the associations between guns and "mentally ill persons" in no way detracts from the dire need to stem gun violence. Yet as we move forward from the recent shameful setbacks in the gun-control debate, we must avoid reproducing historical stereotypes that stigmatize persons with mental illness. This is not to suggest that we should ignore predictive risk factors. But a number of factors other than psychiatric diagnosis—substance use, history of violence, the availability of firearms—are far better markers of potential gun crime.

We must also learn from history that decisions about which crimes American culture diagnoses as "mentally ill" are driven as much by the politics of particular cultural moments as by the actions of individual shooters. Understanding a person's mental state is critical to understanding their actions. But focusing centrally on the psychology of individual assailants ultimately makes it ever-harder to address the larger issues that guns in America represent: the mass psychology of needing so many guns in the first place, or the anxieties, apprehensions, and psychical traumas created by being surrounded by them all the time.

Discussion Questions

1. Is it just or fair to make special gun laws for those who identify as mentally ill or mentally disabled? What's at stake in the debate about gun control and mental illness?

2. What are the three misconceptions about mental illness that are guiding legislative policy about guns? How do they reinforce one another?

Experiencing Disability

19 | The Spoon Theory
Christine Miserandino

My best friend and I were in the diner talking. As usual, it was very late and we were eating French fries with gravy. Like normal girls our age, we spent a lot of time in the diner while in college, and most of the time we spent talking about boys, music, or trivial things, that seemed very important at the time. We never got serious about anything in particular and spent most of our time laughing.

As I went to take some of my medicine with a snack as I usually did, she watched me with an awkward kind of stare, instead of continuing the conversation. She then asked me out of the blue what it felt like to have lupus and be sick. I was shocked not only because she asked the random question, but also because I assumed she knew all there was to know about lupus. She came to doctors with me, she saw me walk with a cane, and throw up in the bathroom. She had seen me cry in pain; what else was there to know?

I started to ramble on about pills, and aches and pains, but she kept pursuing, and didn't seem satisfied with my answers. I was a little surprised as being my roommate in college and friend for years, I thought she already knew the medical definition of lupus. Then she looked at me with a face every sick person knows well, the face of pure curiosity about something no one healthy can truly understand. She asked what it felt like, not physically, but what it felt like to be me, to be sick.

As I tried to gain my composure, I glanced around the table for help or guidance, or at least to stall for time to think. I was trying to find the right words. How do I answer a question I never was able to answer for myself? How do I explain every detail of every day being affected, and give the emotions a sick person goes through with clarity? I could have given up, cracked a joke like I usually do, and changed the subject, but I remember thinking if I don't try to explain this, how could I ever expect her to understand? If I can't explain this to my best friend, how could I explain my world to anyone else? I had to at least try.

At that moment, the spoon theory was born. I quickly grabbed every spoon on the table; hell, I grabbed spoons off of the other tables. I looked at her in the eyes and said "Here you go, you have lupus." She looked at me slightly confused, as anyone would when they are being handed a bouquet of spoons. The cold metal spoons clanked in my hands, as I grouped them together and shoved them into her hands.

I explained that the difference in being sick and being healthy is having to make choices or to consciously think about things when the rest of the world doesn't have to. The healthy have the luxury of a life without choices, a gift most people take for granted.

Most people start the day with an unlimited number of possibilities, and energy to do whatever they desire, especially young people. For the most part, they do not need to worry about the effects of their actions. So for my explanation, I used spoons to convey this point. I wanted something for her to actually hold, for me to then take away, since most people who get sick feel a "loss" of a life they once knew. If I was in control of taking away the spoons, then she would know what it feels like to have someone or something else, in this case lupus, being in control.

She grabbed the spoons with excitement. She didn't understand what I was doing, but she is always up for a good time, so I guess she thought I was cracking a joke of some kind like I usually do when talking about touchy topics. Little did she know how serious I would become.

I asked her to count her spoons. She asked why, and I explained that when you are healthy you expect to have a never-ending supply of "spoons." But when you have to now plan your day, you need to know exactly how many "spoons" you are starting with. It doesn't guarantee that you might not lose some along the way, but at least it helps to know where you are starting. She counted out 12 spoons. She laughed and said she wanted more. I said no, and I knew right away that this little game would work, when she looked disappointed, and we hadn't even started yet. I've wanted more "spoons" for years and haven't found a way yet to get more; why should she? I also told her to always be conscious of how many she had, and not to drop them because she can never forget she has lupus.

I asked her to list off the tasks of her day, including the most simple. As she rattled off daily chores, or just fun things to do, I explained how each one would cost her a spoon. When she jumped right into getting ready for work as her first task of the morning, I cut her off and took away a spoon. I practically jumped down her throat. I said "No! You don't just get up. You have to crack open your eyes, and then realize you are late. You didn't sleep well the night before. You have to crawl out of bed, and then you have to make yourself something to eat before you can do anything else, because if you don't, you can't take your medicine, and if you don't take your medicine you might as well give up all your spoons for today and tomorrow too." I quickly took away a spoon and she realized she hasn't even gotten dressed yet. Showering cost her a spoon, just for washing her hair and shaving her legs. Reaching high and low that early in the morning could actually cost more than one spoon, but I figured I would give her a break; I didn't want to scare her right away. Getting dressed was worth another spoon. I stopped her and broke down every task to show her how every little detail needs to be thought about. You cannot simply just throw clothes on when you are sick. I explained that I have to see what clothes I can physically put on; if my hands hurt that day buttons are out of the question. If I have bruises that day, I need to wear long sleeves, and if I have a fever I need a sweater to stay warm and so on. If my hair is falling out I need to spend more time to look presentable, and then you need to factor in another five minutes for feeling badly that it took you two hours to do all this.

I think she was starting to understand when she theoretically didn't even get to work, and she was left with six spoons. I then explained to her that she needed to choose the rest of her day wisely, since when your "spoons" are gone, they are gone. Sometimes you can borrow against tomorrow's "spoons," but just think how hard tomorrow will be with fewer "spoons." I also needed to explain that a person who is sick always lives with the looming thought that tomorrow may be the day that a cold comes, or an infection, or any number of things that could be very dangerous. So you do not want to run low on "spoons," because you never know when you truly will need them. I didn't want to depress her, but I needed to be realistic, and unfortunately being prepared for the worst is part of a real day for me.

We went through the rest of the day, and she slowly learned that skipping lunch would cost her a spoon, as well as standing on a train, or even typing at her computer too long. She was forced to make choices and think about things differently. Hypothetically, she had to choose not to run errands, so that she could eat dinner that night.

When we got to the end of her pretend day, she said she was hungry. I summarized that she had to eat dinner but she only had one spoon left. If she cooked, she wouldn't have enough energy to clean the pots. If she went out for dinner, she might be too tired to drive home safely. Then I also explained that I didn't even bother to add into this game, that she was so nauseous, that cooking was probably out of the question anyway. So she decided to make soup, it was easy. I then said it is only 7 pm, you have the rest of the night but maybe end up with one spoon, so you can do something fun, or clean your apartment, or do chores, but you can't do it all.

I rarely see her emotional, so when I saw her upset I knew maybe I was getting through to her. I didn't want my friend to be upset, but at the same time I was happy to think finally maybe someone understood me a little bit. She had tears in her eyes and asked quietly "Christine, how do you do it? Do you really do this every day?" I explained that some days were worse than others; some days I have more spoons than most. But I can never make it go away and I can't forget about it. I always have to think about it. I handed her a spoon I had been holding in reserve. I said simply, "I have learned to live life with an extra spoon in my pocket in reserve. You need to always be prepared."

It's hard. The hardest thing I ever had to learn is to slow down and not do everything. I fight this to this day. I hate feeling left out, having to choose to stay home, or to not get things done that I want to. I wanted her to feel that frustration. I wanted her to understand, that everything everyone else does comes so easy, but for me it is one hundred little jobs in one. I need to think about the weather, my temperature that day, and the whole day's plans before I can attack any one given thing. When other people can simply do things, I have to attack them and make a plan as if I am strategizing a war. This lifestyle is the difference between being sick and healthy. It is the beautiful ability to not think and just do. I miss that freedom. I miss never having to count "spoons."

After we were emotional and talked about this for a little while longer, I sensed she was sad. Maybe she finally understood. Maybe she realized that she never could truly and honestly say she understands. But at least now she might not complain so much when I can't go out for dinner some nights, or when I never seem to make it to her house and she always has to drive to mine. I gave her a hug when we walked out of the diner. I had the one spoon in my hand and I said "Don't worry. I see this as a blessing. I have been forced to think about everything I do. Do you know how many spoons people waste every day? I don't have room for wasted time, or wasted 'spoons' and I chose to spend this time with you."

Ever since this night, I have used the spoon theory to explain my life to many people. In fact, my family and friends refer to spoons all the time. It has been a code word for what I can and cannot do. Once people understand the spoon theory they seem to understand me better, but I also think they live their life a little differently too. I think it isn't just good for understanding lupus, but anyone dealing with any disability or illness. I hope they don't take so much for granted or their life in general. I give a piece of myself, in every sense of the word, when I do anything. It has become an inside joke. I have become famous for saying to people jokingly that they should feel special when I spend time with them, because they have one of my "spoons."

Discussion Questions

1. How does Miserando define the difference between being sick and being healthy? Why do the spoons help her explain this to her friend?

2. Why might it be important to try and understand the everyday experiences of someone with disability?

20 | Ableism and a Watershed Experience

Bill Peace

I do not like to use the term ableism.

There is more than a bit of irony in this, and a good friend pointed out recently that ableism is the first entry in the *ABC-CLIO Companion to the Disability Rights Movement* edited by Fred Pelka. For those unfamiliar with this book, it is an invaluable resource. I consult it often and the first entry begins: "Ableism is that set of often contradictory stereotypes about people with disabilities that acts as a barrier to keep them from achieving their full potential as equal citizens in society." What a great start to an encyclopedia type text devoted to disability rights. Yet, this does not address why I do not like the word.

As I thought about writing this entry today, the day before many celebrate May Day, I told my son I was struggling with how to address ableism. Far from a diplomat, he replied "Dad, ableism is a stupid word. Nobody aside from people who know a lot about disability will have any idea what you are talking about. Those people are not the ones that need to understand what ableism is." Leave it to a teen-ager who thinks he has the answer to the world's problems to get down to brass tacks.

While I may not like the word ableism, I certainly was taught what it meant at a young age. In fact, I was taught what ableism means by my mother within months of being paralyzed and well before the word existed.

When I think of the word ableism I think back to the days when I was a newly minted crippled dude. The year was 1978. I was 18 years old and had just emerged from a ten-year medical odyssey that left me paralyzed. I did not have a clue as to which end was up. I was struggling to figure out how to drive with hand controls, take care of my paralyzed body, and return to what I expected to be a normal existence. It did not take me long to realize that a normal life was out of the question. This left me confused, and I had a tendency to avoid social interaction and anything that resembled a confrontation.

I was also worried about returning to school, where I had been known as the kid that was always really sick. And upon my return, I became the kid that used a wheelchair. I was not pleased and felt more than a little sorry for myself.

BOX 20.1

Clinton Brown III suggests that sometimes being disabled is "like being a celebrity, but without the fame and the money." Watch him explain his experiences confronting ableism:

www.youtube.com/watch?v=xprxBBjX_m4

This brings me to the point of this entry: my mother taught me to confront ableism head on.

One day I drove myself to high school in my parents' car and discovered there was no handicapped parking. When I got home I told my mother about this in a woe-is-me fashion designed to prompt sympathy. This went over like a lead balloon. My mother told me in no uncertain terms that rather than whining about the lack of a parking spot for handicapped people, I should do something about it. I replied, "Yeah, what can I do? I am just a student."

She told me, "Tomorrow I want you to drive to school and park in the principal's parking spot. If he has a problem with this, tell him there is no handicapped parking. If he gives you any grief, call me and your father."

I was in my first period class when the principal walked in the door and asked "Who is William Peace and why is his car parked in my spot?"

Stunned silence ensued. I turned red as an apple and was asked to follow him to his office. I felt like a man heading to the gallows and asked to call my mother.

But then a strange thing happened. I told him exactly what my mother told me to say: "I parked in your spot because there is no handicap parking. The day before I parked very far away in the student lot and had a hard time getting to the only accessible school entrance." I dug in my heels and questioned why handicapped parking did not exist. A few minutes later, my mother walked in the door. She gave the principal a withering stare that only a furious mother can produce and that strikes fear into the hearts of others.

Two things dawned on me: first, my parents were behind me 100 percent. Although I could no longer walk, I was still the same person. Second, I realized I had to assert myself. That morning I learned I might be the same person I was before I was paralyzed but my wheelchair radically changed the way I was perceived. My mother used the lack of handicapped parking to force me to acknowledge this fact and assert my rights. By "assert my rights," I mean she taught me to reject ableism. Sure, I was paralyzed, but schools and other institutions had no right to treat me any differently. Basic (and what have become known as "reasonable") accommodations could and should be made. My mother told the principal she and her husband would encourage me to park in his spot every day until the school created handicapped parking. This matter was not subject to discussion, and the sooner handicapped parking was created, the sooner this issue would be resolved.

What happened when my mother and I left the principal's office? I went back to class and my peers were awed by my audacity. News of what I did spread like wildfire. My social status was only enhanced the next day when I drove to school and discovered that next to the principal's parking spot was a newly established area designated handicapped parking. I became a folk hero among my peers. I was the guy that not only had the nerve to park in the principal's parking spot but in less than 24 hours had convinced the school to create handicap parking.

This was a watershed moment in my life. When I saw my mother defend me and force me to assert myself, I knew I would never accept a subservient social status. I could independently manage my own life. If confronted with ignorance and bigotry, I was the one that must demonstrate I had the same rights as any other human. In short, my mother liberated me from an ableist mentality. I learned in a tangible way to reject the "ism" that forms the heart of discriminatory behavior.

Since that day so long ago I have had no qualms about confronting ableism, asserting my inherent civil rights as an American citizen, and rejecting ableist beliefs that sadly remain commonplace some 30 years later. Too bad we cannot clone my parents, who were ahead of their time and knew the importance of disability rights before the concept existed. As one reader of my blog commented, I am very lucky to have won the parent lottery.

Discussion Questions

1. Why does Peace say it's important to "confront ableism head on"? How do perceptions of disabled people change when they demand recognition for disability?

2. Peace opens this chapter by worrying that the term ableism doesn't mean much to people who don't think about disability in the first place. So how might people be liberated from an "ableist mentality" through other means?

21 | O.C.D. in N.Y.C.
Mike Sacks

.

You've seen me. I know you have.

I'm the guy wearing gloves on the subway in October. Or even into April. Perhaps I'm wearing just one glove, allowing my naked hand to turn the pages of a book.

No big deal. Just another one-gloved commuter, heading home.

If it's crowded, you may have noticed me doing my best to "surf," sans contact, until the car comes to a stop, in which case I may knock into a fellow passenger.

Aboveground you may have seen me acting the gentleman, opening doors for others with a special paper towel I carry in my front left pocket for just such a momentous occasion.

No? How about that guy walking quickly ahead of you, the one impishly avoiding sidewalk cracks?

Or perhaps you've noticed a stranger who turns and makes eye contact with you for seemingly no reason. You may have asked, "You got a problem?"

Oh, I definitely have a problem. But it has nothing to do with you, sir or madam. (And, yes, even in my thoughts I refer to you as "sir" and "madam.")

The problem here is what multiple doctors have diagnosed as obsessive-compulsive disorder. You may refer to it by its kicky abbreviation, O.C.D.

I prefer to call it Da Beast.

Da Beast is a creature I have lived with since I was 11, a typical age for O.C.D. to snarl into one's life without invitation or warning.

According to the International O.C.D. Foundation, roughly one in 100 adults suffers from the disorder. Each of us has his or her own obsessive thoughts and fears to contend with. My particular beast of burden is a fear of germs and sickness. It's a popular one, perhaps the most common.

Other obsessions include unwanted thoughts, a fear of harming oneself and religious obsessions, all of which I've struggled with at one point or another.

I wash my hands up to 25 times per day. I perform intricate routines and complicated movements to avoid becoming contaminated. With what, exactly? Nothing specific, just a murky sense of something bad. But I also perform these tasks so that friends and family members—and even potentially you—don't become contaminated.

It's a lot of pressure, but I'm no hero. You can thank me later.

BOX 21.1

Chelsey Thomas lives with Moebius Syndrome, a neurological condition affecting facial expressions and eye movements. She explains what it's like in this video:

www.youtube.com/watch?v=Qh8vxzLirf4

For about half my life, Da Beast and I lived in the suburbs. We were two kooky roommates with occasional squabbles, and I eventually learned to tune it out, much like the news scroll at the bottom of a CNN report. White noise.

The 'burbs are not a bad setting for O.C.D.—serene, very few surprises. A stranger is unlikely to vomit near you. Chances are low that a fellow commuter will sneeze in your face.

New York, where I prefer to live, is another story. It's a difficult city for the disabled, the elderly, the poor and anyone who lives beyond the reach of public transportation. I am able-bodied and relatively young, and I live close to subway stations and bus stops. I'm lucky.

Those who get near me, however, aren't so blessed.

I've fallen into a few subway riders' laps, either after forgetting my pole glove or while attempting to surf. In one instance, I landed in the lap of a large man, spilling his morning coffee onto his work outfit. Before I could explain about Da Beast, in a neutral but almost "What can you do about it?" tone, he had already shoved me into the lap of someone else, who was also not so keen on my sudden, shocking arrival.

One of the intoxicating things about living in the city is that it's forever requiring Da Beast to add new and exciting tics to its arsenal. We're both out of our element, constantly on guard, wending our way through a barrage of horror triggers. New York has become the setting for free immersion therapy.

Two years ago, while I was rushing to meet a friend at a bar, a child vomited close to me. After much thought and contemplation about how I could avoid suffering the same fate in public (and after much trial and error with various tics), I determined that my best course of action would be to perform the following: come to a complete and sudden stop, turn around to face anyone walking close behind me, and stare that person directly in the eye. Without sounding egotistic, I'd like to consider this particular move my "O.C.D. calling card."

As you may have guessed, this series of moves does not come without potential problems.

Beyond the fact that the maneuver is exactly the opposite of what is recommended for New Yorkers—or, for that matter, anyone living anywhere—it is exhausting and time consuming. Also, it's a terrific way to get yelled at, threatened and maybe even punched in the face.

I suppose part of the problem is my need to hold the gaze for as long as possible. I can cut it off only when it feels right. Five seconds? 10 seconds? 30? I do what it takes to guarantee I will never vomit in public. (Again, I'm no hero.)

More than once, a stranger has cocked an arm, ready to unleash a fist on my face. Apologizing profusely helps.

Pretending to search for a lost dog or missing child is also a good gambit, but it can call for unwanted attention—specifically from the police—that I'm not supercomfortable with, especially given my other greatest fear: being locked up. So I often end up muttering something incomprehensible. Or feigning mental illness.

Wait. I have a mental illness.

There is no cure for O.C.D. Researchers remain puzzled by what exactly triggers the disorder, although there is a potential link to childhood strep throat, among other illnesses. Medication helps when it comes to quelling the worst of the impulses, at least for me.

After consuming top doses of Prozac and Wellbutrin for more than four years, I'm proud to say I can once again use a kitchen knife without thinking it may one day be used to stab someone, which is great news but not something to brag about on a dating profile or in my college alumni magazine.

Da Beast may not love this dirty town, but I do. I suppose I could wear a full-body biohazard suit and be done with it (no germs for the rest of my life!), but that would be unwieldy, unsightly and expensive, unless I could find one secondhand. Then again, I'm in no rush to purchase a "gently used" biohazard suit at a stoop sale.

C'mere, we're all in this together. Please stop looking at me like that or, at the very least, try to understand why I seem a little off. Let's make this work. Give me a high-five and let's call it a day.

But elbow to elbow. There we go, thanks.

Discussion Questions

1. Why does Sacks refer to O.C.D. as "Da Beast"? What does the distance between the speaker and his condition tell us about the nature of disability?

2. Sacks writes about how public transportation and a crowded city complicate things for him. What insight does this give us into the relationship between community life and individual experience of a disability?

22

Living With Schizophrenia

The Importance of Routine

Michael Hedrick

I can remember the early days of having schizophrenia. I was so afraid of the implications of subtle body language, like a lingering millisecond of eye contact, the way my feet hit the ground when I walked or the way I held my hands to my side. It was a struggle to go into a store or, really, anywhere I was bound to see another living member of the human species.

With a simple scratch of the head, someone could be telling me to go forward, or that what I was doing was right or wrong, or that they were acknowledging the symbolic crown on my head that made me a king or a prophet. It's not hard to imagine that I was having a tough time in the midst of all the anxiety and delusions.

Several months after my diagnosis, I took a job at a small town newspaper as a reporter. I sat in on City Council meetings, covering issues related to the lowering water table and interviewing local business owners for small blurbs in the local section, all the while wondering if I was uncovering some vague connections to an international conspiracy.

The nights were altogether different. Every day, I would come home to my apartment and smoke pot, then lay on my couch watching television or head out to the bar and get so hammered that I couldn't walk. It's hard to admit, but the only time I felt relaxed was when I was drunk.

I eventually lost my newspaper job, but that wasn't the catalyst for change.

It all came to a head one night in July. I had been out drinking all night and, in a haze, I decided it would be a good idea to drive the two miles back to my apartment. This is something I had done several times before, but it had never dawned on me that it was a serious deal. I thought I was doing well, not swerving and being only several blocks from my house, when I saw flashing lights behind me.

What started as a trip to the bar to unwind ended with me calling my parents to bail me out of jail at 3 AM.

The next year of my life would mean change. I'm not entirely clear on the exact point at which my routine drinking and drug use turned into healthier pursuits. Maybe it was the shock of meeting with a D.U.I. lawyer, or the point after sentencing when I realized I'd be forced to make a daily call, first thing in the morning, to find out if I would have to pee in a cup that day. Maybe it was the fact that I'd need someone else, mainly my mom, to drive me anywhere for the next year. Or perhaps it was the consistent Saturday morning drug and alcohol therapy group or Wednesday and Thursday afternoons of community service that kicked me into a groove.

The groove of it eventually turned into a routine, one that wasn't marked by indulgence but instead by forced commitment that eventually I would grow to respect.

During that time, I quit smoking pot, I quit drinking and I got some of the best sleep I'd gotten since my diagnosis. Trips to the bar on Monday afternoons turned into extended hours at coffee shops where I finished my first novel.

For some reason, it gave me joy to recite my routine to whoever asked. I would wake up at 7, get coffee and a bagel with plain cream cheese, check Facebook, write until I had 1,000 words, get lunch, do errands in the afternoon, return home, get dinner, take my pills (with food), watch TV and get to bed around 9.

It might all sound tremendously boring. But this regimented series of events was always there; they'd always carry over. And with time, it gave me great comfort to not have to deal with the unexpected. I had a set plan for most days, and there was already too much chaos in my head.

I found that I never forgot to take my medicine. I always had at least eight hours of sleep. And I felt much more relaxed and was able to finally wrap my head around my diagnosis. I began to see the world as a mostly random series of events, rather than an overarching conspiracy plot. The healthy routine was integral.

My story, as with so many stories of recovery, isn't over. The biggest things in my life are now my friends and family, my work and my daily routine. I take my meds faithfully, and although I no longer attend regular therapy sessions, I find eight years of living with schizophrenia has made me well equipped to deal with future problems. I still get up early, do my work for the day, hang out with my mom or my friends in the afternoon and then ease into the evening. Most important, I still get to bed by 9 every night. I'm more stable, much healthier, and I'm happy.

The routine of things set a stable foundation for recovery by providing me with familiarity. That familiarity was more than welcome when my mind was unrecognizable.

Discussion Questions

1. Hedrick's story describes how disability can overlap with or manifest in other problems like drug use or inability to hold a job. How can understanding disability help people better understand the source of these problems?

2. Why is routine so important to Hedrick? How can others assist disabled people in the routines that enable their lives?

The Two-In-One

Rod Michalko[1]

> *"What distinguishes men from animals is born of our relationship with them."*
> John Berger, *About Looking*

This work is my attempt to depict my life with Smokie, which I have characterized as a relationship based on the idea of the "alone-together." The alone-together suggests that we possess unity with each other as well as separateness from each other. Our separateness, or difference from each other, originates and is steeped in the distinction between nature and humanity. However else we are together, we are first and foremost "man and dog." We are distinct from one another not simply on the basis that we are two different living creatures, but on the more fundamental level that we are two different species. Smokie is *Canis familiaris* and I am *Homo sapiens*. He is a representative of nature, I of humanity. This marks our fundamental difference.

Some will not be satisfied with this distinction. They are vexed by the question of what distinguishes humanity from nature—in our case, what distinguishes humans from animals. This question presupposes such a distinction, but at the same time it implies a concern for whether or not the distinction is valid or even whether it expresses an anthropocentrism. Even though these concerns are philosophic ones, a program of empirical research has been established as a way to address them. Is it the ability to think that distinguishes humans from animals? The ability to use tools? The ability to speak? The ability to control and manipulate nature? These are but a few of the questions that are raised and addressed by such research. Despite their empirical nature, the posing of these questions presupposes the distinction they are seeking. Without a distinction between human and animals questions about its precise character could not be asked.

The postmodern privileging of perspective influences the motivation for the asking of such questions. Animals and humans alike have a perspective that defines what is real. The postmodern slant on this is that not only are all perspectives equally valid but that any notion of reality can be gleaned only from perspective. This view results in a world of multiple realities in which every reality is as real as every other reality. To privilege one reality over another, from this standpoint, is to be guilty of egocentrism, ethnocentrism, anthropocentrism; the assertion of one reality or one "truth" over another is an illusion animated by hegemonic self-interest.

Regardless of how the distinction between humans and animals is conceived, it is based upon and expresses a relation. My understanding of Smokie, for example, is based upon such a relation. There are times when I trust his judgment more than I do that of a human. When a stranger took my arm and offered to take me through a construction site, I told him, "Let him work." I was not being anthropocentric, but distinguishing between the guiding prowess of a person and that of Smokie—if anything, one might argue that I was guilty of anthropomorphism, of endowing Smokie with human attributes. It was my relation to Smokie—my trust in his loyalty and competence in guiding—that motivated my comment.

As Berger says, "What distinguishes men from animals is born of our relationship with them."[2] My work, both with Smokie and [in writing], presupposes this distinction and this relationship. That I "see" a distinction between humans and animals is grounded in this experience. The relationship of which this is born is crystallized in my reflections upon this experience.

Living With Blindness

I draw a distinction between living *with* blindness and living *in* blindness. This distinction, like the one between humans and animals, was also born of our relationship with it. Whether we live with or in blindness depends on our conception of it.

The conception of blindness as an externally motivated condition which imposes negative effects upon a person results in a life *with* it. The notion of externality is crucial to this concept, for it sees blindness as external to the individual, motivated by disease, accident, or genetics. This makes blindness a condition that imposes itself indiscriminately on individuals, an inadequate physiology which should *naturally* be otherwise. The ability to see, from this perspective, depends on a naturally functioning physiology. Any "act of nature," in this view, is a natural one and thus "mindless." Nature's actions are not based on prejudice or self-interest but are random and indiscriminate. Pollution, for example, is understood as the result of human intervention that causes not only a polluted natural environment but also a polluted version of "natural equality."

This point of view treats blindness as a condition that cannot be blamed on anyone or anything but merely *happens* to people. It is like any other "natural happening" except for one thing—it is a mistake, but a natural one. Nature possesses anomalies, exceptions to the "natural rule." Disease and flawed genes are seen as an anomaly in relation to the natural order of things. Accidents too are often understood as natural occurrences. What accident, for example, wiped out the dinosaurs over 65,000,000 years ago? Was it a giant meteor shower, or was it merely an instance of the way in which evolution naturally works?

Humanity enters the realm of naturally occurring anomalies and accidents in the exclusively human act of interpretation. Human interpretation begins with judging these anomalies as either good or bad. This judgment is based on a presupposed distinction between nature and humanity. Any effect that nature might have on itself is never interpreted as bad. Unpleasant as it may look to human eyes, for example, a lion ripping out the throat of a gazelle is seen as part of the natural order of things; it is interpreted as a good thing insofar as it enables the natural food chain to sustain itself. Even the death of weak and diseased animals is interpreted as "nature's way" of insuring the species' survival. "Nature is therefore something which as it were holds to its own course, and does so in and of itself."[3] In fact, the only bad thing about nature is understood as springing from human intervention. Nature, in this view, possesses an "internal perfection" which, left to its own devices, will take care of itself, even if this process is, as yet, beyond human understanding. The workings of nature can only be seen as "bad" when human beings become part of the equation.

Natural occurrences are not always seen as so benign when they happen to human beings. People see blindness as a mistake, and even though nature, being mindless, cannot be blamed the way a person's self-interest or malice can be blamed, blindness is still seen as a bad thing. Blindness is not merely the unfortunate luck of the "natural draw"; it is the misfortune of the one who draws blindness from nature's deck.

Blindness is not an instance of natural selection and survival, but the human misfortune of having made a "bad draw." A wildebeest has no chance of winning when it draws the natural card of blindness. It must sacrifice its life in order to preserve the strength of its species. A human being who draws the "blind card," on the other hand, has a chance of winning and sacrifices a life of seeing in order to preserve the strength of the human spirit. The person who draws the blind card now focuses on playing the other cards in her or his hand—the cards of hearing, of touching, and especially of the human spirit. Bad card in hand, this person goes on to strengthen the other cards by playing them effectively. Thus humans assert themselves in nature in a way that animals do not. "As human beings we are not wholly accommodated to our natural environment through the mechanisms of instinct and reaction. Precisely this is our 'nature,' that we must assert ourselves over and against nature as far as we can."[4]

The card-playing metaphor depicts what I mean by living *with* blindness. Blindness is reduced to a physical condition with which one must cope and to which one must adjust. The result is a person "who happens to be blind."

Living with blindness requires a separation of an individual from his body. This separation is different from Plato's body/soul distinction or Descartes' body/mind split; it is better characterized as the body/person split. This type of dichotomy, in its modern form, derives from the Enlightenment's separation of reason (the human mind's special capability) and passion, emotion, and instinct (the primitive or animal forces). The Enlightenment's privileging of reason as the distinguishing and animating feature of humankind made the body, symbol of emotion and instinct, a separate and opposing entity. Thus the Age of Reason dichotomized nature and society, and distinguished between laws of nature and laws of society. The key to unlocking both these sets of laws was, of course, human reason.

A similar dichotomy, the body/person split, is essential for a life *with* blindness, for the life of the person "who happens to be blind." Living *with* blindness means understanding blindness as a strictly physical condition of the body—a defective and inadequate physiology of the eye. "Blind eyes" do not function as they were "naturally intended" to do, and the origin of their defect is typically situated within the paradigm of "bodily cause." When this "cause" cannot be located in the body, the person is not considered "really blind," but is suffering from some sort of psychological disorder. However, even psychosomatic blindness falls within the body/person split, as it is yet another sign of the "power of mind," albeit a "mind gone bad."

The Enlightenment's distinction between nature and society supported the belief that nature could be mastered and controlled through the use of reason and its offspring, science and technology. This leads to the interpretation of reason as knowledge and subsequently power.[5] The evolution of human reason, and its mastery of nature, would result in ever increasing human progress, and this belief in progress is the Enlightenment's legacy to us. Living *with* blindness is rooted in just such an understanding of humanity and nature. Human blindness may be a natural happenstance, but it can be known, understood, and to some degree mastered. It can be overcome insofar as collective social life possesses the power of reason. The same understanding does not hold when blindness occurs in a wolf or a gazelle. Natural animal creatures, lacking the power of reason and the ability to create coping technologies, cannot overcome blindness. Instead, nature destroys blindness by destroying those individual creatures "who happen to be blind." The wolf will starve to death; the gazelle will be easy prey to its predators. Living with blindness can occur *only* in human society.

Living with and overcoming blindness is manifest in a variety of ways in our society. There are optical technologies that can maximize any residual vision. Rehabilitation makes it possible to do things without benefit of sight. White canes and dog guides are used as mobility devices that enable blind persons to get around. And, of course, there are various forms of psychotherapy aimed at facilitating an understanding and acceptance of blindness. All of this, together with the human spirit and privileging of personhood, allows blind persons to master blindness through overcoming—that is, to live *with* blindness.

Living In Blindness

Living *in* blindness poses a contrasting interpretation of the relation between nature and society by preserving the distinction between the two without separating them. The "in" and the "with" are intended to represent linguistically the difference between dichotomizing nature and society (the with) and not doing so (the in). Living *in* blindness is an attempt to imagine an alternative to blindness as happenstance.

Happenstance or conditionality is indeed an essential feature of human life. Things do happen to us, beginning with the conditions prevailing at the time and place of our birth. But the interpretation of such conditions represents our need to conceive of the condition Arendt (1958) calls "human." The nature/society distinction is one way to envision the human condition. The Enlightenment recommends living *with* this distinction through the belief that society can master nature. In contrast, living *in* the nature/society distinction imagines it as a discourse. For example, the human understanding of animals is, as Berger suggested, "born of our relation with them" and this relation is born of public discourse about the nature/society distinction. We are distinguishable from nature by virtue of being *in* the midst of this public discourse.

The idea of "many natures"[6] is born of this discourse. But the "pure nature," which these authors reject in favor of these socially constructed "many natures," remains firmly grounded, if not pure, in the nature/society distinction, for without it the social construction of "many natures" would be impossible. The nature/society distinction is the material out of which these many natures are socially constructed.

Social constructionism, however, marks the beginning of the recognition of the nature/society discourse and represents the first step toward a life *in* this discourse. Through the constructionist approach, we can begin to recognize that blindness is not sheerly an objective "natural fact." We see that blindness, like nature itself, is a socially constructed phenomenon that actually produces "many blindnesses." Despite their construction, however, we must still develop a relation to them and must do so in public discourse. We choose one version of blindness over another and insofar as we do so over and over again, the discourse of blindness takes on a moral character. The conception of blindness as a physical condition which can be overcome through the privileging of personhood, a conception held by the disciplines of medicine and rehabilitation, is thus not amoral. Language such as "physical condition," "adjustment," and "rehabilitation," conceal a moral conception of blindness and, to borrow from Matthews, represent the "moral regulation of nature."[7]

Living *in* blindness is to live with the awareness of being in the midst of the moral public discourse of the nature/society distinction. Blindness can remind us of this distinction and of its human origin. Sight loss puts us in mind of the natural way we once saw. It puts us in mind of the naturalness of our bodies and their vulnerability. We feel blindness, think of it, and experience it in an exclusively human way. That blindness has a natural side is a distinctly human depiction. Whatever nature has to say about itself, it says through the mouthpiece of humanity. Since humanity speaks with many voices, there are many natures. "Living with blindness" is one such voice and one such nature. It expresses the nature/ humanity distinction in terms of the necessity of "the-living-with." Nature controls the conditions of life but humanity controls *how* these conditions are lived with. Disrespect for this distinction results in an imbalance of control. The human attempt to control nature has resulted in widespread environmental destruction and the extinction and near extinction of many natural species.

BOX 23.1

What does living in blindness mean for someone who comes into blindness as a teenager or an adult? Read the experience of someone with Usher Syndrome:

www.vox.com/2015/4/10/8365853/blind-vision-loss

The phenomenon of human blindness brings this particular nature/humanity distinction to the fore. It reminds us that nature is in control of the natural conditions of life. As Levin says, vision is a "gift from nature," and as such it may be freely given—or not. When it is not, or when the gift is taken back, we are forcefully reminded of nature's control. Nature gives or revokes vision without regard for our individual interests, purposes, hopes, and fears.

"Living with blindness" is a human response to nature as a distinct entity and as a bearer of gifts. If the gift of vision is withheld or revoked, human society attempts to remedy this anomaly through the unnatural means of medical treatment. If treatment fails, an individual will live without the gift of vision. Living *with* blindness is living *without* vision.

Living *in* blindness, however, requires a different understanding, one that goes beyond coping with and adjusting to blindness. It requires keeping blindness *alive in one's self*. Living *with* blindness raises and immediately solves the problem of blindness by conceiving of it as a condition requiring personal adjustment. Its character is unconditional and unchangeable: There is one blindness and one blindness only.

Living *in* blindness allows for the possibility of many blindnesses. Blindness can be interpreted as dynamic rather than a static phenomenon, and this interpretation flows directly from lived experience. At times blindness is experienced as an unalterable negative condition. At other times, it is experienced as secondary to personhood. At still other times, it is experienced as a tragedy, a stroke of unfairness, payment for wrongdoings, or the bad luck of the draw. But it is also experienced as an occasion for thought. Thinking about blindness permits a blind person to live in the midst of many blindnesses and to claim blindness *as his or her own*.

Thus blindness and humanity belong together in the same way that nature and society do. The nature of blindness as well as the nature of nature are determined by the exclusively human act of interpretation. The existence of many blindnessess and many natures is as natural as the distinction between nature and humanity. As natural as this distinction is, however, we develop a relationship to it that results in the appearance of many blindnesses and many natures.

Conceiving of blindness as though it were a one-dimensional brute fact of physical nature is to abdicate any responsibility for its appearance in the world. This conception results in living *with* blindness in the same way that abdicating responsibility for nature results in living *with* it. We put up with it, we try to master it, we do what we can to adjust to and work around it.

The modern tendency is to attempt to master blindness through adaptive techniques. This approach allows for no other life than the life *with* blindness. Living *in* blindness, however, requires a different interpretive distinction. It requires that humanity recognize its essential responsibility for *any* relation to nature. Such a recognition opens the society/nature distinction to a horizon of possibilities.

The Two-in-One

Through our movement in the world, alone-together, I have come to understand my relationship with Smokie within the conception of the two-in-one. There is my body, my blindness, my nature, and my humanity; there is Smokie's domestication and his body, his nature. He is differentiated from nature by virtue of his domestication and he is differentiated from humanity by virtue of his nature. Smokie is also differentiated from many of his species by virtue of his status as a dog guide. I am differentiated from my society by virtue of my individuality; and, like Smokie, I am also differentiated from many of my species by virtue of my blindness.

Smokie and I are different from most of our respective species by virtue of our togetherness as a dog guide team. Smokie and I live *in* this differentiation. We are alone-together in two ways: We are together in our movement as one and thus alone in the social world, and we are alone by virtue of our belonging to two distinct species, as expressed in the togetherness of the nature/humanity distinction. Thus we are two in the oneness of our togetherness.

This interpretation of the differentiation in the nature/humanity distinction moves the possibility of the relation between nature and humanity beyond the interpretive category of "mastery." Mastery requires that the nature/humanity distinction be interpreted within the "side-by-side." Nature and humanity exist side by side each other, which allows for the possibility of one mastering the other. When humanity is conceived in terms of "mind" and nature in terms of "mindless," it is "natural" for humanity to master nature. Mastery allows nature to be handled and even *owned* by humanity. Nature may be a difficult thing to master and handle, but it is easy to own. We own our bodies, nations own rights to natural resources, and we even own our pets. The best that nature can hope for in this side-by-side relationship is that humanity will be a kind and gentle master.

The two-in-one relation between nature and humanity includes other possibilities. It can be said that I "own" Smokie only in the most technical sense. Someone owns him only insofar as the conventions of our society allow the possibility that one creature can "own" another as property. That I am his master or that I handle him are things that can be said only within the conventional side-by-side nature/humanity relationship.

What there is to be mastered, handled, or owned derives from Smokie and me— alone-together. At times, we conceive of our togetherness in terms of mastering and handling the social world. We get through it, one as blind, the other as dog. We own blindness insofar as we treat it as *belonging* to us. This is one of the possibilities of the two-in-one.

The other and more interesting possibility, however, springs from *our coming in touch with our world.* For this, the ideas of mastery, handling, and ownership are insufficient forms of our relationship. At best, they take on a fluidity that the side-by-side relationship does not permit. At one time, I am master; at another, Smokie is. Now I am handler; now he is. On one occasion, I take ownership for decision-making; on another, Smokie does. Recall that Smokie and I both lead and follow one another. This is a fluid relation that does not apply when leader and follower are understood as static and completely separable entities. Thus mastery, handling, and ownership are situated phenomena and not ontological ones. Our situation originates in our commitment to being in touch with our world.

As we move through our world, Smokie and I are not merely side by side. We move together as one, touching and imagining both each other and our world. Our harmony comes from the contrapuntal relation of the two-in-one interpretation of the nature/humanity distinction. We depict a world to each other generated by our difference and sameness. We communicate this world to one another through the ineffability of the togetherness found in this distinction.

BOX 23.2

Despite the accommodations protected by the ADA, many public places make it difficult for guide dogs and their human counterparts. Read some examples from the life of Stephen Kuusisto:

https://stephenkuusisto.com/2013/10/06/a-guide-dogs-tale/

In her discussion of the two-in-one, Arendt writes: "I am not only for others but for myself, and in this latter case, I clearly am not just one. A difference is inserted into my Oneness."[8] As a blind person, I exist in the midst of "many blindnesses," which are expressed in the multitude of opinions and collective representations my society has of blindness. I am grist for this opinion mill. I receive opinions about blindness from professionals such as ophthalmologists and rehabilitators. My friends and acquaintances give me their opinions. Strangers comment about my blindness as Smokie and I move through the world. The mass media contribute to collective representations. I am certainly for others and clearly not just one.

This multitude of opinion is not restricted to those who are sighted. Blind people have opinions about blindness too. Nor are these opinions generated strictly because they exist in distinction to sight. They exist "not because it has a relation to something lse which is different . . . but because it exists among a plurality of Ideas."[9] Opinions about blindness are not themselves blindness. Its relationship to sight notwithstanding, blindness does not rely on sight for its existence. Blindness is only one of the many things that a society and its people have ideas about. It is only one idea among a plurality of ideas.

It is in the midst of this plurality that I, and all other blind persons, live. Privileging one version of blindness over another does not destroy or escape this plurality. The fact that the modern age conceives of blindness as a physical condition does not mean that blindness cannot be seen otherwise. Blindness as a physical condition is only one of many possible interpretations.

As Smokie and I move through our world, we are constantly in the midst of what others think of blindness. Whether we actually speak to them or not, we do respond to what they think. Our very presence to otherness is always-already a kind of response. Others make sense of us in relation to what they already think of blindness. In this sense, I *am* for others. But, as Arendt says I am also for myself, the one who is blind. But my "one" self too is filled with the plurality of possible blindnesses. The essential difference of my society is inserted, as Arendt suggests, into my "Oneness."

Recognizing, sorting out, and judging the value of all the possible blindnesses that exist requires the kind of thought that Plato (in the *Theaetetus*) made 'Socrates' describe as a dialogue with one's self. A kind of solitude is required that Arendt described as "that human situation in which I keep myself company."[10] This kind of thinking is what Arendt called the "two-in-one."

Smokie and I move through our world *alone-together*, focusing on one another in the midst of the plurality of our world and its many blindnesses. Smokie keeps me company in this estranged familiarity of opinion. I experience my blindness *together* with Smokie in this plurality. My focus is on Smokie and on myself. The world we generate springs from our communication in the midst of the world and from our movement through it.

Smokie is the essential difference "inserted into my Oneness." Who we are together comes from the dialogue between our difference and our sameness. Smokie and I are clearly the "two-in-one." Through our two-in-one Smokie gives me the opportunity to "keep myself company" with thinking about my blindness, its meaning, its various interpretations, and the horizon of possibilities it offers. My life with Smokie has shown me the need to think about blindness and to understand my responsibility for the way blindness appears in the world.

If "you want to think, you must see to it that the two who carry on the dialogue be in good shape, that the partners be *friends*."[11] From the beginning, Smokie demonstrated nothing but his desire to become my friend. He is my partner and the trust, respect, and admiration we have for one another is captured even more in the idea of friendship than in that of a bond. Despite my blindness, Smokie desired this friendship, and this taught me that my blindness is an occasion to be a decisive actor in the world. More than this, however, Smokie's friendship has taught me that I can begin to befriend my blindness and to allow it to keep me company. I am alone-together with Smokie but in solitude with my blindness.

Smokie has reminded me, too, of the value of intimacy. Relationships, even the one between nature and society, are deepened and sustained through intimacy. Sometimes we control and dominate nature; at other times we are controlled and dominated by it. Without intimacy, relations between nature and society become a mere matter of dominance and submission in which "society" dominates and "nature" submits. Intimacy allows the relationship between dominance and submission to become reciprocal, fluid, and dialectical. This is what my life with Smokie has taught me. With his guidance, I have become intimate with him, with my world, and with my blindness.

Discussion Questions

1. What is the idea of being "alone-together," and how does it apply to Michalko and his dog, Smokie? What larger points does he make in describing his relationship to his guide dog?

2. What does it mean to have multiple "blindnesses"?

3. What's the difference between living with blindness and living in blindness? Why is it important that Michalko can "befriend" his blindness?

4. Explain what the concept of the "two-in-one" might contribute to how we think about disability and interpersonal relationships.

Notes

1 Editor's note: This chapter is from Rod Michalko's *The Two-In-One*.
2 Berger, 1980, p. 7.
3 Gadamer 1996, p. 36.
4 Ibid., p. 139.
5 Foucault, 1980.
6 MacNaughten and Urry 1995, p. 207.
7 Matthews, 1996.
8 Arendt, 1971, p. 183.
9 Ibid., p. 184.
10 Ibid., p. 185.
11 Ibid., pp. 187–88.

References

Arendt, Hannah. *The Human Condition*. Chicago: The University of Chicago Press, 1958.

Arendt, Hannah. *The Life of the Mind: Thinking and Willing*. San Diego: Harcourt Brace Jovanovich, 1971.

Berger, John. *About Looking*. New York: Pantheon Books, 1980.

Foucault, Michel. *Power/Knowledge: Selected Interviews and Other Writings, 1972–1977*. New York: Pantheon Books, 1980.

Gadamer, Hans Georg. *Apologia for the Art of Healing*. Stanford University Press, 1996.

Levin, David Michael. *The Opening of Vision: Nihilism and the Postmodern Situation*. New York: Routledge, 1988.

Matthews, David Ralph. "Mere Anarchy? Canada's 'Turbot War' as the Moral Regulation of Nature." *The Canadian Journal of Sociology* 21 (1996): 505–22.

MacNaughten, Phil and John Urry. "Towards a Sociology of Nature." *Sociology* 29 (1995): 203–20.

PART

6

Disability and Culture

If Hollywood's So Creative, Why Can't It Tell New Stories About People With Disabilities?

Alyssa Rosenberg

As the movement for greater inclusiveness in American pop culture has gained steam, one of the most heartening things about it is the way it has expanded. Conversations about the experiences and depictions of women and people of color have become more nuanced and fine-grained, expanding to include the specific challenges that face, say, Asian American actors or African-American women in an industry traditionally dominated by white men.

I've been particularly encouraged by the expanding conversation about the way the way Hollywood treats people with disabilities, a term that is as broad in its own way as a category like people of color. Whether it's the vigorous discussion around *Me Before You,* an adaptation of a novel about a young man with a spinal cord injury, his caregiver and his decision to commit suicide, or the tender storytelling of Pixar's *Finding Dory*, these discussions have illustrated the limits of the industry's storytelling conventions and the desperate need for more parts for actors with disabilities.

> **BOX 24.1**
>
> Like *Finding Dory?* Read more about how the animated hit has become part of disability culture:
>
> **https://disabilityvisibilityproject.com/2016/06/27/finding-dory-disability-culture-and-collective-access/**

Of course, all stories and all parts aren't created equal.

The *Hollywood Reporter* published a terrific deep dive into little people's experiences in the entertainment industry by Seth Abramovitch (see Chapter 25). The piece, which reaches all the way back to the experiences of the actors who worked on "The Wizard of Oz," is wrenching in its portrait of the compromises Abramovitch's subjects have made to be able to stay in the business.

Tony Cox, who starred in "Bad Santa" and had worked on shows like "Rescue Me," told Abramovitch that his first acting teacher told him that "the only thing you'll ever be in is a costume," meaning he would spend his whole career playing costumed elves or lawn jockeys (Cox is black). Abramovitch chronicles the death of Kimberly Tripp, who impersonated Kim Kardashian at a Hollywood cabaret, and the performers, including Miley Cyrus, who have hired little people to perform in their acts.

"Hollywood's little people," Abramovitch writes bluntly, "are at once beholden to the entertainment industry, which remains their biggest employer, and enslaved by its vision of them, which, in 2016, largely remains that of the eager-to-please freak." Getting somewhat more respectful roles can mean playing characters who aren't human at all; Warwick Davis, for example, broke out as the Ewok Wicket in "Return of the Jedi," and showed up as Griphook, one of J.K. Rowling's memorable goblins, in the movie adaptation of "Harry Potter and the Deathly Hallows."

When actors with disabilities, including dwarfism, do get to play recognizably human versions of themselves, rather than comic props, they often do so in stories explicitly about their bodies. Sometimes, those stories treat it as inevitable that people with disabilities will choose to commit suicide. Other times, Hollywood suggests that it's miraculous that people with disabilities manage to get out of bed, work and form romantic relationships and fantasies. As I wrote when *Finding Dory* came out, it's pretty depressing that some of the most adventurous, fully realized characters with disabilities in American popular culture are cartoon fish.

Or, as Sophie Morgan, a model, paraplegic and disability-issues activist, put it in a recent interview with the *Irish Times*: "I would love to switch on my TV and see a disabled person talking about something they are genuinely interested in or acting out a part that doesn't just focus on their impairment."

Since broad definitions of disability which include mental illnesses and issues such as dementia suggest that almost one in five Americans falls into that category, there's no question that people with disabilities are wildly underrepresented in American popular culture. And they are particularly underrepresented if you're looking for stories in which disability is relatively incidental to the plot.

I'm a big advocate for specificity in storytelling, particularly for scripts that acknowledge that people of color, LGBT people, women and members of other underrepresented groups may have different experiences of the world than the straight, white men who are so often Hollywood's default, and thus may approach everything from dating to the workplace in new and different ways.

BOX 24.2

Maysoon Zaid has 99 problems, and cerebral palsy is just one. Watch the comedian deliver a TED Talk about being an entertainer with a disability:

www.ted.com/talks/maysoon_zayid_i_got_99_problems_palsy_is_just_one?language=en

But given that depictions of people with disabilities so often dwell on difference and suggest that a different experience of the world is either crushing or entirely defining, it strikes me that the best possible thing that Hollywood could do for actors with disabilities and audiences at home is to start telling stories about people who work, travel, love and start families, and who just happen to be disabled. If nothing else, don't we deserve a romantic comedy starring Peter Dinklage already?

Discussion Questions

1. Why are people with disabilities expected to play only roles where their disabilities are the focus of their characters?

2. How important is it that Hollywood and other parts of pop culture find ways to represent people with disabilities more often? What can audiences do to demand more for characters with disabilities?

Little People, Big Woes in Hollywood

Low Pay, Degrading Jobs, and a Tragic Death

Seth Abramovitch

Since The Wizard of Oz, *the short-in-stature have flocked to L.A., where work can be found in jobs ranging from human lawn jockey to mini Donald Trump. But the recent death of a 4-foot-1 cabaret act known as "Mini Kim Kardashian" reveals the uncomfortable reality of how slowly things have evolved since the days of the freak show.*

In the basement of the Hollywood Roosevelt Hotel, behind a trick library bookcase, lies the cabaret Beacher's Madhouse. Nightlife impresario Jeff Beacher describes his creation as "circus meets nightclub" and rattles off a litany of A-listers who've popped in over the years—including George Clooney, Sandra Bullock, Quentin Tarantino, Leonardo DiCaprio, Michael B. Jordan and Zac Efron. Running this circus pays; Beacher, 43, says he has amassed a $50 million fortune from his mini-empire. When I visited the club in October, the last time it was operational, the mood inside was raucous, with assorted douchebags pounding $28 cocktails amid a whirlwind of athletic go-go girls, Hollywood Boulevard-caliber costumed characters and little people—about 20 in all—dashing around with vodka bottles in hand. At one point, Ryan Seacrest entered with two beautiful women, a blonde and a brunette, on each arm. Across the room, a neon sign flickered: "MIDGET BAR."

The first act featured two impersonators, introduced as Mini Kanye West and Mini Kim Kardashian, jumping around to "Gold Digger." The crowd ate it up. (Another routine featured the 4-foot-1 Mini Kim "delivering" an even smaller woman, about 2-foot-6, from between her legs.) Later, a little person dressed as an Oompa Loompa, his face painted a Trumpian orange, crossed the room on a ceiling-mounted conveyor belt to deliver a champagne bottle. It was like watching a minstrel show, one with little people painted orange instead of white actors painted black. A discomfiting feeling settled in.

Five months later, I learned that the woman who played Mini Kim (real name: Kimberly Tripp) had died. Her body was found by her boyfriend, Mini Kanye (real name: Ricky Sells Jr.), on the balcony of the Las Vegas apartment they had shared. He had been out of town, competing in a Micro Wrestling Federation event. The couple had moved to Vegas in 2013 to perform at a new Madhouse location in the MGM Grand, where little people offer aerial bottle service after emerging from a faux elephant's rear end.

"I think I could train any midget to perform," Beacher tells me in April. "We do funny performances, whatever's big in pop culture. We had Mini Kim Kardashian, who just passed away." I'd been reluctant to bring Tripp up, as the investigation into her death was ongoing.

"How?" I ask.

"Just old age, unhealthy," he says. "A lot of them don't have long life spans. Little hearts and the whole thing." She was 32.

* * *

For as long as show business has existed, little people have been delighting audiences—usually for the wrong reasons. In the early 1800s, they were billed as "midgets" and put on display alongside oddities like the "Feejee mermaid" in dime museums, precursors to freak shows that served as entertainment for the unwashed masses.

The root of people's fascination with little people is hard to pin down. "There is a psychoanalytic theory that somehow we're attracted to them because we have a fear that we're never going to grow up," says Robert Bogdan, author of the 1990 book *Freak Show*. "But I think that's mostly bullshit. I think people just found them cute."

By the 1840s, P.T. Barnum was operating the biggest dime museum in the country, Barnum's American Museum in New York, and making huge profits off of his midgets. He gave them fake military ranks and royal titles and concocted illustrious backstories. There was the 3-foot-6 Commodore Nutt, who wore a naval uniform and traveled in a tiny carriage shaped like a walnut; Lavinia Warren, a 2-foot-8 fashion plate; and General Tom Thumb, standing 3-foot-4, who was taken by Barnum from his family at age four and whose Napoleon impersonation always killed. At the height of his celebrity, Thumb—who appeared before Queen Victoria and met Abraham Lincoln—was the biggest celebrity in the world.

* * *

205

The politically correct term is "little people," abbreviated to "LPs." "Dwarf" is acceptable, the plural being "dwarfs"—not "dwarves" (which conjures Tolkien or Snow White's pals). "Midget" long has been considered offensive, referred to by many LPs as "the M-word."

More than 200 distinct medical conditions cause dwarfism, but 80 percent of modern cases are achondroplasia. This disorder, which occurs in about 1 in 25,000 births, inhibits the growth of limbs, resulting in adult heights of 4-foot-10 and under, a rate that has remained unchanged for centuries.

Historically, the term "midget" referred specifically to pituitary dwarfism, which produces LPs with proportions similar to average-size adults. Advances in growth-hormone therapies have made that kind of dwarfism extremely rare, though a handful still exist. The most famous of them today is Deep Roy, 58, a veteran actor best known for playing all 165 Oompa Loompas in Tim Burton's 2005 Wonka film *Charlie and the Chocolate Factory.*

"I am proportional and I'm very lucky for that," the 4-foot-4 Roy tells me at a diner a few blocks from his Santa Monica apartment. Kenya-born to Indian parents, Roy dresses dapperly (he shops in the Harrods boys' section) and exudes a put-upon sophistication, which has served his career well. He does not involve himself in little-person organizations ("not my cup of tea") and in fact does not view himself as a little person: "Whether you're a dwarf, whether you're a midget, it's all branding."

According to Stephen Cox, author of *The Munchkins of Oz*, there was a turf war between proportional and disproportionate little people in Hollywood's golden age, and some of those attitudes and resentments still linger. "Midgets felt they were 'above' the dwarfs, and the dwarfs resented that they were not in proportion," says Cox. "In Hollywood, midgets got many more jobs because they were correctly proportioned."

In any case, little people have always been drawn to Hollywood. In the early days, before the nonprofit support group Little People of America (LPA) was founded in the late 1950s, movie sets were one of the few places they could meet people just like them. In Los Angeles, they not only found work—they also fell in love, married and had children. In fact, nearly 20 percent of the 10,000 little people in America call L.A. home.

There's a 50 percent chance that two parents with achondroplasia will produce a child with dwarfism, a 25 percent chance the child will be born average height, and a 25 percent chance the child will not survive at all. It's a risk many LP parents are willing to take, one well documented on current reality television shows with names like *Our Little Family* and *7 Little Johnstons.* (Pituitary dwarfism, by contrast, is not hereditary, though it does tend to recur among siblings.)

Dwarfism is so rare, and a result of so many genetic abnormalities, that it isn't screened for in normal pregnancies. "What might happen is someone would show up for a routine ultrasound," says Colleen Gioffreda, an administrator at Johns Hopkins' skeletal dysplasia center. "They'd see the baby's limbs are shorter and the head is a little bit larger." A test could be given to detect skeletal abnormalities; at that point, the pregnancy would be at least 28 weeks along.

"Little people don't seem to be upset if they have a child with skeletal dysplasia," she says. "It's something they tend to celebrate."

* * *

The Wizard of Oz still holds the record for the most little people in one film. "Legend has it the studio wanted 300 midgets," says Cox.

In the end, MGM had to settle for 124. That's how many perfectly proportional dwarfs Leo Singer, a German-Jewish emigré who collected little people for his traveling review, rounded up. Singer bought LPs outright from the parents, typically poor farmers who had no use for offspring they couldn't put to work. The Singer Midgets were treated pretty well, given salaries, meals, lodging and custom-made wardrobes. They performed in A-level vaudeville theaters and populated such attractions as the Midget Village at the 1933 Chicago World's Fair.

(A similar concept, Kingdom of the Little People, opened in 2010 in China, where tourists pay $9 to watch performances by little people who pretend to live in mushroom-shaped homes. The park has drawn condemnation from LPA president Gary Arnold, who asked, "What is the difference between it and a zoo?")

There were stories that the Munchkin actors, who mostly were put up at the Culver Hotel, got wasted every night and engaged in orgies. Those rumors, refuted by the Munchkins themselves, were seemingly started by the film's producer, Mervyn LeRoy, who pressed crewmembers each morning for gossip about their antics the night before. The stories also were spread by Dorothy herself: In a 1967 TV interview with Jack Paar, Judy Garland called them "little drunks" who "got smashed every night" and had to be rounded up "in butterfly nets."

For their contribution to Hollywood history, the Munchkins were paid less than Dorothy's dog, Toto, who earned $125 per week for her owner and trainer. Singer Midgets were paid $50 per week ($900 in 2016 dollars) and never saw their names on the big screen.

"It was monumental and it will never happen again," Cox says. Today, only one Munchkin survives: Jerry Maren, who played a Lollipop Guild member in green. At 96, his family says he's too frail to submit to an interview.

* * *

On April 7, at the Red Rock Resort in Las Vegas, several hundred LPA members met for the Western states spring regional, where LPs and their families attend panels with names like "Acromesomeliac Meet and Greet" and "LPA Fashion Show: Inspiring Confidence." I was invited by the LPA's treasurer, Thomas Hershey, 53, a former executive at Sony Pictures who oversaw visual effects and postproduction. Hershey, who gets around in a motorized wheelchair, greeted me at the hotel Starbucks.

"I'm undiagnosed," says Hershey, 4-foot-8. "They don't know what kind of dwarfism I have. I have a lot of similarities to achondroplasia, which explains my head." (His skull is slightly misshapen.) "I have a lot of similarities to cerebral palsy, which affects mobility. I may have both." Hershey grew up in Vero Beach, Fla., the son of a lifelong Navy man who specialized in explosives. "He was the head of nuclear materials, so, you tell me."

Gifted in math and computer science, Hershey attended MIT as an undergrad, then moved to L.A. in 1986 to attend UCLA's MBA program. His wife of 13 years, Gina, 3-foot-9, died of ovarian cancer in 2015. These days, Hershey oversees LPA's District 12, which encompasses California and Nevada and has about 700 members, many of whom work in the entertainment industry.

I ask Hershey how the LP community feels about Beacher's Madhouse. "It's a varied reaction," he says. "There are those that don't begrudge anyone entertaining people and taking advantage of their physical attributes. I fall into that camp: Do what you need to do, if you can look yourself in the mirror afterward."

LPA executive director Joanna Campbell, an average-size woman whose daughter was born with dwarfism, tells me the official LPA stance on those kinds of gigs is that "it is their choice. We try to stay overall neutral."

Still, the LPA will not hesitate to step in if it feels that a business is exploiting little people or putting their lives in danger. It recently demanded that a club in Canada put an end to "dwarf tossing," a spectator sport in which LPs are thrown onto mattresses or against Velcro-covered walls. It also sent a letter to a London nightclub that provided costumed dwarfs to VIP tables for an "Alice in Wonderland" night. Neither complaint garnered a response.

Peter Dinklage, arguably the most celebrated LP actor of all time, protested dwarf-tossing in his 2012 Golden Globe acceptance speech for his work as Tyrion Lannister, the scene-stealing character from Game of Thrones. His speech sent viewers to Google the sad tale of Martin Henderson, an LP who was tossed by a drunk man during the Rugby World Cup, rendering him paralyzed.

Dinklage, 47, typically resists being a spokesman for the dwarfism community. ("I can't preach how to be OK with it," he told an interviewer in 2012. "There's days that I'm not.") Still, the 4-foot-5 star, who declined to speak for this story, has several projects relating to his height now in development. One is a biopic of Hervé Villechaize, the *Fantasy Island* star who killed himself in 1993; another is a movie called *O'Lucky Day*, which Dinklage has described as a "very different take" on leprechaun stories.

The LPA hopes that Dinklage's success will help change attitudes in Hollywood. "Maybe now that he has hosted *Saturday Night Live* they'll think twice about the jokes they've made at little people's expense," says Campbell—referring to a running gag in Bill Hader's popular Stefon sketches in which he described "midgets" in demeaning situations. Then there was the scene in Martin Scorsese's *The Wolf of Wall Street* that featured DiCaprio's character, Jordan Belfort, leading his staff in a dwarf-tossing match. LPA leaders pleaded with producers to reconsider, to no avail.

I ask Martin Klebba, the 4-foot-1 actor who plays Marty in the *Pirates of the Caribbean* films (he flies backward after firing a large gun in the 2007 installment *At World's End*) why more LP stars don't speak out against the exploitation of little people.

"What are you going to see?" says Klebba, 47. "A bunch of little people protesting outside the place? Then that will be on the news and look funny to the masses, a bunch of little people waddling around with protest signs."

Arguably, a direct line can be drawn between these performers, typecast as elves and leprechauns, to Hattie McDaniel, Oscar's first African-American acting winner, who played nothing but maids until her death. More than 150 years after Barnum debuted his world-famous midgets, their modern descendants—bereft of good roles, beset by health problems (spinal compression, bone malformation and neurological issues, to name a few), cruelly commoditized and toothlessly defended—remain closer to the past than the future.

So why did I see a minstrel show where others saw a fun night out? Particularly now, with Hollywood on high alert about its representation of marginalized groups, how is it that the hand-wringing never extends to this one—not even among LPs themselves, at least not consistently? Perhaps it's because Hollywood's little people are at once beholden to the entertainment industry, which remains their biggest employer, and enslaved by its vision of them, which, in 2016, largely remains that of the eager-to-please freak.

I bet Kimberly Tripp felt that.

* * *

Tripp's death, which had occurred a few weeks earlier, was on everyone's lips at the LPA conference in Las Vegas. Many attendees knew her or someone who knew her.

"It's almost like we all went to the same school," says Terra Jole, star of *Little Women: L.A.*, a Lifetime reality show in the *Real Housewives* mold. "And if you're a little person in the entertainment industry, 99 percent of the time, I know you. It's very 90210."

Jole, 36, did not envision herself as a reality star. In 2001, against her mother's wishes, she drove from San Antonio to L.A. to pursue a career as a singer. "I was like a vagabond for a hot minute," she says. To pay the bills, she honed an act as a musical impersonator, playing pop sirens like Britney Spears and Lady Gaga. This led her to Beacher's stage—what she calls a "horrible" experience.

"He is a very negative person who is not happy with himself," she says. "I was having to make sure that I got paid ahead of time before I ever did work for him. He would spring surprises on me, like throwing a mini Kevin Federline onstage in the middle of my Britney performance."

Jole and Tripp met at the Madhouse and bonded on the road as dancers for Ozzy Osbourne. Tripp and Beacher didn't share "your normal employer–employee relationship," says Jole, who recalls witnessing Beacher berate Tripp many times. (Beacher insists he never mistreated Tripp in any way.)

Jole and Beacher parted ways in 2009 when Jole was hired to headline a show at Vegas's Planet Hollywood called Little Legends. She claims Beacher saw the move as a betrayal. "He begged for me not to do it," says Jole. "He stalled my contract and called me nasty names over the phone. I had to change my cellphone number."

Beacher laughs off that account. "Miss Jole likes to create drama, as she does on her reality show," he says. "We always have had nothing but love for her. We created spoof skits and characters that we simply told her and the producers that they weren't allowed to use, as they were owned by my theater group."

*   *   *

Tripp isn't the only lost soul. Michael Gilden got one of his big breaks playing an Ewok in 1983's *Return of the Jedi*. Two decades later, his life seemed to be a fairy tale. He was landing roles on *CSI: Crime Scene Investigation* and *NCIS* and was married to LP actress Meredith Eaton, who played William Shatner's love interest on *Boston Legal*. But one day in 2006, Eaton found her husband hanging in their Los Angeles home. He was 44. (Eaton declined to speak for this article.)

There are no medical studies on suicide and depression rates among little people, but the anecdotal evidence is alarming. David Rappaport, a 3-foot-6 English actor who'd starred in Terry Gilliam's 1981 fantasy film *Time Bandits* and recurred on *L.A. Law*, shot himself at the height of his fame in 1990. Three years after that, Villechaize shot himself outside his North Hollywood home, writing in a suicide note that his dwarfism had left him in intolerable physical pain.

"We have plenty of doctors dedicated to orthopedic concerns," Hershey says of LPA's health care program. "But we don't have anyone in our pocket as far as mental health, which is insane."

Substance abuse is common. Henry Nasiff Jr.—known to millions of Howard Stern fans as Hank the Angry Drunken Dwarf—was a regular on the show for years; he'd arrive to the studio each time with a two-liter Sprite bottle filled with vodka. Nasiff, who was not paid for his appearances, would entertain Stern's audience with his self-pitying tales of life as a little person. He died at his parents' home in 2001, with ethanol abuse listed on the death certificate as a contributing factor. He was 39.

Verne Troyer, who grew up in an Amish community in Michigan, has seen lots of drama since his breakthrough role as Mini-Me, a tiny clone of Dr. Evil, in 1999's *Austin Powers: The Spy Who Shagged Me.* "I had a bit of an alcohol problem," the actor says during a visit at his North Hollywood home.

That is an understatement. Troyer, 47, nearly died of alcohol poisoning in 2002 after breaking up with his fiancée of two months, Playboy model Genevieve Gallen. In 2005, he got extremely drunk on VH1's *The Surreal Life* and urinated in the weight room of the home he shared with wrestler Chyna and *The Brady Bunch*'s Christopher Knight, footage of which went viral. In 2008, TMZ released portions of a sex tape he made with his then-girlfriend, 5-foot-6 Ranae Shrider, whom he'd met at the Playboy Mansion. Then in 2009, his ex-girlfriend Yvette Monet filed for a restraining order against him. "That was a bad period in my life," says Troyer of his hard-drinking years. "I've learned from it, and I move on." After two stints in rehab, Troyer, now single, says he's now "sober . . . I mean, I drink occasionally, but not to the extreme that I did."

At 2-foot-8, he is a record holder for being the shortest actor. For his last major role, he played a killer gnome in the 2015 indie horror movie *Gnome Alone.* "I hadn't seen a lot of parts come my way, so I decided just to do it."

Tony Cox knows the routine. The star of the 2003 black comedy *Bad Santa* has had to take his share of costumed roles over the years. His IMDb page includes such parts as "Willy the Ewok," "Midget Nut" and "Lawn Jockey #1," but Cox has earned a reputation in Hollywood as being a true actor's actor. He is set to reprise his breakout role in *Bad Santa 2.*

The 3-foot-6 Cox recalls his first acting class. "The teacher looked at me and said, 'You're black. That's a strike against you,'" Cox recalls. "Then he said, 'Turn around.' I remember feeling like a piece of meat. So I turned around and the guy said, 'The only thing you'll ever be in is a costume.'"

* * *

"Vegas wasn't the right environment for me," Beacher says, munching on a McCarthy salad at the Polo Lounge, where he is a regular (this despite a waning Hollywood boycott of the place; Beacher is not a man of political correctness). "I was drinking and gambling and having a lot of sex with groupies." It was fun, he admits, until he'd grown too fat to have sex.

His drug of choice has always been food ("I have insecurity issues, abandonment issues; I was adopted"). He often ate "six baskets of bread" before settling in for nine-course steak dinners. He tipped the scales at 415 pounds in October 2014, when he checked himself into a holistic resort and dropped 100 pounds. Then Beacher, who is 5-foot-7, had gastric-sleeve surgery, losing another hundred, followed by a procedure that removed the excess skin.

"The whole Vegas lifestyle is based around partying," he says. "It's a very surface, materialistic, lonely, miserable life. I just knew I'd be dead if I stayed. So I walked away from a 20-year, $100 million contract at the Hard Rock." L.A. suits him much better, he says. "I fixed my head. I'm like Bradley Cooper in *Limitless*. Every day I wake up and anything is possible."

Little people weren't always on Beacher's payroll. But a decade ago, Kelly Osbourne, a Madhouse regular, envisioned 21 little people emerging from a giant birthday cake. Determined to service his starry client's needs, Beacher tracked down Tripp. "Mini Kim orchestrated the whole thing. She put this whole troupe together," he says of Tripp, who had died three weeks before our meeting. "Everyone loved her. It's really sad." Osbourne offered to cover cremation costs, but, Beacher says, "I think I'm going to cover it." (He ended up splitting the $2,800 tab with Donny Davis, his LP right-hand man.)

It was Beacher's idea to have LPs suspended from the ceiling. "I just thought of it one day: flying midgets," he recalls. The joke wasn't a cheap one, at least in a literal sense: The rig at the Roosevelt was $250,000 and the one at the MGM Grand cost $700,000. He says it was worth it. "It's pretty f—ing funny."

Mariah Carey and Miley Cyrus are among his best friends, he says, Carey having performed a Christmas concert at the Roosevelt space, Cyrus having celebrated her 21st and 22nd birthdays there. Cyrus also copied and pasted its depraved funhouse aesthetic for her infamous 2013 MTV Video Music Awards performance and Bangerz Tour, hiring away several Beacher's performers.

One non-Beacher's little person, Hollis Jane, blogged of her VMA show with Cyrus: "Standing on that stage in that bear costume was one of the most degrading things I felt like I could ever do." Cyrus waved off the criticism, saying she helps little people "feel sexual and beautiful." (She declined to be interviewed for this story.)

As far as Beacher is concerned, his A-list friendships make him a better man. "I like being friends with Number Ones: the best writers, the best musicians, the best actors. I'm really close with great directors like Brett Ratner and Michael Bay. I'm friends with great doctors and great attorneys. You surround yourself with the best, you become what you surround yourself with, you know?"

I ask him if he'd ever received any complaints about his act.

"Years ago, yes," he replies. "There was a little-person group that would send letters. LPA I think it's called. I think it was about using the word 'midget.' There's nothing derogatory about it. I don't do midget-tossing. My team performs. They're theatrical performers. They are rock stars and get treated like it. TMZ runs that shit all the time."

* * *

"I never deny that I'm a short actor. That was, and it still is, my USP: my unique selling point," says Warwick Davis, a dashing 3-foot-6 movie star who has earned a near-mythic reputation among LP actors. He was discovered by George Lucas, who cast the U.K. native at age 11 to play Wicket, the hero Ewok in *Return of the Jedi*. The part was supposed to be played by Kenny Baker, who also played R2-D2, but Baker fell ill as shooting was about to begin. (Baker died Aug. 13 after a long battle with chronic pulmonary disease. He was 81.)

"A lot of little people can't act, and that's the truth. But Warwick was so good," recalls Tony Cox, who also played an Ewok. "Man, I remember that kid. He could move so good in the costume."

Davis, 46, has dedicated his life to improving conditions for LP actors. In 1995, Davis's father-in-law, a veteran dwarf actor named Peter Burroughs, complained of being "'treated like a commodity.' His agent would ask, 'How many little people do you need?' It was like he was selling fruits or vegetables," Davis recalls. The pair decided to open a theatrical agency, the London-based Willow Management, that specializes in little people actors. Today, they represent about 100 of them, 40 of whom—in what would be the largest LP cast since *The Wizard of Oz*—played Gringotts goblins in *Harry Potter and the Deathly Hallows — Part 2*. Davis played Griphook, the head goblin, among other guises in the film series. Ricky Gervais turned Warwick's colorful existence into a mockumentary series, *Life's Too Short*, which aired on HBO in 2011. In it, the actually upbeat and good-natured Warwick plays a petty, scheming version of himself.

"There's been a lot of talk recently about, is it right to shrink an average-size actor [with digital effects] to fulfill a little-person role?" he says. "On one side, I could say, yeah, you should never do that, you're taking work away from a short actor. Would you cast an average-size actor to play a disabled character in a wheelchair?" (The answer, of course, is yes, as epitomized by the controversy over the recent Emilia Clarke movie *Me Before You.*)

"But at the same time," he continues, "I understand that within the community of short actors, there might not be a performer with the right capabilities, the right attributes."

Warwick's wheelchair comparison is a telling one, as there exists a division within the little people community as to whether to classify dwarfism as a disability. "You can view it as a disease or a difference," the LPA's Campbell told me at the spring regional. "LPA very much views it as a difference."

Danny Woodburn, 52, who played the hot-headed Mickey Abbott on *Seinfeld*, advocates for actors with all disabilities, and counts dwarfism among them.

"People all of a sudden get nervous about employing you," Woodburn says. "In my life I've had probably 30 operations; I've been in four body casts. My particular dwarfism affects everything from my hearing to my eyes to the cartilage in my bones and to my bone strength and development. But I manage and do pretty well. As my Hungarian doctor said to me before he passed away, 'Dwarfs are very hardy people.'"

*   *   *

I return to Beacher's Madhouse nine months after my initial visit for a photo shoot with Jeff Beacher and some of his LP stars: Donny Davis, who plays Mini Donald Trump; the "Amazing" Ali Chapman and her party-animal husband, "Wee" Matt McCarthy, both of whom appeared on A&E's *Freak Show*; and Ricky Sells Jr., aka Mini Kanye West. Sitting among them and looking very uncomfortable is a new addition—Lila Hart, a beautiful, 25-year-old, 4-foot-6 stand-up comedian with spina bifida whom Davis had recently recruited at the Comedy Store.

Two months earlier, on May 20, 2016, the Clark County Coroner had released its findings on Kimberly Tripp. She did not die of "old age," nor did her "tiny heart" give out, as Beacher had suggested at the Polo Lounge. (Little people have the same sized internal organs as non-little people do and, barring any major medical issues, can live into their 80s and beyond.)

Tripp did not commit suicide, nor, as the Las Vegas Police Department had already concluded, was foul play involved. Tripp's death was natural, caused by "complications of chronic alcohol abuse." She had, in effect, during the course of a decade spent as Beacher's Madhouse's biggest little star, slowly drank herself to death.

"She ran this place. Every celebrity loved her. She had a big heart," says Chapman. The 36-year-old Nicki Minaj impersonator giggles as she reminisces about Tripp kicking customers in the head, including John Stamos, while suspended from the ceiling. "She was frustrated. You know, all these drunk people everywhere, and she's dressed like an Oompa Loompa. So she's like, grrr, kicking people in the head." But, Chapman adds, she had never seen Tripp happier than in the months leading to her death. "When she and Ricky got together, well, it was beautiful to see that relationship manifest."

Seated alone on a couch in the far end of the club is Sells. Only 27 and 4-foot-2, Sells has sadness in his eyes but a quiet and confident demeanor.

We speak about wrestling—he's a three-time gold medalist in his league—and the risks of the sport: "One move can end your career. I landed on my head. I landed on my ass. I messed up my knee. People think it's fake, but it's really not." Still, he loves it and relies on it to distract him from his grief, competing in upward of 20 matches a month, held in bars, strip clubs, state fairs, and tattoo and porn conventions.

It was Tripp who convinced Sells to move to L.A. from Austin after they met in 2011 at an LPA convention in Anaheim. "It's tough," he says. "Because I moved out here, well, for her and this job. And now she's not here no more. So, it's like, I'm crying by myself, you know, because my family's in Texas."

Chapman later tells me of her frustrations. "My long-term goal is to be taken seriously and to be a mainstream actress," she says. "Sure, there's Peter Dinklage doing it, but there can be many of us. I mean, I can just be a nurse in a show, or a mom, or a lady walking her dog down the street! Like, do I need to be an elf? Do I need to be a leprechaun?"

Chapman pauses. "But I get it. It's what you do. I mean, here I work at a place and right over there it says 'Midget Bar.'"

I ask her if she ever thought about asking Beacher to take the sign down. "In the beginning, yes," she says. "But I never did. This is his show. I don't have to be here. If I'm offended by that, I can walk out the door. For the things that I get from being here and doing what I do, I overlook it."

Discussion Questions

1. How has the entertainment industry routinely exploited little people, and how do entertainers distinguish between using their physical attributes and participating in stereotypes?

2. What are the complications and dangers for little people in Hollywood, and why is society slow to recognize or ameliorate these issues?

3. Discuss the use of words like "munchkin" or "midget" in describing these entertainers. Why is it important to avoid this terminology?

4. Is there a connection between the limited roles for little people and their struggles to make a living as entertainers? Would more equitable casting lead to better livelihoods?

5. Does the fact that this piece of journalism is written by someone who is not a little person matter to the way the story is told?

The Ethics of Hodor

Disability in *Game of Thrones*

Spencer Kornhaber and Lauryn S. Mayer

Years before Hodor inspired worldwide mourning among *Game of Thrones* fans, he inspired a medical-blog skirmish. In 2014, a few media outlets ran stories diagnosing the character—known for saying only "Hodor" while serving Bran Stark, a highborn child who can't walk—as having expressive aphasia, a neurological condition restricting speech. Some aphasia experts pushed back, saying that while Hodor has often been described as "simple-minded" or "slow of wits," aphasia only affects linguistic communication—not intelligence.

That a fictional stablehand could inspire doctorly debate highlights not only how seriously people take *Game of Thrones*, but how seriously the show and corresponding books take disability. George R.R. Martin's cast is filled with what Tyrion Lannister affectionately terms "cripples, bastards, and broken things" who manage to wield power while facing stigma and physical challenges. Some characters are born different, but more are rendered so by a brutal world, like Bran, Jaime, and the story's various eunuchs and greyscale patients. Hodor's backstory was left sketchy until Sunday's episode revealed his condition to have resulted from Bran controlling his mind during time travel: In a vision of the past, viewers saw a boy named Wylis falling down as if in seizure and repeating "hold the door," the orders he would receive in his dying moment decades later.

In the 2014 scholarly essay "A Song of Ice and Fire's Ethics of Disability," Lauryn S. Mayer of Washington and Jefferson College and Pascal J. Massie of Miami University of Ohio examined the disability themes in George R.R. Martin's book series. They wrote that the saga seemed interested in "dismantling the clichés of disability, examining the costs of ableist ideologies, and uncovering the fear of mortality and vulnerability that compels people to build a wall separating themselves from the disabled."

I spoke with Mayer, an associate professor of English who teaches about medieval and medieval-inspired literature, for her thoughts on Hodor's demise and newly revealed history. This interview has been edited and condensed.

Spencer Kornhaber: What makes *Game of Thrones* interesting in its portrayal of disability?

Lauryn S. Mayer: Medieval and fantasy literature has been noted by a lot of scholars for providing a space to imagine something different: another world—utopian, dystopian—or a particular way of thinking, different social structures, those kinds of things. The thing that I found interesting with Martin was that he takes a world in which people are particularly vulnerable and he plays that up.

Look at Tolkien, for example. If you count up the battles, skirmishes, everything like that [in the *Lord of the Rings* series], the fact that out of the nine [Fellowship of the Ring members], eight of them survived and only one of them is missing a finger is statistically ludicrous. Martin is playing with the idea that because somebody is a hero or a beloved character they are going to live somehow. I used to call that the kids-at-the-end-of-*Jurassic-Park* syndrome: They should have been raptor chow, but we can't have the kids getting killed.

By talking about disability as a very certain set of extreme conditions, we have a tendency of setting up these walls between them and us. But what Martin does is show how very, very fragile the boundaries between wholeness and bodily vulnerability are. Only in a moment you can go from being an "able" person to somebody who is "disabled."

Hodor shows up in the books as somebody who cannot speak anything beyond what we thought was his name. But Martin is very careful to make sure that we know that Hodor can understand people, can follow complex instructions, and has absolutely appropriate emotional reactions to things. This is carried over to the show, too: The actor who plays Hodor spent a lot of time practicing how to say that one word in a way to connote different types of emotions. So it seemed when Pascal and I originally wrote the essay, what we had was somebody who was functionally mute but had an active intelligence. What happens is that he is treated as simply a body to be ordered around.

Part of that obviously is class issues—that's how you treat your servants. But also Martin is playing with the idea of "what do you do when you have someone who seems to have all the tropes of a developmentally disabled individual but he's not [one]?" I thought it was interesting that Hodor keeps saying his name over and over again in a text that is trying to take the disabled out of stereotype and into individuality.

Right now with Hodor, I think it's even sadder. It was made very clear that either Bran or the Three Eyed Raven are responsible for taking a seemingly bright and personable stableboy and turning him into somebody who either can constantly see his own future demise and is so traumatized by it that the only thing he can do is say "hold the door," or somebody who has been stripped of agency to articulate any will of his own other than the purpose for which he has been used.

Kornhaber: There was ambiguity over his mental faculties, and this episode made it clearer that something really was deeply different in him.

Mayer: Yeah. It's very interesting to see the fan reaction to this. He is now either being retroactively rewritten as an automaton whose job was just to hold the door and who now is valorized because of this great sacrificial death—or somebody who is being painted as a Christlike figure who knows perfectly well what his own death is and how horrible it is.

Both of these things bother me a little bit because a character who had the potential to have agency was now turned into one of these other disability tropes: He was a heroic sacrificial figure, or the figure of lost purity and innocence. You see that over and over again in literature, like Dostoyevsky's *The Idiot*, or Lenny in *Of Mice and Men*, or if you want to go into popular culture, *Forrest Gump*.

There's something else: Bran, who of all people should have some empathy for Hodor, is kind of an abusive little shit. Because Martin makes it very clear in the books—and this is another way that Hodor has will and agency—Hodor does not want to be warged into at all. He fights him, but obviously he doesn't have the mental ability that Bran does. And then he curls up like a beaten dog. Hodor could break Bran like a twig, but he doesn't want to be violent; when Samwell gives him those dragonglass weapons, he doesn't want to take them till he's ordered to. And when you get to that scene where he snaps his chains and then snaps his tormenter in half, that's not him, that's Bran. Hodor is horrified by what's happened. Bran's always using an excuse: "I just want to be strong again," "I won't do this for too long"— that's the logic of the abuser.

Hodor's supposed to be loyal anyway. You could just have Bran tell Hodor to hold the door and have him die sacrificially. But I think it's very interesting that the show presents this early violation against a kid who could have grown up to be a perfectly functioning and very colorful adult.

BOX 26.1

What happens when a hit show with a disabled character isn't actually accessible for people with a disability? Read more about the problems with the roll-out of one Netflix show:

www.themarysue.com/daredevil-blind-accessibility/

Kornhaber: The point you made earlier about the show reminding people of their fragility—it seems like this revelation about Hodor's past is another example of that. It wasn't something he was born with.

Mayer: Yeah, and that's the reason, I think, people react so viscerally to the show. Look at the reaction [videos] to any particular horrifying episode of *Game of Thrones*, like Shireen being burned to death or the Red Wedding. If you watch people's body language, they are acting as if they themselves are being physically hurt, right? A lot of them will start curling into themselves. They'll start touching parts of their bodies like you do when you're injured. And if you look at the comments afterwards, you see the kind of thing where [it's like] people dropped something on their foot. A lot of them are not even able to articulate complete sentences: "FUCK THIS FUCKING SHOW!" or "I can't even, I can't, I can't."

When I was driving back from Pittsburgh before I had this interview, I got cut off by a large truck. A three-second miscalculation, and you'd be having this conversation with someone else. And that [feeling], I think, is what Martin does. In terms of disability, it really reminds us of how profoundly vulnerable that we are—that the boundary between the abled and the disabled is so thin.

Kornhaber: And that's, in the end, a good thing for attitudes toward people with disabilities?

Mayer: One of the things I like about Martin is that he doesn't fall into these tropes of disability. Hodor is the closest—I'm kind of disappointed that he fell sort of into the sacrificial Christ trope. But think of the rest of the people who are disabled in the show. I think it's a good thing that Bran is a profoundly complicated individual. He's abusing Hodor but he's not an evil character—he's selfish and lacks empathy on occasion, just like everybody else. [By contrast] imagine what Dickens would have done with him: Tiny Tim.

Tyrion is a dwarf, but he's not so much confined by dwarfishness as much as he is by his own internalization of ableist discourse. Now, again, this cuts across class and cuts across a whole lot of other issues, but I think that there is a huge step forward in the fact that you've got people in here who are disabled, who are complex, sometimes really annoying, sometimes heroic, sometimes selfish, sometimes unselfish. I think Martin is really trying to not put them into types or use them as some symbol for the suffering of humanity or something like that.

Kornhaber: In terms of real medieval history, how would someone like Hodor have been thought about and treated?

Mayer: Well, that's a difficult, complex question. It would depend on a variety of things. Somebody like Hodor, who is of a serving class, who is immensely strong, who, let's say, had some sort of tragic accident—he probably wouldn't be treated too much differently.

He would be considered a useful body, probably tormented by some people, probably helped by others. The medieval church did stress that one was supposed to be Christlike in one's actions, which meant one was supposed to be empathic and compassionate. There might be the kind of thing that surrounded the figure of the fool as someone who may have other wisdom or greater innocence—we get these narratives from places.

I'm leery about any sort of generalization turning medieval people into a homogenous mass. Class does have a huge influence. Courtly literature will usually show lower classes as being inherently less intelligent, less good looking, less able to do things. There's the trope of the kid of the royal blood raised as a peasant but of course you know he's of royal blood because he's so much smarter or whatever. In a lot of cases, medieval courtly literature was self-serving because it was trying to take a class situation and make it an inherent set of qualities. So somebody who was born into a class to serve would probably have automatically been treated as if they were somewhat less mentally capable, which would have been encouraged by the fact that very few of them could read and write.

Kornhaber: One part of the revelation in this last episode was that Hodor became this way through an act of magic. Was there a belief in medieval times that mystical forces were at play in disability?

Mayer: Disability could be seen in a variety of ways. If you're disabled from birth, that might be because your mother had seen some sort of thing that caused an impression on the womb. If you saw a spider when you were pregnant, your kid might be born with extra limbs.

There was also the idea that the state of the body reflected the state of the soul. If you were suddenly disabled, it might be considered a punishment from God because of some sort of aspect of your living. Leprosy, for example, was seen in a lot of cases as a punishment for sexual excess. You lose control of your body parts because you've lost control of your body parts.

[Disability] also might be considered, though, as a privilege because you were living your penance on earth rather than going to purgatory. Going back to the idea of Christ suffering on the cross, it's like, here's your test.

Kornhaber: Can you think of any other historical, mythological, or literary figures that Martin might have been reaching for when coming up with Hodor?

Mayer: I think there's a range of possibilities. Possibly St. Christopher, the person who was carrying Christ on his back. Martin could be [referencing] any one of the service martyrs who devoted their lives to something. Or think of the battle of Thermopylae, where you have 300 Spartans who are being hacked to pieces in order to hold that pass.

Oh, you know what Martin might be thinking of? Princess Bride. Andre the Giant.

Kornhaber: Any other Hodor thoughts?

Mayer: This [Hodor twist] just happened this past Sunday, and already Hodor doorstops are being sold. It's going to be interesting to see how the fans and the audience [talk about] Hodor now. Because even though Martin is very careful to say that Hodor understands what he's doing, he's always seen as the big lovable simpleton, and now, he's being rewritten as a tragic hero. If you take a look at Imgur and various other [memes about Hodor] before this, really in a lot of cases it was mockery. The Hodor rap battle—"worst rap battle ever." Or someone had Hodor's chapter of George R.R. Martin's book: "Hodor, Hodor, Hodor." We're talking about a character who's obviously disabled, and he's a punchline.

That's what I'm worried about: Can we only respect him after he dies in a suitably sacrificial way? I'm not coming down on one side or another on this, because every time you talk about fan reactions you're going to get a huge [range] all the way across the board. But it is an interesting thing to watch. Even some of the articles will say, "He turned from a punchline into a much heavier situation." And I'm like, "Wait a minute, the guy's mute and disabled and obviously there's a mind there, and I think that's tragic even before we realized what has happened."

Discussion Questions

1. How does the fantastic setting of *Game of Thrones* (and other fantasy books or shows) allow us a chance to rethink disability? Discuss how the show also invites us to think about disability in medieval society.

2. Can Hodor teach us anything about vulnerability and interdependence? Does he need to be disabled to do so?

3. If you've seen *Game of Thrones*, can you think of other disabled characters and how their disability is portrayed?

From a Bendy Straw to a Twirly Straw

Growing up Disabled, Transnationally

Shilpaa Anand

Coming of age, as complex as it is, is even more so if one is living with cerebral palsy, is bisexual and depends on one's middle-class Indian caregiver mother. In the 2014 film *Margarita with a Straw*, the main character named Laila has all this complexity in her life as a girl in her late teens growing up in middle-class Delhi. Her life as a young woman with cerebral palsy is a coccooned one, but it has its share of clandestine sexual exploration in the back rooms of the college biology lab with wheelchair-using Dhruv. The frontroom Laila we meet moves about the junior college in her motorized wheelchair, falls in love with the lead singer of the college band, and has her heart broken by him. Does he reject her because of her disability? Is her heartache different because hers is not just a girl's heart broken by a guy, but a disabled girl's heart broken by a nondisabled so-called normal guy? These questions are not conclusively answered and that is what keeps the film from falling into the trap of a typical overcoming-disability narrative.

BOX 27.1

For a sense of what this movie is like, look at the trailer for the film at:

https://youtu.be/yCQjrsV14sl

The film captures the particular Indian flavours of being disabled in an overly caring middle-class family and home, where it seems, as Cohen (1998) has pointed out in a different but related context, disability is not an individual experience but appears to belong to a familial body. Their daily lives are intertwined with Laila's needs and accommodating them to such an extent that her mother's connection with her seems to transcend the limits of an emotional bond in becoming an *aadat* (habit in Urdu), as one of the songs in the film's soundtrack describes her.

In contrast to this familial self that Laila has known all her life is the Americanized independent-individual self into which she learns to grow when she moves to New York to go to university. Laila is settled into an apartment in New York by her mother, who stays with her for a while before leaving her in the care of a professional caregiver. She then lets the caregiver go when her romance with a young woman blossoms. Laila grows into a transnational disabled woman as we see her sell her grandmother's gold necklace to buy an iPad and find the potential of a sexual encounter in everyday proximity with the scribes assigned to her for writing assistance. Before her mother leaves New York she discovers that her daughter has been surfing porn sites on her laptop and, to her utter dismay, Laila tells her mother that she has invaded her privacy. Her mother was clueless about the fact that Laila had begun to explore her sexuality when they were in Delhi. Laila's mother's exasperation is caused by her inability to comprehend how a girl she bathes and grooms can have a private life that does not include her caregiving parent.

At New York University, Laila meets part-Pakistani, part-Bangladeshi Khanum. She is a blind woman, on the picket-line of what looks like an anti-racism demonstration, literally falling into Laila's lap in the post-demonstration, teargas-infested chaos. Khanum's boldness and Laila's diffidence come together in a glorious lesbian romance of jazz, margaritas, picnics in the park, and nightly lovemaking.

The film frames two distinct disability experiences within the circle of the lesbian romance. In a museum in New York, Khanum guides Laila's hands to experience a tactile way of looking at the exhibits, and this turns into a sexually charged moment as Khanum moves her exploring hand up Laila's arm to her face. When Laila flinches, Khanum asks her to relax, saying that it was her turn to look, tactilely, at Laila. Khanum's admiring touch replaces a sighted person's desirous gaze and confuses Laila, who has probably learned in her sighted world to associate desirous touching only with derisive categories of abuse that include being groped or being felt-up. It is also possible that she flinches because she is surprised that anyone can find her desirable. In all of Laila's previous sexual encounters, it is she who had initiated the touching.

Tracing Laila's face with her fingers Khanum, exclaims, "*Kamini!*[1] You're so pretty, dude!" This scene problematizes presumed binaries, such as those between the categories of disabled and normal. While both of them are categorized as disabled, there appears to be a yawning gap between Laila's experience of living with cerebral palsy and Khanum's life as a blind girl. Laila's flinching at Khanum's touch is also indicative of her being unfamiliar with, or ignorant about, what it means to be blind. In another moment when they are lying in the park in New York, Laila enviously comments on how perfect Khanum's body is, telling her that she could be a model. This moment is perhaps reflective of how Laila thinks of her own body as imperfect in a way that conflates the ideal feminine body with the nondisabled body. The moment presents a disabled young woman's yearning for a nondisabled body.

Disabled girlhood, the film confirms, involves learning about one's sexuality in-between and blurred by the lines labeled normal and disabled. On two separate occasions Laila's disabled friends and lovers reprimand her for desiring what appears to count, for her, as normality: wanting to be with and desiring able-bodied friends and able-bodied men. These lines continue to blur her experiences with Khanum and create underlying tension throughout the film. Laila must eventually tell Khanum that she cheated on her and had sex with Jared, the blond scribe she is assigned at the university, only because he was sighted. That blow hurts Khanum as much as any other sighted person's comments on her blindness would have done. What Laila does not say—but is implied in her need to be made love to by Jared—is that she desires, as a person with cerebral palsy, to be validated by a sighted person.

Those who think that the two girls come together because they are both disabled base this assumption on an imagined homogeneity between and among different disabilities. Having one kind of a disability does not necessarily preclude ableism toward another kind.

One of the most common reactions of Indian moviegoers to the film is that it is a bold film to have been made and released in India. Middle-class and urban audiences thought the film was doing things for which India was not yet ready. Was the film bold because it was about queer sex? Was it bold because it shows a young woman masturbating? Was it bold because it shows a disabled woman wanting and enjoying sex? It is very likely that the responses of the moviegoers refer to one or all of these reasons.

Sadly, many disabled people in India were excluded from seeing *Margarita*, this *bold film*. While the very title sets it up as a film about equal access (even if it is access to a margarita, a drink not usually consumed through a straw) the film remained largely inaccessible for wheelchair users, blind people, and sign language users. Although the film crew had unequivocally participated in a campaign called "Mumbai Rising for Disability Access," wheelchair access in India is a complex matter, as pointed out by the film. While most public spaces in the country are inaccessible to wheelchair users, the solution is quite readily available when people willingly offer to lift wheelchairs. The film represents this peculiarly Indian way of making public spaces accessible. As Laila's troubled expression conveys when her chair is being lifted up the college stairway, wheelchair users who wanted to see the film when it was released in theatres were anxious that their only access to the film would include this embarrassingly typical mode of Indian access.

Ironically, the film appeared to go out of its way to become accessible to non-disabled moviegoers by carrying subtitles. These subtitles appeared only for Laila's speech, which would be considered un-understandable for "normal" ears. If the whole film were subtitled, not only would it have become accessible to deaf viewers, but this would also have prevented the film from highlighting Laila's differences in an exclusive way.

Laila returns home for a summer vacation and brings Khanum with her; this, she hopes, will also be the summer of her coming out to her mother as bisexual. But the summer gets complicated. Her mother's cancer returns, Laila becomes her caregiver, and the coming-out is a rocky one. Her relationship with Khanum ends when she reveals that she had cheated on her with Jared. Her mother dies. The film ends with Laila going out to a roof-top restaurant in Delhi. Laila gets her hair styled, wears an orange dress, and gets her father to give her a ride in her mother's minivan to the restaurant where she sits at a table opposite a mirror. She orders her margarita and pulls out of her bag a new kind of straw: a twirly one, as opposed to the usual bendy one she used. The ending of the film is an affirmation of Laila to her self, neither through the caring gaze of her Indian mother, nor through the Americanized and adoring eyes of her former lesbian lover. The Laila she affirms to herself combines the one who is still dependent on private transport that her family facilitates *and* the one who is independent enough to go on a date by herself *and* order an alcoholic beverage.

Margarita is a film about many transitions and makes a case for the fluidity that marks growing up, moving out, and gaining an identity—all significant in the life of a young woman. Laila learns to live her life as one in constant transition between the protected life and the precariously lived one, between being disabled but ableist, between knowing her needs and not giving in to them, and, most importantly, between being a *desi*[2] in New York and being an independent disabled girl in a world of Indian familial bodies. This film offers the scholarship on girlhood and disability in transnational contexts an opportunity to explore the ways in which girlhood and disability constitute each other in relation to different impairment categories in different cultural contexts. *Margarita* enables us to consider and theoretically reflect on an experience that is gendered, corporeally different, and sexualized, as well as geographically and conceptually transnational.

Discussion Questions

1. How is Laila's story a transnational one? How does disability differ between India and New York?

2. Why does Laila seek the love of a nondisabled person at the cost of her other relationships? What might this say about the psychology of ableism?

3. Does it matter that the actress Kalki Koechilin playing Laila is actually not disabled? Does it matter that her parents were non-Indians who came to India in the 1970's from France?

Notes

1   *Kamini* which literally means 'female villain' in Urdu/Hindi is usually used as a term of abuse but is used here by Khanum as an endearment for Laila.
2   *Desi* literally 'local' or 'belonging to one's country' in Hindi but connotes 'being Indian' in standard usage, as in the context of the film.

Reference

Cohen, Lawrence. 1998. *No Aging in India*. New Delhi: Oxford University Press.

The New Kid in Primetime

What *Speechless* Has to Say

Alexander Luft

Midway through the pilot of the 2016 sitcom *Speechless*, JJ DiMeo enters a classroom at his new school. The 16-year-old has cerebral palsy, uses a power wheelchair and is accompanied by an aide. Rolling into this classroom is, for JJ, a lot like *Speechless* rolling into primetime television: they both appear in places where people have imagined disability doesn't exist.

JJ's new teacher urges the class to stand and applaud, but when he notices JJ's wheelchair, he's aghast and tells the students to sit down. He then apologizes to JJ because, as he explains it, they've never had a student like JJ before. And as he tries to explain further, the teacher can't quite bring himself to say the word "disabled." As many physical or environmental barriers might exist for JJ in his new school, he also faces the social barriers that occur when people recognize disability. So the teacher stammers for a second and then falls back on a cliché that rings of inspiration porn, saying: "You are taller sitting down than any of us standing." JJ's new classmates are already prepping him for a run for class president, which prompts JJ to ask, via a laser pointer attached to his head that he can direct at a worded card, why they would do that when they don't even know him.[1]

Just as JJ will encounter all sorts of unrealistic expectations from his classmates, the sitcom itself faces the burden of being what David M. Perry calls "one of the most important shows about disability in the history of television."[2] Historically, disabled people have been vastly underrepresented in popular media, with some studies showing that only around 1 percent of TV characters have a disability. And when disabled people do appear on the small screen, they are most likely relegated to one of a variety of stereotypical roles: as villains, as problems for nondisabled characters to "fix," or as props for nondisabled people to exhibit their empathy. Although there certainly have been notable disabled characters appearing in mainstream scripted television, they are most often secondary characters. Sometimes these unsatisfying roles for disabled characters aren't even played by disabled people but by nondisabled actors who are praised for affecting various impairments.

Speechless, on the other hand, distinguishes itself by placing a disabled character, played by a disabled actor, at the center of its cast. The ABC sitcom makes it clear that disability is more than just a part of JJ's character. Disability is the show's reason for being.

The show's writer, Scott Silveri, grew up with a brother who had cerebral palsy, and the show's DiMeo family is a rough approximation of Silveri's own upbringing. In the pilot, the family has just moved into a shabby house so that JJ can attend the well-funded school where he has been promised a communicative aide. Unlike many people with cerebral palsy who use an Augmentative and Alternative Communication (AAC) device, JJ is portrayed as preferring to use the laser-and-word apparatus to keep other people engaged in conversation with him. Silveri rewrote JJ's character after meeting a woman named Eva Sweeney, whose mother attached a laser pointer to her cap and gave her a new way to communicate. Sweeney, who was brought on as a consultant for *Speechless*, had tried spelling out words by pointing to individual letters (which took too long and was exhausting) or using high-tech AAC devices. She found that pointing to words was more efficient and also helped to keep conversations moving. And so JJ, a boy in search of his "voice," became the newest star in primetime.

BOX 28.1

Meet JJ and the rest of the DiMeo family on the pilot episode of *Speechless*:

http://abc.go.com/shows/speechless/episode-guide/season-01/1-series-premiere-p-i-pilot

JJ's family, led by the feisty Maya DiMeo, talks naturally with JJ, following his laser pointer and translating when necessary. But to make do in the new school environment, JJ needs the help of an aide who can be his "voice." He is initially paired with an older white woman whose cheerful demeanor is misfit to JJ's biting wit and penchant for vulgarity. To the show's credit, we see JJ mistreat this aide (that is to say, a "perfectly behaved" JJ would only reinforce the idea of disabled people as "saints"). The female aide asks to be fired rather than spend more time with the DiMeo family, so JJ approaches the school's groundskeeper, seemingly the community's only black member, to take the job. JJ and Kenneth form a fast friendship by sharing their experiences of tokenism; the rich, white community around them excels at symbolic inclusion but fails to be substantially inclusive, and they both know it.

"It reminds me of when I was a kid," said Cedric Yarborough, who plays the groundskeeper-turned-aide. "My mom would tell me, 'oh wow, we saw a black person on TV. We saw James Brown on television.' So I feel that way with this particular show."[3] Following the successes of *Black-ish* and *Fresh off the Boat*, ABC has implicitly included disability identity as part of its move toward more diverse primetime programming. Viewers with an interest in disability and social justice are watching intently to see if the show succeeds on its own terms rather than simply as a token disability show. Early reviews of the show have been overwhelmingly positive, as many critics laud the perceived authenticity of its characters and the warmth of the family's humor.

And yet *Speechless* isn't without its early detractors or flaws. The show cannot escape being a half-hour family sitcom on a major network; it plays by all the traditional rules of tying up domestic dramas and having a few laughs along the way. Maya DiMeo's belligerence makes her both entertaining and a bit of a one-note character. Even Silveri admits it might be "reductive and insulting to moms [of disabled children] to reduce them simply to that fighting thing. But damn if they don't have it in common."[4] Each episode depends on a small family strife that must be repaired, and the family must be made whole before the credits roll.

In this way, the show's format keeps it always striving for normalization or normalcy, which begs the question of how truly "disabled" a show like *Speechless* can be. Certainly part of the show's success will depend on how faithfully it can represent the lived experience of disability, but it would seem near impossible that one disabled character, who's portrayed as having communication and mobility impairments (while his mother insists repeatedly that he's cognitively "normal") could prove a satisfying representative for a wide variety of disabled people. Why would it be important to be "normal" in one way but not another? Critics have also asked whether an aide is truly a "voice" for JJ and whether having that "voice" could really give him power to represent himself in social institutions.[5] Sitcoms gives us a tidy version of real life, and so *Speechless*, even at its best, gives us only an idealized version of disability and disabled life.

At the same time, it's important for *Speechless* that it can make disability funny— that audiences laugh *about* disability without laughing *at* it. Richard Ellenson, the head of the Cerebral Palsy Foundation and a frequent visitor to the *Speechless* set, puts it this way:

> We need to have a world where we can have safe conversations about disabilities for people with disabilities and people who don't have disabilities. The way to do that is with humor, once you laugh you can say things you can't say any other way.[6]

Perhaps the most telling scene in the pilot episode comes when JJ's father, Jimmy, drives him and his sister, Dylan, to a carnival to track down Maya. Jimmy turns from the driver's seat and tells the kids he'll need one of them to run with him and one to stay and watch the van. "Hmmmm," he says, eyeing JJ in the rear seat, "What might be a good division of labor?" JJ responds with a gesture equivalent to giving his dad the middle finger. Jimmy is, in fact, making fun of his son's mobility impairment. But instead of seeming offensive or ill-conceived, this slight at JJ's expense tells us something authentic about a family living with disability. Like any everyday struggle, living with a disability invites us to either laugh or cry; we're endeared by the DiMeos' choosing the former. Pulling off a disability joke without it seeming mean-spirited or harmful seems like a sign that *Speechless* confronts disability honestly.

Many of the show's jokes seem particularly "accessible" to disabled viewers who will recognize their own lives in the scenes. The show opens with a pair of teenagers gawking at JJ in a parking lot, and he flips them off in reply; public staring is a common experience that many disabled people would know. Kenneth, who would become JJ's aide, uses the word "crippled" in his first scene. This prompts a swift chastisement from Maya, who like many disabled people must explain the history and offensiveness of the term. She also confronts an administrator about the school's plan to have JJ use an entrance ramp used to cart garbage. In Maya's impromptu lecture on "basic human decency," she outlines the difference between garbage and people. These scenes might seem novel to a viewer unaccustomed to arguing for the personhood of disabled people, but they can be parts of everyday life for someone with a disability.

Even as *Speechless* might succeed in terms of representing disability, we might ask whether its off-screen production is as equitable and fair for disabled people. The show's creators have been lauded for bringing disabled actors into the fold, but consider that Silveri, the writer, is nondisabled. And though Micah Fowler, who plays JJ, has cerebral palsy, he is able to speak aloud. Critics would say that Fowler is "cripping up" (adopting an impairment he doesn't actually have) for the role, which ideally could have been reserved for an actor who communicates in a manner similar to JJ. There are countless nondisabled actors who regularly work and have won awards for portraying disabled people while disabled actors struggle to get cast. Disabled people ought to have the chance to work in every part of producing a show like *Speechless,* whether in on-screen roles, behind the cameras or in the editing room. Silveri has publicly discussed plans to incorporate more disabled actors as well as disabled characters, which will better show how JJ, a disabled kid, finds his identity among others in the disabled community.

Primetime television, as much a place of community-forming as any other site in American life, has always imagined a world without disability. Television accounts for more of our leisure time than socializing with real people, which means that our on-screen friends might shape our view of the world more than their flesh-and-blood counterparts. We ought to see and hear from disabled people on our televisions so that we can start to recognize disability everywhere in our lives. Consider again the scene in *Speechless* in which JJ enters his new classroom. The teacher explicitly tells

JJ they've never had a disabled student before, but in real life this would be extremely improbable. Roughly one in five people have a disability at some point in their lives, but it serves the show's plot to think of JJ as an anomaly or as a singular outlier in a world of normalcy. That world is an imaginary one. It seems odd, in fact, that no other characters in the pilot were portrayed as disabled. Just as JJ will certainly strive against the misconceptions of his ableist classmates and community, so too will *Speechless* play out against a backdrop that has long refused to acknowledge this truth: disability has always been with us.

Discussion Questions

1. Is there a difference between a show about a disabled character and a show about disability? Does the difference matter?

2. Discuss how some of the show's jokes might be "accessible" to disabled people. How can we tell the difference between laughing at or laughing about disability?

Notes

1   A later episode in the first season, titled "H-E-Hero," deals explicitly with the idea of inspiration porn, as JJ defines the term for both his aide and a national audience. JJ resents being treated as a "saint" by his classmates and teachers but appreciates his brother's calling-out his flaws.

2   Perry 2016.

3   Hendrickson and Atkinson 2016.

4   NPR 2016.

5   Alper 2016.

6   Hendrickson and Atkinson 2016.

References

Alper, Meryl. "What ABC's New TV Series 'Speechless' Can Tell Us About 'Voice.'" *Vice.* Sept. 21, 2016. Web.

Hendrickson, Molly and Hanna Atkinson. "'Speechless' actor Micah Fowler breaking new ground for actors with cerebral palsy." TheDenverChannel.com. Nov. 9, 2016. Web.

National Public Radio. "ABC's 'Speechless' Looks To Change How Hollywood Depicts Disability." Nov. 10, 2016. Web.

Perry, David M. "Speechless is Breaking New Ground On Television." *The Atlantic.* Sept. 21, 2016. Web.

An Advertising Aesthetic

Real Beauty and Visual Impairment

David Bolt

Foundational to this article, if not to the very discipline of disability studies, are a couple of works on stigma from more than half a century ago. One, the better known book, was a fairly general study of stigma (Goffman, 1963/1968), while the other focused on disability in particular (Hunt, 1966). The latter made the salient point that disabled people were tired of being represented as pitiable objects whose purpose was to elicit funding, as well as being wonderfully courageous examples to the world, and criticized the stereotyped portrayals of popular culture.[1] This sentiment resonated nearly three decades later when advertising was found to contribute to discrimination in two ways: first, people who had impairments were excluded and in some instances deliberately ignored, and second, a distorted view of disability was presented in order to raise money, as in charity campaigns.[2] The issue of stigma loomed large in advertising because, either way, via exclusion or misrepresentation, for people who had impairments that was the effect.

The pitiable misrepresentation of disability was particularly prominent in early charity advertisements. A hallmark of the aesthetic of these advertisements was a stark, usually black and white image of someone who was disabled, with a focus on her or his impairment, the key purpose being to evoke fear and sympathy in the viewer.[3] Unfortunately, until the late 20th century, the representation of disability in advertising was generally restricted to such fundraising campaigns,[4] or at best found in medical and rehabilitation product catalogs, disability magazines, and disability organization posters and brochures.[5] Representations of disability were seldom included in so-called mainstream advertisements.

A more progressive and inclusive approach to disability and advertising became apparent in the late 20th century. Favorable images started to appear in the 1980s[6] and, while "routine pictures of disabled people in advertising" remained "hard to find,"[7] a number of advertisements in the early 1990s included characters who used wheelchairs and were shown as "normal people doing things that normal people do."[8] (By the end of the century, there was a growing list of advertisers who featured disability in their campaigns. This list included Crest, Citibank, Citicorp, Coke, Fuji, IBM, Kmart, Levi's, McDonald's, Nissan, Pacific Telesis, and Target.)[9] Thus, by the 1990s, if not the 1980s, the application of disability in advertising was no longer the sole domain of charity campaigns.

The reason for this progress was not simply a less prejudicial, more informed use of images and ideas. The disabled consumer was said to be coming of age, as companies in the United States and the United Kingdom recognized the profitability of including disability in their advertisements.[10] This recognition was greatly aided by legislation in the form of the Americans with Disability Act (ADA) and the British Disability Discrimination Act (DDA). Moreover, although many businesses started to use disabled models in advertising due to capitalistic motivation (i.e. an awareness not only that there were potential customers who had impairments, but also that diversity enhanced audience reception to the products in question), the crass commercialism produced some good disability images.[11] Albeit due to a desire for profits, companies learned to move away from the use of pity narratives and toward advertisements that were sensitive and accurate, that represented disability as "another slice of life,"[12] progress that was bound to reduce stigmatization.

For all this progress, the portrayal of disability in advertising was far from representative, even in purely quantitative terms. Advertising images that utilized people who had impairments were "few and far between in mainstream media publications."[13] Indeed, although the United States was faster than the United Kingdom to reflect disability in commercial advertising,[14] a two-year quantitative analysis conducted in 1998–1999 found that people who had visible impairments were portrayed "far less frequently in the commercials than their 6.5% of the population as reported by the Census Bureau."[15] In relation to Britain, advertisements on American television were more prevalent and less restricted,[16] but nonetheless harshly underrepresented people who had impairments.

Another representational problem related to questions about if, when, and what impairments were shown. The trouble was that impairments in general were avoided; they were conveniently overlooked or else portrayed so as not to intrude on the viewer's aesthetic consciousness.[17]

Indeed, if and when impairments were visible, they tended to be restricted to a few (if not a couple), for there was an "almost total focus" on wheelchair use and deafness.[18] In other words, in relation to the normative, aesthetic consciousness, some impairments were considered more intrusive than others and avoided accordingly.

Although the disabled consumer was said to be coming of age, the problem of avoidance extended beyond the advertisements in many ways, even when the medium was relatively easy to make accessible, as in the case of the Internet. For example, at the end of the 20th century, according to one study, three out of four banner advertisements in online newspapers failed to provide accessible content by using an informative alternative to image tags.[19] This state of affairs was worsened by a general lack of concern, a form of critical avoidance,[20] for disability in advertising was an important topic seldom discussed.[21] Indeed, although the scope of mass media advertising campaigns was broad by definition, concern within the academy about this level of misrepresentation was slight (judging by the low number of published papers on the topic).

Advertising Now

As we might expect (thanks to disability activism, disability rights, disability advocacy, disability studies, and disability theory), advertising in our own century tends to reflect far more awareness of disability. For example, a qualitative analysis of a selection of Anglo-American advertisements since 1999 finds improvements in the images of disability, including the theme of empowerment, as used by Cingular, and the themes of disability pride and inclusion, as used by Doritos, Marks & Spencer, and HSBC.[22] Such advertisements illustrate a departure from the pitiful, sentimental aesthetic used by charities, representations no longer considered appropriate in societies that are trying to restructure themselves so that those of us who have impairments can compete equally in all facets of life.[23] Indeed, even charity campaigns now often differ greatly from their problematic predecessors; the use of an ableist aesthetic defined by medical tragedy in order to prompt pity is far less evident. In fact, Scope and Mencap, among others, explicitly attack disability discrimination in their advertising, and both promote research and campaigns about social exclusion.[24] In advertising that utilizes disability, then, pity is now far less prominent.

BOX 29.1

There are no bigger advertisements than the commercials during the Superbowl, and many advertisers still rely on feel-good "overcoming" stories for the big game:

> www.salon.com/2015/02/02/inspiration_porn_is_not_okay_
> disability_activists_are_not_impressed_with_feel_good_super_
> bowl_ads/

But in some of its content, advertising that utilizes disability certainly remains problematic. Although departing from the more overt pity narratives, several advertisements adopt antiquated themes that continue to stigmatize those of us who have impairments: among others, Nuveen, HealthExtras, and Bank of America advertisements convey underlying messages that those of us who have impairments are broken, in need of repair, awash in tragedy, or supercrips, put on pedestals for living our lives.[25] Reminiscent of what was carelessly circulated nearly half a century ago, when people who had impairments grew tired of being represented as pitiable or wonderfully courageous,[26] these and other such advertisements follow a binary system in which those of us who have impairments are represented in extreme terms: overtly negative or ostensibly positive.

From all this, we can gather that there is an ableist advertising aesthetic that still resonates in campaigns that employ disability. The nature of this aesthetic can be summarized in relation to five points:

1. **distortion**—usually based on pity, fear, or wonder, a distorted view of people who have impairments is presented;

2. **alterity**—routine, slice of life representations of people who have impairments are not used (instead, Otherness is constructed);

3. **disclosure**—impairments are conveniently overlooked or represented so as not to disrupt the normative aesthetic (alternatively, impairment is such a focus that it becomes reductive and the person effectively becomes displaced);

4. **segregation**—advertisements that feature disability or people who have impairments are not used in mainstream campaigns;

5. **exclusion**—advertisements that feature disability or people who have impairments are carelessly rendered inaccessible.

If only to start the discussion, this problematic profile is a useful instrument in the analysis of recent advertisements, such as those in the Dove trilogy. The key is that regurgitation of the ableist aesthetic demonstrates regression, while departure often reveals progress.

Campaign For Real Beauty

Launched a decade ago, the Dove Campaign for Real Beauty has its genesis in concerns that portrayals of women and girls in popular culture are helping to perpetuate an idea of beauty that is neither authentic nor attainable.[27] The need for authenticity informs not only the selection of women for the advertisements but also the scenarios that are used, as noted by one of the team that developed the campaign in the first instance:

[W]e made a lovely spot with a blind girl to advertise physical deodorant and we could have got her a script and encouraged her to script it, but she is who she is and she talks authentically. And actually, it is manifestly the truth.[28]

The significance of the editing process emerges later in the present chapter, but the point to note here is that although the manifest focus of the campaign is the real beauty of real women, it is criticized in many feminist readings.[29] The fundamental problem is that Dove markets itself as an esteem-building brand based on enhancing women's natural beauty, yet what it sells are beauty products; it is not, therefore, a shining beacon of social change, but a product of corporate aims, implicit in the social problems it seeks to transform.[30] In brief, the campaign for real beauty is part of the very social aesthetic by which women become stereotyped and stigmatized.

This chapter focuses on three Dove advertisements that feature women who have visual impairments. The first advertisement, already mentioned, is for deodorant; the second is for the movement for self-esteem; and the third is for hair color radiance shampoo/conditioner. Aired between 2007 and 2012, all three advertisements depart from the ableist aesthetic insofar as they do contain slice of life representations and are used in a mainstream campaign, facts that should be acknowledged from the outset. However, in relation to distortion and exclusion, the advertisements are far from progressive and even the disclosure of impairment warrants some discussion.

The deodorant advertisement shows a woman who is alone but getting ready to go out with her friends. She tells us that she loves this chance to relax and pamper herself, that she finds the whole experience therapeutic. However, she explains, her deodorant and hair spray must be kept apart to avoid confusion between the two, thereby suggesting that, for her, the purely visible labels are not accessible. This hint toward visual impairment is sustained when we are told that the woman chooses her clothes by how they feel, that she has to be especially careful about using deodorant that leaves marks, and that she puts adhesive tape on the end of her eyeliner so as not to confuse it with lip liner. The woman's impairment ultimately becomes explicit, though, for she asserts that she does most things by touch since losing her sight. Thus, the initial concealment is not simply about protecting the normative aesthetic: it adds punch to the revelation that the woman so preoccupied by looks does not perceive by visual means.

The full power of this punch is captured in the critical term *aesthetic blindness*,[31] which designates the epistemological myth of blindness to aesthetic qualities, whereby visual impairment becomes synonymous with ignorance, and aesthetic qualities are perceived by purely visual means. A consequence of this myth is that aesthetic qualities perceived by other than visual means find expression, indeed legitimation, via visual terms—and, by extension, even the emotions become so framed, as illustrated in the Dove Trilogy.

Aesthetic blindness is implicit in the advertisement for hair color radiance shampoo/conditioner, which focuses on one woman, like the deodorant advertisement, but represents slices, rather than a single slice of life.[32] The woman is shown sitting on a sofa, in the shower, on the beach, in a car, in a boat, in a field, and so on. Again, the ableist aesthetic is not disrupted initially, for there are no signifiers of visual impairment until the woman finally says, "Being blind, I can't physically see the color of my hair." Thus, aesthetic blindness is implicit because, as in the deodorant advertisement, visual impairment is concealed for effect, specifically to bolster the revelation that the woman who has so much to say about beauty does not perceive by visual means.

The movement for self-esteem advertisement is similar insofar as it begins with a woman on her own but, unlike the others, she is not preoccupied with beauty or how she looks. Rather than getting ready for a night out, for example, she is preparing for a game of cricket. The advertisement is also different because instead of concealing her visual impairment in order to reveal it as the narrative unfolds, this woman opens with an explicit reference to when she began to lose her sight. Indeed, where concealment is employed creatively in the other advertisements, in this case there may be a charge of reductionism in the emphasis on visual impairment, a danger of "reducing the complex person to a single attribute."[33] Where the trilogy unifies, however, is in ocularcentrism. Although the woman in the movement for self-esteem advertisement reassures us that she has found her passion in the sport she plays twice a week, the vast majority of her direct (but obviously edited) speech refers or alludes to vision—and, by extension, visual impairment.

If the Dove trilogy is complex in terms of disclosure, it is profoundly problematic in relation to distorted representation. Most explicitly, the woman in the Movement for Self-Esteem advertisement asserts that when she began to lose her sight "it all seemed so dark," thereby illustrating an ocularcentric rendering of visual impairment that invokes the fear of darkness in order to elicit pity. Far more than pity and fear, however, it is wonder that distorts the Dove trilogy's representation of people who have visual impairments. For example, in the deodorant advertisement, the woman says, "I don't know why I use a mirror, I can't see myself," an expression of perplexity that is likely to elicit wonder in the viewer, as the visual domain becomes appropriated by someone who perceives by other means. The use of the mirror resonates with aesthetic blindness, as though beauty must be assessed visually, a suggestion confirmed when the woman finally turns to the camera and asks, "Do I look fit?" The importance of the visual assessment of her beauty thereby becomes explicit, and the implied audience finds a sense of narrative closure, a release from tensions around any suggested departure from ocularcentric aesthetics.

BOX 29.2

Just like in movies and TV shows, ads often restrict disabled people to a few stereotypical roles. Check out this take from a blogger who focuses on disability in advertising:

https://advertisinganddisability.com/2016/08/17/advertising-disability-at-a-crossroads-stop-typecasting-and-using-us-as-props/

The advertisement for the Movement for Self-Esteem is similarly fixated on vision and employs what is sometimes called an overcoming narrative.[34] The woman in the advertisement employs ocularcentric language in order to overcome her visual impairment. "I found my passion," she asserts. "I found the light." At this point, viewers see a sunlit scene that reveals the woman's passion to be cricket. The visual references continue as she says, "I started to see things clearly" and "I don't let my sight get in the way." This contrary reference to "sight" denotes visual impairment, which illustrates the point that "if the actions of disabled individuals are cited as the source of overcoming, then it is only to the extent that they successfully distance themselves from the stigma of their own biologies."[35] The woman's self-esteem depends on her distancing herself from the stigma of her visual impairment. Paradoxically, this narrative about overcoming visual impairment works by rendering the woman's predicament in visual terms. Although the ocularcentric aesthetic ostensibly allows expression of achievement, it necessarily leaves people who have visual impairments wanting.

The use of an overcoming narrative is less explicit in the advertisement for hair color radiance shampoo/conditioner, but the evocation of wonder is nonetheless strong and emanates from the concept of synaesthesia. In a radio program about this advertisement, the creative director Sarah Bamford explains that the idea comes from a briefing with Dove and a color psychologist about a test on someone who is blindfolded and yet can feel if colors are cool or warm.[36]

Indeed, Kate Crofts, the woman in the advertisement, asserts in the same program that she is "acutely aware of the synaesthesia phenomenon of enjoying and experiencing one sense through another."[37] In the advertisement, she tells us that color is sounds, smells, and textures: yellow is sunshine on her face, lemon in her drink, and blue is cool water, air, and sky. She also refers to the pertinence of different colors to different moods, although this point is problematically illustrated via an invocation of stereotypes, whereby blondes are "bubbly and fun and girly," and red hair reveals passion. The supposed significance of color becomes more dramatic when we are told that even normal things become vivid: "It's like the feeling of the sun on my skin or the wind in my hair," "I feel like laughing and dancing," and "I feel beautiful. It makes me happy and I want it to stay that way because I want to feel like that every day." The perception of color becomes paramount, as though sight is the supreme sense by which the other senses are led. The woman perceives by other than visual means, but her very emotions are translated into visual terms.

Adding the proverbial insult to injury, the Dove trilogy is patently problematic in relation to access. Despite late 20th-century legislation, the accessibility of advertising remains an issue for those of us who have visual impairments in the 21st century. Google Adsense, for example, has been found inaccessible because it uses the iframe tag and JavaScript, and as such prevents many screen-readers from being functional in reading the content.[38] The Dove trilogy is comparably inaccessible because there are no audible indications of the products being advertised: in the first advertisement, the product becomes apparent in the form of an image of Dove Invisible, a deodorant that, according to the writing on the screen, keeps the user's "black dress black;" in the second advertisement, the text reads, "Dove movement for self-esteem" and "How do you see the world?"; and in the third advertisement, the text reads "Keep the feeling of freshly colored hair" and "Dove Color Radiance." In the absence of an audible representation of these product names and slogans, the advertisements are essentially inaccessible for those of us who do not perceive by visual means, a scenario that is surely worsened by the fact that the advertisers employ people who have visual impairments and use visual impairment as a theme. After all, the implication is that the advertisers accept the aesthetic blindness implicit in their work and imagine that those of us who have visual impairments necessarily have no interest in a beauty campaign.

Discussion Questions

1. What does Bolt mean when he defines "aesthetic blindness" or calls advertisements "ocularcentric"? What might be unfair about these ads?

2. How do ideas of beauty and gender change the way we think about advertisements? Discuss how disability further complicates these ideas.

Notes

1 Hunt 1966.
2 Barnes 1991.
3 Barnes & Mercer 2003; Hevey 1992.
4 Brolley & Anderson 1986.
5 Thomas 2001.

6   Longmore 1987.

7   Davis 1995, p. 150.

8   Nelson 1996, p. 125.

9   Bainbridge, 1997; Fost, 1998; Haller & Ralph, 2001; Longmore, 1987; Panol & McBride, 2001; Shapiro, 1993; Williams, 1999.

10   Haller & Ralph 2001.

11   Ibid.

12   Ibid.

13   Thomas 2001.

14   Haller & Ralph, 2001; Scott-Parker, 1989.

15   Ganahl & Arbuckle 2001.

16   Haller & Ralph 2001.

17   Barnes, 1991; Thomas, 2001.

18   Haller & Ralph 2001.

19   Thompson & Wassmuth 2001.

20   Bolt 2012.

21   Panol & McBride 2001.

22   Haller & Ralph 2006.

23   Ibid.

24   Shakespeare 2006.

25   Haller & Ralph 2006.

26   Hunt 1966.

27   Etcoff, Orbach, Scott, & D'Agostino 2004.

28   Fielding, Lewis, White, Manfredi, & Scott, 2008.

29   Dye, 2009; Froehlich, 2009; Johnston & Taylor, 2008; Scott & Cloud, 2008.

30   Dye 2009.

31   Bolt 2013.

32   Dove 2012.

33   Garland-Thomson 1997, p. 12.

34   Mitchell & Snyder, 2000; Snyder & Mitchell, 2006.

35   Snyder & Mitchell 2006, p. 208.

36   In Touch 2012.

37   Ibid.

38   Thomson 2006.

References

Bainbridge, J. (1997). Advertising and promotion: Overcoming Ad disabilities. Retrieved from www.marketingmagazine.co.uk/news/53487/

Barnes, C. (1991). Discrimination: Disabled people and the media. *Contact*, 70(Winter), 45–48.

Barnes, C., & Mercer, G. (2003). *Disability*. Cambridge, UK: Polity Press.

Bolt, D. (2012). Social encounters, cultural representation, and critical avoidance. In N. Watson, A. Roulstone, & C. Thomas (Eds.), *Routledge Handbook of Disability Studies* (pp. 287–297). London, England: Routledge.

Bolt, D. (2013). Aesthetic Blindness: Symbolism, Realism, and Reality. *Mosaic* 46(3), 93–108.

Brolley, D., & Anderson, S. (1986). Advertising and attitudes. In M. Nagler (Ed.), *Perspectives on Disability* (pp. 147–150). Palo Alto, CA: Health Markets Research.

Davis, L. J. (1995). *Enforcing Normalcy: Disability, Deafness, and the Body*. London, England: Verso.

Dove. (2012). Feeling is believing with Dove hair colour radiance shampoo/conditioners TV Ad – Kate. Retrieved from www.dove.co.uk/en/Tips-Topics-and-Tools/Videos/Colour-radiance-kate.aspx

Dye, L. (2009). A critique of Dove's campaign for real beauty. *Canadian Journal of Media Studies*, 5(1), 114–128.

Etcoff, N., Orbach, S., Scott, J., & D'Agostino, H. (2004). The real truth about beauty: A global report. *Findings of the Global Study on Women, Beauty and Well-being*. Retrieved from www.clubofamsterdam.com/contentarticles/52%20Beauty/dove_white_paper_final.pdf

Fielding, D., Lewis, D., White, M., Manfredi, A., & Scott, L. (2008). Dove Campaign Roundtable. *Advertising & Society Review*, 9(4).

Fost, D. (1998). The fun factor: Marketing recreation to the disabled. *American Demographics*, 20, 54–58.

Froehlich, K. (2009). Dove: Changing the face of beauty? In *Fresh Ink: Essays from Boston College's firstyear writing seminar* 12(2).

Ganahl, D. J., & Arbuckle, M. (2001). The exclusion of persons with physical disabilities from prime time television advertising: A two-years quantitative analysis. *Disability Studies Quarterly*, 21.

Garland-Thomson, R. (1997). *Extraordinary Bodies: Figuring Physical Disability in American Culture and Literature*. New York, NY: Columbia University Press.

Goffman, E. (1968). *Stigma: Notes on the Management of Spoiled Identity*. Middlesex, UK: Penguin (Original work published 1963).

Haller, B., & Ralph, S. (2001). Profitability, diversity and disability: Images in advertising in the United States of America and Great Britain. *Disability Studies Quarterly*, 21.

Haller, B., & Ralph, S. (2006). Are disability images in advertising becoming bold and daring? An analysis of prominent themes in US and UK campaigns. *Disability Studies Quarterly*, 26(3).

Hevey, D. (1992). *The Creatures Time Forgot: Photography and Disability Imagery*. London, England: Routledge.

Hunt, P. (1966). *Stigma: The Experience of Disability*. London, England: Geoffrey Chapman.

In Touch. (2012). BBC Radio 4, 24 July.

Johnston, J., & Taylor, J. (2008). Feminist consumerism and fat activists: A comparative study of grassroots activism and the Dove real beauty campaign. *Journal of Women in Culture and Society*, 33, 941–966.

Longmore, P. (1987). Screening stereotypes: Images of disabled people in television and motion pictures. In A. Garner & T. Joe (Eds.), *Images of the Disabled, Disability Images* (pp. 5–78). New York, NY: Praeger.

Mitchell, D. T., & Snyder, S. L. (2000). *Narrative Prosthesis: Disability and the Dependencies of Discourse*. Ann Arbor: University of Michigan Press.

Nelson, J. (1996). The invisible cultural group: Images of disability. In P. Lester (Ed.), *Images that Injure: Pictorial Stereotypes in the Media* (pp. 119–125). Westport, CT: Praeger.

Panol, Z. S., & McBride, M. (2001). Disability images in print advertising: Exploring attitudinal impact issues. *Disability Studies Quarterly*, 21.

Scott, J., & Cloud, N. (2008). Reaffirming the ideal: A focus group analysis of the campaign for real beauty. *Advertising & Society Review*, 9(4).

Scott-Parker, S. (1989). *They Aren't In the Brief: Advertising People With Disabilities*. London, England: King's Fund Centre.

Shakespeare, T. (2006). *Disability Rights and Wrongs*. Oxon, UK: Routledge.

Shapiro, J. (1993). *No Pity: People With Disabilities Forging a New Civil Rights Movement*. New York, NY: Times Books.

Snyder, S. L., & Mitchell, D. T. (2006). *Cultural Locations of Disability*. Chicago, IL: University of Chicago Press.

Thomas, L. (2001). Disability is not so beautiful: A semiotic analysis of advertising for rehabilitation goods. *Disability Studies Quarterly*, 21.

Thompson, D. R., & Wassmuth, B. L. (2001). Accessibility of online advertising: A content analysis of alternative text for banner ad images in online newspapers. *Disability Studies Quarterly*, 21.

Thomson, M. (2006). *Accessible Advertising for the Visually Impaired*. Available at: www.bigmouthmedia.com/live/articles/accessible-advertising-for-the-visually-impaired.asp/3387/ (accessed 17 October 2012).

Williams, J. M. (1999). Disabled people work their way up to TV Ads: Madison Ave. has changed its opinion on what plays in the U.S. Retrieved from http://adage.com/article/opinion/disabled-people-work-tv-adsmadison-ave-changed-opinion-plays-u-s/61423

Your Body Isn't Your World

The Heroes of the *Mad Max* Video Game, and Disability

Tauriq Moosa

I noticed a small detail on the opening moments of Avalanche Studio's *Mad Max*: Max was wearing his leg brace. Max first acquires it after his leg is shot and ridden over, at the end of the first film. You don't really see the leg brace in the latest film, *Fury Road*, though it is there.

Though Avalanche's game is not based on the films, it is based in the universe—and chronology isn't exactly a central focus for the franchise ("I can't even work out the chronology [of the original trilogy]," creator George Miller has said). But the leg brace, much like Max's car, has become a central aspect of the character. It was important, and it is significant Avalanche included the leg brace.

It is not merely in the game for aesthetic reasons, either. While playing, I noticed Max doesn't walk like an able-bodied person. He limps slightly when he kicks things and hops for a few seconds to reposition himself. Max leans heavily on his stronger leg when he's in pain, his weaker leg dragging—the sound of the brace banging.

I noticed all this because this is exactly how I move.

I live with chronic pain, originating from my legs. I've learned to manage it, which means knowing which days and which activities will require a walking aid. I've learned to judge distance and effort for different activities.

When I first had pain issues, I would be screaming in pain most nights—but there's nothing you can do when your body becomes a spiky cage. I've become highly efficient at bandaging parts of myself.

It means something to see Max move like me. His is a world dragged to hell, which clings to ghosts of humanity by its fingernails. It's a landscape of the dead and dying. But our hero, one of the few surviving, is someone like me.

An individual who you'd think would be the first gone—not last surviving—due to physical disability. Here was a game presenting Max and saying "He survives." The subtle message, vital message that goes unsaid is the next part:

"And so can you."

BOX 30.1

The Pokemon Go craze inspired many people to explore new areas, but that's not so easy when some places are still inaccessible. For more about the barriers created by augmented reality games, read here:

www.dailydot.com/debug/pokemon-go-disabilities-problematic/

Defined by Dreams, Not Bodies

It's not just Max.

Almost every major character in *Mad Max* is a person with a disability: The first person you meet and constant companion, Chumbucket, has a noticeable outward curvature of his spine; the first Stronghold leader you meet, Jeet, lives with chronic pain that he manages through piercing; the second leader, Gutgash, uses a walking aid and appears to have a missing leg; Pink Eye, the third leader, uses a wheelchair. The wheelchair has wheels so, of course, it also has unnecessary pipes to maintain the aesthetics of *Mad Max*.

What's remarkable about how the game deals with these characters' disability is how unremarkable it all seems. They are not defined by their bodies, chronic pain, walking aids or any other property associated with disability. It is a part of their character, yes, but not their central property.

What does define these characters is how each kindles an obsession of escape, of freedom, in a hopeless world. When Max does mock them, he sneers at them for their pointless pursuits.

Even the villains of the game don't target these characters for their disability, but their refusal to die; they are targeted for their refusal to give in to Max's new nemesis (and son of *Fury Road*'s Immortan Joe) Scrotus and his reign of these lands. There are minor comments made about Chumbucket, but one could easily read these targeting his strange beliefs, not his appearance.

What's amazing is that in this world, people are defined by misplaced dreams, not missing limbs.

Consider Pink Eye: She is an old woman who uses a wheelchair. In our world, this is a person we'd assume requires aid and protection. In the world of *Mad Max*, she's not only a survivor but a feared leader. The first thing she yells at her minions is "Clean up that blood . . . then prepare to spill more!" Max does save her but only, as ever, to use resources she has access to. From then on, she's commanding him.

Seeing characters in wheelchairs who aren't defined completely by that characteristic is still rare. In the video game *Wolfenstein: The New Order*, the character Caroline nearly brought me to tears by describing the same pain I first felt in my legs.

Fiction is a space in which you can create whatever world you want. Avalanche deserves praise for creating a world where people with disabilities are not only treated like everyone else, but are leaders and heroes.

We often hear about games being "power fantasies," and that usually refers to a narrow demographic: young (able-bodied, white, cis, heterosexual) men. These fantasies present strong men doing strong men things: saving women and the world, holding large guns and sometimes walking in slow-motion. When things explode behind them, they often don't turn to look. That's how you know they're cool.

Max the character is also an embodiment of many of these fantasies. He's a brooding loner who is efficient at killing and hand-to-hand combat, proficient with many gadgets, takes allies reluctantly and can't stop thinking about the deaths of loved ones, which seems to be his "motivation." These traits apply to Batman, or nearly any antihero.

But Max and his world is one where people so often caricatured or ignored can be regarded as heroes—indeed, in *Batman*, people with disabilities are often villains and regarded as "freaks." A broken body is often shorthand for broken morals.

Mad Max's treatment of those with disabilities applies to the franchise in general: People like LJ Vaughn, who was born with a missing limb, talked about cosplaying as Furiosa when *Fury Road* was released.

"Watching *Fury Road*, I felt like I was watching my own struggle brought to life (albeit in a very fantastical setting), and I don't think I ever realized how truly profound that could be for me."

Like the characters in the game, Vaughn highlights that Furiosa's missing hand is never what defines her—and, indeed, is never even remarked on, much like the game's characters' disabilities.

"There's no reference made to any tragic backstory regarding her limb," the post states. "We have no idea how she lost it, or if she lost it. It may very well be a birth defect." Wonderfully, you can see what happened when the idea of cosplaying came to fruition.

Mad Max's world is also what allowed an incredibly skilled fan, Ben Carpenter, to use his standing wheelchair to cosplay as Max the Blood Bank himself.

The real world is not designed for differently abled people. I am reminded of this when some buildings only have stairs, but I need to get higher; or when there is no way to travel, unless I use expensive transport; when people take my cane as an excuse to ask extended personal questions about my health; where the idea of chronic pain is unfathomable to those who don't live with it; and where pain is only about crying agony or similar demonstrations of pain reaction, not silent management and medical aid.

We don't need such reminders in fiction, when reality is harsh enough—indeed, fiction can help convey to others what it means to move differently and to be differently abled. It also brings a sense of inclusion, that we're not so alien from everyone else—when we can, in fact, be the stars.

It is wonderful then to see a lead like Max, who—despite having many of the same characteristics of every brooding dude hero—not only is himself a person with a disability, but doesn't dismiss or belittle others because of their disabilities. (Or, particularly in the case of *Fury Road*, their gender.) Even the game's villains don't target people based on their appearance, but their power.

Playing as Max, experiencing characters with disabilities, is a reminder that we can and should create worlds that treat respectfully those so often forgotten—if games want to be more inclusive. It makes us feel welcome, it makes our enjoyment that much more personal: I have little doubt this feeling of empowerment has shaped my perception of what many consider a mediocre game.

While sometimes I want to remember the feeling of running, as with *Mirror's Edge*, it is also wonderful to see that a disability need not be a barrier to being a badass.

Fiction can do that. More importantly, fiction should do that. The real world is reminder enough of how invisible marginalized groups are.

It's lovely to see a major studio deciding someone like me and my friends could be major characters in their game—and not have such characters defined or caricatured by disability.

Discussion Questions

1. Why is it important for disabled people to see video game characters who experience their worlds through disability?

2. What does it mean for the "power fantasy" of a video game to include disability in that fantasy?

Autis(i)m and Representation

Autis(i)m, Disability Simulation Games, and Neurodiversity

Sarah Gibbons

Simulating Autism

Auti-Sim was developed during the 2013 Hacking Health Vancouver hackathon, an event designed to foster collaboration between health experts, programmers, and designers. The first-person simulation game, created in the unity engine and playable in browser, immerses the player in a children's playground and uses overpowering sound effects and visual distortion to raise awareness of auditory hypersensitivity. During my own trial of the game, my first action was to move closer to a circle of kids that I spotted near the play structure. As I approached them, a static television effect overtook the game world and the background chatter intensified.

As I grew closer, walking past and even through some of the faceless children, one child began to chant the alphabet over rising static punctuated by piercing screams. My first impulse was to turn the volume down. I decided that this would count as cheating in the same way that adjusting the brightness control on a television set to reveal enemies in a dark environment is cheating; I needed to find an in-game way to stop the noise. Unlike other games in which challenges can be lessened through manipulating external controls, in *Auti-Sim*, there are no clear objectives that need to be achieved despite the environmental difficulty. Sensory overload is the game and there are no points to be gained or victories to be won. In his developer's blog on Game Jolt, creator Taylan Kadayifcioglu expresses his hesitation surrounding the use of the term "game": "I tried using the words 'simulation' and 'interactive experience', but found that nothing communicated the immersion potential of *Auti-Sim* sufficiently without using the word 'game.'"

Playing *Auti-Sim* clearly calls up the "What is a game?" question that game scholars debate. Like many simulation games, and open world or sandbox games, it lacks a cohesive narrative structure and distinct player objectives. It also isn't—and it's difficult to avoid speaking objectively here—particularly enjoyable to play.

Bracketing off the discussion of whether or not *Auti-Sim* constitutes a game in a strict sense for now, I want to consider the unstated, but clearly implied player objective to stop the noise. During my own game, I stopped myself from turning down my speaker volume, ran away from the children, and retreated behind the bench, where the screaming stopped and the static faded.

Analyzing the game at the level of procedural rhetoric, which Ian Bogost defines as "the practice of persuading through processes in general, and computational processes in particular," the connection between the player's retreat from the playground and the corresponding decrease in noise serves the persuasive function of highlighting how quieter environments may be preferable for people who have hypersensitivity. *Auti-Sim* explores sensory experiences that are often elided in the discourse surrounding autism; Stuart Murray (2012), writing on the history of autism and its cultural representation, explains that, "[a]utism is as often encountered in terms of a response to light, textures, and sounds as it is seen in a love of railway timetables or computer games, and although this is mentioned in passing in diagnostic manuals such as the DSM and ICD, it receives limited focus."[1] At a procedural level, as the player moves away from the source of the visual and audio distortion, the game teaches how children might respond to overwhelming sensory experiences by moving away from large groups and retreating to quiet places. Moving forward, I want to consider the persuasive nature of the game as a disability simulation to suggest other potential narratives that players might construct from *Auti-Sim*.

Disabling the Player

Many player responses to *Auti-Sim* on Game Jolt concern the instructive value of the experience as an exercise in empathy. However, while some players express the extent to which the game is a valuable tool and a viable representation of their own experiences of hypersensitivity, others critique the game on grounds varying from inaccuracy, to the lack of consultation with autistic people during the design process, to the game's representation of autism as a nightmare. Kadayifcioglu responds to concerns regarding inaccuracy and inadequate consultation in his developer's blog, in which he reiterates the 12-hour time constraints he was working within to complete a project that received more immediate attention than he was expecting, and promises to collaborate with individuals on the spectrum to improve the game.

After considering player reviews and responses, the issue that interests me is not the extent to which the game is accurate, since individuals experience hypersensitivity differently, but rather the extent to which *Auti-Sim* induces fear to capture the experience of autistic people. Drawing out the connection between the simulation and horror games, Nathan Grayson of Rock, Paper, Shotgun describes how, "*Auti-Sim* draws on horror game tropes juxtaposed against a bright, idyllic playground environment, to rather brilliant effect." With this comparison in mind, I would like to engage with analyses of disability simulations and the literature of autistic self-advocates to consider another question: Is *Auti-Sim's* representation of autism through recourse to an experience of discomfort that verges on fear compatible with a message of acceptance, and with a call to shape accessible environments?

One of the important messages that disability studies scholars and autistic self-advocates reiterate is that disability should not be understood through the lens of pity. Working against a medical model that suggests that disability is an individual problem, disorder, or defect, many scholars articulate a social model of disability that emphasizes the disabling impact of built environments and social attitudes. Some scholars question the idea of impairment; for example, Shelley Tremain, who exposes the realist ontology that informs our understanding of impairment, explains that our definitions of impairments are not objective, but historically contingent.[2] Tremain and other scholars point toward a generative model of bodily difference. The question with respect to games becomes, can simulation games enable players to explore these alternative models?

Sheryl Burgstahler and Tanis Doe, in their article "Disability-related Simulations: If, When, and How to Use Them in Professional Development," show how simulations can reinforce individual models of disability that overlook the disabling impact of social attitudes. Burgstahler and Doe thus argue that if disability simulations are to be used, they must be designed with attention to disability as a social and political experience. They also caution that trying on disability, by using a wheelchair, wearing a blindfold, or navigating an inaccessible website, does not provide insight into the strategies that individuals develop over time to manage their environments.[3] In other words, the panic that a player might experience may not capture the daily experience of disability, and may reinforce the ableist assumptions that being able-bodied or neurotypical is objectively preferable to being disabled. I think that some player reviews of *Auti-Sim* on Game Jolt (such as, "I feel sorry for children who really have this disease") reflect the concern of scholars and activists that simulations promote pity.

As someone who is committed to understanding autism through a paradigm of neurological diversity, it concerns me that players might conclude that autism is only characterized by suffering. Many autistic self-advocates speak back to discourses that construct autism as a tragic condition that needs to be cured through advancing the concept of neurodiversity. Ari Ne'eman, the president of the Autistic Self-Advocacy network, positions neurodiversity against a deficit model of disability:

The essence of neurodiversity, or neurological diversity, is the idea that the paradigm of acceptance extended towards racial, religious and other similar differences should apply to neurology as well. A relatively new concept, the term originates from conversations held amongst individuals on the autism spectrum in various discussion boards, listservs and other areas of community interaction in the fledgling autistic community. Groups like Autism Network International and, more recently, the Autistic Self Advocacy Network, advocate a new conception of neurological difference along a social rather than a medical paradigm.[4]

The understanding of autism as difference as opposed to defect that Ne'eman articulates here is also central to the message of the YouTube performance piece "In My Language" by Amanda Baggs, an interesting piece to watch in conjunction with "Inside Autism," the video that inspired Kadayifcioglu's *Auti-Sim*. The video is divided into two segments; the first part, "In My Language," captures Baggs interacting with her environment. The video shows her engaging her senses through such actions as stroking the surface of a laptop, pressing her cheek against the page of a book, and waving her hands while making an 'e' sound. In the second part of the video, "A Translation," Baggs uses a text to speech synthesizer to create a monologue that serves as voiceover as she continues in her embodied language. She explains that being sensitive to her surroundings is her way of communicating with the world, stating: "my language is not about designing words or even visual symbols for people to interpret. It is about being in a constant conversation with every aspect of my environment." Her argument that her movement constitutes a language in its own right calls attention to the lack of self-reflection often involved in efforts to teach children to increase their eye contact, or refrain from stimming. (Baggs is one contributor to The Loud Hands Project, a transmedia celebration of autistic culture that addresses this issue.)

BOX 31.1

What does it mean to communicate? Disability points us toward unexpected answers in "In My Language":

www.youtube.com/watch?v=JnylM1hI2jc

I understand that Auti-Sim, in its current form, is limited in its duration and its scope, as it specifically focuses on a child's experience of auditory hypersensitivity. (Although, in the context of controversies concerning corporate charities that focus on autistic children to the exclusion of autistic adults, the decision to feature a child's experience has representational consequences.)[5] However, if the game is to become a tool for professional development, I wonder if future iterations might capture meaningful pleasurable sensory experiences alongside simulating painful or traumatic ones.

Disability Studies and Games Studies

Events like Hacking Health that spawned *Auti-Sim* indicate that researchers are increasingly harnessing the power of games for health care. *Auti-Sim* is an interesting game in this regard because it attempts to intervene at the level of social attitudes, as opposed to directly attempting to change the behavior or communication styles of autistic people. In raising issues surrounding the representation of disability in games, and simulation games specifically, I am not suggesting that games as a medium cannot contribute to a generative discourse on disability; I certainly think that they can. However, I would like to conclude my commentary by expressing my own interest in seeing more research connections between disability studies and games studies at a critical level, alongside ongoing gaming health projects and important efforts to make games accessible for multiple playing styles. (On that note, The AbleGamers Foundation is an excellent resource that outlines accessibility initiatives and offers accessibility reviews of popular games.) I am interested in reading contributions that I have not come across in my own research, and I welcome comments on this topic or any others.

As a literature student, I'm interested in how textual analyses of disability, from David Mitchell and Sharon Snyder's concept of narrative prosthesis to Ato Quayson's aesthetic nervousness, could be redeployed, reframed or extended through a consideration of the intersection between play and narrative. Lennard Davis has suggested that the novel form itself is inextricably tied to ideas of normalcy— what could we say about the form or genre of games?[6] How is overcoming obstacles to complete a game as a disabled character different from reading a narrative about overcoming the body? How does disability function in a role-playing game like *Deus-Ex: Human Revolution* (2011), which involves enhancing the player through biological modifications and prosthetics to proceed through the game? Can science fiction games that increase the difficulty level for players without bodily modifications speak to how our understanding of impairment is historically or environmentally contingent? More broadly, what are the messages, meanings, and stories surrounding disability that we enact, participate in, and produce as creators and players of games?

Discussion Questions

1. How does *Auti-Sim* give players a distorted or particular experience of disability? What are the consequences of thinking about disability this way?

2. Should nondisabled people simulate or "try on" a disability for a short time? Do these simulations aid disabled people or only the nondisabled?

Notes

1   Murray 2012, p. 32.
2   Tremain 2002, p. 34.
3   Burgstahler and Doe 2004, p. 11.
4   Qtd. in Broderick and Ne'eman 2008.
5   Murray 2008, p. 139.
6   Davis 1997, p. 21.

References

Bogost, Ian. *Persuasive Games: The Expressive Power of Video Games.* Cambridge, Mass.: The MIT Press, 2007. Print.

Broderick, Alicia and Ari Ne'eman. "Autism as Metaphor: Narrative and Counter-Narrative." *International Journal of Inclusive Education* 12(5–6): 459–476, 2008. Print.

Burgstahler, Sheryl, and Tanis Doe. "Disability-related Simulations: If, When, and How to Use Them in Professionjal Development." *Review of Disability Studies* 1(2): 4–17, 2004. Web. 8 April 2013.

Davis, Lennard. "Constructing Normalcy: The Bell Curve, the Novel, and the Invention of the Disabled Body in the Nineteenth Century." *The Disability Studies Reader.* New York and London: Routledge, 1997. Print.

Murray, Stuart. *Autism.* New York and London: Routledge, 2012. Print.

——. *Representing Autism: Culture, Narrative, Fascination.* Liverpool: Liverpool University Press, 2008. Print.

Tremain, Shelly. "On the Subject of Impairment." *Disability/Postmodernity.* Eds. Marion Corker and Tom Shakespeare. New York: Continuum, 2002. Print.

Why I'm a Crippled Poet

Steve Kuusisto

I am a poet who's blind—I'm also short, dyspeptic, and addicted to savory treats. I feel better for having said so.

Not long ago I attended a writing conference. A poet who has multiple sclerosis said she didn't want to be a "wheelchair poet," by which (one presumes) she meant she didn't want her writing to be viewed through the lens of disability. Expanding this, I imagine she wouldn't want to be a black poet, a lesbian poet, or a really tall poet. In her view, poetry should be the product of an *ex cathedra* pronouncement—with a stroke of the pen we can erase all the nagging identity markers of humanity.

It's possible to have a disability and live your life pretending you don't have one. Plenty of people have done so. But getting away with this charade in literary terms means the imagination has been suborned—bribed—you've tricked yourself into thinking there's a pot of gold that will be yours but only if there isn't a hint of physical difference in your work. To paraphrase Garrison Keillor: "All the poets are strong, good looking, and above average."

Forget that our nation's greatest poet Emily Dickinson had rod-cone dystrophy and couldn't see in sunlight; forget Walt Whitman's stroke; ignore bi-polar depression in the case of Theodore Roethke and Robert Lowell; dismiss Alexander Pope's spinal disease—I'm sorry this is a long list—Sylvia Plath; Hart Crane; Ann Sexton; Allen Ginsberg; William Carlos Williams; forget them all. Disability doesn't belong in poetry. God help you if you let it in—the critics will dismiss you from the poetry pantheon IN A FLASH since "great" poetry comes from the grandest of all human resources— the dis-embodied mind. (Picture it as a *Star Trek* arrangement, a brain in a plexiglass case with wires emanating from it.)

BOX 32.1

Poetry magazine invited some of the country's leading disabled poets to share their experiences about everything from publishing to accessibility. Read it here:

www.poetryfoundation.org/poetrymagazine/articles/detail/70179

When I went to college in the 1970s English majors were introduced to "New Criticism"—and though this approach to literature was already fading by the time I graduated, the poetry world still has a "New Criticism Hangover." New Criticism argued the study of literature required no knowledge about the writer behind the work. The shaping of words, the wit, the poet's irony, his literary allusions—these were all you had to know to discern meaning—or as I came to call it, the "soft, chewy center" of a poem.

Back then everyone was still under the sway of T.S. Eliot's poem "The Wasteland." We were instructed to read it as a compendium of allusions and to critique it as an allegory of modern exhaustion. No one (and I mean no one) raised his or her hand and said: "Wasn't Eliot's wife in a madhouse when he wrote this; and wasn't he clinically depressed at the time?" We simply talked about the quest for the Holy Grail and the "objective correlative" and, if we were out to impress the prof, we looked up everything in the original Greek.

The New Criticism Hangover (NCH) stipulates you mustn't admit your complaining, belching, limping, loudly breathing, dis-articulated, lumbering body into poems. You may lampoon or parody "other bodies," but this should be reserved for pathos or other symbolic distancing effects.

Many of America's leading poets do this—blindness represents profound isolation; deafness is simply a metaphor for lack of knowledge; deformity is nothing more than a Grand Guignol effect. If you write like a poet who has NCH you must never hint you have a body of your own.

Of course there are messy feminist poets with their leaking womanly poems; and black poets with their jazzy outrages; but the New Critics Hangover School is uncomfortable with all that stuff.

The "wheelchair poet" remark is part of this heritage—it's a highly conscious position—to sequester the outlier body; to keep it in its sarcophagus; to tighten down all the screws.

Me? I'm a messy "wheelchair poet" in the broadest sense. I'm demanding too. I cause trouble in public spaces. I'll make you move your stone lions if they block the damned sidewalk. I'll demand you provide me with a trash can at the Hilton so

I can pick up my dog's shit. If you don't bring me the can, I'll leave the shit right here. I'm loud. I'm really loud. I like hip-hop. I like Mahler symphonies and I turn them way up. I'm a poet who not only admits the defective body into literature—I think the imagination is starving for what that damned body knows. I happen to be blind. What do I know? I know things like this:

"Only Bread, Only Light"

At times the blind see light,
And that moment is the Sistine ceiling,
Grace among buildings—no one asks
For it, no one asks.
After all, this is solitude,
Daylight's finger,
Blake's angel
Parting willow leaves.
I should know better.
Get with the business
Of walking the lovely, satisfied,
Indifferent weather —
Bread baking
On Arthur Avenue
This first warm day of June.
I stand on the corner
For priceless seconds
Now everything to me falls shadow.

Did I mention William Blake? He had a disability too.

Discussion Questions

1. Why does Kuusisto caution against pretending not to be disabled in creative work? What are the consequences of embracing an identity as a "wheelchair poet?"

2. How does Kuusisto understand the relationship between the imagination and the body?

The Disability Yet To Come

33 | Disability Studies in K-12 Education

Linda Ware

Can you recall the first time you heard the word "disabled"? Perhaps you noticed someone who, by virtue of bodily difference, distinct mannerisms or their use of a wheelchair, captured your attention. In your curiosity and naiveté you wondered, "What's wrong with that man?" "Why is she walking that way?" "Is she hurt?" If you were a child at the time, and posed your questions to an adult, in all likelihood, you heard the word "disabled" for the first time, along with the admonishment: "Don't stare! It's not polite." What slowly became obvious was that you could not quite apprehend the word "disabled" in the absence of someone pointing to another person and naming them "disabled."

Every semester I ask students in the undergraduate disability studies courses I teach to reflect on their first memory of disability and to write a personal essay describing that event, or the individual they recall, or any aspect of a memory in response to the writing prompt. Depending on the age of the student, most trace their earliest memory of disability back to a public school context. For many college-age students who completed their K-12 experience in the company of students with disabilities in their classroom, some formed friendships in those early years that continue to this day, others realized career paths they would follow informed by early experiences with disability, and a handful report no prior experience with disability.

And to be sure, "perspective matters!" That is, if you were the non-normative student who was identified with a disability and determined to be in "need of special education" you heard the word "disabled" repeatedly throughout your youth. Yet, even when specified by categorical distinction such as "learning disability," "attention deficit disorder," "oppositional defiant behavior disorder" and so on, such language failed to convey the meaning of "disability." What you came to understand was that you needed "more time" to complete your classwork; that you would spend portions of your school day in special education where you could get extra help to learn; that you might have a team of teachers and staff to help you stay calm and productive throughout the school day, and that all of this was for "your own good." In brief, special education, as you experienced it, was a departure from your general education routines, but it was neither "special" nor "education."

The processes of identification and placement in special education which can provide an array of "services" such as speech and language development support, occupational or physical therapy, adaptive physical education, and so on, unfurls in tandem with the reformulation of the student's identity as "disabled." That is, service provision typically requires the student to leave the general education classroom for "support." This, in turn, compromises naturally developing social engagement opportunities that form throughout the school day with the community of peers and adults in the classroom setting. The delivery of academic content that might be referenced throughout the day is also compromised resulting in instructional gaps as well. Many years later, as adults, students recall such experiences in special education with shame and resentment they now name as being "targeted" by the schools and ultimately by their peers. In all the years that I have made this writing assignment, not one student has offered fond memories of their experience in special education. The notion of "support" failed to register as anything more than exclusion from the mainstream of activity.

In contrast, when siblings or classmates recount memories about their peers or a family member's experiences in special education, they suggest a narrative celebrating the extra "help and support" provided by the schools. Their memory casts special education as the opportunity afforded to ensure individual academic success. Now, when listening to their college-age peers declare that special education was not as beneficial as it was harmful, the exchange proves to be a moment of reckoning with a more critical discussion that explores how special education negatively impacts the healthy development of student identity. For many, up to that moment, there was not a second's thought given to consider this dichotomy. Normative students who witnessed the everyday practices that "othered" their non-normative peers, effectively learned to "silence" their questions and natural curiosity about widespread exclusionary schooling practices. Of course, ableism, ableist oppression, and disability injustice are not commonly explored in public school curriculum even though stigmatizing schooling practices and the segregation that targets disabled students abound. With this as a backdrop I consider the emergence of a new conversation on disability in public school settings, one that is informed by the academic field of "disability studies in education" (DSE).

Changing the Conversation on Disability in K-12 Education

In much the same way that contributors to this *Primer* explore disability from a non-medical model perspective, drawing instead upon social, cultural, historical, discursive, philosophical, literary, aesthetic, artistic, and other academic influences,

DSE deploys a similar critical lens to challenge exclusively medical, scientific, and psychometric models of disability embedded in K-12 educational contexts and teacher preparation. DSE research and scholarship proposes a conversation on disability as a welcome aspect of human difference that must be launched in K-12 education because schools provide our earliest experiences with disability, inclusion, and how we "other." We are motivated by the call to "imagine disability otherwise" (Ware, 2001), a maxim that has been translated in multiple ways and enacted in various contexts to challenge the reductionism and categorical thinking embedded in general and special education classrooms and general and special education teacher preparation.

As proponents of DSE as a new academic field of inquiry, many of us were initially trained to practice K-12 special education as teachers. Over time, we realized that the construction of disability as "problem" and "defect" authored by special education posed a moral challenge to our personal beliefs. That is, we pursued special education with the intention to embrace human variation as a welcome aspect of human difference. To the contrary, we discovered that special education systems challenged our beliefs about how to approach practice, how to support children individually and collectively in educational contexts, and how to support and engage families as allies. We rejected the ideology that has shaped special education since its inception and instead became professors of special education who designed DSE as an alternative approach within teacher preparation in the 1990s.[1] Our research, policy, and advocacy efforts are informed by four guiding tenets that seek to:

- Contextualize disability within political and social spheres.
- Privilege the interest, agendas, and voices of people labeled with disability/disabled people.
- Promote social justice, equitable and inclusive educational opportunities, and full and meaningful access to all aspects of society for people labeled with disability/disabled people.
- Assume competence and reject deficit models of disability.[2]

In a departure from special education's construction of disability-as-problem body/mind, these tenets are broadly conceived and stand apart, if not in opposition to, general and special educational approaches to understanding disability in teacher preparation, and by turns in K-12 education. Discussion follows to reveal how these tenets are enacted in response to three organizing questions developed for consideration in this essay:

1. What do we actually talk about when we talk about disability in K-12 schools?
2. How can disability be considered in the K-12 curriculum?
3. Why are changing cultural meanings of disability relevant now?

Naming Disability—Owing to the Hunt

What do we actually talk about in schools in the example of disability? One might answer, "Well, we actually don't talk about disability in schools! We hunt for it." Owing to the "hunt for disability"[3] in K-12 settings, disability is synonymous with special education, reductionism, and pathology that produce a deficiency discourse informed by labels, categories of difference, needs identification, and resource allocation. We talk about special buses, special classrooms, and special teachers to signify and reify that which is "other" than the "normal" bus, "other" than the "general education" classroom, and "other" than the "regular" education teacher. Disabled students and nondisabled students alike are absorbed into this discursive space wherein it is not uncommon for teachers and administrators to speak informally about "the new LD boy" (not Javier), "the little autistic girl in grade 4" (not Amita), or "one of the BD kids at the middle school" (not Leo). In the course of a school day, teachers and administrators use such language as "shorthand" and are seemingly unaware of its demeaning consequences resulting in the erasure of Javier, Amita, and Leo who lose their identity once categorized as the "other."

DSE scholars critique the institutional hunt for disability in K-12 education that might initially appear benign despite its eugenic roots that shape the attitudes and assumptions embedded in special education to this day.[4] Overly deterministic, institutionally authorized policies and practices transform a student's initial call for learning support to the systematized documentation of learning "needs" that are typically deemed "too taxing" for the general education setting.[5] Exclusion and stigma follow the individual child, often, well beyond the school years. This trajectory has been slow to displace given that special education policy is performed in the absence of contextualizing disability within political and social spheres and uninformed by the institutional and cultural critique advanced by DSE.

At the level of classroom practice DSE researchers integrate the topic of disability within the curriculum and in recognition of the fact that young children's thinking, and the development of ideas about individuals with disabilities in society begin in schools, and increasingly, are driven by media in advance of schooling. In a purposeful departure from the well-entrenched defect discourse on disability, we advance the interests, agendas, and voices of disabled people. School-based DSE researchers explore disability identity, disability history, disability rights, disability in the arts and so on, as powerful interventions to the curriculum, providing an explicit challenge to the metanarrative about disability embedded in education. This becomes just one aspect of a multi-tiered effort to challenge prejudicial thinking about disability—not only in schools—but throughout society.

Reclaiming Disability as Identity

In research designed for primary and elementary school contexts, Santiago Solis (2004) probes the multiple ways that children's literature reifies negative portrayals, misconceptions, and stereotypes of disability. His textual analysis of ten popular children's books captures the subtle workings of ableist assumptions that underwrite a message about disability wherein the qualities of others are "demeaned, stigmatized, ridiculed, feared and degraded" through examples that include "the evil prosthesis of Captain Hook, the sinister hump of Richard III, the pitiable crutch of Tiny Tim, the blind bumbling antics of Mr. Magoo, [and] the comical speech of Porky Pig". Solis calls for teachers to critically consider how exposure to such content can reproduce "unmitigated truths about disability" as children are poised to "perceive" the nature of disability as "beyond doubt [and] begin to speak about disability in categorical, circumscribed and stagnated ways" (n.p.). He further suggests that in the absence of explicit intervention by educators, willing to challenge and engage children through the curriculum, the default belief about difference as problem is "manufactured and immortalized in children's minds" (n.p.).

Others have noted that racism, sexism, ableism, heterosexism, nationalism, linguistic privilege, religious intolerance, and class bias operate unchecked in schools and society. In the absence of a single teacher, or small group of teachers who call such implicit bias into question through intentional instruction, many students complete K-12 education unaware of the ways that inequality is embedded within the curriculum. Solis suggests that in order to productively engage disability beyond the labels and the stratification of difference, educators must have prior exposure to the metanarrative of disability as "defect" so prevalent in society. Yet, this does not figure into teacher preparation in any consistent way. Once teachers are supported to explore literary and visual representations of disability more critically, they quickly recognize that texts once believed to be innocent and compassionate in their treatment of disability amount to little more than an early primer on the deficiency discourse on disability. His suggestion to underscore disability grounded in a "politics of resistance" rather than one rooted in simple stories that maintain nondisabled/disabled dualisms grounded in stereotypes and misconceptions about disability experience serves to pave the path for a revised primer that presumes competence—not deficiency.

Priya Lalvani (2015), self-described as "a disability studies scholar, a teacher educator, and a mother" (n.p.), considers the "silences" perpetuated by a "pervasive master narrative" voiced by teachers who hold that in the instance of disability, "young children don't notice differences among their peers" (n.p.). Like Solis, her research invites teachers to contextualize disability as a sociopolitical rather than a medical phenomenon. Early in her teacher education courses, Lalvani invites master's level students to discuss the ways they might approach disability in their classroom teaching. She finds that most *do not* broach this topic, as if to suggest the mandate for "silence" amounts to a professional disposition. Probing further into this "silence" Lalvani explains to her students that her daughter with Down syndrome is enrolled in a nearby school as one among several visibly disabled students in the district. Every semester she asks, how, as educators, they might explain her daughter's differences to classmates who, in other contexts, express curiosity. She boldly asks her students, "How do you discuss disability as human variations in the classroom?" Clear discomfort follows, until someone offers: "We don't need to say anything—they won't even notice she's different." Others suggest, "They don't ask any questions—children are so accepting." This same logic propels other teachers to claim to "treat 'each student the same'" and so much so that a visitor to their classroom would be "unable to tell which child has a disability" (n.p.).

For Lalvani, these teachers' claims summon an earlier era of "colorblind ideology" when critical race theorists named a similar "silence" in teacher education relative to unwelcomed racialized conversations. Critical race theorists defined "colorblindness" as a "bid for innocence, an attempt to escape our responsibility for our White privilege. By claiming innocence, we reconcile ourselves to racial irresponsibility."[6] Similarly, Lalvani draws parallels to ableist privilege and the silence on disability as profound and troubling. This conflict motivated research with students in her daughter's fourth grade classroom. She probed the purported silence of non-disabled children who "sit alongside a child with a disability in an inclusive classroom" (n.p.). More to the point, she probed how children "gain either meaningful understanding of disability or any genuine appreciation for the diversity within their school community if there are silences around the questions they surely must have." And given her unique position as a parent and researcher, Lalvani further aimed to understand how children with disabilities similar to those of her daughter can even "develop a positive sense of self if one aspect of their experience—or one facet of their identity—is never acknowledged or named?"

Disability-related topics were presented over six weeks of instruction led by Lalvani who met after school with a small group of students comprising her daughter and her peers. Initial discussion was prompted by the students' self-generated questions posed with confidence and clarity. These included a specific question for their friend, Lalvani's daughter: "When did you first know you had Down syndrome?" General questions that followed on their discussion: "Is Down syndrome contagious?" "Do people with disabilities act in different ways or do different things?" "Can someone who does not have Down syndrome have the same symptoms as someone who has Down syndrome?" And questions directed to Priya who was part of the conversation and not simply the teacher authority: "How did you deal with it when Minal was born?" "What was your reaction and how did you knowledgize [sic] yourself?" (Lalvani, n.p.)

Their understanding of disability developed slowly, facilitated by Lalvani, who introduced a perspective on disability, "not as *impairments*—but as the experience of *disablement* (i. e. the attitudinal or systemic barriers faced by people with disabilities, and society's complicity in the existence of these)." Over time, these young students acquired greater ease posing questions about disability and disability identity. They were quick to recognize disability injustice as "bullying" in and outside of the school context, drawing upon anti-bullying campaigns underway nationwide. The students also explored disability history for reference as they created a curriculum component that was ultimately presented to their class. Motivated by curiosity about disability rather than silence, the students revealed the importance of engaging their young minds on this topic.

DSE in an Ever-Changing Cultural Context

In the nearly two decades since the question "Dare we Do Disability Studies?" was first posed, this challenge to both general and special educators has prompted many to revaluate special education's reductionist approach to the understanding of disability (Ware, 2001). Moving "beyond the labels" and informed by inclusive education contexts in an ever-changing cultural context, the value of an applied DSE approach is on the rise. A recent issue of the Bank Street Occasional Paper Series (Valente & Danforth, 2016) featured applied DSE approaches to support inclusive classroom pedagogy. In work described by Ware & Hatz (2016) their multi-pronged approach to the development of curriculum was particularly successful in one middle school setting. Guided by student curiosity, their approach to disability drew heavily upon web-based resources to capitalize on students' increasing consumption of visual media. Although young adult literature also figured into the curriculum, contemporary representations of disability and the actual voices and perspectives of disabled people they met through blogs and YouTube portrayals more readily inspired student questions. Media exemplars featured professional performance by well-known disabled artists and YouTube clips of less famous individuals introduced aspects of disability identity across a wide spectrum of actual lives.

Students and their teachers participated in this collaboration between a classroom teacher and a university professor. Research activities were drawn from district approved "disability-themed" reading material which invoked tired stereotypes of disability as tragic and unfortunate victims of a fate "worse than death" in contrast to media resources informed by the voices of disabled people and their lived experience. These more contemporary accounts provided authenticity that challenged the text-based mis-representation of disability experience. Once again, the resulting curriculum was propelled by student curiosity and previously unasked questions about disability along with those voiced by the teachers participating in parallel dialogues. Similar to earlier research, these middle school students gravitated toward learning something that someone else had decided was not worthy to know.[7] And the teachers realized that although disability is everywhere in K-12 education, it has yet to secure an authorized place in the curriculum. Given that every interaction that occurs in schools involving disabled children serves as an early lesson not only for the disabled child, but also for the nondisabled child who witnesses adult engagement—or its avoidance—in social space, the value of this research was readily acknowledged by all participants.

Jay Dolmage notes on page 30 of this *Primer* that, "rhetorically, the ways we tell 'particular stories' about disability condition our understanding of disability (and thus of all identity and all bodies)." His discussion of the myths, messages, and damaging disability tropes that recur in representations of disability in media over time would be one that educators might find valuable—provided that they were afforded the opportunity to break the silence on disability, informed by critical insights from DSE. Educators would soon realize that "particular stories" are constructed by the "meanings that get written and spoken around, over and into disability" (see Chapter 4). Such is the promise DSE affords to K-12 educators as it engages multi-disciplinary content in ways that might be unfamiliar to educators—but still readily accessible— as the conversation on disability continues to evolve. Where once K-12 education restricted understanding of disability to the discourse authored by the institution of special education, DSE continues to challenge the institution's overt mechanism to constitute the "normative center" as well as its "margins."

Discussion Questions

1. Why does Ware criticize the label "special education"? What problems do disabled students face when put into separate programs?

2. What is the "hunt for disability" and why does it happen in schools? How can educators better understand and approach disability?

3. Why is it important to talk to K-12 students about disability? What can go wrong when operating on the assumption that students should all be treated the same?

Notes

1   David Connor (2014) provides a history of the origins and purposes of the field of DSE from small conference beginnings in 1999 to the present in "The Disability Studies in Education Annual Conference: Exploration of Working within and Against, Special Education" available on-line at http://dsq-sds.org/article/view/4257/3597.

2   The DSE tenets were authored by members of the Disability Studies in Education (DSE) Special Interest Group (SIG) of the American Education Research Association

(AERA). These tenets more succinctly capture DSE efforts to promote the under-standing of disability from a social model perspective drawing on social, cultural, historical, discursive, philosophical, literary, aesthetic, artistic, and other traditions to challenge medical, scientific, and psychological models of disability as they relate to education.

3   Bernadette Baker, the noted curriculum theorist, invoked the notion of the "hunt for disability" in discussion of the ways that schooling systems enact the new eugenics as institutional policy (2002). Baker cited numerous troublesome components of special education including its over-reliance on behaviorism, reductionism, positivism and bureaucratization of policy and practice that revealed its eugenic roots and the motivation for the exclusion of disabled students in the general classroom.

4   Humanities-based Disability Studies scholars Sharon L. Snyder and David T. Mitchell (2006) found, in careful review of primary source material, that the predecessor of today's special education classrooms was the early "ungraded classroom" which they described as "holding tanks for defective students awaiting processing into institutions for the feebleminded" (96). The origins of "special class for defectives" emerged as a practice at the turn of the century that "relieved a burden upon both teachers and students seeking a normal educational model" (96). This perspective was informed by a 1919 report stating, "there remains as justification for the special class the advantage that appeals so much to the school superintendent—it removes the grit from the educational machine, and allows the wheels to run smoothly" (cited in Nash and Porteus, 1919, 2). The separate self-contained classroom remains a fixture in public education today.

5   Among the earliest critiques of the special education identification, classification, and referral process, Ware (1994) drew upon the classic ethnographic research of Hugh Mehan (1993) titled, "Beneath the skin and between the ears: A case study in the politics of representation." He explored the process of identifying those students whose initial call for help and support in the general education classroom would actually reveal the apparatus deployed to probe children for defects. In spite of its powerful critique, Mehan's research and scholarship did not significantly impact the special education literature nor did it impact practice. The institution of special education remains as insular and ignorant of the cultural position taken up by DSE, driven instead by the same justification Snyder and Mitchell (2006) noted as motivation in 1919.

6   Gordon (2005) p. 143.

7   School-based DSE researchers (Baglieri et al., 2011a; 2011b; Ferri, 2006; Ware, 2001; Ware & Valle, 2010) repeatedly find that their research participants, whether they be young children, college students in our courses, or teachers with whom we collaborate in schools, are quick to recognize the importance of their "discovery" of ableism and cultural meanings of disability. It is as if knowledge that was previously deemed irrelevant, or unworthy to know was now revealed to help them make sense of disability oppression previously unnamed. What follows with this discovery is a conviction to probe disability with keen insight and new awareness and consciousness about disability.

References

Baglieri, Susan, Lynn Bejoin, Alicia Broderick, David J. Connor and Jan Weatherly Valle. "Creating alliances against exclusivity: A pathway to educational reform." *Teachers College Record* 113, no. 10 (2011a): 2115–2121. Print.

Baglieri, Susan, Jan Weatherly Valle, David J. Connor and Deborah Gallagher. "Disability Studies in Education: The Need for a Plurality of Perspectives on Disability." *Remedial and Special Education (RASE)*, 32, (2011b): 267–277. Print.

Baker, Bernadette. "The Hunt for Disability: The New Eugenics and the Normalization of school children." *Teachers College Record* 44, (2002): 663–703. Print.

Ferri, Beth. "Teaching to Trouble." In Scot Danforth and Susan L. Gabel (Eds.), *Vital Questions Facing Disability Studies in Education*. New York & London: Peter Lang Publishing. 2006.

Gordon, J. (2005). "Inadvertent complicity: Colorblindness in teacher education." *Educational Studies*, 38(2), 135–153.

Lalvani, Priya. "'We are not aliens': Exploring the Meaning of Disability and the Nature of Belongingness in a Fourth Grade Classroom." *Disability Studies Quarterly Online-Only Journal* 35(4). (2015): n.p. Web. 14 February 2016.

Mehan, Hugh. "Beneath the Skin and Between the Ears: A Case History of the Politics of Representation." In Seth Chailkin and Jean Lave (Eds.), *Understanding Practice: Perspectives on Activity and Context*. Cambridge: Cambridge University Press. 1993.

Nash, A.M. and Porteus, S.D. "Educational treatment of defectives." *Training School Bulletin:* 18 (1919). Vineland, NJ: Vineland Training School.

Snyder, Sharon L. and David T. Mitchell. *Cultural Locations of Disability*. Chicago, IL: University of Chicago Press, 2006.

Solis, Santiago. "The Disabilitymaking Factory: Manufacturing 'Differences' through Children's Literature." *Disability Studies Quarterly Online-Only Journal* 24, no. 1. (2004): n.p. Web. 8 March 2005.

Valente, Joseph M. and Scot Danforth (Eds.), "Life in Inclusive Classrooms: Storytelling with Disability Studies in Education." Bank Street Occasional Paper Series, no. 36 n.p. www.bankstreet.edu/occasional-paper-series/36/?mc_cid=b16cfd9c4b&mc_eid=40adb57a9b.xxx

Ware, Linda. "Opening the Windows of Opportunity: The Challenge of Implementing Change." In Carol A. Thornton and Nancy S. Bley (Eds.), *Windows of Opportunity: Mathematics for Students with Special Needs*. Reston, Virginia: National Council of Teachers of Mathematics. 1994. 393–408.

Ware, Linda. "Writing, Identity, and the Other: Dare We Do Disability Studies?" *Journal of Teacher Education* 52, no. 2 (2001): 107–123.

Ware, Linda and Natalie Hatz. "Teaching Stories: Inclusion/Exclusion and Disability Studies." Bank Street Occasional Paper Series: 36 (2016).

Ware, Linda and Jan Weatherly Valle. "How Do We Begin a Conversation on Disability in Urban Schools?" In Shirley R. Steinberg (Ed.), *19 Urban Questions: Teaching in the City*. New York & London: Peter Lang Publishing. 2010. 113–130. Print.

Presuming Competence

*Douglas Biklen and
Jamie Burke*

The authors of this chapter have known each other for a long time, though when they first met, they could not have imagined that they would be writing together at this juncture, 13 years hence. We first met in Syracuse, New York, at the Jowonio School, a preschool that includes students with and without disabilities. One of us was four years old, the other a university professor in his forties. The latter followed the former around a preschool classroom, recording his every move. The professor watched the 4-year-old student look at pictures on the page of a children's book and then point to letters on an electronic typing device, making words in response to his teacher's questions; the teacher, a young man, alternately held the boy in his lap or sat behind him on a stool, with his hand under the boy's arm as he typed. A few moments later, the professor scurried with the video camera to record a scene of the boy, with both hands held by his teacher, jumping on a mini trampoline.

That video recording did not provide enough data to predict the future for this boy. Would he become an active participant in school life as a teenager? How would his peers receive him? Would teachers in his future grades have ways of involving him in the academic curricula? None of this could be known when he was four years old. Indeed, observers of the video might even wonder how much could really be known about his abilities then, at the age of four. After all, the method of communication that the boy used facilitated communication,[1] was controversial.[2] Not everyone who saw the boy pointing to letters was convinced that he was indeed communicating. It could have been his teacher, they argued, who did the pointing for him. How could you tell? How could you be certain? Was it not wishful thinking to believe that this boy who had very little speech, limited to a few words at a time, could be as smart as the typing suggested? Yet his family and many of his teachers and several key school administrators did give him the benefit of the doubt; they supported his communication training so that today he can type without physical support and also can speak words as he types them as well as read aloud novel text as well as anything he himself has written.[3] In this chapter we talk about the importance of presuming competence of students with disabilities, as for all students, and the link between this concept (presuming competence) and inclusive education. It may be commonplace for parents and early childhood educators to approach non-disabled children as competent—for example, adults routinely gesture, sing, and talk to infants, presuming such children will at some point connect spoken words and visual enactments to things and concepts. Teaching literacy is carried out within the expectation that most, if not all, children are capable of developing literacy skills. Yet with children classified as autistic, it is not uncommon to link early expressive difficulties to a presumption of incompetence. Leading authorities declare 75 percent of persons classified autistic as retarded, linking severity of symptoms with cognitive level.[4] Delays or perceived deficits in language are taken as evidence of intellectual impairment.[5] "There is little doubt," Carpentieri and Morgan declare, "most children with autism suffer from substantial cognitive impairment."[6] Their use of the term "suffer" implies that autism is a kind of wound. Further, Carpentieri and Morgan argue that compared with individuals who test at the same level of cognitive ability/disability, people classified as autistic are more impaired in verbal reasoning abilities. In light of the pessimism that surrounds autism and the intellectual abilities of persons so classified, to presume competence is to step outside of conventional theory and practice.

Why the Theme of Presuming Competence?

The tradition in American education to assume incompetence of students who have severe communication impairments extends beyond autism, and includes those with other developmental disabilities, such as Down syndrome, Rett syndrome, Cri-Du-Chat, and others. This happens through the process of classification. Students "become" mentally retarded on the basis of their performance on intelligence tests and adaptive behavior scales. As an illustration, consider how the American Psychiatric Association's definition of severe retardation declares a person retarded because of difficulties in performance:

> The group with Severe Mental Retardation constitutes 3%–4% of individuals with Mental Retardation. During the early childhood years, they acquire little or no communicative speech. During the school-age period, they may learn to talk and can be trained in elementary selfcare skills. They profit to only a limited extent from instruction in pre-academic subjects, such as familiarity with the alphabet and simple counting, but can master skills such as learning sight reading of some "survival" words. In their adult years, they may be able to perform simple tasks in closely supervised settings.

Most adapt well to life in the community, in group homes or with their families, unless they have an associated handicap that requires specialized nursing or other care.[7]

Schools are the site where labeling most often occurs. Then, once labeled, students are routinely expected to prove that they can benefit from inclusive, academic instruction in order to be maintained in the regular class, often with supportive and specialized services. Specifically, federal regulations read:

1. That to the maximum extent appropriate, children with disabilities, including children in public or private institutions or other care facilities, are educated with children who are nondisabled; and

2. That special classes, separate schooling or other removal of children with disabilities from the regular educational environment occurs only if the nature or severity of the disability is such that education in regular classes with the use of supplementary aids and services cannot be achieved satisfactorily.[8]

Federal courts have found that if a student is determined not to be benefitting from inclusion in the regular class then exclusion is permissible (Hartmann v. Loudoun County Board of Education, 1997). Of course, the problem with this reasoning is that the criterion for inclusion, as for diagnosis of intellectual disability, is a circular one. The very student who has difficulties with performance, including speech, will often be caught in the diagnostic category of severely retarded, not because of any proof about thinking ability, but because of an absence of evidence about his or her thinking ability. Hence the student may be defined as unable to benefit from inclusion. Whereas at one time (i.e., before the passage of federal right-to-education legislation [Education for All Handicapped Children, 1975]) students had to prove their educability, now they must prove their ability to be included. Once diagnosed, the student may be shunted aside into special classes or special schools on the assumption, not proof, that he or she cannot benefit from the same academic instruction enjoyed by nondisabled peers.

This theme, demonstrating-competence-in-order-to-be-granted-it, arises in popular culture as well, for example in the classic *Flowers for Algernon*[9] or its cinematic derivation, *Charly*,[10] where the lead character's intelligence is portrayed as linked to a body that is quick, agile, and immediately responsive or, conversely, plodding, awkward, and only slowly and intermittently able to imagine what the world around him expects. In Levinson's *Rainman* (1988), the main character, Raymond, gets returned to the closed, segregated, disabled-only institution when he dissembles as his toast in a toaster burns and smokes—the implication is that Raymond cannot manage the requisites of daily living and so cannot be part of the everyday world of "normal people." His fate is sealed when he is inarticulate and seemingly unable to speak for himself in response to questions from a psychiatrist who is deciding on where he should be placed.[11]

In short, the outside observer (e.g., teacher, parent, diagnostician, associate) has a choice, to determine either that the person is incompetent (i.e., severely retarded by the APA definition) or to admit that one cannot know another's thinking unless the other can reveal it. The latter is actually the more conservative choice. It refuses to limit opportunity; by presuming competence, it casts the teachers, parents, and others in the role of finding ways to support the person to demonstrate his or her agency.

The notion of presuming competence is not a new one in the field of severe disabilities. Blatt (1999) was one of the first scholars to illustrate this when he pointed out the metaphorical nature of retardation: People labeled mentally retarded, he argued, were about as real as a photograph of a person is a person. To drive home his argument, Blatt notes that prior to Helen Keller becoming an internationally famous writer, speaker, and humanitarian, she was herself believed to be retarded. Only with the help of Anne Sullivan, and the means of communication that Sullivan taught, did Keller escape "being" retarded. It is a special, ethical responsibility, Blatt writes, for the teacher to presume the student's educability. While Anne Sullivan had no way of knowing at the outset of her work that she would enable Keller to become world famous, or even that Keller would learn to read and write, Sullivan was nevertheless obligated to think such accomplishments were possible.

Recently, other scholars have used a similar lens through which to construct educational approaches to students with disabilities,[12] indeed as many have done for conceptualizing education for others who have been traditionally marginalized.[13] For example, the notion of presuming competence implies that educators must assume students can and will change and, that through engagement with the world, will demonstrate complexities of thought and action that could not necessarily be anticipated. Within this frame, difficulties with performance are not presumed to be evidence of intellectual incapacity.[14] Similarly, in a book detailing his work with children whom schools had classified as autistic and severely retarded, Linneman (2001) demonstrates their abilities to work with him on a variety of computer programs where they reveal their interests. Linneman refers to granting a person "mindedness"; his "mindedness"' appears to be analogous to presuming competence. He credits the idea of being open to individuals' competence as crucial to his work. Conversely, "the specter of mental retardation creates an altered set of expectations," he writes, such that the person's mind is thought to be absent or at least "contested territory." Yet if classified as autistic but not mentally retarded, "it is likely that" the mind will be thought to be "present but hidden."[15]

Whether from the perspective that Linneman (2001) refers to as belief in a person's "mindedness," that Blatt (1999) calls "educability,'' that Goode (1992) describes as the "emic" perspective, or that we refer to as "presuming competence," the observer's obligation is not to project an ableist interpretation on something another person does, but rather to presume there must be a rationale or sympathetic explanation for what someone does and then to try to discover it, always from the other person's own perspective. Thus the presumption of competence does not require the teacher's ability to prove its existence or validity in advance; rather it is a stance, an outlook, a framework for educational engagement. As readers will see, this presuming competence lens provides the foundation for the interview that follows.

A Conversation About Inclusive Schooling

The text in this section is a dialogue between the professor and the now high school (soon to be college) student. As will become apparent, the conversation covers not only questions of school organization, the ideology behind everyday educational practice, but also specific descriptions of how the second author experiences school culture as well as particular personal qualities associated with his disability and what he suggests might be changed to create more inclusive schools. Taken as a whole, the discussion itself evidences the possibilities that accrue from presuming competence.

Initial Thoughts on What Makes for an Ideal School

Biklen: Let me begin straightforwardly. If you could design the ideal school, what would it be like?

Burke: What would a school of my dreams look like? Good soft seats and desks that held wonderful books that told of love and kindness. Kids would need to behave in the most kind manner and teasing would be a detention time. Everyone would be asked to join all clubs . . . and pleasing music would play everywhere.

Biklen: Okay, so you want physical comfort but also rich learning. Does your call for no teasing mean that you've encountered teasing?

Burke: Well, I can think of many times, but places where I was teased seemed to be where the others experienced it as well. The lack of speech was an enormous handicap. It made me not sad, but furious. I could not shout at them or harangue them. One terrible time was when I got seated in the back of the school bus. Two bullies told me to jump out the window. Did they think I was stupid? I was vindicated through my typing because the principal listened to me and they were chastised. That example was one, but I was given the opportunity to tell teachers if I was not being called on for sufficient answers. When I had a tough experience in chorus in fourth grade, I was able to talk to my school psychologist who became excellent in facilitating my typing. We shared much in emotional freeing of angry looks at how life dealt me a lousy hand. In the ideal school I would be able to tell my thoughts and troubles when I chose, not when others desire.

Biklen: Are there ways that a school can help you feel confident about your place in it?

Burke: My school is very good and people try both teaching and loving me and my autism. So I think I am fearing less now than younger times of my life. Joy in life as a boy in a journey to a happy life is even a dream now seen. Respect comes with love and understanding each kid's abilities and the desire to teach so therefore teachers must have a desire to teach everyone. They must realize that their dreams are not ours. Ask us what we will need to be an independent person later in our life. Teach good skills in a respectful way. Conversations with me will tell you if I am happy.

Biklen: That seems like such an important principle: Give students a chance to be heard and listen to them! I wonder how we address this issue when some children have trouble speaking or communicating.

Burke: When I was growing up, speaking was so frustrating. I could see the words in my brain but then I realized that making my mouth move would get those letters to come alive, they died as soon as they were born. What made me feel angry was to know that I knew exactly what I was to say and my brain was retreating in defeat. I felt so mad as teachers spoke in their childish voices to me, mothering me, but not educating me.

A Matter of Timing

Biklen: So how do you think these experiences compare to what other students may encounter?

Burke: Perhaps the question should reflect how we differ in the speed of conveying our thoughts. Vocalized thoughts slip quickly and with little prior planning. On my part, I must first have a way to indicate I desire to comment. Then, a facilitator must be available to promptly cue my body to get my communication device (e.g., by gesturing to the computer keyboard). Then I need physical support to type [with certain facilitators such as his mother, Burke types without physical support]. All of this takes too long for typical kids. I have lost many comments that may have engaged friendships because of the complications of this way of communicating. Yet, I am forever pleased to use it to involve my self in the world of my peers.

Teachers can give students a chance to know me. Friends are so hard to keep interested as it takes very much desirous time to type. Kids are mostly good at talking but listening is not an asset they use. If I am able to talk, it still is not very good, as time is fleeting and so are they.

Biklen: So your teachers and fellow students strongly influence how much participation is possible.

Burke: Greatly. The issue is that even though my speed of typing is much faster now, it still is an enormous amount of time in order to type a response to a question. In English class we were studying Shakespeare, I believe it was *Hamlet*. My teacher asked if I could respond to a query about the plot. I was hopeful that she called on me because my knowledge of Shakespeare is fully evident. While typing, the kids were restless and pencils were tapping and the loud sounds of talking distracted me. I needed full concentration, and it's so distracting with the background noises to concentrate on the long English names of the play. I did all right, but could have done better work in a quiet environment. That meant it took me longer to respond. In conversations kids will ask questions and typing is again so much slower than quick use of an athletic tongue which spits out the words without so much as a jog around the jaw. By the time I can formulate a verbal answer, they have left to move onto another class. This leaves me with my response and no one to respond to. It may pop out of the brain even after someone else asks a new question, and I begin it all once more. It's so frustrating to me.

Biklen: A few years ago you wrote, "if homework was told to be done, time more than one day would be given." Is this another aspect of how time to complete a task can inhibit you from achieving what you desire?

Burke: Perhaps it's the enemy of those who cannot execute directly from their initiation direction. I mean that I must read and use both auditory and visual connection. Stimuli are needed in both areas. (Then there is the complication of stamina, or lack of it.) Typing at the end of day exhausts me and my focus. It's like a flea on a dog that's getting wet, always moving to another area of escape. Again, my old participating partner of motor planning inability makes having an adult to keep me on task necessary. I feel it's reasonable and fair to give me an extra day for reports of projects. I must say I rarely, if ever, ask for that accommodation, as it screams of disabled.

Biklen: it seems unfair that a useful accommodation is treated as evidence of inadequacy.

BOX 34.1

Even well-meaning assumptions about disabled students keep them from true classroom inclusion. In this video, Megan Bomgaars tells educators, "Don't Limit Me!":

www.youtube.com/watch?v=9gaSx44pEvk

Ideal Teachers

Biklen: How about the teachers in your school? What should they be like?

Burke: The teachers, good and many of them, would only be as we choose, not assigned by computers. Courses would be chosen by teachers' love of subject and teachers must be excellent in that class (the one chosen).

Biklen: I'm sure most teachers would share your view: Allow them to teach what they care most about. But I sense there is some other reasoning behind your statement.

Burke: It's always curious to me as to why some have chosen this profession. After all, I assume the desire is to impart what they've gone to great monetary debt and great time to learn. Some seem annoyed I am asking to have an additional adult in the room. It is necessary for me to have a facilitator so that I may communicate. Others seem very interested in the curiosities of autism. The best teachers just seem to accept all the variables as nothing that will alter the room, and they demonstrate their love of the knowledge they are teaching. It's a passionate feeling in their delivery and how they seek me out to answer the questions. It's as if we dance in partnership on that floor of knowledge.

Biklen: I know that your mother has been very involved in making sure that teachers know how to support you. Is that part of the ideal teaching equation?

Burke: Well certainly I think politics seem to require people to initiate the uninitiated. I mean, I think that those who know us best and also in our worst state of being can represent us in the way parents want their children to be seen. I think in fairness, [a parent's input] may put the teachers more at ease than a special education teacher. My understanding has been [that] the special education teacher places her or his educational worth on the percentages of acceptance of a kid into regular education classes. The special education teacher very often must try to sell us as worthwhile [for regular class teachers] to take up their effort.

School as a Sensory Field

Biklen: When you first wrote about your ideas for an ideal school, you touched on how you experience your sensory sensitivities. This has often been discussed in other firsthand narratives.[16] You said, "Lunch would be served in a room far from cooking so smells are not sickening. The lunch would be a time for peaceful eating and not loud talking and annoying bells and whistles which split my ears as a sword in use of killing monsters—my ears hear colossally well so noise can be difficult." I am especially interested in this, because it is something that other people with autism have mentioned. But it also may suggest that the busy school could play havoc with your sensory sensitivities. Some might argue that this could justify creating special classrooms and schools less prone to creating sensory overload.

Burke: Total bullshit. Please excuse the term, but I feel it's the end result of ideas ingested that produce a crappy result. What purpose would being exposed to another who hand stims or who has vocal out-thoughts (echolalia)? For me, that would only make my sensory sensitivities higher. It's like a domino, but in reverse order. Setting it off doesn't make it fall lower, but escalates that energy higher. Perhaps the most productive idea is to assist us in lessening the sensitivity. This can be done before classes or exams. It can be done after school. The effects, while taking a certain amount of building up in the brain, will certainly carry over. Treat the difficulties now in order to have a fully functional life after school is done. I am not planning a segregated life for myself. As a young child I often looked to other students' ways of being in order to be a living example of how autism is not fully diving into a shallow pool.

Biklen: Okay. So what are the kinds of strategies that have helped you deal with sensory differences?

Burke: It seems very long ago when this sensory wall was erected. So many perfect therapies that secured through marvelous people have effectively torn down that wall of protection. [My occupational therapist (O.T.)] is serving up the sensory diet of Flow, Infinity Walk, platform swinging while spelling and sequencing. Willbarger Brushing, EFT [emotion freeing therapy], and the love of talking to me as we learn about the brain's ability to redirect and dissipate neurological pathways. [The O.T.] also introduced to me the Listening Therapy music. Listening therapy is a joy. It gives your ears the feeling of reaching the bridge over the missing meaning of sounds. Listening therapy is a grouping of music that has certain frequencies changed. This helped me to integrate my system of midline crossing[17] and helped me to tie my shoes at 15. She has me blow darts through a small tube from a distance to a target on the window. This seems to help my lips form better with more accuracy. At times my ears listen with no difficulty. Other times, I must really focus to hear and make a bridge of sound to cross into the continuation. That seems to help me hear whole words. Before, I would lose certain sounds and the words seemed as garbage to be thrown out with no use to them. You might say I felt I am training my brain to hear better. It helps me to begin to speak better. Also it sends needed rhythm to my speech. I find the classical music best for me. My brain follows the very thorough and detailed patterns.

As for hearing what was said around me, I believe my ears only could hear the strong sounding words, I mean the words that made my ears stretch to listen.

Biklen: Please tell me more about what you just said. Are you now speaking of a sensory and/or processing difficulty with making sense of spoken conversation?

Burke: Yes, the spoken word was so difficult to make clear sense of its purpose. When I was in my tender years, the words were as waves in an ocean, washing over and around me. Soothing, but not making any useful sense.

Biklen: I know you have also tried what people call "sensory integration."

Burke: To me and my brain and body, this is the magnificent therapy that just must never be overlooked. [With that therapy] my body and brain felt more as one unit and not two separate ones. When I would be stressed from demands of staying in the class or the stimulation of too much color in the classroom walls, I could go to the Physical Therapy room and roll in the rainbow barrel or sit on a soft beanbag chair where its firm but soft pressure on my body from all sides would bring control back to me. The desire to scratch or scream to get away was greatly sublimated to just a pesky controllable feeling. It is absolutely paramount that people know that now in my older teenage years my O.T. has assisted me as an angel of mercy in giving me the Listening Therapy and others that have helped me to type much faster and hear better. My typing that was a VW Beetle is now a Lamborghini. It's the grace of faster access to crossing midline. Accessing midline gives me greater ease visually and [that's good, for example, for] doing long calculus problems. It's easier keeping track of the numerical order of problem solving. The readers may not know this, but another vastly helpful therapy has taken the fears that are like a paying customer which ride the autism, and it has left them at the exit gate. This [is] NET [neuro emotional therapy] and kinesiology. Many terrifying fears from those days of frustration and confusion are gone. People must acknowledge that this autism loves to confuse and frighten. Only the person that truly desires to help and not cure [are the ones I require]; they must creatively search all this jumble of wires so inordinately mixed and seek a clear road out from that jumbled mess.

Biklen: Jamie, I know that some people will read what you said earlier about sometimes needing a quiet environment, without the other students' restless tapping of pencils, or away from the busy, sensory overloaded school as an argument in favor of creating and maintaining, separate, disabled-only classes. But if I understand you correctly, your answer to sensory differences is not segregation but access to helpful services such as those of the O.T.

Learning to Speak, a More Valuable Task than Learning to Tie One's Shoes

Biklen: It must have been hard to be aware of what you wanted to say and yet not able to make your speech work, even as nearly everyone else around you was chattering away.

Burke: I understand why kids [with impaired speech] scream. It's frustrating not being able to speak and feeling as a mostly invisible being. Do you know the vintage movie, *The Invisible Man*?[18] That's how I felt. My clothes were there, but the body and the soul felt like nothing. How can you live a life getting treated as that?

Biklen: How did you begin to emerge from that invisibility?

Burke: Understanding that the only way to make this hell a heaven was with speech, I decided to take a risk and began to try just one word. I know my voice sounded foolish, but it felt okay to try. As my bold new hope grew as a fine now true reality, I tried more and felt that heaven moved closer.

Biklen: So this was something you deliberately decided to pursue, even if it was excruciatingly difficult.

Burke: So many things were hard for me to learn. I now think it was so foolish to ask me to learn to tie my shoes. My brain moved into hiding the reason for not being able to do it, but yet my school believed it important mostly as a way to tell you that you are now just greatly smart. Why is shoe tying important compared to the fact that you can't speak? Like saying the letters, mostly there was no pattern to follow in my brain for tying my shoelaces. After much practice, as with my words, it seemed a pattern moved into my brain, giving direction to my hands. I think my music therapy gave help with this. Doesn't tying your shoes mean you are now enclaved in the world of pigtails and basketballs? When a kid can't tie shoes, you know they get frustrated with you, and even though those words of "it doesn't matter" and "we will use Velcro" are heard, your heart feels defeated. I screamed silently, "make my mouth work as my hands; can you idiots not see my struggle to tell you I have so many answers to the questions you place before my face?" Isn't tying the speech to my mouth from my brain more critical to life than making a piece of cotton secure? When I was 15 I tied my shoes and people rejoiced as if I had won an enormous prize in some battle. I laughed at them in my brain. If they knew how ridiculous they seemed. Adults deemed it worthy of such excitement. Mom was happy and dad proud, but my mind believed this excited reaction to tying shoes still foolish.

Biklen: Jamie, I'm embarrassed to tell you how many times I've seen teachers working with students on shoe tying, and yet I never thought much about it, except that it might not be the best use of anyone's time. I wish that I had thought more about what the children must have been thinking. But then there's the problem of how any of us can know what another is thinking if the person cannot speak or otherwise make a choice clear to others. This must have been so hard to you.

Burke: I now think it was a big effort for those who smiled . . . and said, "I know you will speak some day." They did not really believe what they said to my face. I knew their smile hid what they really believed and that sympathy and not belief filled them. Why do all those who have said they are educated in the ways of teaching not know that hope and desire must be moved into place as the pillars of strength first before the floors can be built?

Biklen: Yes, who needs charity if it signals pessimism? So confidence and maybe even security were more what you wanted, to feel secure that you would have chances to grow?

Burke: Security comes from making your choices heard. Choices, even something like selecting a cereal, could be hard. In the morning I was given many silly choices. But as my voice was not a true one, I had to pick the choice I heard. Many times it was not my true choice and both my mom and me were mad if I did not finish the cereal. I mean when you are little and have speech that is only just a few small babyish words, you cannot get yourself unstuck to make a new selection. Like a car that keeps slipping into reverse gear because the track isn't strong enough to move forward. It was impossible to move to a joyful and delicious choice. After I was served, I was furious with myself and mad at mom. Even saying, "do you want something else" didn't help. The gears refused to move. I think many times it felt better to scream and run, than to feel like gagging on the bitter food. Even as the selections were viewed, my brain made only the same choice every day. Many times I desired pancakes but my lousy hand pointed to the bitter choice.

Biklen: Is there anything that a teacher or anyone else could have done to help with this?

Burke: I believe if I had a moveable brain image as a child it would have been easy.

Biklen: What's a "moveable brain image"?

Burke: The moveable brain image came as I learned to watch videos in moving order. Moving order means to me the ability to make things move along in order and not get stuck on an image or phrase that captured my attention.

Biklen: What's an example of this?

Burke: Perhaps getting stuck is the same as getting trapped in a pattern that makes you feel comfortable. In the realm of autistic brains, it's the perfect way to not move forward from the fear of being challenged with a new thought or task that you have no reference for. Being stuck in that pattern is certainly safer than venturing into fear and uncertainty.

Anxiety comes as a regular visitor, just as breathing. I believe my cells have a nucleus filled with it. I think when I was young I walked in a constant pacing to help my body deal with it and I felt my nerves prickle as if a porcupine shot its quills into me. I think that sensory integration . . . has been like a giant Band-Aid to my body. It wraps up the stingers as a ball of cotton and makes things more comfortable for me.

I am now able to handle many situations that would have sent me into man-overboard feeling. One thing that sent me overboard was being asked a question when I felt stressed over the voices asking it. Women have a pitch to their vocal chords that are like vibrato. Sadly, you are expected to respond, but you truly feel as a bird trapped. Fluttering away seems lovely, but the expectation (of others) is a wire cage. Fighting to be appreciated, but longing to escape, I feel I made myself struggle, as this was the way to become competent.

Another time the overboard feeling comes is in tests. I need to focus on the question, work with the difficulty of small print which is black and blurs my eyes. The rustle of papers, pencils, scratching, coughing and scraping chairs, and lights drive me crazy. I do well for the beginning, then it adds up as a bank balance ready to be withdrawn. I am a man overboard awaiting my rescue. But you can't leave, can you, or I will fail. Failing is fundamental, but only for those who aren't in special education designation.

Biklen: Here again, readers might interpret your statements as justification for segregated schooling.

Burke: Segregation equals a distinction of lesser ability. Am I lesser because I get nervous about an exam? Am I deemed less intelligent because my feelings only make passing a higher stakes? I again ask you to think of who is it that has placed this way of evaluating worthiness? Have they placed their feet in my shoes? I would enjoin them to try, and to allow me to view the straightness of their path. Every sensory therapy has bonded my movement pattern stronger to my brain. . . . [This explains how] I have managed to do independent typing. Not every person has received my many therapies that have lessened anxiety. I believe that allows the learning and calming to step forward. It's just like looking to make the brain place the gear in forward, not in reverse.

The idea of school inclusion can be as a lousy or lovely happening. It's really all in the hands of the teachers along with the permission from the big boss, the superintendent. Teachers must be willing to not just give me a desk and then leave me to fill the chair. I need to be asked questions, and given time for my thoughtful answers. Teachers need to become as a conductor, and guide me through the many places I may get lost.

Conclusion

We began this chapter by suggesting that when students and teachers participate in inclusive schooling, they cannot possibly predict what directions it will take them. In particular, when a student has difficulties with speech, as the second author did when he first entered school, teachers cannot know what the student is thinking. This is a situation that demands a kind of compact between teacher and student to choose the most optimistic stance possible, what we have called "presuming competence," within which to effect inclusive education. As it turns out, during his earliest years of being included, Burke understood far more than he was able to express. Fortunately, his mother and a group of teachers and external consultants kept looking for ways that he might communicate. Clearly, his experience stands out as worthy of telling, mainly because it contrasts so vividly with the more common practice of regarding performance difficulties as evidence of incompetence and then expecting little. Pessimistic assessments trigger circumspection about students' potential for learning and lead to diminished expectations—recall for example Burke's account of a curriculum on shoe tying—with little enthusiasm for exploring how students might participate and achieve academically.

The principle of presuming competence leads to consideration of a series of corollaries, each of which can be found in the interview above. These corollaries follow:

- There needs to be a strong commitment to inclusive education that expects student agency, where the participation of the student in the heart of the classroom is a given, not an experiment, and not conditional, and where participation amounts to more than mere physical presence; the student must be seen as someone more than a body to fill the chair. Only then is the stage set for an attitude of problem solving where, when difficulties arise, teachers, teaching consultants, parents, and administrators can work with the child to figure out solutions. Good teaching involves dialogue with the student, for teachers cannot assume they know what students are thinking or aspiring to; as Burke explains above, teachers' "dreams are not ours."

- Disability may cause some students to experience the world in ways that may be dramatically different in degree and even nature from other students. As the above conversation suggests, much of a school administrator's or teacher's work is to find ways of learning about how a student experiences his or her environ-ment. This may involve seeking advice from specialists such as occupational therapists, physical therapists, consultants on anxiety, and people knowledgeable in sensory integration strategies; Burke warns against defining such services as the privilege of middle- and upper-middle-class students. If seen as rightful, schools will aggressively seek out specialized expertise to support students who may benefit from it. It is critically important to remember that difference does not equate with deficit. Unless educators attempt to adapt the school environment, for instance by providing support services that are in response to how students experience social interaction and other environmental characteristics, a student with a disability can indeed be physically present but not really part of the school. Adapting to styles of receiving information effectively, for example by providing visual as well as auditory input, was important for Burke's early education.

- Educators and, especially, specialists are often cast in the role of explaining students to other professionals, to parents, and to themselves. And they are often expected to do so authoritatively. Yet speaking for the other is always problematic. Instead, it would seem best always to seek ways for the other person to explain himself or herself. Schools can provide students with opportunities to be informants about themselves in relation to school culture. Above, Burke notes how the time it takes for him to type his side of conversations affects most of his interactions in school. Particular ways of organizing an environment (rules, standard operating procedures) may privilege some students and disadvantage others, hence the need to analyze how disability may be related to the implicit and explicit rules of a setting. All students could be enlisted to share their thoughts on how the school culture and school practices, including peer-to-peer styles of interaction, can be adapted to enable more democratic participation.

- The idea of "normal" is itself a social construct and can be altered, shifted, and transformed. Hopefully, this chapter will encourage educators to question the very idea of normal. Clearly, ideas of what is possible in regard to human relationships and education do shift within particular historical/cultural moments; and individual teachers, students, researchers, parents, and others can have a part in the reshaping. Although the idea of presuming competence may seem reasonable and advantageous, if introduced to a school where large groups of students are categorized as mentally retarded, this will represent a radical shift in educational ideology. Burke's comments above reveal that even in a school officially committed to inclusion, assumptions of incompetence can still surface— he describes a situation where he was taunted by two students on the school bus. Such events reaffirm the importance of putting disability and ideas of normalcy/difference at the center of conversations concerning school reform; dealing with them is essential to the creation of democratic schooling.

Discussion Questions

1. How do students benefit when educators presume competence rather than focusing on perceived deficits?

2. What does it mean to be truly inclusive in the classroom? Discuss some of Burke's most important concerns about how to best achieve inclusion and aid every student.

3. Why is learning to speak more important than learning to tie one's shoes? How might this idea change our approach to teaching disabled students?

4. What do you make of this chapter's interview format? How might the medium fit its message?

Notes

1 All of the text written by the second author of this chapter was produced after he learned to speak as he typed (he can say the words before and as he types them). In the year prior to our writing this chapter, the student developed the ability to type without any physical support. For all of his writing, the second author had a facilitator sit next to him as he typed. Parts of the discussion were first drafted by the second author for speeches and for an essay that appears in the book, *Autism and the Myth of the Person Alone* (Biklen, 2005), adapted here with permission. Controversy about the method of facilitated communication centers on the question of authorship. It has been shown that a facilitator's physical touch of the typist's hand or arm may influence the person's pointing. A number of studies have demonstrated this fact and/or have failed to validate authorship (Bebko, Perry, & Bryson, 1996; Bomba et al., 1996; Cabay, 1994; Crews et al., 1995; Eberlin et al., 1993; Klewe, 1993; Montee, Miltenberger, & Wittrock, 1995; Moore et al., 1993; Regal, Rooney, & Wandas, 1994; Shane & Kearns, 1994; Smith & Belcher, 1993; Szempruch & Jacobson, 1993; and Wheeler et al., 1993). These studies use one basic type of assessment, namely message passing; that is, the person being assessed was required to convey information that could not be known to the facilitator. Other studies, using a wider range of test situations as well as linguistic analysis and documentation of physical, independent-of-facilitator typing, have successfully demonstrated authorship (Broderick & Kasa-Hendrickson, 2001; Calculator & Singer, 1992; Cardinal, Hanson, & Wakeham, 1996; Emerson, Grayson, & Griffiths, 2001; Janzen-Wilde, Duchan, & Higginbotham, 1995; Niemi & Kärnä-Lin, 2002; Rubin et al., 2001; Sheehan & Matuozzi, 1996; Tuzzi, Cemin, & Castagna, 2004; Weiss, Wagner, & Bauman, 1996; and Zanobini & Scopesi, 2001). The studies by Cardinal and his colleagues (1996), Sheehan and Matuozzi (1996), and Weiss, Wagner, and Bauman (1996) all involved message passing experiments, but unlike many of the assessments in which individuals failed

to demonstrate authorship, these involved extensive testing sessions, with the possible effect of desensitizing the subjects to test anxiety.

2   Beukelman & Mirenda, 1998.

3   Broderick & Kasa-Hendrickson, 2001; Kasa-Hendrickson, Broderick, & Biklen, 2002.

4   Carpentieri & Morgan, 1996; Rapin, 1997.

5   See for example, Jacobson, Mulick, & Schwartz, 1995, and Volkmar & Cohen, 1985.

6   Carpentieri & Morgan, 1996, p. 611.

7   APA 2000, pp. 43–44.

8   Office of Special Education and Rehabilitative Services, 1997.

9   Keyes, 1966.

10 Nelson, 1968.

11 It is perhaps fitting that the psychiatrist is played by the film's director, Barry Levinson, for the film itself, his film, conveys the message that a person who is different belongs in an institution and has no place in the everyday world inhabited by the undiagnosed.

12 Biklen, 1990; Goode, 1992; Kliewer, 1998; Linneman, 2001.

13 See for example, Ashton-Warner, 1963, Freire, 1970.

14 Biklen, 2000.

15 Linneman 2001, p. 183.

16 Rubin, in Biklen, 2005; Jackson, 2002.

17 Crossing midline refers to a person's ability to move an arm from one side of the body to the other, a skill one needs for playing most games and for many other tasks.

18 Whale, 1993.

References

American Psychiatric Association. (2000). *Diagnostic and Statistical Manual of Mental Disorders* (4th ed.). Washington, DC: Author.

Ashton-Warner, S. (1963). *Teacher.* New York: Simon & Schuster.

Bebko, J. M., Perry, A., & Bryson, S. (1996). Multiple method validation study of facilitated communication: II. Individual differences and subgroup results. *Journal of Autism and Developmental Disabilities,* 26(1), 19–42.

Beukelman, D. R., & Mirenda, P. (1998). *Augmentative and Alternative Communication: Management of Severe Communication Disorders in Children and Adults* (2nd ed.). Baltimore, MD: Brookes.

Biklen, D. (1990). Communication unbound: Autism and praxis. *Harvard Educational Review,* 60(3), 291–314.

Biklen, D. (2000). Constructing inclusion: Lessons from critical, disability narratives. *International Journal on Inclusive Education,* 4(4), 337–353.

Biklen, D. (Ed.). (2005). *Autism and the Myth of the Person Alone.* New York: New York University Press.

Blatt, B. (1999) Man through a turned lens. In S. J. Taylor & S. D. Blatt (Eds.), *In Search of the Promised Land: The collected papers of Burton Blatt* (pp. 71–82). Washington, DC: American Association on Mental Deficiency.

Bomba, C., O'Donnell, L., Markowitz, C., & Holmes, D. (1996). Evaluating the impact of facilitated communication on the communicative competence of fourteen students with autism. *Journal of Autism and Developmental Disorders*, 26(1), 43–58.

Broderick, A., & Kasa-Hendrickson, C. (2001). "Say just one word at first": The emergence of reliable speech in a student labeled with autism. *Journal of the Association for Persons with Severe Handicaps*, 26(1), 13–24.

Cabay, M. (1994). A controlled evaluation of facilitated communication using open-ended and fill-in questions. *Journal of Autism and Developmental Disorders*, 24(4), 517–527.

Calculator, S. N., & Singer, K. M. (1992). Preliminary validation of facilitated communication. *Topics in Language Disorders*, 13(1), ix–xvi.

Cardinal, D. N., Hanson, D., & Wakeham, J. (1996). Investigation of authorship in facilitated communication. *Mental Retardation*, 34(4), 231–242.

Carpentierei, S. C., & Morgan, S. B. (1996). Adaptive and intellectual functioning in autistic and nonautistic retarded children. *Journal of Autism and Developmental Disorders*, 26(6), 611–620.

Crews, W. D., Sanders, E. C., Hensley, L. G., Johnson, Y. M., Bonaventura, S., Rhodes, R. D., & Garren, M. (1995). An evaluation of facilitated communication in a group of nonverbal individuals with mental retardation. *Journal of Autism and Developmental Disorders*, 25(2), 205–213.

Eberlin, M., McConnachie, G., Ibel, S., & Volpe, L. (1993). Facilitated communication: A failure to replicate the phenomenon. *Journal of Autism and Developmental Disorders*, 23(3), 507–530.

Education for All Handicapped Children Act. (1975). Pub. L. No. 94-142, 89 Stat. 773, 20 U.S.C. §§1400 et seq.

Emerson, A., Grayson, A., & Griffiths, A. (2001). Can't or won't? Evidence relating to authorship in facilitated communication. *International Journal of Language and Communication Disorders*, 36(Suppl.), 98–103.

Freire, P. (1970). *Pedagogy of the Oppressed.* New York: Herder and Herder.

Goode, D. A. (1992). Who is Bobby? Ideology and method in the discovery of a Down syndrome person's competence. In P. M. Ferguson, D. L. Ferguson, & S. J. Taylor (Eds.), *Interpreting Disability: A Qualitative Reader* (pp. 197–212). New York: Teachers College Press.

Hartmann v. Loudoun County Board of Education. (1997). 118 F.3d 996 (4th Cir.).

Jackson, L. (2002). *Freaks, Geeks & Asperger Syndrome.* New York: Kingsley.

Jacobson, J. W., Mulick, J. A., & Schwartz, A. A. (1995). A history of facilitated communication: Science, pseudoscience, and antiscience. *American Psychologist*, 50(9), 750–765.

Janzen-Wilde, M. L., Duchan, J. F., & Higginbotham, D. J. (1995). Successful use of facilitated communication with an oral child. *Journal of Speech and Hearing Research*, 38(3), 658–676.

Kasa-Hendrickson, C., Broderick, A., Biklen, D. (Producers), & Gambell, J. (Director). (2002). *Inside The Edge*. (VHS). (Available from Syracuse University, 370 Huntington Hall, Syracuse, New York.)

Keyes, D. (1966). *Flowers for Algernon*. New York: Harcourt Brace.

Klewe, L. (1993). An empirical evaluation of spelling boards as a means of communication for the multihandicapped. *Journal of Autism and Developmental Disorders*, 23(3), 559–566.

Kliewer, C. (1998). *Schooling Children with Down Syndrome: Toward an Understanding of Possibility*. New York: Teachers College Press.

Levinson, B. (Director). (1988). *Rainman* [Motion picture]. MGM.

Linneman, R. D. (2001). *Idiots: Stories about Mindedness and Mental Retardation*. New York: Lang.

Montee, B. B., Miltenberger, R. G., & Wittrock, D. (1995). An experimental analysis of facilitated communication. *Journal of Applied Behaviour Analysis*, 28(2), 189–200.

Moore, S., Donovan, B., & Hudson, A. (1993). Brief report: Facilitator-suggested conversational evaluation of facilitated communication. *Journal of Autism and Developmental Disorders*, 23(3), 541–552.

Moore, S., Donovan, B., Hudson, A., Dykstra, J., & Lawrence, J. (1993). Brief report: Evaluation of eight case studies of facilitated communication. *Journal of Autism and Developmental Disorders*, 23(3), 531–539.

Nelson, R. (Director). (1968). *Charly* [Motion picture]. MGM.

Niemi, J., & Kärnä-Lin, E. (2002). Grammar and lexicon in facilitated communication: A linguistic authorship analysis of a Finnish case. *Mental Retardation*, 40(5), 347–357.

Office of Special Education and Rehabilitative Services, Education. (1997). 34 CFR 300.550, 20 U.S.C. §1412(a)(5).

Rapin, I. (1997). Current concepts: Autism. *New England Journal of Medicine*, 33(2), 97–104.

Regal, R. A., Rooney, J. R., & Wandas, T. (1994). Facilitated communication: An experimental evaluation. *Journal of Autism and Developmental Disorders*, 24(3), 345–355.

Rubin, S., Biklen, D., Kasa-Hendrickson, C., Kluth, P., Cardinal, D. N., & Broderick, A. (2001). Independence, participation, and the meaning of intellectual ability. *Disability and Society*, 16(3), 415–429.

Shane, H., & Kearns, K. (1994). An examination of the role of the facilitator in "facilitated communication." *American Journal of Speech-Language Pathology*, 3(3), 48–54.

Sheehan, C. M., & Matuozzi, R. T. (1996). Investigation of the validity of facilitated communication through the disclosure of unknown information. *Mental Retardation*, 34(2), 94–107.

Smith, M. D., & Belcher, R. G. (1993). Brief report: Facilitated communication with adults with autism. *Journal of Autism and Developmental Disorders*, 23(1), 175–183.

Szempruch, J., & Jacobson, J. W. (1993). Evaluating facilitated communications of people with developmental disabilities. *Research in Developmental Disabilities*, 14(4), 253–264.

Tuzzi, A., Cemin, M., & Castagna, M. (2004) "Moved deeply I am": Autistic language in texts produced with FC. *Journées internationales d'Analyse statistique des Données Textuelles*, 7, 1–9.

Volkmar, F. R., & Cohen, D. J. (1985). The experience of infantile autism: A first-person account by Tony W. *Journal of Autism and Developmental Disabilities*, 15, 47–54.

Weiss, M. J. S., Wagner, S. H., & Bauman, M. L. (1996). A validated case study of facilitated communication. *Mental Retardation*, 34(4), 220–230.

Whale, J. (Director). (1933). *The Invisible Man* [Motion picture]. Hollywood: Universal Studios.

Wheeler, D. L., Jacobson, J. W., Paglieri, R. A., & Schwartz, A. (1993). An experimental assessment of facilitated communication. *Mental Retardation*, 31(1), 49–60.

Zanobini, M., & Scopesi, A. (2001). La comunicazione facilitata in un bambino autistico. *Psicologia Clinica dello Sviluppo*, 5(3), 395–421.

35 | Disability and Innovation
Haben Girma[1]

My name is Haben Girma. I work as an accessibility and inclusion advocate, teaching organizations and individuals to design with accessibility in mind.

I'm Deafblind. Deafblindness encompasses a wide spectrum of vision and hearing loss. I have a little bit of hearing, and a little bit of vision. I see maybe about 1 percent of what the average sighted person sees. By identifying as Deafblind, I'm telling the world that I'm part of a community where knowledge gained through touch is equal in value to knowledge gained through sight, sound, or other means. Our world is incredibly diverse, and when we design apps, that celebrate that diversity, and recognize that diversity, we all benefit. So I identify as Deafblind to tell the world to design non-visual access, and non-auditory access to help maximize communication. This is tricky for some people.

One of my best friends, when she first met me, wasn't sure how to say hi. She was sitting next to me in one of our classes at law school. She waved hi, but I couldn't see it. She voiced, "Hi," but I couldn't hear it. It was our first day of international law class, and she wasn't thinking about international law. She was thinking about how to get my attention. After a while, during the class, she came up with a plan. She did the most logical thing for a student. She went onto Facebook and sent me a message saying, "Hi, Haben, I'm sitting right next to you."

Technology has facilitated access to communication for a lot of people. And when apps are designed with accessibility in mind—iMessages, Mail, other communication tools—people with disabilities like myself can use them and are able to connect and share information with people.

I saw that Facebook message my friend sent later, and I reached out to her and we were able to communicate. I explained the various communication methods I use.

Technology facilitates connections when both parties are willing and interested in practicing inclusion. I want to share a photo that highlights some of the communication methods I use. In this photo I'm standing at a table, and I'm reading from a digital Braille display. Digital Braille comes through a device with mechanical pins that pop up to form Braille letters. I read these letters by feeling the dots. Braille is a tool, not a language. I primarily use English Braille. I can read Spanish Braille, and I've seen Braille in many different languages. I was once on a ferry going from Italy to Greece. I remembered feeling a bit lost on the ferry because all of the signs were in Greek Braille. So Braille is a tool and the Braille display is a device that produces this information in Braille.

Also in the photo, President Obama is standing at the table and he's typing on an Apple wireless keyboard. What's being typed is being sent to the digital Braille display. I'm reading what's being typed. This is a communication method that I developed.

Deaf individuals have been developing communication tools for hundreds of years. Communities around the world have developed sign languages. In the United States, the dominant sign language is American Sign Language, which is heavily influenced by French Sign Language.

My brother is Deafblind. When he communicates with me he uses sign language. When he's signing I put my hand over his hand, and feel what he is signing. When he wants to listen to me, he'll put his hand over my hand, and feel what I'm signing. Tactile sign language is another form of communication that has developed, that has been developed by the Deafblind community.

Another form is print on palm, where people write on palms. They could write in English characters, Mandarin, and other forms of characters.

Humans are incredibly creative. We design new ways for each of us to connect and engage and share information.

Another form of communication is dance. Dance is expressed in many different forms. Some Deaf individuals who are sighted will watch the other dancers and will pick up the beats by watching the other dancers. Other individuals will watch the musicians, and pick up the beat by watching the fingers and instruments of the musicians. People are very creative and find solutions.

For me, dance is all about the connection. Salsa is like a kind of sign language. People communicate information, rhythm, beat, music, emotions, through their hands. Some of the signals in salsa are visual, and the people I dance with will switch them around and switch those visual signals to physical signals. Through dance we celebrate joy, connection, and community.

Communities that celebrate diversity will find ways to be inclusive. They'll adapt strategies to make sure everyone can participate and be involved. So dance is one community in which I belong that practices inclusion.

When I join a community the first question people usually ask me is, "How do you communicate?" The second question people usually ask me is, "Have you heard of Helen Keller?"

Helen Keller was an amazing advocate. She lived from 1880 to 1968. She advocated for women's rights, disability rights, workers' rights. She spent her whole life advocating, and yet many stories of Helen reduce her to one theme. She succeeded despite her disability. Disability never holds anyone back. Disability is not something that people need to overcome. The barriers that exist are created by society, and it's up to every single one of us to work together to remove those barriers.

Helen was successful because she was part of communities that chose to practice inclusion. She went to Radcliffe College, and Radcliffe provided books in Braille, and made sure she had interpreters. They worked to ensure access and inclusion.

Not every community practices inclusion. Harvard wouldn't admit Helen. Back then Harvard only admitted men. Helen's disability didn't hold her back. Her gender didn't hold her back. It was the community of Harvard that chose to deny access to women.

As another example, Helen's family would not allow her to experience marriage. Helen fell in love, secretly got engaged, but her family prevented her from marrying the person she loved. Helen's disability didn't stop her from feeling love. She wrote extensively about love. But her family, her community, chose to create insurmountable barriers.

All the barriers that exist are created by society. As members of society, we play a role in removing those barriers and making sure that everyone can access information and opportunities.

We've come a long way since Helen's time. More and more communities celebrate diverse families and relationships. Harvard eventually made the smart decision to open its doors to women. And now technology creates more opportunities for people to connect. I often wonder, what would Helen have accomplished, what freedom would she have enjoyed, if she had access to the world of apps that are accessible to people with disabilities?

One of the features Apple offers for developers is called VoiceOver. VoiceOver is a screen-reader that, when an app is compatible, will produce information in speech or digital Braille for users of the app.

A screen-reader is a program that converts graphical information to speech or digital Braille. The screen-reader on the iPhone is called VoiceOver. VoiceOver also works on the Mac, iPad, and the Apple Watch. So, when I'm using my phone, I use VoiceOver. VoiceOver can speak out loud and send information to the digital Braille display.

VoiceOver has allowed me to access more information: news, mail, and messages, and it's also a way for people to know when friends are at the door.

BOX 35.1

Watch Haben Girma demonstrate accessible technologies during her speech:

www.youtube.com/watch?v=_bC7Mvy7Vn4

Apple has a variety of accessibility features. Another one, support for Dynamic Type. When you support Dynamic Type people who are low vision and need larger font sizes can have better access to your apps. Another feature is Captioning. Support for Captioning allows individuals who are deaf or hard of hearing to access the audio content of your videos. Support for Assistive Devices like Braille displays, switch controls . . . Switch controls benefit individuals with limited mobility. So these are some of the features that, if you design for your apps to be accessible, will allow greater access for people with disabilities. But don't stop there, keep innovating, keep thinking of new ways for people to access your information.

Our goal is to have a world where all the apps in the App Store are accessible. Right now if I need an app for anything from travel to shopping, I need to spend hours looking for an accessible app. And sometimes, there isn't an accessible option. Our goal is to have every app, and I mean every single app, be accessible.

Several years ago, I went to China for the first time. When I arrived in my hotel in Beijing I did what I always do when I go somewhere new. I explored. And while exploring the room, I discovered an unidentifiable object. It felt a little like a piece of fruit, but I'd never seen anything like it before. I was wondering: should I taste it?

I was super curious to find out what it was, but not curious enough to taste an unknown object.

So instead I got out my camera, on my iPhone, took a picture, and texted it to a friend, asking: what on earth is this? Is it safe to eat?

I learned that it was dragon fruit. And I discovered I like dragon fruit. Now I imagine a lot of people thinking, why would a camera app need to be accessible? Why would blind people ever take pictures? We take pictures for the same reasons sighted people take pictures. To capture moments, to share experiences with friends.

Our goal is to make sure all apps are accessible. Try not to make assumptions about what people with disabilities can and can't do. Instead, strive for inclusion. And as you strive for inclusion for your apps, here are a few things to keep in mind.

It helps to plan for accessibility from the start. It's much easier, it saves you resources if you plan for accessibility from the very start. I'll give an example from the physical world. Imagine someone builds a skyscraper but realizes they forgot to put in an elevator. They have to tear down part of the building and then install an elevator. That's more time consuming and drains resources. It would be much easier to just plan for an elevator from the start. Same principle applies in the digital world. You save yourself resources when you can have accessibility from the very start.

And there are engineers with disabilities, designers with disabilities, testers with disabilities to help you with the process. There are also many disability organizations in the U.S. and around the world to help provide feedback. Engage with us from initial design to app updates.

Apple also has a lot of resources to help you with this process. There are online tutorials, documentation, accessibility guidelines for iOS. Tomorrow evening here, at WWDC, we're going to have an accessibility mixer. Come and join us. I'll be there to answer questions, lots of accessibility people will be there, including developers who've gone through this process of making sure their apps are accessible. So these are resources that are available to you and will help you design apps that are accessible.

Accessibility benefits your consumers, but it also benefits you. Accessibility has many benefits for you because people with disabilities are the largest minority group. About 1 in 5 Americans lives with a disability. So when you design with accessibility in mind, you get access to more customers, more people can benefit from your services.

Another thing to keep in mind is accessibility increases access for everyone, including nondisabled users. For example, when you caption your videos, and you add alternative text to your images, more text is associated with your content. And because of that, it's easier for people to find your content through powerful keyword searches. The videos from WWDC are captioned and those captions produce a transcript that anyone can do a keyword search and find exactly where in the video a topic was discussed. This is an example of how a feature that benefits the Deaf community also benefits the greater community.

But the most important point is innovation. Disability drives innovation. When you think about new ways of accessing information, new ways for people to connect, and engage with each other, you're going to find yourself designing the next best thing.

Throughout our history disability has sparked innovation, that benefits all of us today. Many of the products we use today can be traced back to disability.

In 1808, an Italian inventor named Turri built one of the first working typewriters. He wanted a solution for producing print that didn't require vision. That someone can do by touch. Now Turri had a lover who was blind, and he wanted her to be able to write him love letters. So he designed one of the first working typewriters as a possible solution. And now today, around the world, we have lots of touch typists, lots of people who use keyboards without using vision, both sighted typists and blind typists.

More recently, one of the fathers of the Internet, Vinton Cerf, is hard of hearing, and his wife is also hearing impaired, and they were looking for a solution that would allow them to communicate without using hearing. And to communicate from afar. Disability drives innovation, not just by nondisabled inventors but by people with disabilities as well. Vinton ended up developing one of the earliest email protocols, and electronic mail was one way for them to communicate from afar. And now, just about everybody uses email, and sends text messages. Solutions designed with disability in mind end up benefitting the entire community.

Central to innovation is exploration. I'm going to share a photo of a jungle gym. A jungle gym highlights exploration. There are multiple ways to get to the top, there isn't a right or wrong way to climb; there isn't a right or wrong path to take. When I'm climbing I can't see the ropes. This is about 20 feet tall. It's a pyramid-shaped, rope-based jungle gym. When I climb, I reach out, explore, until I find the ropes, until I find the solutions.

There are many, many, many different ways to climb: by touch, by sight, by sound. You could have someone down on the ground offering voice guidance. If you have a mobility disability, you can design an assistive climbing device. Exploration values alternative techniques and the more open you are to seeing the world in multiple perspectives, the more likely you are going to design, develop the next big thing.

One area where we rarely seek innovation is haptics. Haptics is the concept of communicating information through touch. I have an Apple Watch, and it taps my wrist twice when I get a message. That's a form of communication based on haptics, touch.

I recently went surfing, and that whole experience was about haptics. Here's a photo of me on a tandem board. A tandem board is a large board. I'm standing near the front and in the back is the surf instructor, Matt Allen from Maui Surf Academy. He was using tactile signals. I could also feel the power of the waves vibrating through the surf board, the wind, the sun, the cold water. Skin is our largest organ, yet we've barely explored the potential of haptics. There's a lot of potential at this intersection of haptics and technology.

Keep exploring, keep innovating, keep designing apps that are going to increase access for everyone. As you go through this process, engage with the disability community, plan for accessibility from the start and design knowing that it's going to benefit you.

Note

1   Editor's note: These passages were taken from a speech that Haben Girma delivered at the World Wide Developers Conference in 2016.

Discussion Questions

1.   How does accessible technology for disabled people benefit everyone? Discuss some of Girma's examples of these technological advances.

2.   What is haptics? Why might it be the key to future innovations?

"What Will You Gain When You Lose?"

Deafness, Disability Gain, Creativity, and Human Difference

Nicole C.S. Barker

As society frames it, disability is a loss and a deficit—seemingly pathological in its very existence. This is also the personal experience of a large portion of the disability community. Acquired disability is perhaps the best example of this: many people, your author included, experience acquired disability as a profound sense of loss, and a source of despair.

What if, instead, we reframed disability of all kinds as a source of gain, as the Deaf community has? This is a large part of the mission of the disability studies field, seeking to reframe disability as not just a loss, a deficit, but instead an expression of human difference and variation, and thus a valuable part of the human experience.

Each portion of the disabled community expresses their gain differently: each disabling condition has its unique effects, and each individual experiences those effects differently. Disability is by nature diverse, and it is our differences that we have in common.

The impetus toward redefining from loss to gain is perhaps strongest in the Deaf community, which has one of the most, if not the most, strongly codified culture. In fact, Deaf culture actively seeks to portray itself as closer to an ethnic group or even a counter-culture, in part a reaction to the threat posed by the medical establishment toward the existence of the community, by curing the condition, currently best exemplified by the cochlear implant debate.[1]

In response to what is often seen in the Deaf community as a threat to their existence,[2] the Deaf have sought to redefine their experience from the medical term "hearing-loss." They have instead turned the terminology on its head, calling it "Deaf-gain."[3] They argue for their existence as a unique expression of how to look at the human experience.

The Deaf tend to have much greater visual acuity than the hearing populace, a "unique sensory orientation" as Bauman and Murray put it.[4] The culture of the Deaf is much more attuned to sight, as their language system of Sign[5] is entirely visual, expressed in the hands as Sign. Bauman and Murray posit the example that Sign languages have redefined how we think about language, especially within the field of linguistics. They further develop this idea, and ask what has and can come from the Deaf community's unique needs and tendencies.[6]

For one of many instances, there is a fascinating architectural movement[7] being spearheaded at Gallaudet University called "Deaf Space," a very organic, curvilinear, and beautiful system of architectural guidelines designed to maximize the communication of the Deaf.[8] Architecture as it is for the auditory populace is often designed toward maximizing hearing range, or even without concern for maximizing anything other than the generalized "function" of the building—it's only rarely that a room is truly accessible for the Deaf. Deaf Space sought to design around Deaf needs, and yielded a space that is beautiful and functional for the non-Deaf community too.

Let us take another example of something essential to one portion of the disability community that is also beneficial to the nondisabled, from the world of architecture: the case of ramps and other means of mobility accessibility. For people who use wheelchairs, or are otherwise mobility impaired, stairs and even small steps can pose insurmountable difficulties to spatial access. Ramps and elevators are absolutely essential for them to be able to access any space that is raised off ground level. Even for the average, non-mobility-impaired, ramps and elevators are a happy convenience that make life a little easier, especially when a building has many floors, or when a person might need to move a heavy load.

You can thus frame questions of building accessibility as a part of disability gain— many buildings might not routinely have these conveniences were it not for ADA legislation (and indeed many older buildings, exempted from the law, are utterly inaccessible—it was only a step in the right direction, and not a complete societal change).

What is essential for the disabled is beneficial for the nondisabled, too. Thus, this leads to the concept of what a person can gain when they "lose," when a person is or becomes disabled. This is the heart of disability gain: the creativity of working around obstacles, fueled by necessity. It makes us change our perspective from seeing disability as loss and deficit, into gain and creativity. Instead of becoming creative in spite of your disability, you become creative because of it.

However, there is still the ever-present problem of the nondisabled mainstream of society seeing disability as pathological, and at its heart negative. This is rooted in fairly recent history, and tied to the 20th century attitude of medicalizing disability. Michael Oliver discusses this in his 1990 paper, outlining the medical (or, as he refers to it, the individual model) of disability. He defines the medical-individual model of disability as "[locating] the 'problem' of disability within the individual and secondly it sees the causes of this problem as stemming from the functional limitations or psychological losses which are assumed to arise from disability."[9]

Instead, disability studies, Deaf studies, and the disability rights movement have sought to redefine disability as a societal construct: it is not the condition which is disabling, but the society that one lives in and its inadaptability. Oliver defines it thus: "it is not individual limitations, of whatever kind, which are the cause of the problem but society's failure to provide appropriate services and adequately ensure the needs of disabled people are fully taken into account in its social organisation."[10] Society, as it is currently structured, is fundamentally ableist in its constructions.

The conditions that are misnamed disabilities themselves are instead impairing. As Eli Clare defines it, citing another of Oliver's works, impairment is "lacking part or all of a limb, or having a defective limb, organism or mechanism of the body."[11] It is very difficult to differentiate disability from impairment—it is like asking the question about nature and nurture in child development. We are acculturated from the moment we are born, so where can the line truly be drawn, if at all? So too it is with disability and impairment: as bodies and minds cannot truly be separated, and society acts upon the individual, where is it that the line between what is bodily and what is societal can be drawn?[12]

Similarly, what is to be gained from disability cannot be easily delineated. On the one hand, to call impairment and disability only difference and variation in the human experience is to deny the suffering brought about by that very real loss. On the other hand, in order to gain from disability, it cannot be just loss. We have to add on to that definition the creativity, the empowerment of difference that can be had, and the innovation that becomes necessary in the disabled community.

Disability gain is a very new concept still being defined by the disability studies community.[13] Disability gain is, to put it as simply as possible, what good comes of aperson's disability and impairment, that would have been unlikely or impossible otherwise. This can be as little as finding a new friend from a doctor's appointment, or as great as finding a new community and way of life that you would not otherwise have access to. In fact, many of the world's so-called "geniuses" were disabled people, who would not have had many of their formative life experiences were it not for their disabilities.

For instance, Riva Lehrer, the Artist in Residence at Bryn Mawr college, mentioned at the end of one of her talks that much of her family had gone to medical school and ended up in a medical field.[14] She posited that she likely would have followed the same path, and I would argue would have been very unlikely to produce the groundbreaking artwork that she has if she had not been born with spina bifida. She has, however, incorporated her interest in anatomy and the medical into her artwork, and has taught anatomy at several art and medical schools.

Let's also take the work of Mat Fraser into consideration. Without his disability, he would not have developed the innovative and much lauded works that he has as a performance artist[15] had his mother not taken thalidomide while pregnant with him, yielding his phocomelia.

BOX 36.1

Browse the gallery of Riva Lehrer's work at **www.rivalehrerart.com** and Mat Fraser's website at **https://en.wikipedia.org/wiki/Mat_Fraser**

These two artists' work is not in spite of their disability. It is, in some cases arguably, because of their disabilities that their lives have taken this course. They have gained much because of their disabling conditions that would not have existed had they been nondisabled. They took ownership of their conditions, and capitalized on the gains, without disregarding the losses.

However, there are also drawbacks to disability gain. Among other things, the phenomenon of supercripping is pervasive in our society. It is in many ways a cultural trope, that of the "genius cripple," as the pop-culture encyclopedia *TVTropes* has termed it.[16] The phenomenon of the supercrip can be seen as stories of disabled people, with an audience of the nondisabled, that focus on people "overcoming" their disabilities.[17] By nature, these reinforce the superiority of the nondisabled. Eli Clare writes, "They turn individual disabled people, who are simply leading their lives, into symbols of inspiration."[18]

How, then, can a disabled person achieve without it being seen as an opportunity for condescension and reinforcement of ableism by nondisabled people? This is a question we are still in the process of answering, and one that the disability rights movement is seeking to further illuminate. Lehrer and Fraser are, to this author, people who provide a view into how to own their disability and regain control over how they are portrayed by portraying themselves and others with disabilities in ways that are not just disabled but profoundly human, profoundly relatable in their specificity. It is in ownership and creativity that we can begin to change how disability is perceived in society. We can shift from the trope of loss and deficit to human difference and variation by empowering ourselves and making evident the creativity that has come to us because of our disabilities. In this way, we, the members of the disabled and Deaf community, can justify our existence to society, and begin to change the ableist strictures ever present.

Discussion Questions

1. What is disability gain? How does it reorient society's approach to disability?
2. Are there any drawbacks to disability gain? How can we avoid falling into these misconceptions about disability?

Notes

1 Bauman & Murray 2013, 246.
2 The Deaf community has often used racialized language to refer to the threats on their community, in some cases calling the threat of a cure for deafness a "genocide." For a fascinating discussion of Deaf culture, see Andrew Solomon's *Far From the Tree* (Scribner, 2012), Chapter II: Deaf.
3 Bauman & Murray 2013.
4 Ibid, p. 248.
5 Here I have chosen to refer to Sign as group, rather than referring to ASL, BSL, or International. Deaf communities, unconnected by any overarching national culture, have developed hand-based sign languages the world over, often independently. Solomon, for instance, references the case of Kata Kolok, a Balinese sign that developed in one isolated village with a high instance of genetic deafness.
6 An interesting note, further using racialized language: I continuously see and hear discussion of how current American culture, especially the musical culture, appropriates large portions of Black culture, while at the same time societal racism is still strongly present. See, for example the current debates surrounding the Ferguson riots.
7 Clare 2009, pp. 250–51.
8 For reference, see HBHM's Architecture's webpage on the guidelines.
9 Oliver 1990, p.2.
10 Ibid.
11 Clare 2009, pp. 6–8.
12 I heartily suggest that my reader read Eli Clare's work—he puts it much more lyrically than I could hope to, but this is especially evident in the chapter 'The Mountain.'
13 I am endeavoring to define it as I see it. Rosemarie Garland-Thomson, in fact, gave a talk on the subject of disability gain at York University two weeks before this writing.
14 This was mentioned during the question session following her November 20, 2014 talk at Haverford College, "Jarred: A Self Portrait in Formaldehyde."
15 I would also argue that Fraser is amazing in the way he has reclaimed an identity of enfreakment, turning it on its head and playing with his audience. A wonderful video in which he demonstrates this is From Freak to Clique.
16 As accessed Nov. 27, 2014. Perhaps a better explanation, in-wiki, of the concept comes from the page Disability Superpower. Genius Cripple tends to refer more to scientific genius, more than any other kind of distinction.
17 Clare 2009, pp. 2–3.
18 Ibid.

References

Bauman, H-Dirksen L., and Joseph J. Murray. "Deaf Studies in the 21st Century: 'Deaf-Gain' and the Future of Human Diversity." *Disability Studies Reader*. 4th ed. London: Routledge, 2013. 246–260. Print.

Clare, Eli. "The Mountain." *Exile and Pride: Disability, Queerness, and Liberation.* Cambridge, MA: SouthEnd Press, 2009. 1–13. Print.

Oliver, Michael. "The Individual and Social Models of Disability." Joint Workshop of the Living Options Group and the Research Unit of the Royal College of Physicians, July 23, 1990. Print.

Solomon, Andrew. *Far from the Tree: Parents, Children, and the Search for Identity.* New York: Scribner, 2012.

Disability Studies

A New Normal

Cecilia Capuzzi Simon

The temporarily able-bodied, or TABs. That's what disability activists call those who are not physically or mentally impaired. And they like to remind them that disability is a porous state; anyone can enter or leave at any time. Live long enough and you will almost certainly enter it.

That foreboding forecast is driving growth in disability studies, a field that didn't even exist 20 years ago. The reasons are mainly demographic: as the population ages, the number of disabled will grow—by 21 percent between 2007 and 2030, according to the U.S. Census Bureau.

At the other end of the generational spectrum are those raised after the passage of the Americans with Disabilities Act in 1990. They are now in college or entering the work force. They are educated, perhaps without even realizing it, in the politics and realities of disability, having sat in the same classrooms in a more accessible society.

Universities have long studied the disabled in medical and health care curriculums. But when one of the first disability studies programs emerged at Syracuse University in 1994, it was a radical departure from the medical model that had dominated offerings for decades and had approached disability as a deficit that needed fixing.

Like black studies, women's studies and other liberation-movement disciplines, disability studies teaches that it is an unaccepting society that needs normalizing, not the minority group. "Disablement comes from a confluence of social factors that shape one's identity," says Tammy Berberi, president of the Society for Disability Studies. "It is not a distinct physical condition or a private struggle."

What You'll Study

The Modern Language Association, which promotes the study of literature and the humanities, established disability studies in 2005 as a "division of study." This says much about how far the field has come in the last 20 years, and about its mission.

Through courses in disability history, theory, legislation, policy, ethics and the arts, students are taught to think critically about the "lived lives" of the disabled, and to work to improve quality of life and to advocate for civil rights. "It's more than teaching the disabled how to make an omelet," Dr. Berberi says. The emphasis is on applying lessons from the humanities to solving the social struggle at hand.

Steven J. Taylor, who created the Syracuse program, puts it succinctly: "Disability studies starts with accepting the disability. Then it asks the question: 'How do we equalize the playing field?'"

Where You Can Study

Some 35 colleges and universities tackle that question through graduate and under-graduate degrees, minors and certificates. Not all get to the answer in the same way, or agree on what constitutes a successful endgame. Mariette J. Bates, academic director for the program at the City University of New York School of Professional Studies, says the differences stem from a fragmented field ("cognitive doesn't talk to physical, and no one talks to mental") and divergent academic approaches (theoretical versus clinical).

CUNY, Syracuse University and the University of Illinois at Chicago have the oldest and best-known programs. A complete, vetted list can be found on the website for Syracuse's Center on Human Policy, Law and Disability Studies.

BOX 37.1

Explore the variety of disability studies programs currently available in the U.S.:

www.rdsjournal.org/index.php/journal/article/viewFile/23/83

Because of its history and student body, CUNY takes the most applied approach. The program grew from a Kennedy Fellows program in special education and rehabilitative counseling, and 70 percent of those seeking a credential there in disability studies work at service agencies. CUNY started a four-course graduate certificate in 2004 and, because of student demand, created a master's in 2009 and a bachelor's—the first in the field and completely online—in 2012.

Syracuse's program—an undergraduate minor and an advanced certificate—emerged from its school of education at a time when the university was emphasizing educational mainstreaming and dissolving its special education program. At the graduate school level, candidates from any discipline can enroll in the certificate of advanced study, or combine disability studies with law. The only free-standing Ph.D. thus far is at the University of Illinois's Chicago campus.

Why Study It

The rationale for the interdisciplinary approach? Jobs. Disability studies has its greatest impact when taken up with another pursuit, academic or professional, Dr. Taylor says. For doctoral students, an interdisciplinary approach increases the odds of landing an academic appointment, since there are few professorships in disability studies alone.

Graduates can go on to careers in architecture, management, engineering, policy, law, rehabilitative medicine, music and the arts. The most obvious application is in education and human services, including social work and health care, where advancement often requires certification or a graduate degree.

What a credential "signals," says Noam Ostrander, who has a Ph.D. in disability studies from U.I.C. and is director of the Master of Social Work program at DePaul University, "is a nuanced understanding of disability that is not the tragic, scientific model but a progressive model of disability that is more empowering."

Who is Studying It

Joseph Plutz, the coordinator of disability services at the Fashion Institute of Technology, began as an administrative assistant 10 years ago. With a background in finance, 15 years in the corporate world and no formal training in education or social services, he was looking to be promoted to a counselor position. His office coordinator suggested CUNY's certificate, which he earned in 2010. He then continued for a master's. The degree, he said, positioned him to work directly with students, most with cognitive or learning impairments, advising them on course scheduling, time management and ways to advocate for educational and, eventually, on-the-job needs.

The discipline, unsurprisingly, attracts students with disabilities, or those with a disabled loved one. Forty percent of the students in the U.I.C. master's, minor and certificate programs are disabled; about 60 percent of those enrolled in CUNY's bachelor's program have a disability or a disabled child.

April Coughlin has been in a wheelchair since a car accident left her a paraplegic at age six. That didn't stop her from becoming a triathlete wheelchair racer or a middle and high school English teacher. Her six years working in New York City schools galvanized her. She routinely encountered access issues. She was unable to consider jobs in older school buildings, some of which house the city's top schools, because they were not wheelchair accessible. If she couldn't get in to teach in certain schools, she realized, many children with disabilities couldn't learn in them either, or see a person with a disability leading the classroom.

She wove a disability perspective into her literature curriculum, but saw a bigger calling: educating teachers across the board about the needs of students with disabilities. She completed a master's in disability studies at CUNY in 2011 and is a Ph.D. candidate in special education and disability studies at Syracuse. "Disability studies provided me with the language I needed to describe what I had been going through my whole life," she says.

Her goal is to train future educators at the college level. She already has a start. Last summer she was a trainer for New York City Teaching Fellows. She also teaches an online course in disability and embodiment for CUNY, in which she uses memoir writing, videos and film to convey the experience of being disabled.

The best way to learn is from those who have lived it, she says. "I can't help but bring my real-world stories to the classroom. I like to think my disability gives me credibility."

Discussion Questions

1. Why is disability studies growing as a field, and what is expected for its future?
2. Why should we study disability? What do we have to gain?

8

Subject to Debate

38 | Disability and Sexual Objectification

Should disabled women be sexually objectified in the same ways as nondisabled women, or is all sexual objectification unjust?

A. LONGING FOR THE MALE GAZE

by Jennifer Bartlett

When I was in my early 30s, I practiced yoga at a studio in my neighborhood in Brooklyn. On most days, I walked there with two friends—one who was in her 20s and one about my age—but occasionally we each got to class on our own. There was a construction site across the street as part of the growing onslaught of gentrification in the neighborhood. My friends would often complain about being harassed and catcalled by the construction workers—even more so when they wore their yoga clothes. I passed the site day after day without incident.

When I was younger, in my 20s, I was a thin, slight woman. I have also always been beautiful and a nice dresser. I also happen to have cerebral palsy, which affects my motor skills, balance and speech, as it does with most people who have it. It is typically caused by damage to or malformation of the brain during birth or infancy. In my case, my mother's umbilical cord was wrapped around my neck *in utero*. As my mother was unable to have an emergency cesarean section, I was strangled by the cord, and born clinically dead. The temporary lack of oxygen caused damage to a portion of my brain.

Cerebral palsy is not uniform and manifests in a number of ways. It might affect all limbs severely, or just one side of the body; or the effects may be slight, making the disability barely perceptible. It can affect strength, balance and movement; some with the condition may not be able to walk unassisted or care for themselves in typical ways.

To put it bluntly, people with cerebral palsy appear to have strange movements. Since they are not in full control of their muscles, they may have facial expressions or spasticity that most people find surprising, if not unattractive.

People with cerebral palsy are often mistaken for having a mental impairment, although the two are not necessarily linked. I have a speech impediment and awkward gait. My disability is visible, but not necessarily significant. I do have some physical limitations, but am able to do most things that a typical person can do. My primary difficulty has been with people's negative reaction, or what disability studies scholars call the "social construction" of disability. This primarily means that the main challenges disabled people face come from societal prejudice and inaccessible spaces.

Recently, the popular feminist Jessica Valenti published a memoir titled "Sex Object," which focuses on the toll the "male gaze" has taken on her. She wrote an article on this theme for the *New York Times*, "What Does a Lifetime of Leers Do to Us?" Ms. Valenti describes a life of sexual harassment beginning at adolescence. She writes of what seems like countless instances of men exposing themselves to her on the New York City subway. She describes constantly thwarting unwanted advances from men in all areas of her life. Ms. Valenti currently has a 5-year-old daughter, and she wrestles for a way to prepare her child for an onslaught of male harassment. She takes for granted that this will happen.

My experiences have been quite different, nearly the opposite, of Ms. Valenti's and that of most women. I was never hit on or sexually harassed by my professors in college, or later, by my co-workers or superiors. I have not felt as if my male teachers, friends or colleagues thought less of me because of my gender. I've never been aggressively hit on in a bar, despite the fact that I have frequented them alone throughout the years. In fact, I've rarely been approached in a bar at all.

I do remember being sexually harassed by a man on the street. Once. I was 18 years old. I was waiting for a bus, and a man pulled up and offered me a ride in his car. When I declined, he got hostile and asked me if I was wearing panties. I was more startled than anything, and I left the curb to go to the nearby movie theater where my friend worked. I didn't tell my friend what happened, but waited with him for the bus. This was very frightening, but I wouldn't say the incident traumatized me, nor is it something that deeply affected my life. And it happened only once.

Let me rephrase that: It happened only once while I was visibly inhabiting my own body. Virtually, it has been another story.

In 2013, I began experimenting with the dating website OKCupid because I wanted to explore this concept of being desexualized. I created a provocative profile. The photographs were recent, but in photographs, I look "normal." I did not mention that I have cerebral palsy. I wanted to use the opportunity to explore the sexual world as an able-bodied woman, if only online, and see what all the fuss was about.

As a pretend, able-bodied woman, I received all kinds of messages. Men wrote stupid things, aggressive things and provocative things. Often, while I was in a dialogue with a man who didn't know of my impairment, I would disclose it, and almost always, the man vanished, no matter how strong the connection had been beforehand.

After a while, I changed the profile to reflect that I have a disability. Fewer men wrote. Sometimes, no men wrote, depending on the content. But overall, the messages changed. They could be called more respectful. The men who wrote primarily wanted to know how my disability affected me.

This all feels like a political act, and in some ways it is. Strangely, my disability makes me feel as if I have license to play with and deconstruct sexuality in ways I might not have the bravery to do as an able-bodied woman.

I watch men on the street. I will watch a man visually or verbally harass women who pass him. I am invisible enough to do this. Sometimes men look at me, but the reaction is different. There seems to be some level of shame or confusion mixed with the lust in their eyes. Does this mean that I am lucky? Am I blessed to be sexually invisible and given a reprieve from something that has troubled women for centuries?

It certainly does not feel that way. On one hand, I know that I am "lucky" not to be sexually harassed as I navigate the New York City streets. But I am harassed in other ways that feel much more damaging. People stare. People insist that I have God's blessing. People feel most comfortable speaking about me in the third person rather than addressing me directly. It is not uncommon that I will be in a situation where a stranger will talk to the nearest able-bodied person, whether it be a friend or a complete stranger, about me to avoid speaking to me.

I also do understand what it feels like to get attention from the wrong man. It's gross. It's uncomfortable. It's scary and tedious. And in certain cases, traumatic. But I still would much rather have a man make an inappropriate sexual comment than be referred to in the third person or have someone express surprise over the fact that I have a career. The former, unfortunately, feels "normal." The latter makes me feel invisible and is meant for that purpose.

I like it when men look at me. It feels empowering. Frankly, it makes me feel like I'm not being excluded.

B. DISABLED WOMEN AND SEXUAL OBJECTIFICATION (OR THE LACK THEREOF)
from crippledscholar.com

Today in *The New York Times* Opinion pages there was a piece called "Longing for the Male Gaze." It is a personal account of a disabled woman's experiences of not being socially perceived as sexually desirable. I have mixed feelings about the piece.

On one hand, while it is reasonably well known that disabled people are viewed as nonsexual by default, there is very little available on the lived experience of not being accepted as an attractive, sexual being. This piece challenges that trend and does so in *The New York Times*.

On the other hand, much of the framing of the piece is problematic. It focuses less on being seen as attractive and sexual within interpersonal relationships and more on not being treated as a sexual object. Jennifer Bartlett (the author) focuses on her lack of experiences with catcalling and other forms of sexual harassment.

This is problematic for a couple of reasons. For one it gives a lot of social power and validation to harmful social interactions. For another, the author actively plays "oppression Olympics" between sexism/misogyny and ableism. In so doing she fundamentally fails to comprehend the very real harm that can come from catcalling and other forms of sexual harassment.

I do understand her frustration with the fact that disabled women are left out of the sexual objectification faced by our nondisabled peers. It is a catch-22 of intersectional oppression that even being denied an oppressive force usually experienced by part of your identity as a result of its intersection with disability is in fact further oppression.

That disabled women are often denied sexual objectification only shows how disability has denied us the ability to live up to social and cultural understandings of gender presentation and punishes us by denying us not only the consequences of being sexually objectified but also of simply being seen as fully women.

That is a conversation that hasn't happened enough and needs to.

Unfortunately, Bartlett is not starting that conversation. She instead writes almost longingly of being sexually objectified as though being seen as worthy of catcalling would also mean she was worthy of being seen as a sexual being in healthier interpersonal interactions. Unfortunately, in this she is probably right.

That however does not negate the issue of her downplaying the seriousness and real dangers of sexual harassment and catcalling. She writes,

On one hand, I know that I am "lucky" not to be sexually harassed as I navigate the New York City streets. But I am harassed in other ways that feel much more damaging. People stare. People insist that I have God's blessing. People feel most comfortable speaking about me in the third person rather than addressing me directly. It is not uncommon that I will be in a situation where a stranger will talk to the nearest able-bodied person, whether it be a friend or a complete stranger, about me to avoid speaking to me.

I also do understand what it feels like to get attention from the wrong man. It's gross. It's uncomfortable. It's scary and tedious. And in certain cases, traumatic. But I still would much rather have a man make an inappropriate sexual comment than be referred to in the third person or have someone express surprise over the fact that I have a career. The former, unfortunately, feels "normal." The latter makes me feel invisible and is meant for that purpose.

She does acknowledge that attention from the "wrong" men can be scary but still positions it as preferable to the erasure of the ableist interactions she does experience more frequently.

I would however argue that catcalling and sexual harassment are an erasure of the humanity and personhood of women. They can also be deadly.

Like Bartlett I am a woman with cerebral palsy. However, I have not lived a life as free of catcalling and sexual harassment as she describes her life to have been. I have also experienced the stares, question, prayers and being ignored in favor of nondisabled companions. But I am not going to say that one is preferable to the other.

In every single incident of street harassment that I have experienced, I have felt either utterly dehumanized or genuinely threatened. I however cannot say that I have left every dehumanizing disability-specific negative interaction feeling totally safe either.

Being a disabled woman who has experienced street harassment, I can also attest to the fact that it hasn't done anything for my being accepted as a sexual being by society. In fact it is sometimes used to reinforce the fact that I'm generally not viewed as sexual.

As I've written about before, as a result of my disabilities I am not able to perform femininity to cultural expectations. This has resulted in men yelling questions like "are you a man or woman?" at me out of car windows or men foregoing the question altogether and simply loudly debating the question as I walk by.

When the harassment is actually sexually suggestive it's threatening. Like the time I was lost in downtown Winnipeg at night and someone came up to me while I was trying to get my bearings, told me I was beautiful and requested that I go home with him. Luckily when I visibly recoiled he moved on. This interaction was immediately followed by a second man who had witnessed the interaction using it as an excuse to get way to close to me in order to say, "Well, that was creepy wasn't it?"

These interactions didn't affirm my femininity despite my disability. They made me terrified. The fact that I am also disabled and less physically able to run away or fight only exacerbated that fear.

So while I agree that in many ways the ability to be viewed as a sexual object is also tied to the more benign assessments on who gets viewed as a sexual being, I do not agree with Bartlett's downplaying of the harm of sexual harassment.

Sexual harassment, when coupled with disability, does not actually reinforce a disabled sexual identity in a culture that continues to ignore that disabled people are sexual beings. Downplaying the harm of street harassment not only erases the real harm it causes nondisabled women who experience it regularly but also ignores that some disabled women do experience it and that it only makes them less safe, not more fully human.

39 | **Sexual Surrogacy**

Should disabled people have free access to sexual surrogates, or is sexual surrogacy a form of sex work that potentially exploits both parties?

DISABILITY AND PAYING FOR SEX

from unlockingwords.wordpress.com

Firstly – is sex a right?

Are we all entitled to have sex? I firmly believe we should all have the option of having a good sex life. We should all be able to choose to have sex in the context of a mutually beneficial situation where no one involved is forced, coerced or has no real alternative.

Which brings me to sex workers. This is a huge topic with so many different perspectives, including from people who freely chose to work in the sex industry. There are, however, many people who are forced, coerced or have no real choice. Women can get trapped in the sex industry, and this has to be an important part of any conversation around the right to have sex. However they've entered, or whatever the reason they stay in sex work, we need to ensure that our desire for sex doesn't further exploit sex workers. Whether it's through trafficking or sex slavery, through being willfully misled or because they need the money, or whether they've got addictions which need feeding, or even in situations as complicated as a history of abuse which makes them feel like they have no other option, sex workers deserve the same respect as anyone else.

Sex Workers and Sex Surrogates

Within the context of disabled people paying for sex, the phrase "sex surrogates" comes up a lot. What does this mean?

Sex workers—a sex worker is anyone who works in the sex industry (e.g. porn actors, prostitutes, lap dancers, phone sex workers, sex surrogates). The predominant definition requires the worker to be involved in "sexually explicit behavior."

Sex therapists—licensed mental-health professionals; think *counselor*. A sex therapist will not have sex with or engage in any sexual activity with the client.

Sex surrogates—a surrogate does engage in sexual activity with the client. They aren't (or don't have to be) medical professionals, but they do engage in work which addresses particular sexual difficulties such as erectile dysfunction, anxiety, or lack of confidence. Think of this more like a way of being able to practice sex or masturbation with the support of someone. There is an International Professional Surrogates Association which offers training for surrogates.

Should Disabled People Be Able to Pay For Sex?

Firstly, who would be allowed? Would you have to show that you receive disability related benefits? Prove that you're disabled? How do invisible disabilities factor into this? Would it just be for people who've proven they can't find a partner? How would people with mental illness show that they were eligible? What would happen to people who faked disability in order to be legally allowed to use a prostitute?

OK, so that was a bit of playing the devil's advocate, but this is a hugely complicated issue. If you decide that yes, disabled people can pay for sex, you then have a whole load of logistics and specifics to sort out. Especially if you're also in a society where nondisabled people aren't allowed to pay for sex.

Rewinding a bit, let's look at the arguments for and against disabled people paying for sex.

Arguments For

Rachel Watton, from the Australian organization Touching Base, believes for people with disabilities, being able to pay for sex is a right. She acknowledges that society should change but feels that in the meantime sex should be available.

Forty-four percent of people in a *Guardian* poll said they had never had sex with someone with a physical disability and probably wouldn't. Those odds don't work well for a disabled person looking for a shag.

Watton stars in a documentary, *Scarlet Road*, about her life with Touching Base and providing sex to disabled people. The film doesn't address the issues that some sex workers face in terms of exploitation; indeed, the white sex workers featured appear to dismiss and invalidate the experiences of exploited workers. I was pleased to see that disabled people were included in the documentary, but the language used about them wasn't always so positive. The word "they" to refer to all disabled people was used a lot, as was "deserving," which to me can conjure up ideas of pity and can feel demeaning. Why do I deserve sex more than the next person? Does my disability make me that special?

However, *Scarlet Road* wasn't all bad. It talked about developing training for sex workers who were working with disabled people. This included things like manual handling and ways of communicating. This has potential to lead to resources and a bank of knowledge for disabled people and their partners.

Within this discussion, the most important voices are those of disabled people and the sex workers. *Disability Now* conducted a survey in 2005 which revealed that 22 percent of disabled male respondents (compared to an estimated 10 percent if you look at the whole male population) reported having paid for sexual services, compared to just 1 percent of disabled women. Similarly, just 16 percent of disabled women had considered paying for sex compared to nearly 38 percent of disabled men. This figure increases if you ask about paying to see specially trained sex workers.

Would legalizing sex work for disabled clients make the industry safer for the sex workers? The pros and cons of legalization are far too big a discussion to go into in this blog, but it is an important part of the conversation so I'd highly suggest going away and doing some reading about it.

What about the therapeutic benefits of sex? Orgasms can help reduce pain; being touched in a non-functional way can have mental-health benefits, and sex can be relaxing.

Would allowing disabled people to pay for sex normalize the idea of disabled people as sexual beings? Or would it make it easier to see us as "freaks"?

Examples of Where This Already Happens

Mark O'Brien, a disabled writer, wrote:

> I wanted to be loved . . . held, caressed, and valued. But my self-hatred and fear were too intense. I doubted I deserved to be loved . . . Most of the disabled people I knew . . . were sexually active, including disabled people as deformed as I. But nothing ever happened.

O'Brien went on to see a sex surrogate and lost his virginity with her.

In Holland and Denmark, support needed around sexuality and sex is something which social workers discuss with their disabled clients and have funded visits to sex workers or sex assistants.

A sexual assistant is a Dutch model which seems to offer a non-penetrative sexual service, instead more focused on erotic massage and teaching. Some sites suggest no kissing, no oral sex and no penetration. Perhaps a sex surrogate lite?

The horrifically named White Hands offer a masturbation service to disabled men in Japan (I'm hoping something got lost in translation of the name because there are some troubling connotations with its English version). The video I watched spoke of clients who didn't understand their sexual urges and desires and who got confused or ended up hurting themselves because they didn't know what to do with their feelings. The service appears to help clients understand how to react to sexual urges as well as providing masturbation for physically disabled men. From my perspective, it felt rather clinical, slightly reminiscent of the Victorian woman going to her doctor to have her hysteria treated by orgasm.

And Against . . .

Returning to Rachel Watton's stance on the issue—society should change, but until it does, sex should be purchasable. An argument could be made that providing the service could hinder or prevent society from changing. It puts a bandage over the issue and means that it's less visible. Disabled people have a means of having sex, so society no longer needs to address discrimination or perceptions of disabled people.

Legalizing paying for sex for disabled people is a way of ignoring the issue of disability and sexuality; society doesn't need to change because we can get sex at a brothel (assuming it's accessible of course!). It's an attempt to pacify us. It also assumes that disabled people are only looking for the physical side of sex and that we don't want or don't deserve an intimate relationship. It feels like allowing sex work for disabled people checks off the box of the functional desire for sex and allows society to ignore the need for intimacy, which would require a lot more change and participation of society to achieve.

Allowing disabled people to pay for sex focuses heavily on the individual disabled people who may want to use this service and adapting things for them rather than on changing society. This approach feels much more in line with the medical model approach of disability: something is at fault with this person—let's fix them rather than addressing how disability is perceived and how we are disabled by society. If disabled people were seen as accepted members of the community, would we even be having this discussion?

In an *Atlantic* article, Alex Ghenis and Mik Scarlet echo this tokenistic gesture and the troubling implications on how we're seen by others.

Alex Ghenis, an American disability advocate and former dating and relationships columnist says of paying for sex: "It commodifies sex in terms of an action. It makes it so society can check this box that men are getting laid, so we don't have to have broader social change—we are giving them sex through a brothel, so we don't have to change our social attitudes around socially excluded people with disabilities . . . And it pities and coddles us, as if we are being given things that will assuage us . . . rather than have society change around us."

Mik Scarlet, a disabled TV presenter and musician: "Imagine this, I'm disabled, growing up in Luton, and it's now legal for me to go to a brothel—to have sex for money—because apparently that's the only way I'm going to lose my virginity. Instantly, my relationship with sex is distorted, and it means that everyone I meet afterwards is going to say, 'He's disabled, that means he's paid for sex; I don't want to go to bed with someone who's paid for it.' You've reinforced the fact that you can't give it away because you've paid for it. We are reinforcing the idea that some people are too hideous and too disabled to have sex like the rest of us, and so they have to pay for it."

Paying for sex risks making us more "other." It could demean our (unpaid for) sexual experiences—the idea that if you're disabled, you've probably had to pay for sex and if you've paid for sex, the experience is therefore lesser. Paying for sex could further marginalize people with disability. It reinforces the idea we are too ugly, too broken, too disabled to have sex and not pay. It also makes us "special," a subset of society who are "allowed" to buy sex. It feels like a strange extension of the charity model of care.

Paying for sex is also expensive, especially if your disability means you can't work or you live in poverty. This could result in more division within the disabled community—a tier where more privileged disabled people can afford to pay for sex and less privileged can't. Some people would argue that benefits shouldn't be spent on sex, but I don't feel you can police what people do with their money. Some countries do pay for disabled people to access sex services rather than the disabled person paying themselves.

There is also potential for sex workers who specialize in sex with disabled people to be seen as a higher class of sex worker. An elevated role. Or by allowing sex workers for disabled people, the argument for sex work more generally could be justified.

When it comes to consent, there are the issues of the sex worker (are they freely consenting to the work they're doing?) as well as issues of consent for the disabled person. If you happen to have seen *Who's Driving Doug*, you may recall a scene where Doug (a disabled man) has been bought a prostitute by his driver. He seems reluctant to make use of this "present" but ends up going ahead with encouragement from the driver, his friend and the worker (who possibly wouldn't get paid otherwise?). Whilst I think it was a consensual act, it highlighted the pressures that can lead to coerced consent. Feeling that peer pressure means you can't refuse: spending the money and then changing your mind or feeling you can't call a stop to things. Consider the pressure society puts on people to lose their virginity, or situations where someone is nonverbal and someone else decides that of course this person would want to use a sex worker because it's "normal" to have sex. What about situations involving dementia or other memory issues? And what if someone appears to be consenting but actually doesn't have the mental capacity to do so? And communication issues?

All About the (Straight) Men?

Perhaps unsurprisingly, most of the information around this topic I could find is focused on disabled men. From what I could find, there are far more female sex surrogates, which suggests that it's easier for straight men to find someone. Something I read also suggested that disabled women felt more at risk of abuse from male sex workers than disabled men with female sex workers.

And in Conclusion . . .

I'm not actually going to conclude anything. It's a complicated, multi-faceted topic, and there's too much I still don't know and I still have too many questions. I hope that this post has raised some of the arguments for and concerns with the idea of sex workers for disabled people.

Prenatal Testing and Abortion

Should expectant mothers screen for disease and disability, or does this practice threaten the lives of disabled people before they're even born?

A. THE BENEFITS OF PRENATAL TESTING
from WhatToExpect.com

If you're nearing the end of your first trimester, your doctor has likely already mentioned prenatal testing. And if you're like most new parents, you might be wondering what it's all about—and whether it's for you. While most pregnant women receive high-level screens for some chromosomal abnormalities with their first trimester blood work, your doctor may suggest more specific screenings—including noninvasive prenatal testing (NIPT) and nuchal translucency (NT)—toward the end of your first trimester, especially if you're considered high-risk (you're over 35 or have a family history of genetic birth defects). These tests don't look for every possible disorder, though they do help identify the most common ones.

The decision to get tested is totally up to you, so talk to your doctor about your options. In the meantime, here are a few advantages of prenatal screenings to consider:

You May Feel More Relaxed If You're Informed

In the vast majority of cases, prenatal testing will tell you that your baby is almost certainly developing normally, and that peace of mind is priceless. Luckily, the latest testing is more accurate than ever—so while a false positive result can happen, it's increasingly less likely. Keep in mind: a positive result on a prenatal screening still doesn't mean your baby definitely has a certain condition (prenatal screenings can't diagnose a condition; they only tell you your baby's risk of having it). If you test positive, your doctor will discuss best next steps, which usually involve meeting with a genetic counselor and opting for invasive prenatal tests (like amniocentesis or chorionic villus sampling) that can diagnose the condition with certainty.

If an abnormality is detected, there are benefits to knowing in advance of your baby's birthday, too.

You Can Arrange for Procedures During Pregnancy

If your baby has an abnormality that can be addressed while you're still pregnant, knowing before you go into labor can be a big advantage: In some cases, you can take action. If your doctor finds a serious heart condition, for example, you may be able to opt for a pre-birth procedure to correct it, if necessary, rather than waiting until after your baby is born. Or, a specialist can be on hand soon after you deliver to help.

You Put Time on Your Side

Knowing you're expecting a child with special needs gives you time to prepare—both emotionally and practically. You can:

• Get informed. Talk to genetic counselors and doctors specializing in your child's condition and ask where you can get more information. By researching the condition now, you and your partner will better understand it and feel better prepared for your child's arrival.

• Seek out counseling and support groups. A condition-specific support group with other parents in the same situation provides community and answers. St. Joseph's Hospital in Orange, NJ holds regular "perinatal collaborative conferences" to help parents realistically plan a course of action for lethal defects like trisomy 13. The 22Q Foundation helps inform and support families with a child born with the 22q microdeletion, while the National Down Syndrome Society links parents to local support groups.

• Give birth at the right facility. Depending on your child's condition, you may want to arrange to give birth at a specialized hospital. What's more, many of these hospitals that cater to high-risk births already have support groups in their community outreach programs.

- Arrange special care for your child. Lining up a pediatrician with specialized training while you're still pregnant guarantees care specific to your little one's condition from the day he arrives.

You Can Treat a Condition That Doctors Might Not Otherwise Detect at Birth

Even if you'll love the baby no matter the results of a genetic test, some conditions aren't obvious at birth or even months later, like 22q. Without screening, your child could have symptoms that take longer to pinpoint and treat. Prenatal screenings, however, can help you to discover conditions early, so your child can receive treatment from the moment she's born. This, in turn, can sometimes help prevent symptoms. In the case of 22q, your child could have difficulty maintaining calcium or immune system deficiencies—but by knowing about the condition at birth, doctors can immediately begin monitoring your child's calcium levels or avoid giving her vaccines (which can be deadly).

Parenthood is always a journey into the unknown, but prenatal testing allows for a little more control and reassurance. Though it's very likely your baby will be born healthy and normal, modern technology can help you to make the choices that are best for you and your family.

B. DISABLED U.K. LAWMAKER: END ABORTION DISCRIMINATION AGAINST DISABLED

by Michael Tennant

Declaring current abortion law in the United Kingdom "eugenic," Lord Kevin Shinkwin offered an impassioned speech urging passage of a bill he introduced to put an end to the law's "corrosive, unjust and deeply discriminatory" language that permits aborting a disabled baby right up to the time of his birth while restricting the time during which a healthy baby may be aborted.

"From this disabled person's perspective, there is a stark anomaly, an inconsistency in the law, whereby discrimination on grounds of disability is both prohibited in law after birth yet, confusingly, actually enshrined in law at the very point at which the discrimination begins, at source, before birth," Shinkwin, who has the genetic disorder brittle bone disease, said during his opening remarks on the second reading of his Abortion (Disability Equality) Bill in the House of Lords.

The U.K.'s Abortion Act of 1967 permits the abortion of babies during their first 24 weeks of gestation. Section 1(1)(d) of the act, however, also allows for abortion at any time prior to delivery, not just the first 24 weeks, if "there is a substantial risk that if the child were born it would suffer from such physical or mental abnormalities as to be seriously handicapped."

"It is illegal for an unborn human being to have their life ended by abortion beyond 24 weeks, but if they have a disability their life can be ended right up to birth by law. Where is the consistency, the justice or the equality in that?" Shinkwin asked when introducing the bill earlier this year.

"If anyone thinks such obvious discrimination is acceptable, I respectfully invite them to imagine the outcry if the same were applied to skin color or sexual orientation. Such discrimination would rightly be regarded as outrageous."

Whether or not one finds discrimination on particular grounds to be "outrageous" and worthy of legal prohibition when applied to those who have been born, the fact is that the U.K. government does indeed have various laws prohibiting such discrimination while simultaneously encouraging discrimination against disabled babies in the womb.

"Our legislation currently affords unborn disabled babies significantly less protection than that which is afforded those who are able bodied," Lord David Alton said in his remarks supporting Shinkwin's bill. "Paradoxically, we will campaign and raise our voices for wheelchair ramps to be placed on public buildings but fail to uphold the innate right to life itself of the disabled person who uses that wheelchair."

The Lords are not speaking hypothetically. With the increase in prenatal screenings for various disabilities has indeed come an increase in abortions to prevent the "unfit" from being born—a practice "of which a particular regime of the 1930s and 1940s would heartily approve," Shinkwin pointedly observed.

"For unborn babies whose disability is detected, a mother's womb has become an increasingly dangerous place," he averred.

Citing statistics from the Department of Health—statistics that a 2014 review found were likely too low because of underreporting—Shinkwin noted that the number of abortions after 24 weeks on the grounds of disability had increased 271 percent over the last 20 years and 56 percent in just the last five. The overall number of abortions on the grounds of disability, regardless of the point of gestation at which they occurred, has grown by 68 percent over the last 10 years. Over one-fifth of the unborn terminated in 2015 were aborted because they had Down syndrome. Alton pointed out that already about 90 percent of Down syndrome babies are aborted; that rate is almost certain to rise even higher once the government implements a new technique that can detect the condition in unborn babies with 99-percent accuracy. In addition, Shinkwin said, last year 11 babies were aborted because they had cleft lip or palate despite the fact that such a condition can now be easily corrected via surgery.

"I find the contrast between the 0.3-percent decline over the last decade in the number of overall abortions and the rise in the number of abortions on unborn babies detected with a disability alarming and deeply offensive," Shinkwin added.

"What does it say about us and our society," inquired Alton, "when amniocentesis and other tests are used as part of [a]search and destroy mission with barely a murmur of dissent?"

Alton pointed to government reports showing that parents in the U.K. are routinely pressured into aborting their babies if prenatal tests detect any disabilities. Mothers reported that their doctors became angry with them for refusing to abort; one said her doctor "threatened that all medical help would be denied." Those who gave birth to disabled children claimed they were later criticized by their doctors for having failed to abort. One parent said, "I have heard views expressed that suggest my child is seen as a drain on resources."

This is hardly unexpected in a country in which the government owns and operates the health care system. And doctors, having become agents of the state rather than advocates for their patients, are only too willing to go along with the program.

"As a disabled person," said Shinkwin, "I am a prime candidate for abortion on the grounds of disability. I admit that I would like to say to the eugenicists in the Department of Health and those who obviously fail to appreciate the enormity of what is being perpetrated in our name: 'How dare you? How dare you wipe us out as mere conditions?'"

Of course, as Shinkwin well understands, they "dare" because the practice of aborting disabled babies has become "normalized," even expected. "I suggest that, collectively, we are in denial about the consequences of the choices we have made," he maintained.

One of those consequences, remarked Alton, is that the disabled who are born are viewed with disdain. "What does it say to the survivors—those who have been inconsiderate enough to avoid the perfection test and have somehow managed to slip through the net?" he asked.

Shinkwin recognizes that his bill, which would strike Section 1(1)(d) of the Abortion Act, will not put an end to the practice of aborting babies because of detected disabilities, but it will at least restrict the time period in which they may be aborted, putting them on an equal footing with nondisabled babies. Moreover, wrote *Live Action News*, "If passed, Lord Shinkwin's bill could be the most significant pro-life legislation since abortion was legalized in the UK."

# Assisted Suicide

Should people be allowed to seek assistance in ending their lives, or does legalizing assisted suicide present too great a threat to vulnerable people?

A. THE DANGER OF ASSISTED SUICIDE LAWS
by Marilyn Golden

My heart goes out to Brittany Maynard, who is dying of brain cancer and who wrote last week about her desire for what is often referred to as "death with dignity."

Yet while I have every sympathy for her situation, it is important to remember that for every case such as this, there are hundreds—or thousands—more people who could be significantly harmed if assisted suicide is legal.

The legalization of assisted suicide always appears acceptable when the focus is solely on an individual. But it is important to remember that doing so would have repercussions across all of society, and would put many people at risk of immense harm. After all, not every terminal prognosis is correct, and not everyone has a loving husband, family or support system.

As an advocate working on behalf of disability rights for 37 years, and as someone who uses a wheelchair, I am all too familiar with the explicit and implicit pressures faced by people living with chronic or serious disability or disease. But the reality is that legalizing assisted suicide is a deadly mix with the broken, profit-driven health care system we have in the United States.

At less than $300, assisted suicide is, to put it bluntly, the cheapest treatment for a terminal illness. This means that in places where assisted suicide is legal, coercion is not even necessary. If life-sustaining expensive treatment is denied or even merely delayed, patients will be steered toward assisted suicide, where it is legal.

This problem applies to government-funded health care as well.

In 2008 came the story that Barbara Wagner, a Springfield, Oregon, woman diagnosed with lung cancer and prescribed a chemotherapy drug by her personal physician, had reportedly received a letter from the Oregon Health Plan stating that her chemotherapy treatment would not be covered. She said she was told that instead, they would pay for, among other things, her assisted suicide.

"To say to someone: 'We'll pay for you to die, but not for you to live'—it's cruel," she said.

Another Oregon resident, 53-year-old Randy Stroup, was diagnosed with prostate cancer. Like Wagner, Stroup was reportedly denied approval of his prescribed chemotherapy treatment and instead offered coverage for assisted suicide.

Meanwhile, where assisted suicide is legal, an heir or abusive caregiver may steer someone toward assisted suicide, witness the request, pick up the lethal dose, and even give the drug—no witnesses are required at the death, so who would know? This can occur despite the fact that diagnoses of terminal illness are often wrong, leading people to give up on treatment and lose good years of their lives.

True, "safeguards" have been put in place where assisted suicide is legal. But in practical terms, they provide no protection. For example, people with a history of depression and suicide attempts have received the lethal drugs. Michael Freeland of Oregon reportedly had a 40-year history of significant depression, yet he received lethal drugs in Oregon.

These risks are simply not worth the price of assisted suicide.

Available data suggests that pain is rarely the reason why people choose assisted suicide. Instead, most people do so because they fear burdening their families or becoming disabled or dependent.

Anyone dying in discomfort that is not otherwise relievable, may legally today, in all 50 states, receive palliative sedation, wherein the patient is sedated to the point at which the discomfort is relieved while the dying process takes place peacefully. This means that today there is a legal solution to painful and uncomfortable deaths, one that does not raise the very serious problems of legalizing assisted suicide.

The debate about assisted suicide is not new, but voters and elected officials grow very wary of it when they learn the facts. Just in 2014 alone, assisted suicide bills were rejected in Massachusetts, New Hampshire, and Connecticut, and stalled in New Jersey, due to bipartisan, grassroots opposition from a broad coalition of groups spanning the political spectrum from left to right, including disability rights organizations, medical professionals and associations, palliative care specialists, hospice workers, and faith-based organizations.

Assisted suicide is a unique issue that breaks down ideological boundaries and requires us to consider those potentially most vulnerable in our society.

All this means that we should, as a society, strive for better options to address the fear and uncertainty articulated by Brittany Maynard. But if assisted suicide is legal, some people's lives will be ended without their consent, through mistakes and abuse. No safeguards have ever been enacted or proposed that can properly prevent this outcome, one that can never be undone.

Ultimately, when looking at the bigger picture, and not just individual cases, one thing becomes clear: Any benefits from assisted suicide are simply not worth the real and significant risks of this dangerous public policy.

B. ASSISTED SUICIDE SHOULD BE LEGAL
by Rafia Zakaria

On Oct. 12, 2014, Brittany Maynard, 29, who suffers from inoperable terminal brain cancer, announced plans to voluntarily end her life. Maynard's diagnosis means she will eventually lose all cognitive capabilities. Refusing aggressive chemotherapy treatment, Maynard decided to move to Oregon, where physician-assisted suicide is legal. Under Oregon's Death With Dignity Act, mentally competent terminally ill patients with less than six months to live can elect when to die by taking lethal doses of prescribed drugs. With only a month left to live, Maynard has made her death into a campaign for terminally ill patients' right to die.

However, her decision has been met with fervent opposition from disability rights advocates and religious conservatives. The freedom to live according to one's beliefs and choices is duly recognized and celebrated in the United States. But terminally ill patients who wish to choose death with dignity versus a painful and prolonged end often face an enormous challenge even to obtain life-ending drugs. Denying mentally capable individuals the right to end their lives in a peaceful manner is a denial of their individual rights to self-determination and freedom of choice.

Oregon is one of only five U.S. states—along with Vermont, Washington, Montana and New Mexico—that allow medically assisted suicide. In the rest of the country, assisting people with suicide (even if they are terminally ill) is a crime. Maynard's campaign highlights just how intrusive and unfair the laws criminalizing assisted suicide are for terminally ill patients and their families. For one, these patients must accept and live with their diagnosis. Second, asking a loved one to help end their suffering bears the cost of exposing them to the threat of prosecution and jail time.

The fear of prosecution for family members who help terminally ill patients is not theoretical. Last year Barbara Mancini, a 57-year-old nurse in Pennsylvania, was prosecuted for handing her father, John Yourshaw, a lethal dose of morphine. Yourshaw was a home hospice patient in failing health and had repeatedly expressed to family members his wish to die. Mancini was charged with a felony after an autopsy showed that her father died from a morphine overdose. The case was eventually dismissed but not before costing Mancini her job and more than $100,000 in legal fees.

Fear of prosecution is not the only hurdle facing advocates of death with dignity. Disability rights activists and religious conservatives have been very vocal about the ethics regarding assisted suicide laws. "There are hundreds—or thousands—more people who could be significantly harmed if assisted suicide is legal," Marilyn Golden, a senior policy analyst at the Disability Rights Education and Defense Fund, wrote in response to Maynard's announcement. Golden maintains that prognoses of terminal illness are often wrong and the disabled or terminally ill may be encouraged to choose assisted suicide for cost reasons. She adds that dying from illness is not necessarily painful because of "palliative sedation."

To be sure, there may be terminally ill patients who wish to cling to the possibility of incorrect diagnosis. But most people are convinced of their fatal prognosis, given the advances in medical technology. Besides, there is scant evidence of misuse and no local movements to repeal the laws in states that have death with dignity statutes.

Golden's assertions regarding treatment costs as a factor in choosing assisted death, particularly for the poor, also do not hold up. A 2007 study published by *The Journal of Medical Ethics* found "no evidence of heightened risk for the elderly, women, the uninsured, people with low educational status, the poor, the physically disabled or chronically ill, minors, people with psychiatric illnesses, including depression, or racial or ethnic minorities" from the death with dignity statutes in Oregon and the Netherlands.

The criticisms of disability rights advocates suffer from one central contradiction. They claim to protect the terminally ill (who are also often disabled) by insuring that they do not get steered into ending their lives. But that argument takes the crucial decision of choosing death with dignity away from the very people they purport to advocate for. Death with dignity statutes such as the one in Oregon allow cognitively capable patients to decide when and how to end their lives, regardless of their physical abilities. Hence, opposing physician-assisted suicide denies those disabled by terminal illness the right to control their deaths despite the fact that they suffer no cognitive impairment.

Support For the Right To Die

Religious conservatives oppose assisted death on the basis of their beliefs about the worth of life and the meaning of suffering. For example, Kara Tippetts, a devout Christian who is terminally ill, acknowledged in a letter to Maynard the pain of knowing one's days are numbered. "But it was never intended for us to decide when that last breath is breathed," wrote Tippetts. "Brittany, when we trust Jesus to be the carrier, protector, redeemer of our hearts, death is no longer dying. My heart longs for you to know this truth, this love, this forever living." As with most religious opponents of assisted suicide, Tippets applies her own definitions of the transcendent value of suffering and the existence of an afterlife on others, including those with differing views.

But none of these arguments are new. What is new, however, is the number of people who are engaged in the right-to-die debate because of Maynard's decision. A recent Gallup survey shows that seven out of ten Americans polled supported some form of physician-assisted suicide. It's a dramatic increase from just over 50 percent in 1970s. Legislatures in Hawaii, Kansas, Massachusetts, New Jersey and Pennsylvania have recently introduced death with dignity bills, with votes in New Jersey and Pennsylvania expected this year. Maynard's campaign may serve as the catalyst for other states to consider similar laws.

A handful of European countries—the Netherlands, Belgium, Switzerland and Luxembourg—have legalized physician-assisted death. But the U.S. doesn't have to look that far for examples. On Oct. 15 the Canadian Supreme Court heard oral arguments on reversing a two-decade-old precedent, which would decriminalize assisted death and even permit physician-assisted suicide.

As the representative from Quebec, which has already legalized the measure, rightly noted, death is part of life, and assistance in death is not suicide but should more accurately be described as end-of-life care. Unfortunately, that kind of thoughtful debate continues to be absent from our discourse in the United States, where death with dignity is often not an option for the terminally ill.

42 | Cochlear Implants

Do cochlear implants endanger the future of the Deaf community, or should people use this technology to improve hearing?

A. INFANTS MAY BENEFIT FROM ADVANCED COCHLEAR IMPLANTS

by Brian Owens

Cochlear implants are powerful tools for people with hearing loss. Using electrodes implanted in the ear that transmit sound directly to the brain, they can give even the profoundly deaf a sense of sound.

But their success often depends on how early the implants are placed. People who are born deaf and receive implants as adults have worse outcomes than those who are fitted with the implants as children, said Andrea Warner-Czyz, an audiologist at the University of Texas at Dallas who studies development in children with hearing loss.

This is at least partly because as people with hearing loss grow older, the parts of their brain that are normally used to process sounds are reassigned to other jobs, such as visual processing. Once these reassignments occur, it is difficult to re-train them to do anything else.

The brains of children, by contrast, are much more flexible, and can adapt quickly to process the signals coming from their implants, so cochlear implants are most successful when implanted at a young age.

The Food and Drug Administration advises that children should be at least 12 months old before receiving a cochlear implant, but Warner-Czyz wondered whether they would benefit from receiving the implants even earlier.

"We always want to push the envelope, we're trying to figure out if we get them implants before 12 months, is that going to be better?" she said. Some children do receive their implants earlier than the FDA-approved age.

The question that Warner-Czyz wanted to answer was: Can infants at that age properly process the information from the implants? She and her colleagues explored this question in a study recently published in the *Journal of the Acoustical Society of America*.

Cochlear implants have two main parts. First, sound is collected by a microphone that sits outside the ear like a traditional hearing aid. The sound signal is analyzed in a speech processor where it is coded for intensity, frequency and duration. Then, the coded signal is transmitted across the skin to an array of electrodes that have been surgically implanted in the cochlea, which is located in the inner ear. That array directly stimulates the auditory nerve to transmit the sound signal to the brain.

But the implants do not reproduce sounds exactly. The implant groups similar sounds into channels, collecting information on the sounds' general frequencies, but losing their finer details. The more channels there are, the more information is provided about the sounds. Typical implants have between 12 and 22 channels. Those are more than enough for adults, who only need eight or nine channels to understand speech. But younger people, whose brains are less developed, need more. Pre-schoolers need between 12 and 16 channels to reliably understand speech.

So Warner-Czyz wanted to find out whether infants, whose brains are even less developed, would need even more information to distinguish different sounds.

She took a group of 6-month-old children with normal hearing and played them one of two sounds, either "ti" or "ta." Once they became accustomed to that sound, they listened to a series of both sounds; this time, the sounds were played either through a normal speaker, or processed by an audio device known as a vocoder to sound like a 16- or 32-channel cochlear implant, to see if the children could tell the difference.

When the sounds were unprocessed, or played through 32 channels, the children could easily distinguish between the two sounds. But with 16 channels, they could not.

"Infants may need more information than cochlear implants are able to give them at this time," said Warner-Czyz.

Having more channels could help.

"If we can increase the channels, and improve the signal that they're getting, then maybe we can improve the outcomes for language and speech and hearing for those getting implants at early ages," she explained.

Mario Svirsky, a speech and hearing scientist at New York University in New York City, said that the work tells us important things about how infants understand degraded speech, but he cautions that the standard method of using a vocoder to mimic what a cochlear implant user hears is "woefully inadequate."

"Given how poorly validated, or even downright inappropriate, noise vocoders are as models of cochlear implants, I don't think the study allows you to draw any conclusions regarding the optimal number of electrodes in cochlear implants for children," he said.

Warner-Czyz acknowledges that the method does not perfectly mimic a cochlear implant, and her findings do not necessarily mean that more electrodes would be needed in the ear. The software that runs the speech processor can be configured to provide more detailed information through "virtual channels."

But most importantly, her work shows that a person's brain development should be taken into consideration when making decisions about when and how to use implants.

"Right now we're using a one-size-fits-all strategy for people with cochlear implants, rather than basing it on developmental age," she said.

B. UNDERSTANDING DEAFNESS: NOT EVERYONE WANTS TO BE "FIXED"
by Allegra Ringo

When the police showed up, there were maybe 50 protesters, most of them Deaf, outside the Omni Hotel in downtown Los Angeles. Officers stepped out of their squad cars—four in total—and spoke to the protesters through an American Sign Language interpreter. They soon left amicably, though, apparently having not found much that needed policing.

The protesters were rallying against the Listening and Spoken Language Symposium, an annual event put on by the Alexander Graham Bell Association for the Deaf and Hard of Hearing (AGB). The symposium featured speakers, workshops, and product displays centered around the topic of, as you may have guessed, listening and spoken language. Many of the sponsors and exhibitors were affiliated with companies that sell cochlear implants, surgically implanted devices that allow a Deaf or hard-of-hearing person to hear (to varying degrees).

The protesters were angry, but acting peacefully. The majority of them were Deaf. (Yes, with a capital D. In the book *America: Voices from a Culture*, Carol Padden and Tom Humphries explain, "We use the lowercase deaf when referring to the audiological condition of not hearing, and the uppercase Deaf when referring to a particular group of deaf people who share a language– American Sign Language (ASL) – and a culture.")

The AGB has a complicated history with members of Deaf culture. AGB's stated mission is to "[help] families, health care providers and education professionals under-stand childhood hearing loss and the importance of early diagnosis and intervention." Their preferred methods for doing so emphasize spoken language, and de-emphasize the use of ASL. In practice, this translates to teaching communication methods like lip reading, learning to speak (by imitating breathing patterns and mouth shapes) and, relatively recently, using cochlear implant technology.

AGB's reasons for their oral focus depend who you ask. When reached for comment, Susan Boswell, director of communications and marketing for AGB, told me that AGB "supports the development of spoken language through evidence-based practices focusing on the use of audition and appropriate technologies." When I asked Ruthie Jordan, a Deaf activist who runs Audism Free America and helped organize the rally against AGB, she told me the reason is much more bottom-line. (I spoke with Ruthie and other Deaf people at the rally through my interpreter, Drew Tolson, who was extremely helpful.)

Ruthie's take is that AGB "[Makes] money . . . by miseducating the parents of Deaf children." Like many others at the rally, Ruthie feels that AGB takes advantage of the fact that hearing parents may not understand how a Deaf child can lead a functional, fulfilling life. A hearing parent in this situation may be easily convinced that a cochlear implant and an oral-based approach is the only legitimate option.

AGB's "listening and spoken language"-based approach comes out of the school of oralism, which aims to educate Deaf children through the use of oral speech and lip reading (as opposed to manualism, which advocates for the primary use of ASL in Deaf education). The goals of oralism may not sound controversial to most hearing people, but oralism has a long and problematic history.

In the 1860s, Alexander Graham Bell was a prominent oralist, and to some, an important figure in the spreading of audism—the belief that it is inherently better to be able to speak and hear. Although he surely thought otherwise, Bell had an ugly relationship with the Deaf community. Though his mother and wife were Deaf, he was intent on wiping out "hereditary deafness." He removed Deaf faculty from schools, demanded the same schools stop their use of ASL, and advocated against "deaf intermarriage."

Bell was also involved in the Eugenics movement, serving for a time as chairman of the board of scientific advisers to the Eugenics Record Office.

In 1880, prompted by talks between Bell and other prominent figures in deaf education, 164 delegates met for the Second International Congress on Education of the Deaf. Only one of the delegates was deaf. At the conference, a resolution was passed that banned sign language in schools, in an effort to encourage spoken language skills, and thus "[restore] the deaf-mute to society." Other passages in the resolution urge us to "[consider] the incontestable superiority of speech over signs," and argue that teaching deaf people to speak English will "[give them] a more perfect knowledge of language." After its passage, schools in Europe and the United States ceased all use of sign language.

Given this history, some Deaf people feel that oralism is rooted in audism. Some argue that the sentiment of needing to "restore [Deaf people] to society" still underlies the AGB and companies affiliated with them. In fact, many Deaf people and Deaf allies, like the ones at the rally, strongly oppose the AGB and their affiliates. These people argue that the AGB and its affiliates propagate practices that harm Deaf people, all for the sake of making money. And indeed, AGB has a financial stake in the sales of cochlear implants as well as other "hearing technology."

In addition to running an academy that trains teachers in oral-based educational methods, AGB "provides advertising opportunities to companies seeking to promote their products to individuals who are deaf and hard of hearing." According to AGB's website, one of their "partners in hearing" is Med-El, a large manufacturer of cochlear implants. As I mentioned earlier, the exhibitors and sponsors for their 2013 symposium include a long list of companies who sell or otherwise advocate for cochlear implant technology: Advanced Bionics, Cochlear America, the American Cochlear Implant Alliance, and many others.

Those who oppose the AGB's practices argue that this is a large coalition of companies that stand to benefit from the sale of cochlear implants. This, they argue, is a conflict of interest, and renders any information distributed by these companies untrustworthy. Ruthie Jordan told me she feels that AGB is "miseducating the parents of Deaf children . . . [AGB is] earning their millions by perpetuating misinformation. They are using the ears and the bodies of Deaf people to make themselves rich." She thinks AGB's actions are "only related to spoken language and 'fixing' Deaf people . . . they see Deaf people as sick, disabled, as having a deficit."

Many within Deaf culture feel similarly. They argue that the AGB harms Deaf communities by propagating large amounts of information about oralist methods—including cochlear implants—and treating ASL as "less than" spoken English.

The controversy is sometimes difficult for hearing people to understand. Hearing people often assume that Deaf people would naturally want to take advantage of any method that could lead them to become part of the hearing world—especially cochlear implants, the most advanced hearing technology we have. In reality, that assumption is far from true. To members of Deaf culture, American Sign Language is a cultural cornerstone. Because Deaf children who receive cochlear implants at a young age will likely be educated in the oralist method, they are less likely to learn ASL during their early years, which are the most critical years of language acquisition. For some Deaf parents, that would result in a child who speaks a different language than they do. Understandably, some see this as a loss of culture—one that, in some cases, has been passed down through generations. What may seem to a hearing person like an opportunity may be seen by some Deaf people as a loss.

The debate stems from a fundamental disagreement: one group sees deafness as a disability, and the other group sees it as a culture. The trouble is that the former group holds a disproportionate amount of power, and the latter group are the ones affected.

Jeff DuPree volunteers with Audism Free America, and is a proud sixth-generation Deaf person. I spoke with him through an interpreter at the symposium. Jeff told me,

> My whole life I've lived as a Deaf person. I married a Deaf person, I've worked and associated with Deaf people, and I've had no problem in this world. So why are organizations like this trying to take away my right to live the way I want to live, my right to raise my children the way I feel they should be raised?

It's not an easy question to answer. For their part, AGB maintains that they are simply advocates for the Deaf and hard of hearing. They point to the many people who, they argue, they have helped, by giving them information, grants, or general guidance related to cochlear implants and overall oral-focused education. AGB's website states that they "[Help] to ensure that every child and adult with hearing loss has the opportunity to listen, talk and thrive in mainstream society."

That's not a disingenuous statement. The question is whether the affected people are receiving the full truth about "mainstream society."

43 | Nondisabled Actors in Disabled Roles

Should audiences reject nondisabled actors who "crip up" for roles, or should disabled roles be open to all kinds of performers?

A. WE WOULDN'T ACCEPT ACTORS BLACKING UP, SO WHY APPLAUD "CRIPPING UP"?

by Frances Ryan

"If you do a film about the Holocaust, you're guaranteed an Oscar," goes the famous Kate Winslet joke in *Extras*. The same can be said for an actor doing a film about disability. Unless you're a disabled actor, that is. Then you're lucky to even get the part.

In 2014, when Eddie Redmayne won a Golden Globe for his portrayal of Stephen Hawking in *The Theory of Everything*, he became the latest in a long line of nondisabled actors to portray disabled characters. And to walk away—literally—with an award for doing so. From Daniel Day Lewis in *My Left Foot* to Dustin Hoffman in *Rain Man*, the ability to play "disability" is a definite asset for an actor, a source of genuine acclaim.

But is this as harmless as mainstream audiences seem to see it? While "blacking up" is rightly now greeted with outrage, "cripping up" is still greeted with awards. Is there actually much difference between the two? In both cases, actors use prosthetics or props to alter their appearance in order to look like someone from a minority group. In both cases they often manipulate their voice or body to mimic them. They take a job from an actor who genuinely has that characteristic, and, in doing so, perpetuate that group's underrepresentation in the industry. They do it for the entertainment of crowds who, by and large, are part of the majority group.

The explanations for "cripping up" are obvious. The entertainment industry is a business, after all, and stars sell. When Daniel Radcliffe played a disabled orphan in *The Cripple of Inishmaan* this won more headlines for the production than if a disabled, lesser-known actor had been cast. On a practical level too, perhaps hiring a non-disabled actor is easier. The ability to walk allows Redmayne to portray Hawking before being diagnosed with motor neurone disease. But I can't get away from the fact that, if these arguments were made for white actors "playing black," our outrage would be so great that the scenes would be left on the cutting room floor.

There's a theory of why nondisabled actors playing disabled characters leads to success: audiences find it reassuring. Christopher Shinn, a playwright who had a below-the-knee amputation, describes the act of watching a disabled character being played by an actor who we know is really fit and well as allowing society's "fear and loathing around disability" to be "magically transcended."

When it comes down to it, Shinn says, "pop culture is more interested in disability as a metaphor than in disability as something that happens to real people."

After all, disabled characters create powerful images and sentiments for audiences. They can symbolize the triumph of the human spirit over so-called "adversity." They can represent what it is to be "different" in some way, an outsider or an underdog who ultimately becomes inspirational. These are universal feelings every audience member can identify with. And there is something a little comforting in knowing, as we watch the star jump around the red carpet, that none of it—the pain or negativity we still associate with disability—was real.

Perhaps that's part of the problem. Perhaps as a society we see disability as a painful external extra rather than a proud, integral part of a person, and so it doesn't seem quite as insulting to have nondisabled actors don prosthetics or get up from a wheelchair when the director yells "cut." But for many disabled people in the audience, this is watching another person fake their identity. When it comes to race, we believe it is wrong for the story of someone from a minority to be depicted by a member of the dominant group for mass entertainment. But we don't grant disabled people the same right to self-representation.

Perhaps it is time to think before we next applaud "cripping up." Disabled people's lives are more than something for nondisabled actors to play at.

B. ABLE-BODIED ACTORS IN DISABLED ROLES: MODERN-DAY "BLACKING UP" . . . OR IS IT?

by Tony Seymour

Eddie Redmayne recently received a Golden Globe and a good deal of well-deserved praise for his role as the young Stephen Hawking in James Marsh's *The Theory of Everything*. The film charts the young physicist, who developed motor neurone disease

(MND), whilst courting his first wife. It has already attracted critical acclaim around the world, notching up no less than ten BAFTA nominations and five Academy Awards nominations. However, it has not escaped criticism. Some have cited the film as yet another example where disabled actors have been overlooked in favor of their able-bodied counterparts. Is this true? Is playing a disabled character the equivalent of "blacking up"? Or a guaranteed way to secure a stash of accolades? Should disabled roles simply be the preserve of disabled actors?

Frances Ryan's recent article in the *Guardian* suggested that Eddie Redmayne's Golden Globe-winning performance of the disabled Professor Stephen Hawking was the equivalent to "blacking up."

I took this and the other points made in the column very seriously. After all, as a disabled person myself and writer of *The Mermaid in The Gherkin Jar*, I wrestled with similar issues when working with Northern Rose in bringing the story to the stage. Christopher, the disabled little boy in the book, is currently played by an able-bodied actor and I still wonder what a disabled person might think of this, were he or she to see the full studio production at The Lowry Theatre in September 2015.

The reality of casting the stage production of *The Mermaid in the Gherkin Jar* is perhaps similar to Eddie Redmayne's role in *The Theory of Everything*. In the film, Redmayne must play both the able-bodied Stephen Hawking before his MND diagnosis as well as the increasingly crippled scientist, once the disease starts to take hold. Similarly, the actor playing Christopher in *The Mermaid in the Gherkin Jar* must play able-bodied as well as disabled roles. Therefore the part of Christopher must be adopted by someone capable of slipping between disabled and nondisabled personas.

I thought reading Ryan's article might cause me to doubt this. On the contrary, it only served to assure me that disabled people are not the only ones capable of playing physically challenged parts.

A number of key points can be distilled from her column, which I will attempt to look at in turn:

1. An able-bodied actor taking on the persona of a disabled person is the equivalent of a white person wearing make-up to play a black person;

2. Playing a disabled character is a good way of securing an Oscar or some other such award;

3. Able-bodied people feel more comfortable seeing disabled roles portrayed by able-bodied actors;

4. Giving disabled roles to able-bodied actors is robbing disabled actors of a role which is rightfully theirs, denying them the right of self-representation and further perpetuating the exclusion of disabled actors from the stage; and

5. It is wrong for someone from a minority group to be depicted by someone from a majority group for mass entertainment.

1. Is "Cripping Up" the Modern Day Equivalent of "Blacking Up?"

The first observation to make here is that Frances Ryan only seems concerned with physically disabled people. No mention is made of roles involving those with severe mental or behavioral problems. So, whilst it is acceptable for a mentally balanced person to play a manic depressive or paranoid schizophrenic, it is wrong to allow an able-bodied actor to portray a disabled character. Why? I'm not exactly sure. It seems to be an issue of perception and visual impact.

Writing as a disabled person with mild cerebral palsy, I have read the multitude of comments which followed Frances Ryan's article on the *Guardian* website. I have also researched a host of other opinions held by writers and social commentators on the issue. As such, I am only too aware of how serious and sensitive this matter is and how some disabled people may feel offended by comments which they perceive as going to the core of who they are.

However, having thought hard on this point for a couple of days, I have come to the firm conclusion that I absolutely cannot agree that the act of so-called "cripping up" is the equivalent of "blacking up" for stage and screen (at least not in the way that Frances Ryan implies).

"Blacking Up" as a Derisive Act of Racism

The practice of white actors donning makeup to assume the personas of black characters was widespread in the early 20th century where blacks were patronizingly perceived as simple, servile human beings or figures of comical derision. In other words, the roles perpetuated racism and the erroneous belief that black people or any ethnic minority for that matter, were somehow inferior to the white majority. Back then, society actively alienated and discriminated against black people.

But Modern Day "Blacking Up" Still Occurs

As Ryan asserts, the kind of "blacking up" that occurred all those years ago to poke fun and belittle black society has rightly stopped. But this is not to suggest that "blacking up" does not happen at all to enable an actor to more accurately assume a role. Sir Ben Kingsley won an Oscar for his interpretation of Mahatama Gandhi in the 1982 film of the same name. Perhaps the fact that his father was Indian helped to silence any critics, though the Yorkshire-born actor still had to wear a considerable amount of makeup for the role.

To say that wearing makeup to more accurately portray a role is an inexcusable act of bigotry seems rather exaggerated. The so called "blacking up" which occurred in *Gandhi* was not some racist act aimed at arrogantly excluding ethnic minorities from cinema, it was the result of the late Lord Attenborough's desire to accurately depict one of the most famous freedom fighters of all time. In other words, to make Sir Ben Kingsley's characterization of Gandhi more convincing.

Eddie Redmayne was cast to play the brilliant physician because, like Sir Ben Kingsley, he is a talented actor with a proven track record. It is also apparent from the screen shots that his physicality is very similar to the young professor. He is a good "fit" and believable in the role.

For these reasons the so called "cripping up" of actors to play roles such as Stephen Hawking in *The Theory of Everything* or Christie Brown in *My Left Foot* is little if anything to do with the kind of motives behind "blacking up" which occurred so many years ago. It is in fact, more as a result of the actor's intention to transform him or herself into that role, in the same way as he or she might wear a befitting costume.

2. The Use of Disability to Guarantee an Award

There are many occasions where playing a physically disabled person has led to an award. The examples are numerous. However, there is a danger that pointing this out time and again begins to sound just a little cynical, if not bitter.

I don't know the criteria on which awards are presented, but I should guess they run a little deeper than an actor faking a limp or a stumbling gait. One thing is for certain, approaching topics such as disability is almost certainly quite a challenge, not just for the actor, but for the director and producers involved.

It must be the case that, in making a film such as *The Theory of Everything*, those involved wanted to be as thorough as possible in understanding the nature of Hawking's disease. That probably explains the months of research conducted by Eddie Redmayne. Amongst other things, he studied MND and visited patients who had this condition. Before even attempting to mimic the physical symptoms, a great deal of time was spent understanding what it was to have the disease. Surely that difficult challenge, if executed well, is worth an Oscar.

To turn the argument on its head, are we saying that a great actor, who happened to have MND, would stand no chance of an award were they to play a young Stephen Hawking with the same disease?

I would agree that many actors have certainly won awards on the back of portraying disabled characters, but this is not because it is not a cop out. It is because it is a tough challenge where the able-bodied actor must really be at the top of their game to carry it off successfully. If they do, it is only right that they receive the acclaim they deserve.

3. Able-Bodied People Feel More Comfortable Seeing Disabled Roles Portrayed by Able-Bodied Actors

I agree with Frances Ryan here. Hand on heart, there are times when I have found it hard speaking with people with severe physical impairments. It's a devastating reality with which we'd rather not deal, so I can understand how it's more reassuring to see an able-bodied actor walk away from a disabled part. Nobody likes to face a harsh truth. That does not mean we should not confront it at all, of course. Nevertheless, there are numerous films where the use of an actor and the illusion of make-believe elicits a sense of relief such as seeing brutal re-enacted scenes of the Holocaust or apartheid.

4. Giving Disabled Roles to Able-Bodied Actors is Robbing Disabled Actors of a Role Which is Rightfully Theirs

I have already touched on the fact that there is more to playing a physically disabled character than simply "cripping up." Pretending to have the same physical handicap is not enough. The actor must be convincing. He or she must engage with the audience so that they buy into the story. In other words, they must draw on their subtle skills as actors to cast the magic that is necessary to make a tale genuine. If all that is needed to play a character with a given physical disability is personal experience of the same handicap, then this would give a very narrow, almost blinkered view of what it is to be an actor.

A Shortage of Disabled Actors

Furthermore, one cannot ignore the financial perspective. Producers must make a film or theatre performance pay and so, like it or not, they require personalities who attract the crowds. To be fair, this is something that Frances Ryan readily understands.

But the criticism that able-bodied actors automatically win disabled roles over and above their disabled-bodied counterparts also seems to imply that there is a rich seam of well-known disabled talent just waiting to fill any role depicting physical impairment. This is simply not true.

The only agency which focuses on representing disabled actors in the U.K., of which I am aware, is the VisABLE Model Agency run by Louise Dyson. The agency represents well known disabled actors such as Colin Young, who played a key role in the BBC's *Call The Midwife*. VisABLE is an excellent resource for any casting director looking to hire a disabled actor, but that does not mean it is always easy to find someone for a specific role.

For instance, the role of Christopher in the physical theatre production of *The Mermaid in the Gherkin Jar* would require someone with cerebral palsy who is also capable of performing the other able-bodied elements of the piece. As someone with Christopher's condition, I can assure the reader that this is something which is really rather difficult.

On this point, one actor I did have in mind for the role of Christopher was R.J. Mitte, star of the hugely successful U.S. series, *Breaking Bad*. In many ways he would be absolutely perfect, but I doubt the production company could afford his fee. Not at the moment anyway! Furthermore, there is no guarantee that such an actor would want to audition for the part. An actor's career flourishes as his roles become more and more varied. Would any actor with a disability really be content being the "go-to" man or woman for any piece involving physical impairment? I think not.

The assumption that there is a multitude of eager actors who are missing out on plum disabled roles played by able-bodied, award-hungry actors is misleading. These roles are actually relatively few and far between and arguably not enough to sustain any acting career.

Why is Disability so Precious?

Perhaps the point that Frances Ryan made which I found most difficult to agree with was her comment that seeing an able-bodied person assuming a disabled persona is "for many people in the audience" the same as "watching another person fake their identity."

The obvious point here is that faking another identity is exactly what acting is all about. Moreover, why shouldn't able-bodied actors play disabled roles? Are these parts so sacred as to suggest that no able-bodied person could possibly interpret them accurately? I have watched a number of films depicting disability and I have never felt that my own identity as a disabled person was being faked. The idea is frankly absurd.

Mental disability has often been portrayed by healthy actors without the likes of Mencap taking to the street claiming the collective identity of their membership has somehow been faked. What is the real difference with physical disability? I just can't see it.

5. It is Wrong for the Story of Someone From a Minority to be Depicted by a Member of the Dominant Group for Mass Entertainment

This statement would be beyond debate should any theatrical role be used by a "dominant group" to somehow belittle or undermine a minority. But, as I have already mentioned, this was not the case in roles such as *Gandhi*. Far from being an insulting portrayal of the Indian revolutionary, Sir Ben Kingley's interpretation was arguably a powerful and insightful piece of acting, worthy of great praise.

Similarly, Eddie Redmayne's portrayal of Stephen Hawking and Daniel Day Lewis's role in *My Left Foot*, to name but two, could hardly be argued in terms of a majority group capitalizing on a minority group for the sake of entertainment. I am personally thankful that actors and directors see these stories as so important that they must be told and I am happy to see them gain further publicity through their connection with famous faces.

The Harsh Reality of Disability in Film

There was a time when there were hardly any black actors in cinema, because the barriers toward them were so great. Over time the barriers to such actors broke down and more and more black artists as well as players from other ethnic minorities emerged.

The same will happen, to an extent, with disabled actors and stars like R.J. Mitte and Colin Young will, no doubt, lead the way. However they will always be few and far between. There is a very real and harsh truth to face—disabled people will always exist in far fewer numbers comparative to other minority groups, and the nature of having a disability will make it more difficult to play a wide variety of roles resulting in the majority of them losing out on blockbuster scripts.

An actor with severe cerebral palsy or MS might be able to play the role of Stephen Hawking in a wheelchair, but would find it impossible to pass off an able-bodied Cambridge student before MND took hold. An actor such as R.J. Mitte could have perhaps been a good call as an alternative for Eddie Redmayne, though bizarrely he would have to "crip down" for the first part of the film and "crip up" for the latter part. Is there any real difference? Also, as previously discussed, there is more to playing any role than simply being able to mimic the physical attributes of the character.

Similarly, casting Christopher for *The Mermaid in the Gherkin Jar* is not as simple as hiring the first actor one can find with cerebral palsy or a similar condition. After all, CP itself is a broad church that affects different people in different ways. Colin Young (although I thought about it) would have not been suitable as he wouldn't have been able to execute the more physically demanding able-bodied parts of the piece. This is a real shame as I think other aspects of his physicality would have been an excellent fit. Perhaps there are other actors out there with a milder form of cerebral palsy, but would they have had the same facial and physical characteristics as our current cast member?

The danger here is that in trying to use a disabled actor, the piece may alter in a way that was not truly intended. This, as a writer, I will always resist. Furthermore, and I may well be lambasted for making this point, if we focus on the disability itself too closely, there is actually the real risk that the piece becomes just about that—disability.

Conclusion

At first blush, Frances Ryan's article in the *Guardian* makes some strong points, but this is only because they appeal to our sense of outrage by hooking into emotive topics like racism. In reality, there is little in her article that holds water.

I've dealt with disability all my life and can honestly say I have never felt offended when an actor receives an award for "cripping up." Nor have I felt anger that the casting of an able-bodied person has somehow deprived me of my right to self-expression. On the other hand, I would feel far more disappointed if I watched a film that failed to deliver simply because of some misguided act of "positive discrimination."

Don't get me wrong, I would like to see more disabled actors in film. I want to see more talent agencies like VisABLE introducing actors into theatre casts and onto film sets. People need to see disability represented on TV and in the cinema as general roles. I can even see some disabled actors taking on far bigger parts.

But the reality of it is that those best suited to developing a mainstream career in entertainment are those at the periphery of disability, such as R.J. Mitte, who can keep their symptoms under control. This in turn allows them to play a wider variety of roles, even perhaps able-bodied parts. Having said that, the irony is that I doubt that any such individual would wish to base their career entirely on roles made possible because of their disability.

Sources

Chapter 1. Davis, Lennard J. "Introduction." Original to this volume.

Chapter 2. Garland-Thomson, Rosemarie. "Becoming Disabled." *The New York Times.* 19 August 2016. Web.

Chapter 3. Linton, Simi. "Reassigning Meaning" in *Claiming Disability: Knowledge and Identity.* New York: New York University Press (1998): pp. 8–17.

Chapter 4. Dolmage, Jay. "Disability Rhetoric." Original to this volume—though it is essentially material from his book: Dolmage, Jay. *Disability Rhetoric.* Syracuse University Press (2014).

Chapter 5. Omanksy, Beth and Karen Rosenblum. "Bringing Disability into the Sociological Frame: A comparison of disability with race, sex, and sexual orientation statuses." *Disability and Society* 16: 1 (2001): pp. 5–19. Note: the authors rewrote/edited portions of the source article for this volume.

Chapter 6. Silberman, Steve. "Neurodiversity Rewires Conventional Thinking About Brains." Wired.com. 16 April 2013. Web.

Chapter 7. Padden, Carol A. "Talking Culture: Deaf People and Disability Studies." *PMLA,* vol. 120, no. 2, 2005, pp. 508–513.

Chapter 8. Leahy, Morgan. "Stop Sharing Those Feel-Good Cochlear Implant Videos." *The Establishment.* 17 August 2016. Web.

Chapter 9. Groce, Nora. "Everyone Here Spoke Sign Language." *Natural History* (June 1980): pp. 10–16.

Chapter 10. Burch, Susan and Kim E. Nielsen. "History" in *Key Words for Disability Studies* ed. by David Serlin, Rachel Adams and Benjamin Reiss. New York: New York University Press (2015).

Chapter 11. Baynton, Douglas C. "Defectives in the Land: Disability and American Immigration Policy, 1882–1924." *Journal of American Ethnic History*, vol. 24, no. 3, 2005, pp. 31–44.

Chapter 12. Carey, Allison C. *On the Margins of Citizenship: Intellectual Disability and Civil Rights in Twentieth-Century America.* Temple University Press (2010).

Chapter 13. Erevelles, Nirmala. "Disability and Race." Original to this volume.

Chapter 14. Schalk, Sami. "Coming to Claim Crip: Disidentification with/in Disability Studies." *Disability Studies Quarterly* 33:2 (2013). Web.

Chapter 15. Mingus, Mia. "Moving Toward the Ugly: A Politic Beyond Desirability." Web blog post. *Leaving Evidence.* 22 August 2011 at leavingevidence.wordpress.com.

Chapter 16. Ralph, Laurence. "What Wounds Enable: The Politics of Disability and Violence in Chicago." *Disability Studies Quarterly* 32:3 (2012). Web.

Chapter 17. Perry, David M. and Lawrence Carter-Long. "How Misunderstanding Disability Leads to Police Violence." *The Atlantic.* 6 May 2014. Web.

Chapter 18. Metzl, Jonathan. "Let's talk about guns, but stop stereotyping the mentally ill." MSNBC.com. 10 September 2013. Web.

Chapter 19. Miserandino, Christine. "The Spoon Theory." Web blog post at butyou dontlooksick.com.

Chapter 20. Peace, Bill. "Ableism and a Water Shed Experience." Web blog post. *Bad Cripple.* 30 April 2009 at badcripple.blogspot.com.

Chapter 21. Sacks, Mike. "O.C.D. in N.Y.C." *The New York Times.* 11 August 2016. Web.

Chapter 22. Hedrick, Michael. "Living with Schizophrenia: The Importance of Routine." *The New York Times* Well Blog. 4 September 2014. Web.

Chapter 23. Michalko, Rod. *The Two in One.* Temple University Press (1999).

Chapter 24. Rosenberg, Alyssa. "If Hollywood's so creative, why can't it tell new stories about people with disabilities?" *The Washington Post.* 29 August 2016. Web.

Chapter 25. Abramovich, Seth. "Little People, Big Woes in Hollywood: Low Pay, Degrading Jobs and a Tragic Death." *The Hollywood Reporter.* 25 August 2016. Web.

Chapter 26. Kornhaber, Spencer and Lauryn S. Mayer. "The Ethics of Hodor." *The Atlantic.* 27 May 2016. Web.

Chapter 27. Anand, Shilpaa. "From a Bendy Straw to a Twirly Straw: Growing up Disabled, Transnationally." *Girlhood Studies* 9:1 (2016).

Chapter 28. Luft, Alexander. "The New Kid in Primetime: What *Speechless* Has to Say." Original to this volume.

Chapter 29. Bolt, David. "An advertising aesthetic: Real Beauty and visual impairment." *British Journal of Visual Impairment* 32:1 (2014): pp. 25–32.

Chapter 30. Moosa, Tauriq. "Your body isn't your world: The heroes of *Mad Max* and disability." *Polygon.* 21 September 2015. Web.

Chapter 31. Gibbons, Sarah. "Autis(i)m and Representation: *Auti-Sim,* Disability Simulation Games, and Neurodiversity." *First Person Scholar.* 1 May 2013. Web.

Chapter 32. Kuusisto, Stepen. "Why I'm a Crippled Poet." Web blog post. *Planet of the Blind.* 25 April 2014 at stephenkuusisto.com.

Chapter 33. Ware, Linda. "Disability Studies in K-12 Education." Original to this volume.

Chapter 34. Biklen, Douglas and Jamie Burke. "Presuming Competence." *Equality and Excellence in Education* 39:2 (2006): pp. 166–175.

Chapter 35. Girma, Haben. "Disability and Innovation: The Universal Benefits of Accessible Design." Apple Worldwide Developers Conference 2016. Web.

Chapter 36. Barker, Nicole C.S. "'What Will You Gain When You Lose?': Disability Gain, Creativity, & Human Difference." *Serendip Studio.* 28 November 2014 at serendip. brynmawr.edu.

Chapter 37. Capuzzi Simon, Cecila. "Disability Studies: A New Normal." *The New York Times.* 1 November 2013. Web.

Chapter 38. Bartlett, Jennifer. "Longing for the Male Gaze." *The New York Times.* 21 September 2016. Web.

Crippledscholar.com. "Disabled Women and Sexual Objectification (or the Lack Thereof)." Web blog post. 21 September 2016.

Chapter 39. Unlocking Words. "Disability and paying for sex." Web blog post. 27 July 2016 at unlockingwords.wordpress.com.

Chapter 40. What to Expect. "The Benefits of Prenatal Testing." 23 March 2017 at whattoexpect.com.

Tennant, Michael. "Disabled U.K. Lawmaker: End Abortion Discrimination Against the Disabled." *The New American.* 25 October 2016. Web.

Chapter 41. Golden, Marilyn. "The danger of assisted suicide laws." CNN. 14 October 2014 at edition.cnn.com.

Zakaria, Rafia. "Assisted suicide should be legal." Al Jazeera America. 24 October 2014 at america.aljazeera.com.

Chapter 42. Owens, Brian. "Infants May Benefit from Advanced Cochlear Implants." *Inside Science.* 28 May 2014. Web.

Ringo, Allegra. "Understanding Deafness: Not Everyone Wants to Be 'Fixed.'" *The Atlantic.* 9 August 2014. Web.

Chapter 43. Ryan, Frances. "We Wouldn't Accept Actors Blacking Up, So Why Applaud 'Cripping Up?'" *The Guardian.* 13 January 2015. Web.

Seymour, Tony. "Able-Bodied Actors in Disabled Roles: Modern-day 'Blacking Up' . . . Or Is It?" Web blog post. 18 January 2015 at themermaidinthegherkinjar.com.

Index

Page numbers with "n" refer to notes.

62823993R00204

Made in the USA
Columbia, SC
05 July 2019